Foundational Theology

Francis Schüssler Fiorenza

FOUNDATIONAL THEOLOGY

JESUS AND THE CHURCH

CROSSROAD · NEW YORK

1992
The Crossroad Publishing Company
370 Lexington Avenue, New York, N.Y. 10017

ISBN 0-8245-0706-1 (pbk.)

Printed in the United States of America

Library of Congress Cataloging in Publication Data

Fiorenza, Francis Schüssler.
    Foundational theology.
    Includes bibliographical references.
    1. Theology, Doctrinal.   2. Hermeneutics.
3. Jesus Christ—Resurrection.   4. Church.
5. Mission of the church.   I. Title.
BT75.2.F56 1984   230'.2   84-7764
ISBN 0-8245-0494-1

To
My friends and colleagues in
The Department of Theology
The Catholic University of America

Contents

Preface

Much theological debate centers on foundational theology. Historical and philosophical criticisms have demolished traditional solutions, and these criticisms have posed new problems. They have raised and left unresolved issues specific to foundational theology. But more importantly, they have challenged the nature and structure of foundational theology and have questioned its very methods and goals. The very name, fundamental or foundational theology, appears to be in dispute. This volume, therefore, seeks to discuss some of these most controverted issues and to analyze the nature of foundational theology itself.

Since a confusion of terminology exists, the term "fundamental theology" will be used to characterize all traditional conceptions of fundamental theology as a distinct and independent discipline from systematic theology. The term "foundational theology" will be used to express my own proposal of foundational theology as a reconstructive hermeneutic. Such a choice is not completely arbitrary. Bernard Lonergan has used the term "foundational theology" as distinct from "dialectics" to express the discipline's theological rather than apologetical character. Peter Hodgson has selected the term "foundational theology" to avoid the associations that have historically related fundamental theology to a type of natural theology. Although my proposal of foundational theology as a reconstructive hermeneutic differs from their conceptions, it also seeks to avoid the identification of fundamental theology with apologetics as well as to elaborate the theological nature of the discipline. For this reason, the ascription "foundational theology" to characterize my own proposal and the ascription "fundamental theology" to characterize most of the traditional proposals appear justified and should help eliminate much terminological confusion.

Four distinct foundational theological problems are analyzed: the resurrection of Jesus, the foundation of the Church, the mission of the Church, and the nature of fundamental/foundational theology. Each makes up a separate section, follows a similar pattern, and can be read independently of the others. After sketching the historical emergence of the theological issue, each section first surveys traditional and contemporary options, then offers some constructive proposals by applying recent hermeneutical theory. In each section, the analysis of contemporary theological approaches and the constructive proposals are placed in different chapters so that the reader can clearly distinguish the survey of the state of the question from my own suggestions for new directions.

The reader might expect that the first section will deal with the nature of foundational theology. However, the historical detail, philosophical analyses, and methodological reflections made the material less immediately relevant and intelligible than the concrete issues of the resurrection of Jesus and the foundation and mission of the Church. Following the advice of several readers, I have removed this "dragon in the gate" so that the methodological analysis is the fourth and final section. Not only pedagogical but also methodological reasons urge this relocation. One can move from the abstract to the concrete or from the concrete to the abstract. The latter has distinct advantages. After a method has been practiced, it not only can be better understood but also its success can be more appropriately judged. The final section will, therefore, clarify the theoretical issues raised or implied in the previous sections. It will also, I trust, be more convincing after the fruitfulness of the method has been demonstrated for the three concrete foundational theological issues.

The resurrection of Jesus, treated in Part I, formed the cornerstone of traditional fundamental theology. Jesus' resurrection was not simply a creedal belief to be historically demonstrated, but a foundational belief. Once demonstrated, it legitimated Jesus as the divine legate and thereby grounded the truth of the Christian Church and its creeds. Traditional fundamental theology, therefore, appealed to the resurrection of Jesus not so much as an object of faith but rather as a ground of faith. Chapter 1 surveys three approaches to the resurrection: the traditional, the transcendental, and the historical-critical. I examine each of these to show how diverse historical and methodological presuppositions determine not only their view of Jesus' resurrection but also their basic conception of fundamental theology. Chapter 2 proposes a hermeneutical approach to the resurrection that takes into account the distinct role of testimony, the relation between

literary form and revelatory content, and the foundational significance of the diverse New Testament texts.

The foundation of the Church, treated in Part II, has been posed
as a historical question within traditional fundamental theology. Did
the earthly Jesus explicitly will and intend to institute a permanent
Church? So formulated, the question gave rise to the modernist controversies and has remained a thorny issue within contemporary theology. In addition, this historical question, even when not explicitly
discussed, is at the basis of many of the current controversies surrounding ecclesiastical discipline, the ordination of women, papal
primacy, the number of sacraments, and authority within the
Church.

Traditional fundamental theology developed a historical demonstration that Jesus did indeed establish a Church and even a particular
church order. Transcendental fundamental theology has sought to
complement the historical argument through an indirect approach
and an appeal to the phenomenological structures of human community. Modern historical-critical approaches have developed notions of
a pneumatological and postresurrection foundation of the Church. In
developing foundational theology as a reconstructive hermeneutic, I
attempt not to bypass the historical relation between the earthly Jesus
and the postresurrection Christian communities, but rather to view
the problem as one of religious identity and reception. As a problem
of identity and meaning, the foundation of the Church is understood
not primarily in terms of historical intentionality, but as the hermeneutical reception of the identity that came to the fore in the vision,
life, and praxis of Jesus.

Part III deals with the mission of the Church. In traditional fundamental theology, the Church's mission was treated briefly and suc-
cinctly. Jesus not only founded the Church but also gave it a supernatural goal and a spiritual mission. A social mission or a political
ministry was neither proper nor constitutive for the Church. Today,
the emergence of political theology and liberation theology has made
the question of the Church's mission especially controversial. Various
theological attempts have been made to integrate the Church's social
mission by using the categories of substitute mission, unofficial mission, or partial mission. These attempts prove to be inadequate because they fail to deal with the foundational issue of the Church's
religious identity. The mission of the Church is not just an ecclesiological problem, but a fundamental theological issue, for it bears upon
how religious and Christian identity is conceived in theory and
praxis. Just as the issue of Christian identity is central to the theologi-

cal interpretation of the resurrection of Jesus and the foundation of the Church, so too it is central to the issue of the Church's social and political mission.

Foundational theology entails a reconstructive interpretation of the intertwining of Christian vision and social praxis. The Church's praxis that flows from its Christian faith and vision not only expresses its religious identity but is a foundational and validating warrant of that identity. Praxis is not simply the application of theory; it is intrinsically interconnected with theory as a source of the discovery of self-identity and as a warrant for the veracity of that identity. Consequently, the theological problem of the foundation of the Church is closely linked to the problem of the Church's mission. When the meaning and nature of the Church's mission is resolved, then the issue of the Church's foundation will be resolved.

The fourth and final part discusses the emergence, characteristics, and presuppositions of fundamental theology. Since many of the presuppositions implicit within fundamental theology can be made explicit only through an analysis of its historical roots, our study begins in chapter 9 with an "archaeology" of the discipline. This investigation uncovers three distinct conceptions of fundamental theology that eventually merged in the classic understanding of fundamental theology as an independent theological discipline with the twofold task of defending the truth of the Christian religion and of establishing the foundation of Christian theology. The next chapter then surveys the presuppositions not only of classical but also of contemporary fundamental theology with specific emphasis upon the criteria of truth employed. This chapter challenges the adequacy of correspondence and coherence theories of truth and it critiques the dominant method of correlation within fundamental theology.

The final chapter proposes a conception of foundational theology as a reconstructive hermeneutic that entails three distinct elements: hermeneutical reconstruction, retroductive warrants, and background theories. In working out this conception, I first outline the criticisms that have been raised against foundationalism within contemporary American philosophy. The validity of these criticisms rests on the hermeneutical dimension of any appeal to experience or to tradition. Consequently, foundational theology cannot directly and immediately appeal to tradition or to experience alone, but must seek a reflective equilibrium between hermeneutical reconstruction, retroductive warrants, and relevant background theories. All three elements must be taken into account if foundational theology is not to fall into a foundationalism with merely limited and specific conditions of truth. Since these three elements have been elaborated in the specific issues of the resurrection of Jesus, the foundation of the Church, and the mission of the Church, their systematic elaboration in the final section provides the theoretical basis for the position and methods advanced in regard to the concrete controversial issues. At the same time, I trust, my explanations will clarify my advocacy of a foundational theology that avoids the pitfalls of foundationalism.

I owe thanks to many persons, most of all to Justus George Lawler. His suggestions have been helpful and his encouragement, indispensable. Above and beyond his editorial advice, I owe him a special debt. His own writings had strongly influenced me when I was a beginning student of theology. Long before it was fashionable, he spoke out against the morality and rationality of a nuclear defense; long before others, he spoke out against American militarism and against the injustices that we ourselves commit. A foundational theology that argues for the interrelation between the truth claims of the Christian vision and the praxis of justice owes no small debt to the intellectual vision of Justus George Lawler.

In addition, special thanks are due to Frank Oveis for his unflagging editorial assistance and his supportive encouragement. If publishers are awarded halos for patience and the willingness to publish serious theological works, then Werner Linz's shines out like a beacon. A special word of thanks is also due to Ulla Schnell.

Several friends and colleagues have made comments on individual sections. I am especially grateful for the comments of Gregory Baum, Raymond Brown, Charles Curran, Avery Dulles, John Ford, Elizabeth Johnson, Catherine LaCugna, David Power, and Edward Schillebeeckx. Doctoral students at Catholic University have made me much more reflective through their probing criticisms. Of these I am especially grateful to Mary Catherine Hilkert, Richard Miller, and Ellen Snee.

The American Association of Theological Schools has under the guidance of its director, Dr. Leon Pacala, begun a program of research awards on issues of theological education. I am especially grateful to him and to the Association that gave me the opportunity for research into the origins of foundational theology and for discussions on it with Joseph Hough, David Kelsey, Douglas Meeks, Barbara Wheeler, and Leon Pacala. Their comments and suggestions have been immensely helpful. Parts of the chapter on the Church's mission were given as the John Kelly Lectures on Social Justice at St. Michael's, the University of Toronto, and at several other universities. An earlier and much shorter version appeared in *Theological Studies*, edited by

Walter Burghardt, and received the award of the College Theology Society for the best essay published in theology in 1982. I am thankful to the society's president, Roger Van Allen, and the chairperson of the award committee, Joseph La Barge.

I want to thank the graduate students at Catholic University who helped with the proofreading of the galleys: Joseph Bagiackas, Diana Hayes, Ralph McMichael, and Sally Ann McReynolds.

Elisabeth Schüssler Fiorenza and I have discussed the positions taken in this book. We have often disagreed. Where I have heeded her advice the volume has been improved. Where I have not, well. . . . Christina has been a source of encouragement and has even suggested a much more appropriate title for the volume. But it is much too similar to the title of her mother's volume to be used.

This book is dedicated to my colleagues in the Department of Theology at Catholic University of America. Their personal friendship, supportive encouragement, and theological comradeship has made this volume possible and has meant much more to me than they themselves realize. I am happy that the volume's publication coincides with the centenary of the decision by Third Plenary Council of Baltimore in 1884 to establish a School of Theology in Washington, D.C.

Abbreviations

The abbreviations used in the notes are those published annually in the "Instructions for Contributors" of *Theological Studies* and *Harvard Theological Review*. In the few cases where they differ, *HTR* has been followed as the more common practice (e.g., *Th* instead of *T* for *Theology*). The following abbreviations, which are not included in the common list, are used here:

FThS	Freiburger theologische Studien
FTS	Frankfurter theologische Studien
FZPhTh	*Freiburger Zeitschrift für Philosophie und Theologie*
HJ	*Historisches Jahrbuch*
JP	*Journal of Philosophy*
LThPh	*Laval Théologie et philosophie*
Proceedings CTSA	*Proceedings of the Catholic Theological Society of America*
QD	Quaestiones Disputatae
TRE	*Theologischen Realenzyklopädie*
TThS	Trierer theologische Studien
TTS	Tübinger theologische Studien

PART I

THE
RESURRECTION
OF JESUS

Introduction

In Christianity the resurrection of Jesus has been more than a historical claim about a past event for which the evidence has been weighed; it has been more than an individual dogmatic belief that has been more or less adequately interpreted. Instead, the resurrection of Jesus has been foundational. The Pauline statement "if Christ has not been raised, then our preaching is in vain and your faith is in vain" (1 Cor 15:14), has been taken quite seriously by the traditional fundamental theology that has placed the defense of the resurrection of Jesus at the center of the defense of the truth of Christianity.

The situation that contemporary theology faces is in respect to Jesus' resurrection quite unique. On the one hand, the Pauline statement affirms the centrality of the resurrection of Jesus for faith. The tradition of much Christian theology has reaffirmed that centrality. On the other hand, critical historians have challenged the validity of the historical demonstrations of the resurrection; theologians have radically reinterpreted it; and even Christian apologists have questioned whether the resurrection of Jesus should have such central and foundational significance for the truth of Christianity. In this situation, theology has to grapple not only with the problems raised by historical accounts of the emergence of the belief in Jesus' resurrection but must resolve the extent to which Jesus' resurrection should be foundational to a defense of Christianity.

The relation between fundamental theology and Jesus' resurrection will be explicated in this section. First it will show how the resurrection of Jesus functioned as the cornerstone of traditional fundamental theology and how the demonstration of the facticity and truth of the resurrection was to function as the foundation of Christian faith and theology. After a survey of the historical criticisms that have made evident the weaknesses of the traditional fundamental theological approach, attention will be given to two contemporary endeavors within fundamental theology. Contemporary transcendental fundamental theology advances an indirect and existential approach to Jesus' resurrection and provides a radical reinterpretation of its nature and function. In the last decade a new historical-critical approach to fundamental theology and Jesus' resurrection has been developed. Underlying many of the current controversies in christology this approach has emphasized the life of Jesus rather than the appearances after Easter as the foundation for the belief in the resurrection of Jesus. Finally, developing the proposal of foundational theology as a reconstructive hermeneutic, the diverse New Testament texts on the resurrection of Jesus will be analyzed.

Chapter 1

Fundamental Theology and the Resurrection of Jesus

Throughout the history of Christianity individual apologies were written for Christianity and individual Christian beliefs were defended.[1] Although the resurrection of Jesus was defended along with these other beliefs, it did not have the centrality that it came to occupy in modern fundamental theology and has held up until contemporary times. In fact, the resurrection of Jesus had become so central to the modern defense of Christianity that its defense not only stood at the core of the development of fundamental theology as a theological discipline, but determined how the very enterprise was carried out.[2] This centrality and significance of the resurrection of Jesus within fundamental theology can be traced through three distinct types of modern fundamental theology: the traditional historical fundamental theology; the transcendental fundamental theology; and a very recent historical-critical approach to the resurrection as a fundamental theological issue.

Traditional Fundamental Theology

The Enlightenment rejected the claim of a special divine intervention or a supernatural revelation. It therefore denied the reality of miracles and especially the miracle of the resurrection of Jesus. Since fundamental theology developed in opposition to the Enlightenment, it developed certain characteristics from its anti-Enlightenment stance. These characteristics affected not only the method of fundamental theology in general, but also the specific treatment of Jesus' resurrection. Thus a correlation exists between the method of traditional fundamental theology and its approach to the resurrection.

Its Characteristics in Relation to the Resurrection

One of the distinctive characteristics of fundamental theology was its independence as a theological discipline seeking to provide a complete foundation for the Christian religion. This characteristic differentiated fundamental theology from previous apologies, for these previous apologies had very specific goals. Tertullian's *Apology* sought to refute the accusation that Christian practices were evil. Eusebius of Caesarea's *The Preparation of the Gospel* sought to show that Christians did not abandon Greek philosophical wisdom, whereas his *The Proof of the Gospel* was directed against the accusation of infidelity to Jewish thought. Even more comprehensive apologies like St. Augustine's *City of God* and St. Thomas's *Summa Contra Gentiles* were directed against specific errors and specific contexts.[3]

In its attempted refutation of the Enlightenment, fundamental theology sought to provide a foundation for all of Christian faith and theology.[4] Since it saw the Enlightenment critique of revealed religions as a critique of this very foundation, it sought to demonstrate the possibility, existence, and necessity of revelation[5] through a threefold division of revelation: revelation in general, Christian revelation, and Catholic revelation.[6]

The central section on Christian revelation defended not only the possibility of revelation but also the de facto reality of revelation. Within this central section the resurrection of Jesus was indeed the linchpin, for the demonstration of the truth of Jesus' resurrection would amount not only to a proof of the historical facticity of revelation but also would constitute a proof of the truth and reality of Christian revelation. Since the resurrection of Jesus was the ultimate example of divine intervention in history, the proof of its truth amounted to the proof of Christian revelation.

Since traditional fundamental theology considered the resurrection of Jesus as an event in history that demonstrated the truth of a historical revelation, it sought to develop an appropriate method of demonstration—a historical demonstration. This reliance on historical demonstration was the second characteristic affecting not only its method but also its approach to the resurrection. After a philosophical argument for the possibility of revelation, fundamental theology sought to prove the existence of revelation by an ascending set of historical arguments. It argued from the existence of messianic prophecies to their historical fulfillment in Jesus. Then it argued from the facticity of Jesus' miracles and of his prediction of the resurrection to the real occurrence of a physical resurrection. The resurrection was therefore the ultimate proof of Jesus' divine mission, for it was the greatest of miracles which had come to pass as predicted.

Traditional fundamental theology relied on this historical demonstration as an objective method. If the historical objectivism of the Enlightenment sought to undermine Christianity's claim to a supernatural reveleation, then fundamental theology sought to counter the critique with a historical objectivism based upon the existence of certain "historical facts"—such as the empty grave—that demonstrate the truth of the resurrection and the facticity of relevation.[7] Although outstanding theologians such as Johann von Drey and Johann Ehrlich criticized this historical objectivism and positivism,[8] it nevertheless became the dominant method of the Roman School, the Latin manuals, and was at the basis of the argumentation in Vatican I's constitution on faith.

A third characteristic was the extrinsicism of its method or its reliance on external authority. Although this extrinsicism had its roots within medieval theology, it became radicalized within the development of fundamental theology. Medieval scholastics assumed that the truths of faith were essentially obscure, that is, they were not in themselves intelligible.[9] The basis for the truth of creedal beliefs, therefore, must be sought outside of the intelligibility grasped by human reason. Despite the harmony between faith and reason, reason did not measure up to the objects of faith. Human reason could in some way comprehend revealed truths, but it could not of itself justify the adherence of faith. The justification of the revealed truths, therefore, did not stem from the truths themselves, but rather from the veracity of those revealing the truths.

Traditional fundamental theology explicated this notion of justification. The impetus was provided by Petrus Maria Gazzaniga (1722–1799), an Austrian Dominican. In his arguments for the facticity of divine revelation, Gazzaniga distinguished between internal and external criteria. The internal criteria were holiness and sublimity, whereas the external criteria were prophecy and miracle.[10] The resurrection of Jesus was, therefore, the highpoint of the external criteria. Considered not as an object of faith, it was an external criterion that demonstrated the veracity of Jesus and the truth of his revelation. It was this distinction between internal and external criteria and its use to demonstrate the truth of Christ's revelation that became the dominant approach of the theology incorporated into Vatican I.[11]

The distinctive characteristics of this fundamental theological approach led to the centrality of the resurrection of Jesus. It was not only the highpoint of the historical demonstration but also the ultimate foundation of this demonstration. The Old Testament prophecies,[12] as well as Jesus' own prophecies, all pointed to the resurrection. Moreover, the resurrection was seen not only as the culmination of Jesus' miracles but also as an absolute and incontestable miracle. If natural explanations could be given for some miracles, no such explanation could be given for the resurrection of Jesus after three days of burial. The resurrection was, therefore, described by Gazzaniga as the greatest of all miracles (*miraculum omnium maximum*) that legitimated the New Testament and Jesus' divine mission.[13]

The Resurrection of Jesus within Fundamental Theology

The apologetical use of the resurrection within fundamental theology marked a decisive transformation. Although so common as to appear traditional, the apologetical use of the resurrection is in reality a shift from the previous theological locus of the resurrection. The early church fathers, both in the apostolic and postapostolic periods, did not concentrate on the resurrection of Jesus as an isolated historical demonstration of the supernatural truth of Christianity. Instead, they related it to the Christian belief in the future resurrection of the dead. Since they confronted the gnostic interpretation of the resurrection, the church fathers underscored the significance of the Incarnation and interpreted the resurrection from the perspective of the Incarnation.[14]

Medieval theologians likewise did not treat the miracle of the resurrection as the foundational fact that demonstrated the truth of all theology. Instead, the resurrection was located within christology. Thomas Aquinas's *Summa Theologiae* deals with Jesus' resurrection primarily as one of the mysteries of Jesus' life. Its locus is theological and sacramental. It does not serve as a historical demonstration of Jesus' divine mission.[15] The appearances of the Risen One are not so much strict proofs as they are signs to Jesus' disciples.

The fundamental theology developed in the Latin manuals and in the Roman School has had an ironic history. It sought primarily to retrieve Thomism; yet, in fact, it differed radically from Thomas. Whereas Thomas viewed the resurrection as central to christology and drew out its consequences for grace and salvation, traditional fundamental theology reduced Jesus' resurrection to apologetics and saw it primarily as an external criterion of the truth of Christianity.

The most widely used textbook in the 1950s and 1960s faithfully represented this fundamental theology: it devoted less than a page to the resurrection in its treatment of christology because it had limited its discussion to the demonstration of the resurrection's historical facticity and apologetical function.[16]

Another decisive change took place. Not only did traditional fundamental theology view the resurrection of Jesus primarily as an apologetical proof of Christianity rather than as a central mystery of the life of Jesus, but also it transformed the traditional distinction between the proper ground of faith and the extrinsic reasons of credibility. The proper ground of faith has been considered to be the authority of God testifying and guaranteeing the truth of revelation. The extrinsic ground of credibility had consisted of the reasons that were based on historical demonstration.[17] In fundamental theology the decisive criteria of the credibility of Jesus' divine mandate and relevation became reduced to the "historical facts" of the empty grave and the appearances. Both became "facts" that can be demonstrated by impartial historical science.[18] They are not objects of belief, but the grounds of faith. They constitute the foundation of Christianity, the basis of its revelation, and the ground of its theology and faith.

Historical Critique of the Traditional Apologetic

The structure of this modern fundamental theology eventually collapsed. Since it was built upon historical arguments and facts, the historical method itself undermined such a theology. Its view of the resurrection as a fact was open to the ridicule of Adolf Harnack who quipped in his *History of Dogma* that when faced with "the assertion that the resurrection of Christ is the most certain fact in the history of the world, one does not know whether he should marvel more at its thoughtlessness or its unbelief."[19] The application of the historical method to the Gospel texts made it no longer possible to view the resurrection of Jesus as "the most certain fact in the history of the world."

Historical criticism undercut the major arguments of this fundamental theology. Historical research questioned the apologetic value of the messianic prophecies that referred primarily to their own contemporary time rather than to the events of Jesus' life. They should therefore be interpreted within their own historical context, except for some possible "fuller sense" (*sensus plenior*) that would not allow an apologetic demonstration.[20] The Gospel authors had used the Old Testament to explain the meaning of Jesus so that what was considered to be messianic was primarily determined by the evangelists themselves.[21]

The historical-critical method likewise undermined the apologetic function of miracles. Since comparative studies had shown that the cities of antiquity were crowded with miracle workers, the apologetic appeal to the miracles of Jesus was weakened.[22] Theology, moreover, became increasingly aware of the significance of Lessing's distinction between miracles and the reports of miracles. The immediate and direct experience of a miracle differs from reports about miracles, especially for apologetics where the credibility of the reports is subject to debate.[23]

Moreover, historical research had shown that the Gospels themselves did not understand the miracles primarily in their apologetical function.[24] Fundamental theology viewed the miracles of Jesus primarily as supernatural interventions that broke through the natural order. They were historically verifiable and therefore could serve as certain proofs of the divine and supernatural mission of Jesus. Against the naturalism of the Enlightenment, this fundamental theology argues that the miracles were supernatural events that demonstrated the supernatural revelation of Christianity. The Gospels, however, did not view the miracles foremost as events that were contrary to nature or as demonstrations of the supernaturalness of Jesus' revelation. Instead, they proclaimed Jesus' miracles as intrinsic to his revelation and as signs of the breaking in of God's kingdom. Although miracles have some apologetic function with the Gospel traditions, their role within the Gospels is very complex.[25] Some traditions within the Gospels do indeed stress the miraculous; other traditions minimize and criticize this usage. Nevertheless, the Gospels do not view miracles as apologetical proofs that can be demonstrated prior to faith, but as signs of the kingdom for those who believe.

Centrality of the Empty Tomb

For our purposes, what is significant is how in this theology two foundational pillars supported belief in the resurrection: the empty grave and the accounts of the resurrection appearances.[26] Belief in the resurrection was supported by both; nevertheless, the empty tomb became the main argument, for it demonstrated the reality of the resurrection appearances.[27] Several reasons explain the primary emphasis given to the empty tomb. The historical origin of the belief in the resurrection was attributed to the discovery of the tomb. Because the first disciples discovered the tomb empty, they came to believe in the resurrection. Moreover, the empty tomb appeared to be more easily verified as a historical fact. Appearances could be discounted as subjective experiences, whereas an empty tomb could not. In addition, the empty tomb demonstrated the truth of the proclamation of the appearances since the resurrection could not have been preached in Jerusalem unless the tomb had in fact been empty. Finally, the empty tomb proved that the resurrection of Jesus was corporeal and physical.[28] In the face of the objection that the resurrection was a spiritual resurrection or that the appearances were spiritual rather than physical, the empty tomb stood as the certain fact that spoke against these theories.[29] The empty tomb provided the foundation for the belief in the resurrection of Jesus; it demonstrated the truth of this resurrection; and it made evident the physical reality of this resurrection. As the basis of Christian belief in the appearances of Jesus and in his resurrection, the empty tomb was at the center of fundamental theology.

Critique of the Empty Tomb Apologetic

Since this fundamental theology was based upon historicity, its validity stood or fell with the historicity of the empty tomb. The criticisms raised against this position came first from an analysis of the New Testament texts themselves and their literary history.[30] The New Testament texts referring to the empty tomb are not the earliest documents, but rather the latest texts. The formula of 1 Cor 15:3b–5 does not refer to the empty tomb even though Paul's line of argument would have been strengthened by such a reference.[31] Perhaps as some critics have claimed it was unknown to Paul? In response, it could be claimed that the formula represented a creedal formula and not an apologetical argument. Some of the traditions contained in 1 Cor 15 indicate that Paul did presuppose a corporeal resurrection. But such a response would not make the empty tomb the historical foundation of belief, rather Paul's faith and the creedal beliefs of the early Christian communities.

Further, the question arises from an analysis of the New Testament texts whether the discovery of the empty tomb was the cause or the origin of the belief in the resurrection. The discovery of the empty tomb in itself does not, according to the New Testament evidence, demonstrate Jesus' resurrection.[32] Other explanations could be given of the tomb's emptiness. The New Testament texts themselves underscore that faith came not through the discovery of the empty tomb but through an experience of the Risen One. If the empty tomb was not the cause of belief in Jesus' resurrection at that time, then it could be questioned whether historical arguments for the veracity of the empty tomb traditions can serve as the foundational cause of Christian faith today.

The differences among the accounts and the embellishments of the later accounts raise the questions whether the reports of the discovery of the empty tomb derived from apologetic interests, cultic etiology, theological reflection on the appearances, or whether they had a kernel of truth underlying all the diversity.[34] Nevertheless, a uniformity exists in all the texts that a tomb was discovered. Moreover, the reports relate that women had discovered the empty tomb. That such a role was attributed to women could not be due to the creativity of the early Church but speaks for the basic historicity of the reports. The pros and cons of all these historical arguments cannot be explored further here. They do show that historical reasons speak for and against the use of the empty tomb as a "certain demonstration" of the truth of the resurrection.

In its argumentation, traditional fundamental theology combined and mixed together several distinct issues: the genetic, historical, and functional. These issues should be kept distinct. The genetic question (Was the discovery of the empty tomb the cause and origin of belief in the resurrection?) is distinct from the historical question (Was the tomb discovered to be empty?). Moreover, both the genetic and the historical questions are distinct from the functional question as to whether the empty tomb can have the apologetical role that it played in traditional fundamental theology to demonstrate not only the truth of the resurrection but also that of Christianity itself.

Historical research appears to have reached a twofold consensus: in regard to the genetic question, the discovery of the empty tomb did not in itself cause the belief in the resurrection; in regard to the historical question, it appears that the traditions claiming that the tomb was discovered at an early date are later literary texts that probably contain historically reliable traditions. The functional issue remains:[35] Should a fundamental theology be based upon the empty tomb if it did not originally generate the belief in the resurrection and if its historical veracity is at the best only probable? A negative conclusion would not deny the resurrection or the discovery of the empty tomb, but it would deny that fundamental theology should seek to establish the resurrection faith exclusively and primarily through a historical demonstration of the empty tomb. Such a fundamental theology insufficiently stressed the meaning of the resurrection and the function of the appearances because it concentrated on the empty tomb and reduced the resurrection to an external criterion of truth.

Transcendental Fundamental Theology

Transcendental fundamental theology sought to overcome the historical objectivism of traditional fundamental theology. It maintained that the "traditional" fundamental theology was really a modern phenomenon since its basic structures had emerged only in the eighteenth and nineteenth centuries and it argued further that the Roman School and the tradition of the manuals were caught up in the historical objectivism of the very position that they sought to refute. Although transcendental fundamental theology has its antecedents in the nineteenth century and in the "Blondelian Shift" as expressed in the classic 1896 "Essay on Apologetics,"[36] its most consistent development and extension to all themes and topics of theology have been achieved by Karl Rahner. Not only has he worked out the implications of Kant's transcendental philosophy but also he has combined them with an anthropological appropriation of Martin Heidegger's early "existential" categories.[37] It is especially in regard to the resurrection of Jesus that Rahner has shown the advantages and fertility (also the weaknesses) of transcendental fundamental theology. Whereas traditional fundamental theology emphasized the independence of the ground of faith, the significance of extrinsic authority, the possibility of a historical demonstration, and the facticity of the empty tomb, transcendental fundamental theology seeks to interrelate object and ground of faith, to propose an indirect approach and a transcendental deduction, and to reinterpret the meaning and significance of the resurrection.

Resurrection as Object or Ground of Faith?

Traditional fundamental theology sought to demonstrate the truth of Christian revelation prior to dogmatic theology and strove to ground Christianity independent of faith. Transcendental fundamental theology, however, sought to explicate existential grounds that are not prior to, but drawn from the very formal structures of dogmatic theology and of the Christian faith itself.[38] This transcendental approach significantly modifies the understanding of the resurrection as the ground of faith.[39] Since contemporary experience encounters the resurrection more as a scandal of faith than as a reason for faith, the resurrection is more an object of faith (what is to be believed) than a ground of faith (the basis or proof of what is to be believed). Consequently, the resurrection should not be seen as a foundation that is external to faith. Instead, it grounds faith primarily as an object of faith as, for example, in friendship mutual love and trust are both ground and object of friendship. The resurrection does not extrinsically ground faith *apart from* faith but only *in* faith.[40] Thus every ground of faith is at the same time an object of faith, but not every object of faith is necessarily a ground of faith. How the resurrection as an object of faith is also the ground of faith becomes evident in the use of an indirect approach and a transcendental method within theology.

Necessity of an Indirect Method

The use of an indirect method is the second major difference between the two theologies. It contrasts with the previous appeal to historical demonstration.[41] The transcendental approach emphasizes that the contemporary situation of theology has radically changed from the past because of the pluralism of diverse philosophical standpoints and the emergence of highly technical specializations. If previously a theologian could be in control of scholastic philosophy with its common questions and conceptions, today no one individual can master all the diverse philosophical currents operative in theology. If formerly a theologian had a command of the basic historical research, today, as a result of the expansion of knowledge, a theologian can master only a limited specialized field. If up to the nineteenth century systematic theologians lectured not only on systematic issues but also on biblical studies, today a New Testament scholar may be a specialist only in one narrow field, the synoptics, Pauline studies, or intertestamental literature. If previously a systematic theologian could discuss the central Pauline text of 1 Cor 15:3–5 on the resurrection, today only a specialized New Testament scholar with a knowledge both of languages (Greek, Aramaic) and of Pauline studies can do so.

Such reflections challenge the function of historical demonstration within fundamental theology. Since the historical method has become so specialized and can be mastered only by the expert, how can it establish the reason for faith of the ordinary Christian or even the ordinary theologian? For these reasons, as Rahner advocates, an indirect approach must complement the historical approach by appealing to human and existential Christian experience.

If theologians had previously disparaged such an approach as an argument ad hominem that had less than scientific validity, Rahner now praises it, as not only more accessible to the average Christian but also as more revelatory than the historical and scientific methods.[42] This suggestion betrays the influence of Heidegger's philosophy upon Rahner's conception of theology[43]; in *What Is Metaphysis?* Heidegger emphasizes that reflection about Being is more than categorical reflection.[44] Philosophical thinking about Being becomes in theology the thinking about God. Such thinking goes back to foundational issues, and a person should have the courage to go beyond the scientific and be willing not only to face limited and specialized questions but also to ask about the very ground of Being. Consequently, an indirect method that would explicate the relation between human existence and the truth of the Christian faith would not be less theological than a historical method because less specialized. It would be more theological because more foundational.[45]

Correlation between Jesus' Resurrection and Human Experience

This indirect and nonscientific approach to the resurrection employs primarily a transcendental method to overcome the extrinsicism of the previous apologetic. The transcendental method demonstrates the correlation between the human experience of grace and Christian belief in the resurrection.[46] For Rahner, the primary task of fundamental theology is to uncover the correlation between the formal structures of Christian experience and the content of Christian revelation.[47] The human experience of openness toward the infinite and the human experience of the dynamism toward the absolute move human beings to search through history for the presence of this absolute and ultimately to discover that presence in the Christian proclamation. Christian revelation is the symbolic expression in history of the expectations implicit in the human experience of grace.

This transcendental analysis, then, elaborates the relation between the resurrection and the human experience of grace in time and freedom. Human beings experience time as the opportunity for freedom and responsibility; temporality or temporal succession makes possible freedom and decisions. In every act of freedom and choice there is an implicit affirmation of values, an implicit affirmation of that which transcends the temporal. Present in every act of freedom is, therefore, the hope for the endurance and permanence of all dimensions of human reality. Every act of freedom implicitly affirms not simply the immortality of the soul, but total personal permanence, including the corporeal dimension of personhood.[48]

This transcendental analysis contrasts with the previous extrinsicism and reliance on external criteria within fundamental theology. The resurrection of Jesus grounds Christian faith not because of reasons independent of faith, but rather as an object and part of faith. The ground of faith is reached only in and through faith and yet this provides a true grounding. A mutual interaction takes place between the transcendental experience of grace and the historical proclamation of the resurrection. It is a mutual interaction between the transcendental affirmation of personal permanence and the concrete historical manifestation of that permanence in the resurrection of Jesus. The resurrection of Jesus as a real symbol and as an object of Christian faith grounds Christian faith because it historically manifests the permanence for which human beings hope. What has taken place in the history of Jesus explicates the eternal permanence implied in all free human decisions.[49]

This existential approach radically changes the locus and value of the empty tomb and the appearances to the disciples. If they had a basic function in the previous fundamental theology, they now have a secondary function. The first witnesses and disciples stand in a relation to the resurrection that is similar to ours, since for them the resurrection is both an object and ground of faith. Their transcendental experience relates similarly to their belief in the resurrection. Rahner interprets even the resurrection experience in a similar manner:

> Hence they [resurrection accounts] are to be explained as secondary literary and dramatic embellishments of the original experience that "Jesus is alive," rather than as descriptions of the experience itself in its real and original nature. So far as the nature of this experience is accessible to us, it is to be explained after the manner of our experience of the powerful Spirit of the living Lord rather than in a way which either likens this experience too closely to mystical visions of an imaginative kind in later times, or understands it as an almost physical sense experience.[50]

The disciples' original experience is not a sense experience of Jesus as someone who has reached fulfillment, for such a sense experience would reduce the manifestation of the resurrection to a normal and ordinary profane sense experience.[51] Nevertheless, a significant difference exists between the first witnesses and us. Their faith in Jesus as risen is *a ground* of our faith because their first witness is prior to our experience. Their belief encourages us to enter into the structure of their faith.[52]

Jesus' Resurrection as Definitive Manifestation of Grace

The last characteristic of this existential fundamental theology is its interpretation of the resurrection as the definitive manifestation of

God's grace revealing the finality of life.[53] The previous fundamental theology emphasized the empty tomb as a historical proof because it interpreted the resurrection primarily as a physical miracle that took place after death. Existential fundamental theology emphasizes that the resurrection is not so much a separate physical fact as it is Jesus' entry into the permanent fulfillment and culmination of his life. The resurrection is viewed not as a separate and additional event to the death of Jesus, but rather as the manifestation of the meaning—and of his death as the ultimacy—of his life.[54] The resurrection, therefore, is not so much a physical miracle that demonstrates the credibility of the message, but rather the manifestation of the unity of revelation and history. The unity between grace and history is expressed in the resurrection insofar as the unity between God and humanity that takes place in grace reaches its culmination in the resurrection. God's divine historical act of accepting the humanity of Jesus in his suffering and death is an act of solidarity that becomes manifest in the resurrection.[55]

From the point of view of fundamental theology, the difference between the previous fundamental theology and transcendental fundamental theology can be illustrated by the distinction between truth and meaning. Since the previous fundamental theology saw the demonstration of the fact of the empty tomb as the foundation of the truth of the resurrection, it argued that the veracity of this fact was the foundation of the truth of Christianity's supernatural revelation. In contrast, existential fundamental theology underscores the meaningfulness of the resurrection in its intrinsic revelatory significance. The resurrection is meaningful as an existential affirmation and as a historical manifestation of the achievement of the finality of life in history. This fundamental theology does not deny the facticity of the resurrection; rather, it emphasizes that its significance is the historical manifestation of a Christian existential truth.

Although the originality of this reinterpretation of the resurrection is incontestable, two critical objections can be raised against its method and interpretation. In its awareness of the complexity of scientific scholarship, the indirect approach overlooks how scientific formulations are often generally accepted in a popularized form. A fundamental theology must therefore interrelate the historical and the existential much more than the transcendental indirect method does. An individual, for example, may not be aware of all the current scientific theories about the origin of the universe, of life, and of the human race. Nevertheless, because of the general acceptance of such scientific theories, a theology of creation must come to terms with the relevant scientific data if it is to be credible even to that person. It does not suffice to appeal to the experience of creatureliness to defend the creative activity of God. The experience of creatureliness must be correlated with contemporary scientific rationality in its specialized and popularized forms.

Likewise, the indirect correlation between the historical and the existential does not remove the need for a historical treatment of the belief in Jesus' resurrection. Rahner concedes that such a historical fundamental theology is still needed. But, in fact, he does not rely on historical research to contextualize the meaning of the resurrection for the earliest disciples. Instead, he starts out from our contemporary human experience of temporality and freedom. The genetic and historical issues of the truth of Jesus' resurrection are almost collapsed into the functional issue of existential meaningfulness. This approach does not reconstruct the diverse truth and meaning claims of the different testimonies of faith in Jesus' resurrection.[56] If the older fundamental theology collapsed the genetic and the functional issues into the historical question, the existential transcendental approach coalesces the genetic and historical into the functional.

A Contemporary Historical-Critical Approach

Recently, a new fundamental theological approach has emerged that explicitly rejects the traditional apologetical demonstration of the resurrection. Whereas modern fundamental theology emphasized the empty tomb and the transcendental approach explicated the existential significance of the appearances of the Risen Christ, this new fundamental theology rejects the significance of both the empty tomb and the appearances. By means of historical-critical exegesis it seeks to establish a new foundation for the resurrection not with the appearances but with the life of Jesus.

This fundamental theology grounds belief in the resurrection *during and not after* the lifetime of Jesus. The exegetical analyses of Willi Marxsen, Ulrich Wilckens, and especially Klaus Berger have influenced Roman Catholic scholars such as Rudolf Pesch, Edward Schillebeeckx, and others[57] to develop diverse positions of what in many ways is a common approach, which even a critic, Anton Vögtle, claims "is in a decisive way superior to all previous solutions of this explanatory direction."[58] It marshals exegetical, historical, and systematic arguments not just to give a new interpretation of the New Testament accounts of the resurrection but to establish a new apologetical front. Much of the criticism of Schillebeeckx's *Jesus* has been engendered precisely by his use of this approach to the resurrection.[59] The decisive innovation is the critique of the foundational significance of the appearances and the appeal to the life and preaching of Jesus for that foundation. Its rejection of the apologetical function of the empty tomb for contemporary fundamental theology is not new since, with few exceptions, that became the common consensus after the demise of modern fundamental theology.[60] Previously, however, the historical critique of the appearances as foundational had been associated not with the development of a new apologetics for the resurrection, but with the denial of belief in the resurrection.[61] It is therefore important to grasp *why* this approach rejects the appearances as the foundation of the belief in the resurrection and *how* it attempts to establish a new foundation for the resurrection in the life of Jesus.

Rejection of the Appearances as Foundational

At first glance this approach appears contrary to the New Testament reports of the centrality of the appearances to the early Christian kerygma. Nevertheless, this apologetic offers three basic arguments why the appearances according to the New Testament reports themselves should not be given a foundational or apologetical foundation. Although each of these arguments and their interpretations can be challenged, the conceptions of Pesch and Schillebeeckx will be presented before any attempt is made to evaluate them.

First, the New Testament accounts themselves do not claim that the appearances caused the emergence of the faith in the resurrection. Rudolf Pesch argues that the New Testament does not report the appearances of the Risen Lord as demonstrations or as proofs of the resurrection. Instead, they presuppose that the belief in the resurrection/exaltation of Jesus had already taken place. Pesch claims "even the Gospel accounts of the appearances altogether narrate the appearances of Jesus not as encounters that have established the belief in the resurrection. In every case they presuppose the faith in the resurrection. They confirm and develop it. And they commission the disciples."[62] No indication is given in the New Testament, he claims, that the disciples first came to a belief in the resurrection of Jesus as the result of the Easter appearances.

Second, the New Testament accounts of the resurrection appearances represent later texts that were composed only after the emergence of the belief in the resurrection/ascension. Earlier texts refer to the resurrection/ascension without grounding the resurrection in the appearances. Moreover, the New Testament formula "he appeared" was written not in order to explain how the first disciples came to believe in the resurrection, but rather to explain their legitimacy as apostles. It justifies the commissioning of various individuals as apostles.[63] Since the intention of the phrase is to describe the legitimacy of the apostolic commissioning, to read it as an apologetical proof or as a genetic explanation of the resurrection is therefore to read it against its grain.[64]

Third, the central kergymatic formula within the New Testament, 1 Cor 15:5 ("he appeared to Cephas, then to the Twelve"), should not be interpreted as a visual phenomenon, sense experience, or ocular perception, but as a manifestation, as in the revelation of a truth. The passive form of the verb *oraō, ōphthē*, with the dative construction is commonly translated here as "appeared to."[65] But the Greek Bible uses this verb so broadly that it does not necessarily imply visual experience, even though it can include it. Moreover, since *ōphthē* rather than *eidon* ("to see") is used, Pesch suggests that it should be understood not so much that Jesus was seen by Cephas and the Twelve as that he was revealed to them. Furthermore, following Marxsen, he argues that Gal 1:16 should be used to interpret 1 Cor 15 where Paul refers to his conversion as a revelation. And he alleges as additional support the use in Mark 16:12,14 and John 21:14 of *phaneroun* to mean "being made manifest."[66] The use in the Old Testament of visionary language suggests not so much the act of seeing as a vocational commission.[67] For these reasons, Pesch interprets "he appeared" as a legitimation formula rather than as a vision. In his response to critics he is more cautious but states that even if the phrase were to refer to a vision, "the vision did not occasion the origin of the Easter faith, but confirmed this faith."[68]

Foundation in the Life of Jesus

Since neither the empty tomb nor the appearances have genetically caused the early Christian faith in the resurrection of Jesus but already presuppose it, this approach looks to the life of Jesus for the origin as well as the foundation of the belief in Jesus' resurrection. On the basis of several historical hypotheses, it argues that at the time of Jesus a general and widespread expectation existed that a messianic prophet would be sent. This prophet would be martyred and would after his death be raised from the dead and taken to heaven. Evidence for such a widespread popular belief existed prior to Jesus[69] and is even found in Mark 6:14 ("Some said, John the baptizer has been raised from the dead"). The Jewish tradition of the martyrdom and resurrection of eschatological figures (Elijah and Enoch) had in Jesus' lifetime been applied to the fate of John the baptizer. This widespread belief therefore provided the conceptual horizon for the emergence of the belief in Jesus' resurrection.

Pesch's Hypothesis

The argument is as follows: since the death and resurrection of martyred prophets were widespread, since Jesus understood himself as such a prophet, and since his disciples shared this belief, then their belief in the resurrection has its foundation not on the time after the death of Jesus but during his ministry when they came to believe in Jesus as the end-time eschatological prophet.[70] The faith of the disciples in Jesus as an eschatological prophet was neither changed nor shattered by his death. Just as the disciples of John the baptizer could, even after his death, still endure in their faith, believe in his resurrection, and become missionaries and baptize (Acts 19:1–7), so too could the disciples of Jesus remain faithful to their belief in him and his message after his death. Their faith in Jesus prior to his death and after his death remains basically the same. Moreover, Pesch argues that in fact Jesus at the last supper instructed his disciples concerning his death,[71] and they were able to accept this instruction because the Jewish tradition of the death and exaltation of Enoch and Elijah had already provided them with models to understand the fate of Jesus.

What took place after the death of Jesus? In regard to the disciples, they gathered together, reflected on his life, and continued to believe in Jesus. Luke 22:31 is taken to indicate that Peter's faith was not shaken so that he strengthened the others and gathered them together. The disciples expressed their continued faith in Jesus as the eschatological prophet who would be martyred and exalted through their proclamation of the resurrection. The formula "he appeared" expresses the manifestation and revelation of the truth of Jesus. The special reference to Peter indicates his leadership in gathering them together.[72] In short, it was not the appearances that gave rise to the resurrection, but rather the prophetic life-style and fate of Jesus. The appearances are literary devices used to express the disciples' continued belief in Jesus and their further reflection on his fate.

Schillebeeckx's Hypothesis

Since Schillebeeckx's position has been closely associated with Pesch's view, the agreements and differences should be noted.[73] First, both reject the empty tomb or the appearances as either an

apologetical foundation of the faith in the resurrection or as a historical genetical explanation of the origin of that faith. In fact, Schillebeeckx notes that to assume pneumatic experiences led to the emergence of the faith in the resurrection is to postulate what needs to be
explained: the gathered community. "The reassembly of the disciples
is precisely what has to be explained. Appearance stories and accounts of the empty tomb assure the fact of the reassembled community and its Christological kerygma."[74] Moreover, whereas in his response to his critics Pesch carefully distinguishes between "he
appeared" as a legimation formula and the appearance accounts,
Schillebeeckx maintains, "it should be noted that initially the appearances are not reported with any apologetic purpose in view, as a kind
of proof of Jesus' resurrection. At issue is the legitimation of the
apostolic missionary mandate, not some confirmation of the resurrection's having taken place."[75]

Second, Schillebeeckx also seeks a foundation for the belief in the
resurrection in the life of Jesus, but he differs by appealing to a post-
Easter "conversion experience." Using the exegetical studies of
Berger, Nickelsburg, and Ruppert,[76] he argues that at the time of
Jesus belief in the martyrdom and vindication of God's eschatological
prophet was not only current but also formed Jesus' self-understanding. Therefore, the post-Easter understanding of Jesus "is not just a
vision born of faith and based solely on the disciples' Easter experience; it is his self-understanding that creates the possibility and lays
the foundation of the subsequent interpretation by the Christians."[77]

Although much more cautious than Pesch in attributing a pre-
Easter prediction of his death to Jesus and much more aware of the
shattering negativity of his death, Schillebeeckx still maintains that
Jesus' death did not lead to "a loss of faith."[78] Moreover, a challenge
is placed to exegetes "who start from the death of Jesus as the point of
disjunction" to explain "why, when John the Baptist had been be-
headed, his movement was able simply to continue on Jewish
ground."[79] Therefore, Schillebeeckx argues that the Easter christology with its belief in the resurrection of Jesus "was originally
grounded in and justified by the Christians' identifying the person of
Jesus with the eschatological prophet."[80]

Even though Jesus' life provides the foundation and ground for
this identification, only after the death of Jesus, only after his life is
completed, does this identification take place. This is the decisive
difference between Pesch and Schillebeeckx. Whereas Pesch maintains that the belief in Jesus prior to the death continues and is only
modified and further explicated after his death, Schillebeeckx postu-

lates a conversion experience. Despite their commitment to Jesus, the disciples do not comprehend Jesus' own self-understanding as an eschatological prophet who would be martyred. Only after his death and only "after the first shock of his dying, the memory of Jesus' life and especially of the last supper must have played a vital role in the process of their conversion to faith in Jesus as the Christ."[81]

After the death of Jesus, the disciples undergo a "conversion experience." It is caused by a divine act of grace and forgiveness and occurs in their further reflection upon the life and death of Jesus. This conversion experience is constituted not only by the awareness that they have been forgiven for their frailty at the time of Jesus' death but also by the belief that Jesus is the prophet whom God has vindicated. Just what leads to this conversion experience is not clear. Augustin Schmied writes of Schillebeeckx, "he would like to indicate that as the locus and source of the faith in the resurrection 'more normal' and more human processes came into question as disclosure-situations for a completely new knowledge of Christ."[82] Such an interpretation reads into Schillebeeckx's brief remarks what is left open. He does not exactly determine the source of the conversion experience except to emphasize that it results from an act of God and from recollections of the life of Jesus.[83]

Since the conversion experience involves coming to believe in Jesus as the vindicated eschatological prophet, the question is what precisely does this identification entail for Jesus. Here Schillebeeckx selects a particular exegetical option—not a dominant opinion today—that not only separates the notion of exaltation from that of resurrection, but places the notion of exaltation prior to that of resurrection and separates a "simple exaltation" in heaven (immediately after death) from an "exaltation as enthronement at the right hand of the father" (at the parousia).[84] In developing this exegetical tradition, the following historical reconstruction is suggested: after the death of Jesus, the disciples had a conversion experience; they first identified Jesus as the end-time humiliated and exalted prophet; then they expressly explicated this belief as either exaltation or as resurrection; finally, they not only identified exaltation, resurrection, and enthronement but also further explicated the notion of resurrection with the category of appearances.

In response to his critics, Schillebeeckx wavers. On the one hand, he affirms that the identification of Jesus as the eschatological prophet with the one who is to come is the matrix for all other beliefs, including the resurrection belief. On the other hand, he argues that his emphasis upon the diversity of early Christian beliefs intends to affirm that in some traditions the resurrection was the earliest belief, whereas in other traditions (the majority of traditions) the exaltation was the earliest belief.[85] Only at a later stage in the development of traditions are the resurrection and exaltation in power identified. It is this final development, however, that Schillebeeckx takes as normative for systematic theology in its understanding of the resurrection of Jesus.[86]

Unfortunately, Schillebeeckx's emphasis upon the diversity of conceptions has led to severe misinterpretations and unjust criticisms. When he claims that the resurrection was unknown in some early Christian traditions or when he claims that the conversion experience led to the identification of Jesus as the humiliated and exalted prophet, he is not denying that the early Christians believed that Jesus still lives; he is denying only that a particular notion of the resurrection was present. He distinguishes sharply between resurrection and exaltation in order to prevent resurrection from being understood as resuscitation. When he claims that the resurrection was unknown, he means a resurrection as resuscitation, but not a resurrection understood as exaltation.[87]

Implications for Fundamental Theology

Despite differences, Pesch and Schillebeeckx have developed a new fundamental theological approach to the resurrection.[88] Both reject the empty tomb and the appearances as the ground of belief in the resurrection; both assert that the life, ministry, and self-understanding of Jesus provide the foundation for faith in the resurrection. Such an approach contrasts starkly with the modern apologetic attempt to base the belief in the resurrection upon a historical demonstration of the veracity of the empty tomb and the appearances. Belief in the resurrection, Pesch and Schillebeeckx assert, is prior to the appearance traditions. This approach goes even beyond the existential fundamental theology that sought to interpret the appearance of Jesus as both the object and ground of the Christian faith, even though it acknowledged the literary nature of the appearance accounts. This new approach, however, rejects the notion that the appearances are the object and ground of Christian faith. In Schillebeeckx's words, "the appearances as such are, after all, not an *object* of Christian faith."[89] Moreover, whereas the existential fundamental theology illumined the transcendental horizon for belief in the resurrection, this historical approach highlights the horizon of the first disciples in their encounter with the historical Jesus, especially the horizon of their expectations of a latter-day prophet.

This emphasis upon the life and fate of Jesus rather than on the empty tomb or on the appearances as the ground of belief in the resurrection has fundamental theological significance insofar as the claim is then advanced that practically no difference exists between the first disciples and us in regard to that belief.[90] Fundamental theology had previously underscored this difference insofar as the experience of the empty tomb and of the appearances gave rise to the belief in the resurrection preceded both traditions.[91] Insofar as the experi-first disciples. Since all other generations of Christians did not have access to this experience, their faith was based upon the testimony of the first disciples. The approach of Schillebeeckx and Pesch, however, emphasizes that the life of Jesus is the ground of the resurrection belief. Therefore, just as we have no access to the empty tomb or to the appearances, so too did the first disciples not have first an experience of the empty tomb or appearances, but rather their belief in the resurrection preceded both traditions.[91] Insofar as the experience of grace and reflection upon the life of Jesus ground and cause belief in the resurrection, the faith of succeeding generations of Christians has the same structure since it too rests on the experience of grace and on reflection on the life and fate of Jesus.

Since such an approach approximates the emphasis upon the historical Jesus of nineteenth-century Protestant liberalism, the label of liberalism has been attached to it by some as strongly as it has been rejected by others.[92] De facto, within the nineteenth century, Schleiermacher, Ritschl, and Herrmann, and in our century Tillich and Ebeling have sought to ground the faith of Christianity not in the resurrection, but in the life and ministry of Jesus.[93] For Schleiermacher, it was Jesus' consciousness of God, for Herrmann, his inner personality, and for Ebeling, it was the faith of Jesus.[94]

This new approach, however, does differ, for it seeks to combine the historical question of the emergence of faith in the resurrection with the historical question about Jesus' self-understanding, life-praxis, and fate in order to resolve the issue of the foundation not only of Christianity but of the resurrection. Insofar as Schillebeeckx emphasizes the uniqueness of Jesus' consciousness of God as *abba* and his mystical experience as both the ground of God's being in him and the result of God's presence in him, he approaches the position of Schleiermacher.[95] Nevertheless, Schillebeeckx radically affirms Jesus' continued personal existence and his historical analysis is not simply the old quest for the historical Jesus.[96] He seeks to mediate between the empiricism of historical research and the fideism of a faith stance alone. Historical research uncovers beneath the layers of tradition the self-understanding of the historical Jesus and the faith of the first disciples. This method is in Schillebeekcx's words, *fides quaerens intellectum historicum* ("faith seeking historical understanding").[97]

This fundamental theological approach has several important advantages. Against a prevalent skepticism, it seeks to link the early Christian kerygma with the life and ministry of Jesus. Consequently, a commitment to the Risen Lord is a commitment to the life, preaching, and fate of the historical Jesus. The kerygma about Christ does not stand in isolation from the historical Jesus.[98] Further, it underscores not only the complexity and diversity of the early Christian creeds about Jesus but also emphasizes that the various conceptions of Jesus' fate, exaltation, rapture, enthronement, and resurrection should be understood against the background of diverse traditions at the time of Jesus. Finally, it drives home that the resurrection should not simply be conceived of as physical miracle that so stuns the disciples that no room is left for faith. Instead, the resurrection of Jesus implies an encounter involving subjective conversion, a revelation of the meaning of Jesus, a commission to proclaim, a response in faith, a new view of the life and fate of Jesus.

Unresolved Issues

Several important objections, both historical and fundamental theological, can be raised against this new approach:

Most significantly, the interpretation of the New Testament data is based upon questionable hypotheses, interpretations, and selections. First, the assumptions that there was an expectation of the death and resurrection of an eschatological prophet and that this expectation was widespread in Palestine prior to the time of Jesus—both assumptions have been challenged by exegetes Eduard Schweizer, Martin Hengel, Johannes Nützel, and Ulrich Kellermann.[99] They argue that the data are much later than the New Testament and therefore do not demonstrate a pre-Christian horizon. Second, the listing of the various appearances and witnesses does serve as proof of the reality of the resurrection and not simply as a legitimation formula.[100] Third, the approach appears to operate on the hypothesis that Mark and the synoptics contain historical traditions that represent earlier stages than the pre-Pauline formula and hymns. Hence the formula material of the Pauline writings is neglected. Fourth, Schillebeeckx's use of the three accounts of Paul's conversion in Acts to illustrate the Easter experience is questionable on two accounts. As he himself admits, much of the material in the Lukan accounts represents Lukan theology. In addition, a difference exists between the disciples and Paul. The disciples knew the earthly Jesus, they were committed to him during his ministry so that their post-Easter experience is less appropriately a conversion experience than an "identity manifestation."[101]

In terms of fundamental theology, this new approach therefore has not only not resolved the genetic issue of the origin of the resurrection faith, but it appears to have reduced the foundational issue to the genetic issue. Has it explained sufficiently how faith in the resurrection of Jesus emerged? Even if we grant that Mark tended to overemphasize the failure of the disciples at the death of Jesus in order to underscore that true discipleship is an imitative suffering, and even if we grant that belief in a humiliated and exalted prophet was current in Palestine, we would still question whether it has adequately explained the continuation of the belief in Jesus after his death—a belief not just in exaltation but also in appearances. Pesch refers to "continued reflection" and Schillebeeckx refers to a "conversion experience" as an act of God. Does not the appeal to an act of God as causing a conversion experience appear as illusive unless it illustrates how the act of God occurred in time and space?[102]

A more significant criticism relates to how this approach brings together the foundational and the genetic issue. Even if the appeal to the pre-Easter horizon of the disciples helps explain the post-Easter faith of the first disciples, does it help to found our belief in the resurrection of Jesus? Is not the problem of the foundation of the resurrection pushed back from the post-Easter to the pre-Easter period but not really resolved. To argue that the disciples had adequate categories from their tradition that made their belief more intelligible, meaningful, and credible does not eo ipso make this belief more meaningful and intelligible for us today. In fact, the attempt to show the pre-Christian horizon for such a belief actually undercuts their fundamental theological assertion that we are in a structurally similar position as the first disciples. We would then be at a disadvantage insofar as their apocalyptic world view may not be our world view. The foundational issue of the faith in the resurrection requires that this faith not only be linked with the intellectual horizons of the first disciples but also with our intellectual horizons.

Modern fundamental theology sought to demonstrate the resurrection as a historical fact that could be made credible independently of human faith. Existential fundamental theology interrelated the object and ground of faith by showing how the resurrection was meaningfully related to human aspirations. But, as we have already argued, this existential solution collapses both the genetic question (how did faith in the resurrection emerge) with the foundational question (of its truth and credibility) and with the question of its meaningfulness.[103] The proposed historical approach with its emphasis upon the pre-Easter horizon merges the issue of meaningfulness and the foundational question into the genetic question. By showing the meaning of Jesus for universal history, Schillebeeckx does indeed go beyond this identification and beyond making Jesus' life the ground of our faith in the resurrection itself. Nevertheless, in criticizing the foundational significance of the empty tomb and the appearances, the mainstays of previous apologetics, this new historical-critical approach does not resolve the question, but actually makes it more acute. The historical and fundamental theological weaknesses of this approach make necessary both a different conception of fundamental theology and a different approach to the resurrection.

Chapter 2

A Reconstructive Hermeneutic of Jesus' Resurrection

Testimony and Historical Argumentation

The problem of the resurrection of Jesus for fundamental theology is that if universal laws of historical demonstration, if a general existential anthropology, or if previous apocalyptic thought-horizons are used to ground the resurrection of Jesus, the danger exists that the historical uniqueness of the resurrection will be downplayed and its attestability only through believing Christian witnesses will be minimized. On the other hand, if the uniqueness of the resurrection is overemphasized, then the danger exists that the belief will not be linked up with human history, meaning, and expectations. Christian faith proclaims the resurrection of Jesus both as a singular event in history and as an event with universal significance.

In order to take into account this dilemma of fundamental theology and of the previous positions, this concluding section of Part I will outline a reconstructive approach[104] to the resurrection that will analyze the hermeneutical significance of testimony and will discuss the nature of historical narrative. Then it will survey two distinct literary genres of New Testament testimony of the resurrection, and finally relate the meaning disclosed within the Christian testimonies with human experience in a way that differs from the three previously discussed approaches.

The Hermeneutics of Testimony

A central problem of belief in the resurrection is the extent to which our general experience does not illumine either its meaning or its truth claim. To speak about the resurrection of Jesus does not involve saying that something universally known and experienced has happened to Jesus. For example, we have a general knowledge of pneumonia so that when we state that someone is sick from pneumonia our language is informative because we are simply moving from the general to the particular. In contrast, to affirm the resurrection of Jesus from the dead does not involve affirming a particular example of what we already know. In fact, what we may think about the resurrection of the dead is, as much if not even more, dependent upon what we proclaim has happened to Jesus, than is the reverse. Today we do not so much go from a knowledge of what the resurrection of the dead means to a proclamation that this has happened to Jesus as we move from the belief in the resurrection of Jesus to the belief in the resurrection of the dead. Our understanding of the former molds our understanding of the latter.

This problem of meaning points to the necessity of taking into account certain developments in hermeneutics. Recently Paul Ricoeur has outlined a conception of revelation and revelatory discourse based upon the category of testimony.[105] He argues that neither the example nor the symbol but only testimony can fulfill the role of an experience of the absolute.

The example is an individual case subsumed under a general law. Therefore, an example illustrates in a particular case what is common or universal. It manifests what is the general norm, but not what is the exception to the norm by transcending it. What the general norm does not justify doesn't come to the fore in the example. Nor does a symbol suffice as a category for the experience of the absolute. Despite its richness of multivalent imagery, a symbol does not point to the concrete particular or to the individual historical moment. A symbol is ordered to meaning rather than to the historical. If the example is the category of historical understanding, then one misses the significance of the claim that the resurrection of Jesus transcends the common and general. If the symbol is taken as the category to understand the resurrection, then the claim of the historical particularity of Jesus' resurrection is neglected.

Testimony, however, attests to a concrete singular event. It invests a moment of history with absolute character. An example that merely exemplifies a universal law or a symbol that symbolizes a universal meaning does not of itself need testimony. But an event of singular transcendence needs testimony. Such testimony provides two elements. It presents a content that needs to be interpreted and it calls for an interpretation. In language that Paul Ricoeur borrows from Jean Nabert, two elements are needed, "the exegesis of the historic testimony of the absolute and the exegesis of the self in the criteriology of the divine."[106]

Ever since Lessing criticized an apologetics based upon reports of prophecies and miracles, testimony has lost its standing within theology. His distinction between immediate and direct experience of miracles, and historical reports about miracles has led to an emphasis upon experience and to a devaluation of testimony.[107] Despite the significance of Lessing's distinction, what his critique overlooks is that testimony is not simply a report about what happened; rather, testimony brings to expression the meaning of what happened. The meaning and significance of an event do not exist independently and isolated from the testimony about the event. Instead, the meaning and significance of the event emerge in the testimony about the event.

Since the content of testimony points to the singular historical and since it discloses the meaning of the event, the criteria of testimony are complex. They are not simply criteria of correspondence between reports and events independent of interpretation. Instead, the criteria of testimony entail the ability to provide an intelligible narrative and the personal authenticity of the individual. In addition, a testimony's ability to disclose the meaning of an event in a way that is both theoretically and practically illuminating belongs to the criteria of the truth of the testimony.[108] For these reasons, it is necessary to look more closely at the resurrection in the light of the issues relating to historical testimony, the disclosure of meaning, and its illuminating foundational significance.

Historical Testimonies

An important issue is whether the testimony about the resurrection qualifies as history, as opposed to fiction or legend. A realistic novel may provide a coherent picture and a consistent narrative and yet still not be qualified as historical. Ernst Troeltsch's famous principles (criticism, analogy, and correlation) point out not only the probability of all historical knowledge but also the necessity of historical events to stand in analogy to other events and to stand in a chain of cause and effect within the historical order.[109] Historians agree that for a narrative to be historical it must be located within time and space and must be analogous to other events within the human world. Moreover, the event must be capable of proof through unprejudicial evidence and public accessibility.[110]

The complexity of historical knowledge and of historical events makes these criteria especially complex in dealing with singular events which are publicly inaccessible. Since history must deal with all events, historical thinking would require an openness to the uniqueness of certain past events. No historian should rule out a priori the possibility of such events. Historical knowledge must face the challenge of comprehending the genuinely unique.[111] Likewise, a historical narrative of the sequence of events is forced to offer an interpretation, even where certain events or some evidence is not publicly accessible. Faced with this challenge, a philosopher of history, W. B. Gallie, suggests that an account of an event can be considered historical if it is built out of materials that are publicly accessible, and if it provides the best narrative account of what has taken place even if all the evidence or all the events are not publicly accessible.[112]

For example, a political decision may have been made for reasons and motives not publicly accessible, but the conditions prior to the decision and the consequences of the decision are accessible. A historian reconstructs an account that gives the best narrative continuity between all the events so that his/her narrative structure appears as the most plausible explanation. The historian's narrative account is then considered historical not because all events or evidence are publicly accessible nor because neutral witnesses can be provided, but because it provides the most consistent account of what has taken place.

If the above brief suggestions are applied to the issue of the historicity of the resurrection accounts, then these accounts cannot be characterized simply as fictional, legendary, or even mythical in the sense of unhistorical. Nor, however, can they be considered historical in the sense that the empty tomb was a publicly accessible fact in Jerusalem which demonstrated the truth of the resurrection. Such an argument overlooked the theological orientation of the accounts themselves, their production by believing witnesses, and the possibility that the resurrection was preached first in Galilee and not in Jerusalem.[113]

If these accounts, however, are approached not as unhistorical nor as neutral historical documents, but as confessional narratives, the question can still be put to them: how do they link what is historically accessible to what is not? How do they disclose the meaning of what appears to escape the criteria of analogy, correlation, and accessibility? The historical issue would then become not whether the documents have a demonstrative force and apologetic function independently of faith, but whether they give the most appropriate narrative accounts of extant publicly accessible materials and whether these accounts disclose the meaning of events in relation to reality and human existence.

What is historically accessible are the facts of the execution of Jesus and the first disciples' proclamation of Jesus. The historian is faced with an unknown X about what took place between the death of Jesus and the early Christian proclamation. The New Testament testimonies of what took place provide for many Christians the most consistent narrative accounts that explain the emergence of the Christian faith in Jesus despite the shock of his death on the cross. But these narrative accounts propose an event that transcends normal expectations and they lack analogies in our everyday experience. Rather than exclude a priori such testimonies, it would be more appropriate first to analyze them in their diverse literary forms.

New Testament Testimonies

Since an exegesis of all the various New Testament accounts cannot be given here, I will discuss briefly two diverse sets of texts: the short formula material within the Pauline writings and the appearance traditions within the Gospel writings. These discussions will illustrate an approach that differs not only from those of modern and transcendental fundamental theology but also from the method used by Schillebeeckx. For example, he does not focus on the short formulas as the earliest texts but seeks to uncover the earliest traditions from his analysis of the Gospel materials. Moreover, he uses the Lukan accounts of Paul's conversion in Acts to obtain a basic model for understanding the meaning of the "Easter experience," rather than exploring the appearance traditions within the Gospel materials for their fundamental theological significance.

Short Formulas

The earliest texts are the short formulas. These formulas show a development from one verse eulogies, or homologies, to several verse credo formulas.[114] The earliest formula is the one member clause, "God has raised Jesus from the dead," which occurs eight times in the New Testament (Rom 4:24b; 8:11a and 11b; 2 Cor 4:14; Gal 1:1;

Eph 1:20; Col 2:12; 1 Pet 1:21). It describes God as the active subject of a past action (aorist): God has taken Jesus from the realm of the dead.[115]

The one verse formula has the literary form of a *eulogy*, a form of praise and prayer within liturgical service. Eulogies were introductions or conclusions to psalms that praise God. The formula, a participial phrase, is used as a predicate of God.[116] Its parallel to Old Testament Jewish prayer and liturgical practice points to its meaning. The formula is primarily a *theo*-logical affirmation and only indirectly a christological statement. The Christian community continues the Israelite belief in God's power over life and death, and praises God for the exercise of this power in regard to Jesus. Since the formula is so theocentrically oriented, it does not result from a long development but stands at the very beginning of the Christian understanding of the resurrection, and not merely the resurrection of Jesus as a past event, but as an affirmation of the reality of God's deed and power. It affirms that God as the all-determining power over life and death has intervened for Jesus.

Next to these early one verse formulas are the two verse formulas that explicate the Christian faith and are known as *credo* or *pistis* formulas, for example, Rom 1:3 and 10:9.[117] The two member formula of 1 Thess 1:9f. illustrates how the terminology of preaching and faith (v. 9) is combined with the resurrection formula, "and to wait for his Son from heaven, whom he raised from the dead, Jesus who delivers us from the wrath to come." (v. 10).[118] If the one verse eulogy was theocentric, this formula adds an explicitly christological emphasis. This creedal formula probably became a part of missionary preaching or of a baptismal liturgy within Hellenistic Jewish Christianity.

It is theologically significant that God's raising of Jesus from the dead (resurrection) is associated with Jesus' enthronement in power, and is the basis of his ability to intercede for the Christian community (exaltation). Moreover, the intercession is future oriented: he delivers the community from the wrath to come and the community awaits his descent from heaven. The formula expresses an early stage of theological development: it views salvation as a future event and it emphasizes God's action in raising Jesus. The power of God in Jesus' resurrection becomes the eschatological power of Jesus.[119]

1 Cor 15 stands at the center of pre-Pauline tradition and Pauline theology. The four member creedal formula of 1 Cor 15:3a–5[120] should be considered only after the above one- and two-member formulas and not before them since it represents a later and more developed stage. Paul quotes these verses as a formula of the tradition within the

context of a defense of his own apostolic mission and of the resurrection of the dead. To the creedal formula in verses 3a–5, "that Christ died for our sins in accordance with the scriptures, and that he was buried, that he was raised on the third day in accordance with the scriptures, and that he appeared to Cephas, then to the twelve," he adds verses 6–8: "Then he appeared to more than five-hundred brethren at one time. . . . Then he appeared to James, then to all the apostles. Last of all, as to one untimely born, he appeared also to me." Paul alone of all the New Testament writers advances such a first person claim and yet he places his testimony within the tradition of the other witnesses.

The interpretation of both the traditional formula and of Paul's extension of it to himself should not be contrasted but correlated. To interpret "he appeared" not as a visual experience but as a revelation or to explain it not as a testimony to the resurrection but as a legitimation of Paul's apostleship separates what should be linked.[121] The reference in verse 6 to the "more than five hundred" makes improbable any explanation of the formula exclusively as a formula of apostolic legitimation. When the verb "he appeared" (*ōphthē*) was used in the Septuagint with the prepositions *pros* or *en*, the visual element was not weakened but strengthened. Likewise, appearance terminology was used in the Septuagint with a visual element, for example, Tob 12:22 (the appearance of Raphael) and 2 Macc 3:23–24 (the horseman).

The proper correlation between Paul's own explanations in Gal 1:15 and 1 Cor 9 and the text of the creedal formula in 1 Cor 15 is even more significant. In Gal 1:1 Paul proclaims that he has received his gospel not from human hands but through a revelation of Jesus Christ. His claim has been either contrasted with 1 Cor 15 or has been interpreted incorrectly to mean "he appeared" as an internal revelation or a mystical experience.

A correlation rather than a contrast is required for two reasons. First, recent research has indicated that the "revelation" (*apocalypsis*) in Galatians should not be understood as an intellectual insight, a mystical experience, or a religious conversion.[122] Paul uses language in Gal 1 that he used elsewhere to refer to the making manifest or to the unveiling of end-time events. Within an apocalyptic tradition, it refers to the unveiling of end-time events and heavenly conditions.[123] Moreover, his language is similar to the language of the tradition in Q (the source common to Luke and Matthew) that refers to Jesus' eschatological role as the son of God.[124]

Second, Paul's statements in Gal 1:15f. and 1 Cor 9:1 indicate that he understood his calling to apostleship analogously to the prophetic vocation.[125] He explicitly uses the terminology of the vocational theophany (e.g., Isa 61:1, 5). Just as the prophetic mission was inaugurated by a theophany, so too does his apostolic mission begin with a christophany. The revelation to Paul of Jesus as God's son and of Jesus' eschatological role constitutes the meaning of the christophany that establishes Paul's apostleship. Not simply his apostolic legitimation but as the analogy to the prophetic vocation indicates a revelation is at stake. Consequently, precisely because Jesus' status and role have become manifest to Paul, he is empowered to proclaim the gospel of Jesus Christ.

The fundamental theological problem meshes with the historical question: how are the statements of the resurrection of Jesus (the doxological, proclamatory, and creedal formulas) related to the claims of the revelation and manifestation (*apocalypsis*) of Jesus as God's son? Our analysis of the literary forms and traditions shows that the resurrection formulas and the "Jesus-revelation" testimony represent independent literary traditions and have different contexts. Several important fundamental theological consequences result from this analysis.

First, this analysis dismisses the claim that the resurrection is only an interpretation of a revelatory experience. No literary evidence exists that the resurrection formula exists only as an interpretative model of the revelatory experience. Second, the antiquity of the resurrection formula shows that belief in the resurrection is as early as belief in the exaltation or the expectation of the son of man. Third, this testimony to a manifestation and revelation of Jesus should not be reduced to a belief in the resurrection. Such a reduction occurs when today's horizon and questions dominate. Belief in the resurrection of Jesus alone does not fully explain the development of early Christianity. In the tradition of the humiliation and exaltation of the "righteous sufferer" or the "martyr-prophet," the resurrection/exaltation would legitimate the teaching, piety, and life of the righteous person and prophet, but it would not make them into the eschatological son of man or into the messiah.[126] The proclamation of Jesus as the Christ and as the son of man is a proclamation that goes far beyond that of resurrection. The resurrection would of itself be an insufficient foundation for such beliefs. Consequently, the pre-Easter traditions of the righteous sufferer or the martyr-prophet do not suffice to explain the rise of early christology and the decisive eschatological role attributed to Jesus.

The fundamental theological issue of the resurrection of Jesus obtains its proper perspective when the literary traditions of the resurrection formulas and of the revelation of Jesus are seen as involving more than the continued personal existence of Jesus. The belief that Jesus lives is, at the same time, a belief that the ultimate power of life, God, has not only raised Jesus from the dead but has made Jesus the decisive eschatological instance. Belief in the resurrection of Jesus entails a vision of reality, a vision of the presence of God's power, that not only illumines the life and faith of Jesus but also grounds the mission of the Church. This vision gives new meaning to Jesus' life and at the same time provides a meaning for the Church and its mission—as the Gospel accounts make evident.

Gospel Appearance Narratives

The short formulas are the earliest New Testament texts about the resurrection of Jesus, and the Gospel narratives of the appearances and of the empty tomb narratives are among the latest. Several recent monographs have analyzed in detail these complex accounts.[127] The following presentation is limited to summary points made with a view to raising the fundamental theological issue.

Several characteristics appear in most of the Gospel appearance narratives. They are anthropomorphic appearances as distinguished from heavenly radiance or shining light appearances.[128] Whereas in Acts Paul sees only a light or hears a voice, the Gospels narrate that Jesus appeared in an anthropomorphic form. In addition, despite structural similarities to the Greco-Roman appearances of divine men, the Gospel descriptions borrow most heavily from the literary form of the Old Testament accounts of anthropomorphic theophanies. Finally, the accounts are permeated with the motifs of apologetics, commission, and identity. A distinction is often made between appearances to individuals and groups:[129] whereas Jesus appears to the gathered group of disciples as a recognizable figure and commissions them, he seems not to be recognized by individuals and only later do they recognize him. Nevertheless, in almost all the stories the identity motif is present because even in appearances to the group he is either not recognized or recognized only with doubt and suspicion, so that he must confirm his identity before commissioning them.

The apologetic motif comes to the fore in the stories about the discovery of the empty tomb,[130] the references to the fulfillment of the Scriptures, and the proliferation of the number of witnesses.[131] Although this apologetic motif is also present within the appearance accounts themselves, there the identity and commissioning motifs dominate. The significance of the identity motif is blurred if, as in the modern apologetic, the resurrection is considered primarily as a supernatural miracle attested by appearances. If the modern apologetic sought to demonstrate the supernatural character of the resurrection, the identity motif within the appearance narratives basically serves to demonstrate the humanity of the Risen Lord. What is stressed is not so much the risen status of Jesus. Rather, his human reality and identity with the historical Jesus is emphasized. Luke 24:36–43 shows that what appears it not a spirit; he affirms its fleshly reality, and underscores its identity with the earthly Jesus.[132] Likewise, John 20:20 emphasizes the corporeal reality of the risen Jesus[133] to make an anti-Docetic point. What is emphasized is that the Jesus the disciples have seen is in his humanity identical with the historical Jesus.

The meaning of the appearance narratives lies in the combination of the motifs of commissioning and of identity.[134] Matthew's description of the commissioning underscores the power and presence of the Risen Lord in the Church as the ground of its universal mission. Since Luke associates apostleship with witness to the resurrection, he has the appearances stretch out over a longer period of time. The Risen Lord opens the meaning of the Scriptures and establishes the Church so that a new stage of salvation history begins. John's Gospel relates the commissioning to the forgiveness of sin.

The combination of the motifs of commissioning and identity show that the basic goal of the appearance stories is not to prove the resurrection of Jesus but to show the link between the Church's mission and the historical Jesus. The identity of the Risen Lord with the historical Jesus is the key to the appearance stories.

Testimony and Ground of Faith

Faith in the resurrection has its ground within these testimonies rather than outside of them. Such a suggestion affects how we understand not only these testimonies but also fundamental theology. It differs from what has been emphasized in the approaches discussed earlier. The modern apologetic grounded belief in the resurrection not so much in the testimonies themselves as in the public accessible data to which they referred or in the authority of God as their ultimate author. For the existential apologetic, the resurrection was both the object and ground of Christian faith because the anthropological hope in eternal permanency comes to expression in the Christian historical hope in Jesus' resurrection. The texts are only secondary embellishments of a primary experience. For the historical approach, the ground of faith was neither the appearances nor the doxological formulas; rather, Jesus' self-understanding and the disciples' conversion experience to Jesus that resulted from God's grace and provided the basis of the New Testament testimonies. My proposal that the testimonies themselves are the ground of faith in the resurrection entails specific positions on two issues: the relation between literary form and revelatory content; and the interrelation between interpretation, experience, and faith.

Literary Form and Revelatory Content

The diverse literary forms (eulogic and creedal formulas within the Pauline letters and androcentric narratives within the Gospel accounts) have each a particular situation, function, and meaning. Whereas the eulogic formulas were located within the liturgical service and the creedal formulas within the missionary proclamation or baptismal liturgy, the appearances have been seen (since Martin Dibelius) as examples, paradigms, or illustrations of the kerygma in graphic imagery. Yet this is too simplistic for the appearance narratives do not merely embellish the kerygma; instead, they contain distinct traditions with a specific form and content.

A correspondence exists between the form of literary discourse and its content. The hymnic and creedal formulas in the Pauline letters refer to God's deed of raising Jesus from the dead. Just as the Pauline letters do not narrate the life and history of Jesus, these creedal formulas do not describe and relate appearance stories. But just as the Gospel materials go back and describe the life and ministry of Jesus, so too the Gospel accounts spell out the revelation of Jesus in androcentric theophanies. Similarly, the Pauline references to the revelation of Jesus combine revelation and commissioning as do the Gospel accounts. But whereas the Pauline letters do not describe the theophanic commissioning, the Gospel narratives do and thereby secure more clearly the Church's identity and foundation with its belief in the Risen Lord as the historical Jesus.

The importance of attending to the diversity of original religious discourse has been noted by Paul Ricoeur.[135] An interpretation of revelation should heed the diverse modalities of religious discourse within a community's language of faith so as to avoid an a priori reduction of revelation to merely one particular mode of religious discourse. Whereas traditional conceptions of revelation have re-ferred primarily to the prophetic experience or to a lesser extent to historical experience, they have neglected sapiential, prescriptive, and hymnic forms of discourse as keys to understanding the content and nature or revelation.

Hymnic discourse not only addresses God, but it also expresses personal and communitarian sentiments. It not only refers to objective action, but it also utters subjective dispositions. In giving thanks, in praising, and in supplicating, the communities are manifesting something about their own state of existence, so that these acts are in a sense self-transformative. *Narrative* discourse differs.[136] It emphasizes the acting subject of the discourse. A narrative has a beginning, a course, and an end. A historical narrative relates how the foundational identity moves forward with continuity and constitutes a specific history.

The resurrection accounts can be better understood through this distinction of literary forms. It is the nature of narrative to focus on the subject of action, the foundational beginning, and the continuity of identity; and the Gospel accounts can be seen to reflect these characteristics. They relate the resurrection of Jesus as manifestations of Jesus, they focus on the identity and continuity between the historical Jesus and the manifestation of the Risen Lord, and they portray the foundational significance of these stories for the emerging Church. The hymnic accounts, however, do not have such characteristics. Their literary form as hymnic discourse determines how they express the event and experience of the resurrection. If one were to conclude that the Gospel materials are unhistorical because their narrative descriptions do not appear in the hymnic material, then one would overlook the necessary interrelation between the structure of literary form and the content expressed in that form. Likewise, the attempt to uncover a primal experience underneath such literary forms overlooks the fact that experiences take place only within interpretation and that meaning is expressed through literary forms.

Intepretation and Experience

The hymnic and creedal testimonies disclosed the meaning of Jesus' resurrection as the manifestation of God's power over life and death. Paul interpreted this power as the saving ground of human hope. The Gospel narratives linked this hope with the historical Jesus and with the beginning of the Church insofar as they used narratives expressing a historical identity and linked these narratives with those of commissioning disciples and of founding a Church.

Interpretation and experience are such that one cannot isolate an experience from its interpretation as if the experience were prior to the interpretation.[137] Instead, the interpretation of an experience is integral to the experience itself and, in some way, constitutive of the experience. The early Christian experiences of the resurrection are not experiences that can be isolated and viewed independently of the interpretation of those experiences. Therefore, the diversity of testimonies, first in various types of oral tradition and then in various literary and oral forms are, in part, the very experience itself.

The attempt to get behind these testimonies does not enable us to say more but to say less than they do. This point, often controverted and counter to recent approaches to the resurrection, can be illustrated with reference to the doctrine of God before applying it to the resurrection of Jesus. The image and the language of personhood is applied to God not only in narrative language, but also in technical theological language. Yet personhood as a relational notion implies finitude and therefore can be applied only inadequately to God. But to avoid applying the word *personal* to God would result in conceiving of God not as more than personal, but as less than personal. Consequently, the use of personal language for God is indispensable for an understanding of God.

It is likewise with the resurrection narratives. Hymnic language, creedal formulas, apocalyptic traditions, and androcentric theophanies are all diverse forms, both in their oral and literary state, which express the meaning of Jesus' resurrection. In each of these diverse forms the meaning of the resurrection is brought to the fore. Attempts to get behind this diversity and to refer to the resurrection as an apologetic fact, transcendental experience, or as a conversion experience do not say more but less about the meaning of Jesus' resurrection. The traditional fundamental theological emphasis upon the empty tomb tended to reduce the resurrection of Jesus to mere resuscitation. The transcendental and existential approach tended to equate the resurrection with the full realization of human freedom and temporality. The recent emphasis upon the experience of the Risen One as a conversion experience underscores the triumph of grace over sin and guilt, but insufficiently explores and explicates the reality of the resurrection for Jesus. The problem underlying all these approaches stems from inadequately taking into account the interrelation between oral and literary forms and their revelatory content and from inadequately exploring how the interpretation of the resurrection in these forms constitutes the experience of the meaning of Jesus' resurrection.

Foundational Theology and Faith in Jesus' Resurrection

Foundational theology undertakes several distinct tasks: the reconstructive interpretation of the Christian tradition or of a Christian belief; an analysis of the retroductive warrants in support of that tradition or belief; and a discussion of the relevant background theories. Each of these must be brought into critical and reflective equilibrium with the others since they may not only support but also critique and modify each other. It is therefore necessary to look at belief in Jesus' resurrection with explicit reference to the foundational theological task.

The reconstruction of the New Testament texts about Jesus' resurrection distinguished two genres: the doxological and the narrative. The analysis of these texts, moreover, uncovered a form, content, and meaning that does not coincide with the apologetical tenor of modern fundamental theology. Even when these texts do contain apologetical motifs, they are quite different in direction from the modern apologetic. It is therefore important to outline the contours of the vision of Christian faith expressed in the doxological and narrative statements about the resurrection.

The faith in the resurrection of Jesus expressed in the doxological statements is laced with apocalyptic motifs and with belief in God's covenant fidelity. This context combines apocalyptic motifs of God's vindicating judgment, the establishment of God's kingdom, and the resurrection of the dead. The belief in the resurrection of the dead occurs in relation to the belief in God's fidelity to the covenant. This belief is a part of the belief in God's saving action and of God's vindication of the injustices against righteous persons, wise persons, and martyrs. The resurrection of the dead demonstrates God's fidelity especially to those who have suffered unjustly.

The correlation between the belief in the eschatological establishment of God's reign and the historical manifestation of God's justice provides the immediate context of the early Christian communities' creedal and proclamation formulas of the resurrection of Jesus. As baptismal and proclamation formulas, they express the central affirmation of Christian faith and locate it in the inaugural rite of baptism and in the very act of proclamation.

It is important that belief in God's saving act regarding Jesus is not simply the affirmation of an isolated datum within history; rather, this belief forges a vision of all reality in relation to historical reality. Expressed in the affirmation of Jesus' resurrection is a vision which shows all reality to be meaningful because, in the end, goodness and justice as the final ground of reality triumph over evil and injustice. Belief in the resurrection of Jesus, therefore, is not simply a belief in a historical event that stands isolated in the past and separated from our present view of reality; it is a vision and a view of the total meaning of reality. And it is this vision that is brought out by the early creedal formulas.

At the same time, the linking of this vision in the narrative accounts points to the life-praxis of the historical Jesus and to his death on the cross that resulted from that life-praxis. These narrative accounts link resurrection not only to the life-praxis of the historical Jesus but also to the origin of the Church. Consequently, what is affirmed in the accounts of the resurrection is not only an ultimate vision of reality in which justice triumphs over injustice but also a vision of reality that is linked to the concrete historical Jesus and to the origin and mission of the Church.

This reconstruction of the meaning of the New Testament affirmations points to the difference between the treatment of modern fundamental theology and the New Testament narrative accounts. Each takes an almost contrary direction. In its polemic against deism, modern fundamental theology emphasized that the resurrection of Jesus was a supernatural event and an external criterion of revelation that transcended the possibilities of nature. But the tendency of the narrative accounts within the New Testament pointed in a different direction. These texts underscored the identity between the experienced Risen One and the historical Jesus. They emphasized continuity rather than discontinuity. These texts stress a corporeal realism not in order to emphasize the otherness of the resurrection, but in order to ward off any spiritualistic or dualistic interpretation of reality and in order to assert a continuity between the earthly and the Risen Jesus. In addition, as the analysis of the texts has shown the move from the doxological to the narrative texts combined apocalyptic expectation and its emphasis upon God's coming rule with the history of the earthly Jesus and with the beginning history of the Christian communities.

A reconstructive analysis of the meaning of a Christian belief does not suffice for fundamental theology. It is also necessary to ask what are the retroductive warrants for this belief and what relevant background theories must be taken into consideration. In regard to the consequences of the belief in Jesus' resurrection, several important explanations have recently been developed: the offering or individual consolation, the building up of community, or the providing of a meaning of all reality in the face of the evils and injustices of the world.

The first has been developed by Wayne Meeks in his recent analysis of the social background to Paul's theology. He argues that the belief in Jesus' resurrection led to the emotional appeal of Christianity because it offered consolation in the face of anxiety in the ancient world. In his opinion, "one effect of the belief in Jesus' death and resurrection was to provide a powerful warrant for a hope of life after death for the believers."[138] This warrant was powerful and popular, for classicists have recently pointed out that it is doubtful whether a common belief in personal immortality was widespread at that time in the ancient world. In fact, Ramsay MacMullin claims that "assurances of immortality prove unexpectedly hard to find in the evidence. Even the longing for it is not much attested."[139] Consequently, Meeks suggests that the effect and meaning of statements about the resurrection in 1 Thess 4:13–18 lie in that it is a "consolation passage."[140]

In his analysis of the diverse creeds, Helmut Koester underscores their ecclesial aspect.[141] It was precisely the proclamation of the death and resurrection of Jesus that had as its social consequence the building up of the community. Such proclamation of the death and resurrection of Jesus at first did not refer to the life of Jesus, but since it took the suffering and death of Jesus seriously, it gave an impetus to the later development of the narration of the life of Jesus. In Pauline theology, moreover, the proclamation of the death and resurrection of Jesus became associated with the concepts of "ecclesia," "Body of Christ," and of being "in Christ."[142] This association was pivotal for the development of the self-understanding of the community.

A third contemporary interpretation points up the significance of the resurrection in relation to the problem of evil and justice.[143] To illustrate this interpretation Karl Martin Fischer takes, as an example, the very complex and controverted text of Rev 11:3–13, a test linking the notion of God's justice with the resurrection of the dead. Using older sources, but containing christological influences, Rev 11:3–13 relates how two eschatological witnesses will prophesy for 1262 days. If anyone does injustice against them, then he or she will be punished. The beast kills the witnesses, but the spirit of life from God raises them up after three and a half days. They ascend to heaven and are thereby vindicated before their enemies who watch them. The act of raising them is associated with the act of judgment against the enemies of God, whereas the remnant of God remains and gives honor to God. Fischer sees this text as exemplifying a response to the problem of evil in the world. The consequence of belief in the resurrection is therefore, for Fischer, to provide a meaning for evil in the world by presenting a belief not just in an individual event but in an event that inaugurates the eschatological vindication of God.

The interpretation that appears most adequate would in my opinion combine all three interpretations. An interpretation of the resurrection of Jesus with primary reference to the consolation of personal immortality and with reference to the suffering life of Jesus and the problem of injustice in the world borders on a Feuerbachian and Marxian interpretation of Christianity. The interpretation of the consequences of the resurrection belief in relation to the eschatological vindication of the end-time does not sufficiently underscore the historical and community-building function of that belief. Consequently, the interpretation suggested in my analysis of the doxological and narrative forms underscored how the individual and eschatological hope was rooted in relation to the historical life of Jesus, the commission of the community, and the task of linking the Church with the life-praxis of Jesus.

Belief in Jesus' resurrection as belief in God's justice that vindicated the life and praxis of Jesus had the effect of affirming that life and praxis. The belief therefore led the disciples to focus further on the meaning of Jesus' historical life, on their own rootedness in that life, and on its community-forming dimensions. The movement from the resurrection of Jesus to the history of Jesus' life-praxis has significance for the foundation of the community, its existence and mission. The Church's religious identity and social mission is a further realization of Jesus' life and praxis as vindicated by God.

The task of foundational theology involves more than the reconstruction of the Christian vision and the consequences of this vision for faith, it is also necessary to discuss the relevant background theories. Otherwise the danger exists that the argument will be circular and a mere "narrow equilibrium" between faith and its praxis will be elaborated. It is also necessary to relate the faith to those relevant background theories affecting the truth. For Jesus' resurrection two such background theories come into play: the validity of the historical argument for Jesus' resurrection and the possibility of any resurrection in view of what is known about the laws of nature. Since our interpretation of the resurrection of Jesus pointed to the distinct literary forms with their doxological and narrative content and focused on the relation between religious identity and historical identity, the relevant background theory discussed at the beginning of this chapter concerned the nature of historical testimony and its importance for underscoring the presence of the singular within history.

Since my analysis concentrated on the problems of identity, historical testimony, and mission rather than on the antideism problematic of modern fundamental theology, the relevant background theories about the laws of nature were not discussed. In contemporary theology significant discussions have developed such theories that offer an alternative to the mechanistic interpretation prevalent within the world view of deism. Rahner's understanding of the dialectical relation between spirit and nature, Pannenberg's understanding of causality and contingency in his theology of nature, and process theology's appropriation of Whiteheadian categories would all constitute important elements in such background theories of nature.[144] And they are indeed relevant to a treatment of the resurrection within foundational theology. This chapter's emphasis upon the importance of testimony within historical argumentation, the relation between literary form and revelatory content, and the possible consequences of resurrection belief for one's relation to the world moves in a different direction from the antideist polemic of fundamental theology. Although a further analysis of that problem is significant, it would go beyond the focus and limits of the present analysis.

Foundational theology has a reconstructive task of interpreting the tradition and of considering the retroductive warrants and relevant background theories.[145] This foundational task is not, as the term might suggest, that of the builder laying a foundation in bedrock or that of the archaeologist digging down to the lowest stratum but that of the interpreter seeking to convey the meaning of a past event and experience, seeking to translate its illuminative and liberating vision, and seeking to elucidate its transformative consequences for human life.

NOTES

1. See Avery Dulles, *A History of Apologetics* (Philadelphia: Westminster, 1971) and *Apologetics and the Biblical Christ* (Woodstock, Md.: Woodstock, 1963).

2. See Claude Geffré, "Recent Developments in Fundamental Theology," in his *A New Age in Theology* (New York: Paulist, 1974).

3. See Léonce de Grandmaison, "Sur l'apologétique de S. Thomas," *NRTh* 39 (1907) 65–74 and 121–30.

4. The first example of an independent apologetics published as a separate treatise under the title "True Religion" was Ignatius Neubauer's *Vera religio indicata contra omnis generis incredulos* (Würzburg, 1771). It was also published under the title *Tractatus de religione* as vol. 1 of the influential 14-volume Jesuit dogmatic series of Würzburg, *Theologia Wirceburgensis* (1766–1811; vol. 1 Paris, 1771; 2nd ed. 1852). See Part IV for the historical background of this development.

5. This anti-Enlightenment defense of revelation is the center of Johann Sebastian Drey's development of an independent apologetic. See the historical introduction to the first volume of his 3-volume *Apologetik* (Mainz, 1838; reprint Frankfurt: Minerva, 1967).

6. Pierre Charron, *Les trois vérités* (Bordeaux, 1594). The same triple division was also used by Hugo Grotius in *De veritate religionis christianae* (1627).

7. Even the 1950 edition of Reginald Garrigou-Lagrange's *De revelatione* (Rome: F. Ferrari, 3rd ed.) affirms that the resurrection is a historical certitude: "Historice certum est . . . Christum resurrexisse" (p. 320).

8. See Drey, *Apologetik*, 1:55–78; and Clemens Engling, *Die Bedeutung der Theologie für philosophische Theoriebildung und gesellschaftliche Praxis* (Göttingen: Vandenhoeck und Ruprecht, 1977), for the attempt of Johann Nepomuk Ehrlich (1810–1864) to give fundamental theology a new foundation over against previous objectivism and positivism.

9. Albert Lang, *Die Entfaltung des apologetischen Problems in der Scholastik des Mittelalters* (Freiburg: Herder, 1962) and *Die Wege der Glaubensbegründung in den Scholastikern des 14. Jahrhunderts* (Beiträge der Geschichte der Philosophie und Theologie des Mittelalters, 3, 1/2; Münster: Aschendorff, 1930).

10. Gazzaniga taught dogmatic theology at the University of Vienna. His *Praelectiones theologicae* (first published between 1788 and 1793) were reprinted often until 1831; our reference is to the 3rd ed. (Venice, 1803), p. 70.

11. For the interpretation of Vatican I, see Hermann J. Pottmeyer, *Der Glaube vor dem Anspruch der Wissenschaft. Die Konstitution über den katholischen Glauben "Dei Filius" des 1. Vatikanischen Konzils* (Freiburg: Herder, 1968). Vatican I takes over not only Gazzaniga's use of internal and external criteria but also the threefold demonstration. See Pottmeyer, pp. 107–20.

12. Quite often Pss 15:9–11 and 2:10–13 were interpreted as predictions of the resurrection. See Michael Joseph Cantley, *The Use of Messianic Prophecy in Apologetics* (Studies in Sacred Theology, Second Series, no. 167; Washington, D.C.: Catholic Univ. Press, 1966), pp. 79ff. For a general critique of the apologetical use of prophecies, see Bruce Vawter, "Messianic Prophecies in Apologetics," *Proceedings CTSA* 4 (1959).

13. Gazzaniga, *Praelectiones*, p. 115.

14. See Reinhart Staats, "Auferstehung Jesu Christi. Alte Kirche," *TRE* 4 (Berlin: de Gruyter, 1979), pp. 513–29. For the controversy with gnosticism concerning the resurrection, see Klaus Koschorke, *Die Polemik der Gnostiker gegen das kirchliche Christentum* (Nag Hammadi Studies 12; Leiden: Brill, 1978).

15. Questions 53–56 discuss the resurrection of Christ. For a discussion of the theological rather than apologetic interpretation of the resurrection in Thomas, see William Van Roo, "The Resurrection of Christ, Instrumental Cause of Grace," *Greg* 39 (1958) 271–84.

16. J. Solano, *Summa Sacrae Theologiae per Patres S.J. Facultatem Theol. in Hispania Professores*, vol. 3 (Madrid: BAC, 1956, 3rd ed.).

17. For this development, see Peter Eicher, *Offenbarung* (Munich: Kösel, 1977), pp. 80–162; and the earlier classic work of Roger Aubert, *Le problème de l'acte de foi* (Louvain: Warny, 1950, 2nd ed.).

18. Even as recently as the 1959 edition of Adolf Tanquerey's *Synopsis Theologiae Dogmaticae Fundamentalis* (rev. J. B. Bord; Tournai: Desclée), pp. 317ff., the resurrection is described as a historical fact (*factum historicum quod est miraculum physici ordinis*) and a

miracle of the physical order. The argument is divided into fact and exposition of fact. It concludes that the resurrection is the most certain fact (*factum certissimum*) that should convince all persons (p. 333).

19. Trans. Neil Buchanan from the 3rd German ed. (New York: Dover, 1961; reprint of 1900 ed.), 1:85, n. 1.

20. See Bruce Vawter, "Messianic Prophecies" (cited in n. 12 above). In regard to *sensus plenior*, cf. the differences between Raymond Brown (*CBQ* 25 [1963] 262–85) and Bruce Vawter (*CBQ* 26 [1964]) as well as James M. Robinson (*CBQ* 27 [1965] 6–27) and Raymond Brown (*EthL* 43 [1967] 460–69).

21. See the argument against David Freidrich Strauss by Johannes Evangelist von Kuhn, *Das Leben Jesu, wissenschaftlich bearbeitet* (Mainz, 1838).

22. For a pithy discussion of the parallels to Jesus' resurrection in antiquity that points out the differences, see Arthur Darby Nock "A Note on the Resurrection," in *Early Gentile Christianity and Its Hellenistic Background* (New York: Harper, 1964), pp. 105–8.

23. See Gotthold Ephraim Lessing, "On the Proof of the Spirit and of Power," in *Theological Writings*, ed. Henry Chadwick (Stanford, Calif.: Stanford Univ. Press, 1957), pp. 51–56; for commentary, see Henry E. Allison, *Lessing and the Enlightenment* (Ann Arbor: Univ. of Michigan Press, 1966).

24. Reginald H. Fuller, *Interpreting the Miracles* (London: SCM, 1966); Alan Richardson, *The Miracle Stories of the Gospels* (London: SCM, 1941; reprint 1969); and Alfred Suhl, *Der Wunderbegriff im Neuen Testament* (Wege der Forschung, 295; Frankfurt: Wissenschaftliche Buchgesellschaft, 1980).

25. See Elisabeth Schüssler Fiorenza, ed., *Aspects of Religious Propaganda in Judaism and Early Christianity* (Notre Dame: Univ. of Notre Dame Press, 1976). For New Testament and especially Mark, see Karl Kertelge, *Die Wunder Jesu im Markusevangelium* (SANT 12; Munich: Kösel, 1970); for John see J. Becker, "Wunder und Christologie. Zum literarkritischen und christologischen Problem der Wunder im Johannesevangelium," reprinted in Suhl (cited in the previous note). For a recent discussion of the systematic issues, see Bela Weissmahr, *Gottes Wirken in der Welt* (FTS 15; Frankfurt: Knecht, 1973).

26. For a textbook representing the approach of this apologetic, see Gerhard Van Noort, *Dogmatic Theology*, vol. 1, *The True Religion*, ed. J. P. Verhaar, trans. John J. Castelot and William R. Murphy (Westminster, Md.: Newman, 1955), pp. 166–87.

27. "The most important fact, one thoroughly established, is that Christ's tomb, though shut tight by a huge rock and guarded by solders, was empty on the third day" (ibid., p. 172).

28. Ibid., p. 173. Rationalist theories of hallucination and imaginary vision are refuted by the empty tomb.

29. The theory of a spiritual appearance is rejected by means of the empty tomb by Garrigou-Lagrange (*De revelatione*, 2:326).

30. I do not mean to deny that philosophical presuppositions have often been involved, but the problems also arise from historical, literary, and comparative studies. For a survey of how literary criticism, form criticism, and the history of religious posed distinct problems for modern apologetics, see Paul De Haes, *La résurrection de Jesus dans l'apologétique des cinquante dernières années* (Rome: Gregorian Univ., 1953).

31. For a chronological survey of the development of the New Testament accounts of the resurrection, see Reginald H. Fuller, *The Formation of the Resurrection Narratives* (New York: Macmillan, 1971); pp. 9–49 deal with 1 Cor 15:3–7.

32. Hans von Campenhausen emphasizes very strongly the historicity of the early discovery of the empty tomb and yet does not equate this discovery with faith in the resurrection itself ("The Events of Easter and the Empty Tomb," in *Tradition and Life in the Church* [Philadelphia: Fortress, 1968], pp. 42–89).

33. See Vögtle's analysis of the significance of the empty tomb in Anton Vögtle and Rudolf Pesch, *Wie kam es zum Osterglauben?* (Düsseldorf: Patmos, 1975).

34. Concerning the aetiological thesis, see especially L. Schenke, *Auferstehungs-*

verkündigung und leeres Grab (SBS 33; Stuttgart: KBW, 1968). See also Jacob Kremer, *Das älteste Zeugnis von der Auferstehung* (SBS 17; Stuttgart: KBW, 1966); and for Kremer's response to Schenke, his "Die Überlieferung vom leeren Grab," in . . . *denn sie werden leben* (Stuttgart: KBW, 1972), pp. 72–75.

35. Elisabeth Schüssler Fiorenza, " 'You are not to be called Father': Early Christian History in a Feminist Perspective," *Cross Currents* 29 (1979) 301–23; and E. L. Bode, *The Gospel Account of the Women's Easter Visit to the Tomb of Jesus* (Rome: Angelicum, 1970).

36. *The Letter on Apologetics and History and Dogma* (New York: Holt, Rinehart and Winston, 1964). For a perceptive application of the "Blondelian Shift" to all the major themes of theology, see Gregory Baum, *Man Becoming* (New York: Herder and Herder, 1971). Of additional importance for the development of fundamental theology in the twentieth century was the influential article by Pierre Rousselot, "Les yeux de la foi," *RechSR* (1910) 241–59 and 444–75.

37. See my introduction, "Karl Rahner and the Kantian Problematic," in Karl Rahner, *Spirit in the World* (New York: Herder and Herder, 1971), pp. xix–xlv, for a discussion of the influence of Kant, Maréchal, and Heidegger on Rahner's theology.

38. Karl Rahner, "Formal and Fundamental Theology" and "Transcendental Theology," in *Encyclopedia of Theology: The Concise Sacramentum Mundi*, ed. Karl Rahner (New York: Seabury, 1975), pp. 524–25 and 1748–51; "Reflections on Methodology in Theology," in *Theological Investigations* 11 (New York: Seabury, 1974), pp. 68–114; and "Theology and Anthropology," in *Theological Investigations* 9 (New York: Herder and Herder, 1972), pp. 28–45.

39. Rahner, "Jesus' Resurrection," in *Theological Investigations* 17 (New York: Seabury, 1981), pp. 16–23, and his earlier "Dogmatic Questions on Easter," in *Theological Investigations* 4 (Baltimore: Helicon, 1966), pp. 121–33, and "Hope and Easter," in *Christian at the Crossroads* (New York: Seabury, 1975), pp. 87–93.

40. Rahner, *Foundations of Christian Faith: An Introduction to the Idea of Christianity* (New York: Seabury, 1978), pp. 243–45.

41. Rahner, "Reflections on a New Task for Fundamental Theology," in *Theological Investigations* 16 (New York: Seabury, 1979), pp. 156–66; "Pluralism in Theology and the Unity of the Creed in the Church," in *Theological Investigations* 11 (New York: Seabury, 1974), pp. 3–23.

42. See Rahner's defense of the indirect method in "Reflections on Methodology in Theology" (cited in n. 38 above), esp. pp. 70–84.

43. See the important but critical study of Peter Eicher, *Die anthropologische Wende: Karl Rahners philosophischer Weg vom Wesen des Menschen zur personalen Existenz* (Freibourg: Universitätsverlage, 1970). For a contrary and more balanced interpretation, see Klaus P. Fischer, *Der Mensch als Geheimnis: Die Anthropologie Karl Rahners* (Freiburg: Herder, 1974), who emphasizes the background of Rahner's work on spirituality.

44. In Martin Heidegger, *Basic Writings* (New York: Harper and Row, 1977), pp. 91–112. This essay was originally Heidegger's inaugural lecture in Freiburg at the time Karl Rahner was a student there. On page 96, Heidegger refers to the diversity of scientific fields, the multiplicity of disciplines, and the exactitude of sciences. He uses the question of nothing to argue against the limitation to scientific questions. In *Discourse on Thinking* (New York: Harper and Row, 1966), he calls for a "meditative thinking" instead of the dominant "calculating thinking" (pp. 46–57).

45. See Rahner's important letter to Klaus Fischer in which he explains why he is not a scholar and most of his writings are "unscientific" (in Fischer, *Der Mensch*, pp. 400–410).

46. For two excellent and complementary surveys of Rahner's methodology, see Anne Carr, *The Theological Method of Karl Rahner* (Missoula, Mont.: Scholars, 1977), for a study of the philosophical categories; and James J. Bacik, *Apologetics and the Eclipse of Mystery* (Notre Dame: Univ. of Notre Dame Press, 1980), for an analysis of Rahner's concept of mystagogy.

47. See the careful analysis by Elmar Mitterstieler, *Christliche Glaube als Bestätigung des Menschen. Zur 'fides quaerens intellectum' in der Theologie Rahners* (Frankfurt: Knecht, 1975).

48. See Rahner, "Resurrection," in *Sacramentum Mundi* 5 (New York: 1970), pp. 323–24, and *Foundations*, pp. 266–74.

49. *Foundations*, pp. 238–40.

50. *Foundations*, p. 276.

51. *Foundations*, pp. 241–42. See also Karl-Heinz Weger, "Auferstehung. Zumutung oder Fundament des Glaubens?" *Stimmen der Zeit* 193 (1975) 219–27. For the uniqueness of Jesus' resurrection, see Rahner "Auferstehung Christi," *LThK* 1:1038–39; E.T. "Resurrection, I. Resurrection of Christ," in *Encyclopedia of Theology*, pp. 1430–42.

52. Rahner, "Jesus' Resurrection" (cited in n. 39 above).

53. John P. Galvin points out in his excellent survey, "The Resurrection of Jesus in Contemporary Catholic Systematics" (*HeyJ* 20 [1979] 123–45], that Rahner's christology has shifted its emphasis from the incarnation to the resurrection. However, it should be noted that Rahner's interpretation of the resurrection views it as the culmination of God's grace and presence in grace in the incarnation.

54. Because Rahner's interpretation of the resurrection connects so intimately the death and resurrection of Jesus, he has been accused by Wolfhart Pannenberg of being very close to Rudolf Bultmann's position (see Pannenberg, "Dogmatische Erwägungen zur Auferstehung Jesu" *KD* 14 [1968] 105, n. 2, and "Tod und Auferstehung in der Sicht christlicher Dogmatik," *KD* 20 [1974] 175–77). Yet it should not be overlooked how closely Bultmann and Rahner follow a Johannine interpretation of the death and resurrection of Jesus (see J. Forestell, *The Word of the Cross and Salvation as Revelation in the Fourth Gospel* [An Bib 57; Rome: Biblical Institute Press, 1974]). For different christological traditions within the Johannine school itself, see Raymond E. Brown, *The Community of the Beloved Disciple* (New York: Paulist, 1979).

55. Rahner, "Gnade als Mitte menschlicher Existenz," in *Herausforderung des Christens* (Freiburg: Herder, 1975).

56. I have made similar criticism of Rahner's approach to the historical foundation of the Church in "Seminar on Rahner's Ecclesiology: Jesus and the Foundation of the Church—An Analysis of the Hermeneutical Issues," *Proceedings CTSA* 33 (1978) 229–54.

57. See Rudolf Pesch, "Zur Entstehung des Glaubens an die Auferstehung Jesu. Ein Vorschlag zur Diskussion," *ThQ* 153 (1973) 201–28; and contributions in the same issue of *ThQ* by Kasper, Schelke, Stuhlmacher, Hengel, and Pesch's response, pp. 229–83. See also Willi Marxsen *The Resurrection of Jesus of Nazareth* (Philadelphia: Fortress, 1970); Ulrich Wilckens, *Resurrection* (Atlanta: John Knox, 1978); and Klaus Berger, *Die Auferstehung des Propheten und die Erhöhung des Menschensohnes* (SUNT 13; Göttingen: Vandenhoeck und Ruprecht, 1976). For Edward Schillebeeckx, see *Jesus* (New York: Seabury, 1979) and *Christ* (New York: Seabury, 1980); also Franz Schupp, *Vermittlung im Fragment. Überlegungen zur Christologie* (Innsbruck: Universtität Innsbruck, 1975), pp. 30–37.

58. Vögtle and Pesch, *Wie kam es zum Osterglauben?*, pp. 29–30.

59. Schillebeeckx's response in *Interim Report on the Books Jesus and Christ* (New York: Crossroad, 1981) correctly notes the differences between Pesch and himself. In responding to Kasper that he had been unaware of Pesch's thesis and the Tübingen discussion, Schillebeeckx, however, overlooks the fact that the one exegete most quoted is Klaus Berger whose opinions in *Die Auferstehung des Propheten* were partially anticipated in his "Die königliche Messiastradition des Neuen Testaments," *NTS* 20 (1973/74) 1–44, *Die Gesetzauslegung Jesu* (WMANT 40; Neukirchen-Vluyn: Neukirchener Verlag, 1972), and *Die Amen-Worte Jesu* (BZNW 39; Berlin: Walter de Gruyter, 1970).

60. Wolfhart Pannenberg's use of the empty tomb or a historical apologetic represents a major exception in contemporary Christology (*Jesus—God and Man* [Philadelphia: Westminster, 1968], pp. 88–106).

61. David Friedrich Strauss, *The Life of Jesus Critically Examined*, trans. George Eliot (Philadelphia: Fortress, 1972; reprint of 1892 ed.; 1st ed. 1835), pp. 709–44.

62. Pesch, "Zur Entstehung," p. 216.

63. Ibid., pp. 212–18. See Wilckens, p. 114: "The appearances are thus not really *testimonies* to the resurrection, but rather *credentials* proving the identity and authority of the men who because of their heavenly authorization had permanent authority in the church" (Wilcken's empasis). Wilckens overlooks the appearances to women.

64. Pesch argues that contrary to Kasper he does not consider the appearances as such as legitimation, only the "he appeared" formula ("Stellungnahme zu den Diskussionbeiträgen," *ThQ* 153 [1973] 270–83).

65. Pesch, "Zur Entstehung," p. 217. Pesch is heavily reliant on the studies of Michaelis, especially his Kittel dictionary article.

66. For arguments against such a nonvisual interpretation of "he appeared," see Raymond E. Brown, *The Virginal Conception and Bodily Resurrection of Jesus* (New York: Paulist, 1973), pp. 89–92.

67. See Pesch's further documentation in "Materialien und Bemerkugen zur Entstehung und Sinn des Osterglaubens" (in *Wie kam es*, pp. 135–84) where he discusses individually the work of Friedrich Ellermeier, Johannes Lindblom, Ernst Benz, Herbert Mölle, Norbert Lohfink, and Manuel Oliva to make his point.

68. Ibid., p. 152.

69. Klaus Berger, *Auferstehung* (cited in n. 57 above), pp. 9–150. For a criticism of Berger's data as insufficient and as chronically later than alleged, see Ulrich Kellermann, *Auferstanden in den Himmel. 2 Makkabäer 7 und die Auferstehung der Märtyrer* (SBS 95; Stuttgart: KBW, 1979), pp. 140–42; Johannes M. Nützel, "Zum Schicksal der eschatologischen Propheten," *BZ* 20 (1976) 59–64; and Eduard Schweizer's review in *ThLZ* 103 (1978) 874–78.

70. Pesch, "Zur Entstehung," pp. 222–26.

71. Rudolf Pesch, *Das Abendmahl und Jesu Todesverständnis* (QD 80; Freiburg: Herder, 1979). See the critical analysis by Ferdinand Hahn, "Das Abendmahl und Jesu Todesverständnis," *TRev* 76 (1980) 265–72.

72. Rudolf Pesch, "Das Messiasbekenntnis des Petrus (MK 8, 27–30). Neuverhandlung einer alten Frage," *BZ* 17 (1973) 178–95 and 18 (1974) 20–31, and "Die Passion des Menschensohnes. Eine Studie zu den Menschensohnworten der vormarkinischen Passionsgeschichte," in *Jesus und der Menschensohn* ed. R. Pesch and R. Schnackenburg (Freiburg: Herder, 1975). For a sympathetic survey of Pesch's position within current options, see John Galvin, "Jesus' Approach to Death: An Examination of Some Recent Studies," *TS* 41 (1980) 713–44.

73. Walter Kasper's criticisms of Schillebeeckx tend to identify Schillebeeckx and Pesch. See Kasper, "Liberale Christologie: Zum Jesus-Buch von Edward Schillebeeckx," *EvK* 6 (1976) 357–60; and Schillebeeckx's response in *Interim*, pp. 90–92.

74. *Jesus*, p. 382.

75. *Jesus*, p. 354.

76. Klaus Berger, "Zum traditionsgeschichtlichen Hintergrund christologischer Hoheitistitel," *NTS* 17 (1970/71) 391–425, and "Die königlichen Messiastraditionen des neuen Testaments," *NTS* 20 (1973/74) 1–44; George W. E. Nickelsburg, *Resurrection, Immortality, and Eternal Life in Intertestamental Judaism* (Cambridge, Mass.: Harvard Univ. Press, 1972); Lothar Ruppert, *Jesus als der leidende Gerechte?* (SBS 59; Stuttgart: KBW, 1972).

77. *Jesus*, pp. 311–12.

78. *Jesus*, p. 387.

79. *Jesus*, p. 393.

80. *Jesus*, p. 497.

81. *Jesus*, p. 312. See also p. 640: "The Christian 'disclosure' experience therefore presupposes the life of Jesus as a whole. Only with Jesus' death, the conclusion of his earthly life, can our account of Jesus begin."

82. "Ostererscheinungen—Ostererfahrung. Zu einer neuen Sicht ihres Verhältnisses," *Theologie der Gegenwart* 19 (1976) 46–53, here p. 49.

83. For Schillebeeckx's extended treatment of "Easter experience," see *Jesus*, pp. 379–97, and the clarifying addition to the Dutch 2nd ed. on pp. 644–50 of the English

translation. For some clarifications in response to critics, see *Interim*, esp. pp. 147f., nn. 43 and 46.

84. In this regard, Schillebeeckx is strongly influenced by Ferdinand Hahn (*The Titles of Jesus in Christology* [Cleveland: World, 1969]) and the development of Hahn's interpretation of Mark's understanding of exaltation by Theodore J. Weeden (*Mark: Traditions in Conflict* [Philadelphia: Fortress, 1971]). Schillebeeckx does not reflect on how idiosyncratic Weeden's position is and although is aware of Vielhauer's criticisms of Hahn does not really take them into account except for Hahn's associations of exaltation with delay of the parousia. See Philip Vielhauer, "Ein Weg zur Neutestamentlichen Christologie? Prüfung der Thesen Ferdinand Hahn," in *Aufsätze zum Neuen Testament* (Munich: Chr. Kaiser, 1965); W. Thüsing, "Erhöhungsvorstellung und Parusieerwartung in der ältesten nachösterlichen Christologie," *BZ* 11 (1967) 216–19 and 12 (1968) 226–28.

85. Cf. *Interim*, pp. 71–72 with 83–86.

86. See *Jesus*, pp. 640–43, with the subtitle "Salvation in Jesus or in the Crucified-and-Risen One?" The criticisms of Kasper and Löser seem to have overlooked this section. See also pp. 648–50.

87. On the relation between resurrection and exaltation, see *Jesus*, pp. 533–44.

88. For discussions of the fundamental theological relevance of Pesch's proposal, see Adolf Kolping, "Zur Entstehung des Glaubens an die Auferstehung Jesu," *MThZ* 26 (1975) 56–69; Wilhelm Breuning, "Aktive Proexistenz—Die Vermittlung Jesu durch Jesus selbst," *TTHZ* 83 (1974) 193–213; Augustin Schmied, "Auferstehungsglaube ohne Ostererscheinungen?" *Theologie der Gegenwart* 17 (1974) 46–51, and "Auferstehungsglaube heute und die ursprüngliche Ostererfahrung," *Theologie der Gegenwart* 20 (1977) 43–50; Jacob Kremer, "Enststehung und Inhalt des Osterglaubens," *TRev* 72 (1976) 1–14; and John Galvin, "Resurrection as Theologia Crucis Jesu: The Foundational Christology of Rudolf Pesch," *TS* 38 (1977) 513–25.

89. *Jesus*, p. 710, n. 119.

90. "Despite the unrepeatable and peculiar status of the first apostles, who had known Jesus before his death, the way the apostles then found reason for 'becoming Christians' does not differ so very much in fundamentals from our way now" (*Jesus*, p. 647). For Pesch, see *Zur Entstehung*, p. 227, especially the reference to Seckler's letter.

91. See Schillebeeckx's nuanced response to Descamps in *Interim*, pp. 74–90.

92. Walter Kasper, "Liberale Christologie," pp. 357–60; and in regard to Pesch, see Kasper's "Der Glaube an die Auferstehung vor dem Forum historischer Kritik," *ThQ* 153 (1973) 220–41. For Schillebeeckx's response, see *Interim*, pp. 27–35.

93. See the survey by Hans Grass, "Glaubensgrund und Glaubensgedanken," and "Zur Begründung des Osterglaubens," both in *Theologie und Kritik* (Göttingen: Vandenhoeck und Ruprecht, 1969), pp. 28–37 and 180–94. See also the final chapter of his *Ostergeschehen und Osterberichte* (Göttingen: Vandenhoeck und Ruprecht, 1964), pp. 257–87. Joachim Gnilka points out the similarities between Tillich's "restitution theory" and Pesch's position ("Auferstehung Jesus," in *Wer ist doch Dieser? Die Frage nach Jesus heute* [Munich: Don Bosco, 1976], pp. 30–40).

94. For contemporary formulations of this position, see Van A. Harvey, *The Historian and the Believer* (New York: Macmillan, 1966), pp. 246–91; and James P. Mackey, *Jesus the Man and the Myth* (New York: Paulist, 1979). Pesch himself refers to Ebeling for a systematic grounding of his fundamental theological position (*Wie kam es*, pp. 175–81).

95. For Schleiermacher's defense of his christology, see Friedrich Schleiermacher, *On the Glaubenslehre*, trans. James Duke and Francis Fiorenza (AAR Texts and Translation 3; Chico, Calif.: Scholars, 1981).

96. Schillebeeckx is not completely consistent in his methodology. On the one hand, the impact of Jesus upon the believing community is the norm; on the other, he does attempt to get back to Jesus' self-understanding and abba experience. See Francis Fiorenza, "Christology after Vatican II," *The Ecumenist* 18 (1980) 81–89.

97. Edward Schillebeeckx, "Fides quaerens intellectum historicum," *NedThTs* 29 (1975) 332–49.

98. See my critique of Rahner, Bultmann, Moltmann, and Pannenberg on this point, in "Critical Social Theory and Christology," *Proceedings CTSA* 30 (1975) 63–110.

99. See n. 69 above for the references to Kellermann, Nützel, and Schweitzer. For Martin Hengel, see his "Ist der Osterglaube noch zu retten?" *TQ* 153 (1973) 252–69.

100. Rudolf Bultmann even criticizes Paul for attempting a proof in 1 Cor 15. See his "Karl Barth, *The Resurrection of the Dead,*" in *Faith and Understanding* (New York: Harper and Row, 1966).

101. Grass had earlier argued that the appearance narratives are not so much conversion experiences or even narratives of experiences as they are epiphany stories of Jesus (*Ostergeschehen*, p. 327).

102. Schillebeeckx's failure to specify further the tangible causes of the "conversion experience" recalls to mind the debate between the Dominicans and Jesuits at the beginning of this century on the analysis of the act of faith. In his response to critics, he has modified his explanation; see *Interim*, p. 147, n. 43.

103. For the differences between meaning, meaningfulness, and truth, see Jürgen Habermas, "Wahrheitstheorien," in *Wirklichkeit und Reflexion*, ed. H. Fahrenbach (Pfullingen: Neske, 1973), pp. 211–65.

104. For the concept of fundamental theology as "reconstructive," see Francis Schüssler Fiorenza, "Political Theology as Foundational Theology," *Proceedings CTSA* 32 (1977) 142–77.

105. "Toward a Hermeneutic of the Idea of Revelation" and "The Hermeneutics of Testimony," in his *Essays on Biblical Interpretation*, ed. Lewis S. Mudge (Philadelphia: Fortress, 1980), pp. 73–153. Ricoeur relies on the work of Jean Nabert, *Le Désir de Dieu* (Paris: Aubier, 1966).

106. Ibid, p. 143.

107. G. E. Lessing, "On the Proof of the Spirit and of Power," in *Theological Writings* (cited in n. 23 above), pp. 51–56.

108. See the perceptive remarks of Avery Dulles, "Fundamental Theology and the Dynamics of Conversion," *The Thomist* 45 (1981) 175–93.

109. See Ernst Troeltsch, *Gesammelte Schriften*, vol. 2 (Tübingen: J. C. B. Mohr 1913), pp. 729–53.

110. See R. G. Collingwood, *The Idea of History* (Oxford: Oxford Univ. Press, 1946); and the collection by Patrick Gardiner, *Theories of History* (Glencoe, Ill.: Free Press, 1959).

111. Richard R. Niebuhr, *Resurrection and Historical Reason* (New York: Scribners, 1957). See the criticisms of this position by Harvey, *The Historian*, pp. 2–126.

112. W. B. Gallie, *Philosophy and the Historical Understanding* (New York: Schocken, 1964).

113. Wolfgang Nauck distinguishes between early missionary preaching and community preaching in order to claim that the empty tomb played a role only in the missionary preaching ("Die Bedeutung des leeren Grabes für den Glauben an den Auferstandenen," *ZNW* 47 [1956] 243–67, esp. pp. 260f.). For Vögtle's consideration of the various possibilities, see *Wie kam es*, pp. 87–89 and 97.

114. See Hans Conzelmann, "Was glaubte die frühe Christenheit?" in *Theologie als Schriftauslegung* (Munich: Chr. Kaiser, 1974), pp. 106–19, for the distinction between a homology and a credo formula. Whereas the homology is a liturgical acclamation of the Lord, a credo formula is a short summary of the main contents of salvation history— e.g., death and resurrection of Jesus—that is used at baptism. See also Werner Kramer, *Christ, Lord, Son of God* (London: SCM, 1966), who distinguished between homology and pistis-formula; Reinhard Deichgräber, *Gotteshymnus und Christus in der frühen Christenheit* (Göttingen: Vandenhoeck und Ruprecht, 1967); and Klaus Wengst, *Christologische Lieder des Urchristentums* (Gütersloh: Gerd Mohn, 1972). Despite differences of terminology, the above research points to the resurrection one-verse formula as the oldest form of tradition. Schillebeeckx follows the contrary opinion of Gerhard Kegel in *Auferstehung Jesu, Auferstehung der Toten* (Gütersloh: Gerd Mohn, 1970).

115. See the short but important essay by Rudolph Schnackenburg, "Zur Assage-

weise 'Jesus ist (von den Toten) auferstanden,'" *BZ* 13 (1969) 1–17, especially for his criticism of Willi Marxsen and Philip Seidensticker.

116. Jürgen Becker, "Das Gottesbild Jesu und die älteste Auslegung von Ostern," in *Jesus Christus in Historie und Theologie*, ed. Georg Strecker (Tübingen: J. C. B. Mohr, 1975), pp. 105–25; and Gerhard Delling, "Partizipiale Gottesprädikationen in den Briefen des NT," *StTh* 17 (1963) 1–59.

117. See Jürgen Becker, *Auferstehung der Toten im Urchistentum* (Stuttgart: KBW, 1976), esp. pp. 18–31.

118. Gerhard Friedrich, "Ein Tauflied hellenistischer Judenchristen, 1 Thess 1, 9f.," *ThZ* 21 (1965) 502–16. See also Paul Langevin, "Le Seígneur Jésus selon un texte prépaulinien, 1 Th 1, 9–10," *Sciences Ecclésiastique* 17 (1965) 263–383.

119. See the relevant discussion of Phil 3:10 by Joseph Fitzmyer, " 'To Know Him and the Power of His Resurrection' (Phil 3:10)," in his *To Advance the Gospel* (New York: Crossroad, 1981), pp. 202–17.

120. For a discussion of this formula within the content of the whole of 1 Cor 15, see Hans Conzelmann, *1 Corinthians* (Hermeneia; Philadelphia: Fortress, 1976), pp. 248–93; see esp. bibliographical notes 15 and 54. For a careful comparison of Bultmann, Ebeling, and Pannenberg on 1 Cor 15, see Klaus Kienzler, *Logic der Auferstehung* (Freiburg: Herder, 1976).

121. Against Wilhelm Michaelis's interpretation of "he appeared," see Karl H. Rengstorf, *Die Auferstehung Jesu* (Witten-Ruhr: Luther, 1960), pp. 117–27; and Elpidius Pax, *Epiphaneia* (Münster: Aschendorff, 1955). For the use in the Septuagint, see André Pelletier, "Les apparitions du ressuscité en termes de la Septante," *Bib* 51 (1970) 76–79.

122. See Hans Dieter Betz, *Galatians* (Philadelphia: Fortress, 1979), pp. 62–74.

123. Karl Kertelge, "Apokalypsis Jesou Christou (Gal 1, 12)," in *Neues Testament und Kirche*, ed. Joachim Gnilka (Freiburg: Herder, 1974), pp. 266–81. See also Jacques Dupont, "La révélation du Fils de Dieu en faveur de Pierre (Mt 16, 17) et de Paul (Gal 1, 16)," *RechSR* 52 (1964) 411–20.

124. Paul Hoffman, *Studien zur Theologie der Logienquelle* (Münster: Aschendorff, 1972), pp. 102–42, and "Die Offenbarung des Sohnes," *Kairos* (1970) 270–88.

125. Ferdinand Hahn, "Der Apostolat im Urchristentum. Seine Eigenart und seine Voraussetzunge," *KD* 20 (1974) 54–77. See also Traugott Holtz, "Zum Selbstverständnis des Apostels Paulus, *ThLZ* 91 (1966) 321–30, who focuses almost exclusively on Deutero-Isaiah.

126. Martin Hengel, *The Atonement* (Philadelphia: Fortress, 1981), pp. 40–43 and 48–50.

127. See the works already cited by Brown, Evans, Fuller, and Grass.

128. Berger points out how light is generally associated with the title Lord whereas a revelation with the title Son of God (*Auferstehung*, pp. 209–21).

129. This distinction is crucial to Josef Alsup's division of the species into individual and group appearances (*The Post-Resurrection Appearance Stories of the Gospel Tradition* [Stuttgart: Calwer, 1974]). Rudolf Bultmann notes how the identity motif is present in most of the stories (*The History of the Synoptic Tradition* [New York: Harper and Row, 1976], pp. 284–91).

130. See E. Bickermann "Das leere Grab," *ZNW* 23 (1924) 281–92, for the emphasis on the apologetic motif. In comparison, see Nauck, "Die Bedeutung," pp. 243–67.

131. Berger, *Auferstehung*, pp. 154–72.

132. See Gerhard Friedrich, "Lk 9, 51 und die Entrückungschristologie des Lukas," in *Orienterung an Jesus* (Freiburg: Herder, 1972), pp. 48–77, here p. 59.

133. See Berger, *Aufterstehung*, pp. 577f. See also Charles Kannengiesser's notion of "evangelical realism" in *Foi en la résurrection. Résurrection de la foi* (Paris: Beauchesne, 1974), pp. 111–46.

134. For the redactional emphasis, see Paul Hoffmann, "Auferstehung Jesu Christi" *TRE* 4 (1979), esp. pp. 497–529; cf. also Normal Perrin, *The Resurrection according to Matthew, Mark, and Luke* (Philadelphia: Fortress, 1977).

135. "Toward a Hermeneutic," pp. 75–95.

136. See Paul Ricoeur, "The Narrative Function," in *Hermeneutics and the Human Sciences*, ed. John B. Thompson (New York: Cambridge Univ. Press, 1981), pp. 274–96.

137. See, for a different interpretation, Edward Schillebeeckx, *Interim Report*, pp. 10–19, and *Christ*, pp. 40–64. Although Schillebeeckx emphasizes the interweaving of revelation and experience and of experience and interpretation, he stresses that interpretation is permeated with exchangeable models and does not sufficiently explore how the literary form, interpretation, and experience are interwoven.

138. "The Social Context of Pauline Theology," *Interpretation* 36 (1982) 266–77, here p. 274.

139. Ramsay MacMullen, *Paganism in the Roman Empire* (New Haven: Yale Univ. Press, 1981), pp. 136f. See also E. R. Dodds, *Pagan and Christian in an Age of Anxiety* (Cambridge: Cambridge Univ. Press, 1965).

140. "Social Context," p. 274. For a full development of Meeks's use of social context, see his *The First Urban Christians: The Social World of the Apostle Paul* (New Haven: Yale Univ. Press, 1983).

141. See Helmut Koester and James M. Robinson, *Trajectories Through Early Christianity* (Philadelphia: Fortress, 1971), esp. pp. 223–29.

142. See Part III on the foundation of the Church.

143. *Das Ostergeschehen* (Göttingen: Vandenhoeck und Ruprecht, 1978), pp. 91–96.

144. *Foundations*, pp. 258–64; Wolfhart Pannenberg et al., *Erwägungen zur einer Theologie der Natur* (Gütersloh: Gerd Mohn, 1970), pp. 33–80; and David Ray Griffin, *A Process Christology* (Philadelphia: Westminster, 1973).

145. See my "Political Theology as Foundational Theology" (cited in n. 104 above), pp. 174–77, for the distinction between critical and reconstructive; and see also chapter 11 below for the meaning of reflective equilibrium, warrants, and background theories and their role in foundational theology.

PART II

THE
FOUNDATION
OF THE CHURCH

Introduction

The foundation of the Church was the second major issue of traditional fundamental theology. Along with the resurrection of Jesus it formed the core of the central historical demonstration. After the traditional fundamental theology had argued that Jesus was the divine legate in view of his fulfillment of Old Testament prophecies and his performance of miracles, especially his own resurrection, it then argued that Jesus had instituted a Church with papacy, ministry, and sacraments. Jesus' institution of the Church was not a matter of belief as an object of faith, but it was a historical fact which could be historically demonstrated. It would therefore serve as a ground rather than an object of faith. It was the task of fundamental theology to carry out this historical demonstration and to show how the institution of the Church was the ground of Catholic faith.

But just as historical criticism challenged the apologetic use of the resurrection of Jesus within fundamental theology, so too has it challenged the possibility of a historical demonstration that Jesus explicitly willed to institute a Church. This challenge went much deeper than the confessional controversies of the fifteenth, sixteenth, and seventeenth centuries. If Roman Catholics and Protestants had then debated which church order was divinely willed, they now had to face the common challenge laid down by the Enlightenment and by historical studies whether any church could claim with legitimacy to have Jesus as its founder. The challenge was not only whether the Church's foundation was historically demonstrable but also whether Jesus even intended to found a Church. The confessional debates about particulars of church order and of ministry are relatively secondary to the fundamental challenge whether Christianity as an ecclesial Christianity is a legitimate continuation of Jesus' vision and praxis.

Chapter 3

The Church's Foundation as a Fundamental Theological Issue

The Emergence and Nature of the Problem

In the eighteenth century, Hermann Samuel Reimarus argued in an essay published by Gotthold Ephraim Lessing, "The Goal of Jesus and His Disciples," that Jesus' aim, shared by his apostles, was not to establish a Church or even a separate religious community, but to reestablish the Davidic kingdom on Palestinian soil.[1] Jesus allegedly failed in this goal, and only after his execution and as a result of deception did the disciples propagate the notion of a Church. Such a charge has been continually repeated and it has just as often been refuted. The question of the foundation of the Church came to be controverted not in relation to a political interpretation of Jesus' preaching, but rather to an eschatological interpretation.[2]

The controversy at the beginning of this century, associated with modernism and with the discovery of the eschatological meaning of Jesus' preaching, is the watershed for the contemporary treatment of the relation between Jesus and the Church.[3] The problem as formulated then remains the same for us today: how does Jesus' eschatological preaching and imminent expectation allow for the foundation of a continuing Church? Moreover, during this controversy a catchphrase was born that still lives on and hovers over the debates.

The Birth of a Slogan

At the turn of the century, during the academic winter semester of 1899–1900, Adolf von Harnack delivered a set of lectures at the University of Berlin on the essence of Christianity (*Das Wesen des Christentums*). Their publication in 1900 attracted considerable attention: an English translation appeared a year later under the title *What Is Christianity?*[4]; a French translation, within two years; and the German edition itself underwent fourteen printings in two decades.

To the questions What is Christianity? What is the essence of Christianity?[5] Harnack had a clear-cut, even simple answer. Christianity had an essence which could be distilled from the preaching of Jesus. It was neither a metaphysical system nor a philosophy nor even a set of value judgments, but Jesus' preaching of the kingdom of God. Unfortunately the meaning of that preaching has been misunderstood. What, in fact, had been the husk of the message was taken as its kernel. Harnack, therefore, searched for the essence of Jesus' preaching. Adopting the methodological principle that the essence is determined by the specific difference, Harnack argued that the meaning of Jesus' preaching can be ascertained if its specific difference from its Jewish environment is uncovered. The apocalyptic elements of this preaching, also present in the religious tradition and in the preaching of John the baptizer, should therefore be excised. They do not constitute the novel and original element of Jesus' preaching.

The kingdom of God as the rule of God in the hearts of individual men and women constitutes this originality: God and the individual, the individual soul and God, are at the center of Jesus' message. When Jesus preached the kingdom, he did not refer to some apocalyptic cosmic event of the end-time nor did he point to some future institutional Church. Instead, he called for conversion, he proclaimed the reign of God's forgiveness in the hearts and souls of individuals.

The Church as an institution with its hierarchy, dogmas, and rituals does not belong to the essence of Christianity. Jesus' gospel had one aim: "As a Gospel it has only *one*—the finding of the living God, the finding of Him by every individual as his God, and as the source of strength and joy and peace."[6] Harnack taught that the gospel was essentially an internal, spiritual reality. The visible community that developed is not the Church of faith itself, but rather a form of its earthly realization. Consequently, its external forms are not primary. Although necessary embodiments of the gospel, these external forms are, in Harnack's opinion, deficient: intellectual creeds replaced immediate experience; individual laws were the countenance that the commandment of love took; and an organized hierarchical institution grew out of the community of disciples.

In May of 1902, a French translation of Harnack's work appeared that was favorably received by many Catholics, but not by Alfred

Loisy. Interrupting his work on an apology for Catholicism and using some of its material, Loisy wrote *The Gospel and the Church* ostensibly as a refutation of Harnack.[7] He sought to counter Harnack's interpretation of the kingdom proclamation; he wrote to overcome the contrast between the historical Jesus and the emergent Roman Catholic Church.[8] Yet his sentence, "Jesus foretold the Kingdom, and it was the church that came," has become a slogan expressing the contrast between Jesus' preaching and the existing Church. This slogan has remained in currency. In *Outline of the Theology of the New Testament*, Hans Conzelmann writes: "Liberal theologians drew from [the] inauthenticity [of Matt 18:17] the conclusion that Loisy put so perversely, Jesus expected the kingdom of God—and the church came. This statement is historically correct."[9] Likewise, Gerhard Ebeling's new dogmatics cites Loisy on the chasm between the kingdom and the Church.[10]

The Gospel and the Church advanced an eschatological interpretation of Jesus' preaching. It accepted Johannes Weiss's criticisms of the moral interpretation of God's reign prevalent within nineteenth-century liberalism.[11] These criticisms had dealt the deathblow to the moral and ecclesial interpretation of God's reign within historical scholarship, even if that scholarship has wavered in explaining just what is meant by an eschatological interpretation.[12]

Although Loisy put forward his eschatological interpretation of Jesus' proclamation against Harnack, it has been suggested that he is not as far from Harnack as one might suspect or even as Loisy leads one to suspect.[13] While it is true that Loisy refuses to identify God's reign with a moral kingdom in the hearts of individuals, he also disallows an identification of kingdom and Church. A chasm seems to exist between Jesus and the institutional Church for Loisy as well as for Harnack.[14] But their respective positions are so much more nuanced that they are thereby only loosely described. For Harnack, the gospel has need of a Church because the believer cannot discover within herself or himself the means of salvation. The gospel is not to be reduced to an individualistic mysticism. For Loisy, a fundamental continuity exists between the proclamation of the kingdom and the emergence of the Church because the existence of the Church is a necessary condition of the possibility of the continued preaching of the kingdom. Without the Church, the proclamation of God's reign would no longer continue.

Categories of functional identity and organic development are used by Loisy to explain the relation between Jesus, his proclamation of the kingdom, and the Church.[15] The hope expressed in Jesus' preaching is the hope propagated after the resurrection and on its basis. The Church, however, as the necessary condition for the continued preaching of the kingdom, is not a new creation that has sprung up after Jesus, but is the organic development of the seeds already planted by Jesus. Partly by necessary adaptation to external conditions, partly by internal assimilation, the pattern set already during the lifetime of Jesus unfolds. The gospel becomes the Church. The Church's distinctive government evolved from the clear distinction between the apostolic college and the ordinary disciple. The primacy of the pope developed out of Peter's leadership of the Twelve. The episcopal responsibility for local dioceses continues the apostolic responsibility for order in the earliest Christian communities. The episcopal exercise of excommunication grows out of the apostolic practice of receiving converts into the community and of excluding unworthy members from it. The present Church, therefore, not only continues to proclaim the hope contained in Jesus' preaching, but it also continued the pattern established at the time of Jesus.[16]

Loisy had maintained that Jesus selected the Twelve—he does not distinguish between the Twelve and the apostles as is commonly done today—and gave them a mission so that he had "associated them, directly and effectively, with His ministry."[17] Moreover, he gave priority to Peter, a priority not stemming from the priority of his conversion, but from Jesus' explicit designation.[18] Although the post-Easter Church is based upon faith in Jesus as the Christ, it owes its historical foundation to the actions of Jesus prior to his death. Loisy's defense of Catholic ecclesial existence was not merely a criticism of Protestant liberalism; it sought to grapple with the problems raised by the eschatological interpretation of the kingdom proclamation.

Loisy, however, did not affirm that Jesus established a constitutional charter or formally inaugurated the Church. "It is certain, for instance, that Jesus did not systematize beforehand the constitution of the Church as that of a government established on earth and destined to endure for a long series of centuries."[19] Consequently, despite its defense of Roman Catholicism and its argument for the development of hierarchical structures and religious dogmas, Loisy's book was condemned on 17 January 1903 by Cardinal Richard of Paris.[20]

The phrase, "Jesus foretold the kingdom, and it was the Church that came," was to become the slogan that has since dominated the discussion.[21] Indeed, Loisy's book presented a twofold challenge to theology. The historical question about the relation between the

Church and the earthly Jesus came to the forefront as a *modern contro-versy* within theology and especially within Roman Catholic theology. At the same time, the historical question posed a problem for *funda-mental theology*, for Loisy had argued that it was not possible to dem-onstrate historically that Jesus had intended to found the Church. The institution of the Church was in Loisy's opinion "not a tangible fact for the historian."[22] The divine foundation of the Church has shifted from a ground of faith to an object of faith. It is primarily faith in Jesus as the Christ that founds the Church.[23] Just as the resurrec-tion of Jesus has been challenged as a ground of faith so too the historical origin of the Church appears to have been moved from the domain of foundations to that of faith. The second pillar of modern fundamental theology thus seems to have collapsed.

A Modern Controversy

The storm of controversy about the foundation of the Church struck with such fury during the period of modernism because two currents within theology were clashing with each other. From one direction came the development of fundamental theology as an apologetic dis-cipline, increasingly structuring itself around the historical demon-stration of the foundation of the Church by Jesus. Vatican I's defini-tion of papal primacy and infallibility intensified this direction so that historical demonstration focused more and more on the foundation of the papacy by the historical Jesus. From the other direction came the increasing use of the historical-critical method. It not only questioned the use of Gospel texts as proof texts with its distinction between historical and dogmatic methodology, but with its study of the apoca-lyptic dimension of Jesus' proclamation it challenged the historical claim that Jesus intended to establish a Church.

How modern the historical critical questioning of the foundation of the Church is can be seen by a history of the exegesis of Matt 16:17–19. Critics such as David Friedrich Strauss, Ferdinand Baur, and Ernest Renan did not question the authenticity of the text. Although Christian Weisse had first doubted the authenticity in 1838, in 1856 he reconsidered and judged it genuine. In the second half of the nine-teenth century, several scholars (Bianchi-Giovini, Edmond, Schérer, Gustave d'Eichthal, Heinrich Julius Holtzmann) questioned its au-thenticity and suggested that the text was an interpolation. Toward the end of the century, the authenticity was textually challenged by Adolf von Harnack, Daniel Völter, and others. However, the eschato-logical issue that came to the fore at the turn of the century was to become decisive. The history of religion attack could easily be dismantled, but the challenge raised by "thoroughgoing and consistent eschatology" remains today.[24] Alfred Loisy's interpretation of Matt 16:17–19 and 18:17 pointed to the discrepancy between Jesus' expectation of an imminent end and the idea of a permanently enduring institution.[25]

Although the foundation of the Church is presupposed in many official Catholic teachings, it has become an object of explicit discussion and intentional decision only in very recent times. The Council of Trent affirmed that Jesus established the seven sacraments; Vatican I promulgated the institution of the papacy; and Leo XIII referred to the institution of a perennial and living magisterium.[26] These presuppose that Christ had indeed established a Church; it is an uncontested truth. Specific controversial issues, but not the foundation of the Church itself were open to debate. In its guidelines for the interpretation of dogmatic statements, *Mysterium ecclesiae* suggested that they be interpreted precisely in relation to the specific historical issue, dogmatic controversy, and religious issue that they sought to resolve. Issues not yet raised should not be considered resolved in completely different contexts.[27]

Nevertheless, the challenge of Loisy's eschatological interpretation of Jesus' preaching provoked definite magisterial responses. In *Lamentabili,* issued by the Holy Office on 3 July 1907, sixty-five "modernist" propositions were condemned, many directed explicitly against Loisy.[28] The fifty-second is of particular relevance here: "It was foreign to the mind of Christ to establish a Church as a society that would endure on earth through the long centuries because in the mind of Christ the Kingdom of Heaven was always identified with the end of the world that would soon come."[29] This condemnation was viewed by other modernists such as George Tyrrell[30] and Ernesto Buonaiuti[31] as directed at the tension between Jesus' eschatological proclamation and the foundation of an enduring institution.

Lamentabili condemned several other propositions that could easily be lifted from Loisy's writings.[32] It condemned the opinion that the organic constitution of the Church was not immutable and was subject to change as every other human society. It rejected the opinion that dogmas, sacraments, even the Church's hierarchy are Christian interpretations and developments of the tiny seed that was hidden in the gospel and grew through external accretions and came in time to fruition. It censured the opinion that Peter was not aware of his primacy and that the Roman see became the primary see as a result of political developments rather than of divine providence.

These condemnations were accepted and approved by Pope Pius X. His encyclical *Pascendi dominici gregis,* issued on 8 September 1907, sought to distill a unified philosophical system from such diverse historical opinions.[33] He attributed a system of immanentism and pantheism to modernism. This system was at the basis of all modernist teaching. It maintained that religious doctrines were neither supernatural nor real, but symbolic. The scholarly judgments about the historical evolution of the Church, its magisterium, doctrines, and sacraments and the opinion that these later developments go only mediately back to the historical Jesus are less the result of historical research than an expression of this philosophical immanentism.

In 1910, Pope Pius X required the "Oath against Modernism" of pastors, confessors, preachers, religious superiors, professors in philosophical and theological seminaries, and of all advancing to major orders. This oath was directed toward the very issues of the foundation of the Church. It required the individual to affirm: "I believe with equally firm faith that the Church, the guardian and teacher of the revealed word, was personally instituted by the real and historical Christ, when he lived among us, and that the Church was built upon Peter, the principle of the apostolic hierarchy, and his successors for the duration of time."[34] The same oath also sought to buttress the traditional fundamental theology and required the affirmation that miracles and prophecies served as criteria of the demonstration of the truth of revelation.[35] Moreover, under the direction of Monsignor Umberto Benigni, a secret society was established known as *Sodalitium Pianum* or *La Sapinière* to ferret out as "modernists" anyone purportedly holding or teaching anything contrary to the above affirmations.

The way in which the papal documents link the historical, theological, and philosophical make the meaning of their condemnation of certain modernist opinions not unambiguous. They excluded developmental views as reflecting an immanentism that reduces the Church to the level of any other organization. They rejected the symbolic interpretation of the religious doctrine as an interpretation denying their reality and truth. They viewed the explanation of historical growth with reference to external factors as the elimination of the religious distinctiveness of the Church. Since these condemnations intertwine pantheism, immanentism, and secularism with this historical position, it becomes difficult to evaluate the condemnations when these interconnections are not made. If the symbolic and realistic are not contraries, if external influences and divine origin are not exclusives, and if development and religious distinctiveness are not opposites, then the point of the condemnation becomes questionable and ambiguous.

At the same time that these pronouncements were made on the foundation of the Church, the Pontifical Biblical Commission issued several statements regarding diverse historical biblical questions and regarding the methodology of biblical studies themselves. These ranged from the authorship of the Pentateuch to the authorship of John's Gospel. Later documents of the Biblical Commission and Vatican II's Constitution on Divine Revelation have fundamentally revised and annulled the methodological presuppositions of the 1907 and 1910 pronouncements.[36] But none of the condemnations in regard to the foundation of the Church in either *Lamentabili* or *Pascendi* has been explicitly retracted.[37]

Therefore, the condemnations occasioned by the modernist controversy stand in force, but they stand in a twilight zone. On the one hand, they represent a long-standing and traditional belief of Catholicism about the foundation of the Church, the historical origins of the papacy, and the divine institution of the hierarchy. On the other hand, the Church's official documents have now defended a historical methodology as applied to the Scriptures that calls for a radical revision of how these beliefs have been used in traditional fundamental theology as an apologetic for a particular confessional stance.

The Foundation of the Church within Fundamental Theology

The modernist controversy about the foundation of the Church was so virulent because it touched all areas of theology: ecclesiology, christology, sacramental theology, eschatology, and so on. Not a single theological discipline was unaffected by the results of the discovery of the eschatological nature of Jesus' proclamation of God's reign. Moreover, the issue of the foundation of the Church affected the very roots of fundamental theology for several reasons. It was pivotal for the structure and development of fundamental theology; it was at the center of the apologetic endeavors within fundamental theology; and it raised the basic issue of the meaning of the Christian vision.

First of all, in developing as a distinct theological discipline, fundamental theology had as its goal not only to establish the truth of the Catholic faith but also to lay the foundations of systematic theology.[38] Such a double goal explains the emphasis given to the issue of the foundation of the Church. As the resurrection of Jesus functioned to demonstrate the existence and truth of Christian revelation, the demonstration that Jesus founded the Roman Catholic Church sought to

secure the truth of Catholicism. Just as the resurrection, as a historically demonstrable truth, established the legitimacy of Jesus, the historical demonstration that Jesus founded a Church and constituted
the papacy was to establish the legitimacy of the Church, the divine
right of Catholic church order, and the veracity of all Catholic teachings.

Consequently, the historical demonstration had another function: it also served to provide the basis for a specific conception of
systematic theology. Since fundamental theology culminated in a
demonstration of the foundation of the Church and more especially
of the foundation of a magisterium to which the deposit of faith was
entrusted,[39] systematic theology could develop independently as a
magisterial dogmatic theology. It primarily explained and interpreted
magisterial teaching, while it dispensed with fundamental theological
reflections. The truths of systematic theology had already been established in principle by fundamental theology which has produced a
historical demonstration of Jesus' institution of the Church's magisterium. Systematic theology primarily explicated both the meaning and
truth of Christian doctrine through its qualification, interpretation,
and explication of magisterial pronouncements. It was the historical
demonstration of the foundation of the Church and of an ecclesial
magisterium that made possible a sharp distinction between fundamental theology and systematic theology.

The issue of the foundation of the Church occupied a crucial role
within fundamental theology because fundamental theology incorporated within itself the confessional controversies of the previous centuries. Since the time of the Reformation differences among Roman
Catholics, Lutherans, and Calvinists were largely based upon what
had allegedly been divinely instituted. Each confession traced back its
church order to Jesus and used similar, if not synonymous, terms
such as "divine right," "divine institution," "divine law," and "divine ordination."[40] Each confession was confident not only that Jesus
had founded a Church, but that he had established a very specific
kind of Church order.

The appeal to what Christ instituted is central to Roman Catholic,
Lutheran, and Calvinist traditions. In the Roman Catholic tradition,
the last three ecumenical councils have appealed to an institution by
the historical Jesus in order to justify Roman Catholic church order
and liturgical practice. The Council of Trent affirmed in general the
medieval theological opinion that Jesus had instituted all seven sacraments.[41] This general affirmation was supported more cautiously in

the individual canons dealing with matrimony, holy orders, the anointing of the sick, and sacramental confession.[42] Moreover, it was affirmed that the Eucharist was instituted by Jesus as a sacrifice.[43] Likewise, the Church's hierarchical ministry with its distinct grades resulted from divine institution.[44] In *Pastor aeternus*, Vatican I proclaimed that Christ directly and immediately gave to Simon Peter the primacy of a true and proper jurisdiction over the whole Church. Moreover, the Roman pontiff is a perpetual successor to Peter in primacy over the Church by the institution of Christ himself, or *jure divino*.[45] This teaching is reaffirmed by Vatican II's teaching that the bishops are also by divine institution the successors of the apostles and, as members of the apostolic college, have by Christ's institution care for the whole Church. The various ministries in the Church are themselves *ex divina institutione*.[46]

Similar appeals are made in the Lutheran and Calvinist traditions for their own church orders. Luther insisted that Christ commissioned the Church to preach, instituted the sacraments of baptism and Eucharist, and established the pastoral office. However, this pastoral office does not have special power status nor do bishops have jurisdiction by divine institution. The Lutheran creedal statements and Lutheran theology specify as divinely instituted the Church, the ministry of the word of God, and the sacraments, though, of course, they reject the supremacy of the bishop of Rome.[47] Calvin, also referring to the institution by Christ, explains that Christ not only gave his Church a permanent constitution but also established holy ordinances such as sacramental ministry, preaching, and the community of prayer.[48]

All these confessional debates presupposed one truth: Jesus had founded not only a Church but also the constitutive elements of that Church. These constitutive elements were therefore established by divine law. Although some caution existed in particular cases about the direct reference to the historical Jesus,[49] the foundation of a particular church order was the central point of the controversy. The foundation of the Church was presupposed. In the development from apologetical theology to fundamental theology, therefore, the central task of fundamental theology remained not so much to demonstrate that Jesus founded a Church, but to prove that Jesus established a particular Church with a definite structure. Even today, in the ecumenical (and even intramural) debates about the ordination of women, the argument is advanced about Jesus' attitude toward his Church and its order.[50]

Thus the modern controversy about whether Jesus founded a Church at all in view of his eschatological proclamation, therefore, undercuts all of these specific arguments about church order and sacramental institution. If Jesus' expectation of an imminent end excluded the possibility of any intention to establish a Church, then arguments based upon a conception of divine institution with reference to the intention of the historical Jesus become pointless for each position on the ecumenical spectrum.

Finally, the foundation of the Church should be central to fundamental theology for a third reason, although this reason has been insufficiently explored both in traditional and contemporary accounts of fundamental theology. Traditional fundamental theology saw the foundation of the Church as an apologetic and controversial issue because it grounded systematic theology and defended a particular church order. The foundation of the Church concerns, however, not merely the historical issue about Jesus' intention during his lifetime to institute a Church or a particular church order, but also the large systematic issue of the meaning of Jesus and of Christianity. In what does the Christian vision consist? What is the reality of Christianity? How does the historical development of ecclesial Christianity relate to Jesus and to the vision present in his preaching and in his life-praxis?

The relation between ecclesial Christian existence and Jesus' meaning and significance has been discussed in relation to certain particular issues. At the turn of this century the debate focused on the moral or eschatological interpretation of Jesus' preaching as it affected the development of dogma and institutional structures. The fundamental issue also surfaced in the famous debate between Rudolf Sohm and Harnack. For Sohm, the Church is primarily charismatic. It arises from the enthusiasm caused by the presence of God and God's spirit. There is no room for ecclesiastical law. For Harnack primitive Christianity had from its very beginning rules that led to full legal regulations.[51]

The debate at the time of neo-orthodoxy focused on the relation between the historical Jesus and the kergymatic Christ. Is there not only a factual continuity between the Church's proclamation of Christ and Jesus' own self-understanding and proclamation but also an objective continuity? The debate between Rudolf Bultmann and his students with their new quest for the historical Jesus was not simply a historical debate about whether the Gospel sources allow a reconstruction of Jesus' self-understanding or proclamation but also a debate about the nature of the continuity between Jesus and ecclesial Christianity.[52]

The eschatological interpretation of Jesus' proclamation is also entailed in the current controversy over political and liberation theologies. Ecclesial Christianity has developed not only creeds and institutional structures but also a social and a political ministry. Since political and liberation theology emphasize the Church's social and political mission, they often confront the criticism that Jesus did not preach some kind of humanly realizable political kingdom, but only an eschatological one. He was not a zealot but a prophet. He did not advocate social justice through legislative reform, but proclaimed God's coming reign. The challenge of the eschatological interpretation of Jesus' proclamation, therefore, affects not only the emergence of the Church as an enduring institution; it concerns not only the constitution of office and of creed for the Church; it also contests the social and political ministry of the Church.[53]

At stake in all these controversies is the nature of the continuity between Jesus' vision and praxis and the Christian community's reception of Jesus in its own developing vision and praxis. If fundamental theology does not have as its method and goal the apologetic proof of Christianity through a historical demonstration or a transcendental deduction, but seeks to unfold the disclosure power of the Christian vision and praxis, then the issue of the foundation of the Church will be viewed increasingly in relation to the issues of the nature of the Christian vision and the legitimacy of its praxis.

Fundamental Theological Options

The two following chapters will analyze the various approaches of fundamental theology to the issue of the foundation of the Church. Initially, the classic historical demonstration developed in modern fundamental theology after the modernist crisis will be outlined and critiqued as inadequate. The inability of this approach to achieve what it set as its goal raises anew the problem posed by Loisy; if the institution of the Church is "not a tangible fact for the historian," then it is more "an object of faith than a demonstration of faith."[54] So framed, this question asks whether the foundation of the Church can even be a part of fundamental theology.

Therefore, it becomes important to analyze how transcendental and existential theology developed a formal-fundamental theology with an indirect method. This method seeks to take seriously Loisy's claim. Yet at the same time, it develops the foundation of the Church as an issue within fundamental theology.

Whether transcendental fundamental theology complements or

bypasses the historical issue, it remains necessary for fundamental theology to come to terms with the historical problem of the relation between Jesus and the Church. Two historical proposals have emerged. One locates the origin of the Church in the intention of the earthly Jesus. At the beginning of his ministry Jesus did not intend to establish a Church, but toward the end he laid the foundations for a Church insofar as he gathered disciples, urged the celebration of commemorative meals, and deliberately prepared for an "interim community" of the end-time. The other approach focuses on the postresurrectional emergence of the Church as a result of the activity of the Spirit and of Peter. The Church was not explicitly intended by the earthly Jesus even in the form of an "interim community."

These approaches raise important questions about the meaning of the Church in relation to the historical Jesus. The balance of this chapter will therefore explore the hermeneutical problems entailed in any discussion of the foundation of the Church, especially those problems relating agency and intention, the meaning of continuity, and the nature of reception. It will show how foundational theology as a reconstructive hermeneutic avoids the pitfalls of the traditional and contemporary historical demonstrations. Moreover, instead of proposing only an indirect or existential approach to the foundation of the Church, a reconstructive hermeneutic of the Church's foundation should elaborate the historical and theological continuity between the vision and praxis of Jesus and that of the early Christian communities.

Traditional Fundamental Theology and the Foundation of the Church

As noted above, fundamental theology has viewed the foundation of the Church by the earthly Jesus as a historically demonstrable fact. Although historical-critical scholarship during the modernist controversy challenged such a conviction, Roman Catholic fundamental theology continued to argue that it was historically possible to demonstrate such a foundation of the Church and so emphasized this historical demonstration that it became the high-point of fundamental theology. Pervasiveness of this historical demonstration makes it imperative to analyse how it understood the foundation of the Church; what its historical arguments were; and how its probative character has been challenged by contemporary biblical scholarship.

Notion of Foundation of the Church

Fundamental theology usually referred to the Church as instituted by Christ. The contemporary distinction between (earthly or historical) Jesus and (kerygmatic) Christ was not made. Instead, the words *Jesus* and *Christ* were, in the tradition of this fundamental theology, applied indiscriminately to the earthly Jesus. As far as the act of foundation itself, the manualist tradition used the terms *instituere, fundare,* and *aedificare* to express Jesus' direct intention and explicit will to "institute," "found," and "build" a Church. Jesus is the efficient cause of the Church not only because he formed it but because he instituted the Church itself and its various constitutive elements. Jesus instituted the Church, as the leading textbook of the 1950s stated, "with a free, authoritative, and express will to constitute something with determinateness and stability in the moral and juridical order."[55]

In describing the foundation of the Church as "instituted by Christ," this tradition of fundamental theology carefully distinguished between "to institute" and "to constitute."[56] To constitute is to give a particular shape and form to what was already established and existent. To institute, however, is to bring something into existence through an efficient cause. Jesus, therefore, did not merely give a particular shape and form to the Church. He brought it into existence.

The conceptual framework implicit in this explanation of the foundation of the Church is the Aristotelian system of four causes.[57] These four causes (efficient, formal, material, and final) explain the Church's constitution, existence, properties, and goal. The material cause is the plurality of believers that make up the Church, whereas the final cause is the sanctification of these members that are now enabled to participate in eternal life.[58] The formal and efficient causes, however, are the most significant categories for understanding of the Church. The formal cause—here defined as the hierarchy—is that which makes the Church what it is. The material cause, the plurality of believers, is only the material, or "stuff," out of which the Church is made. These believers do not make the Church into Church, for only the hierarchical structure provides the formal unity which makes it into a specific entity. The papacy as the formal cause of unity, therefore, most probably makes the Church to be the Church. Thus, the foundation of the Church is the foundation of the hierarchy—in particular the papacy.[59]

Christ is the efficient cause of the Church. Indeed, as the ultimate efficient cause,[60] he calls together the plurality of believers that make up the material cause of the Church and he institutes the hierarchy as the form of the Church. Christ does not merely form or shape the Church, he brings it into existence. The hierarchy, acting as a secondary cause, forms the Church and especially the laity who make up only the material of the Church.[61]

This use of Aristotelian categories of causality was exemplified in G. Paris's *De vera Christi ecclesia* and culminated in Charles Journet's projected four-volume work in which each of the volumes was to focus on a single cause.[62] This neoscholastic approach dominated modern fundamental theology. Although it contained elements that went beyond the use of the four categories (for example, the conception of the Church as the mystical Body of Christ), the Church was viewed primarily in these Aristotelian terms.[63] Even the use of body-soul imagery to clarify the visible reality of the Church was cast within this neoscholastic framework of causality. Thus, the conception of the Church determined the conception of its historical demonstration. The Church was a visible institution insofar as it consisted of visible human persons as believers (material cause), insofar as it was made distinct and visible under the direction of the hierarchy (formal cause) for the sake of salvation (final cause), and insofar as it was founded by Jesus (efficient cause).

Jesus' efficient causality in instituting the Church was further specified. On one hand this tradition of fundamental theology maintained that Jesus did not institute the Church through a single act or at one particular time, but through several "instituting actions" or "founding acts" that took place at different times.[64] On the other hand, since it viewed the hierarchy as the formal unity of the Church, it necessarily underscored two specific acts as constitutive: (1) the appointment of Peter as primate and ruler of the Church as a monarchical society; (2) the selection, instruction, and mission of the Twelve. They are given the deposit of faith with the fullness of revelation along with the threefold power and authority to teach, sanctify, and rule.

This tradition also considered other actions to be foundational,[65] for example, the institution of the Eucharist as the new covenant and cult, the institution of the sacraments, and the tripartite division of orders into bishops, priests, and deacons. But these actions, although alleged to be historical, were all placed in the background. The appointment of Peter as primate was in the forefront. For in the framework of Aristotelian causality, Peter was the highest visible sign of the unity of the Church and was the formal cause of the unity of the apostolic college.[66] Only within the formal unity incorporated in Peter could the apostolic power of teaching, sanctifying, and ruling take place. Therefore, Peter's appointment by Jesus must be historically demonstrated if this fundamental theology were to demonstrate that Jesus as efficient cause instituted the Church.

Fundamental theology, however, faced a diversity of seemingly contradictory scriptural texts. Although these texts occasioned the debate about when Jesus actually instituted the Church,[67] the common opinion that emerged posited a basic continuity among the various foundational acts of Jesus. It used the categories of preparation, institution, and promulgation to unify diverse statements. In regard to Peter, it used the category of promise and actual conferral.

Consequently, common opinion envisioned the foundation of the Church in three stages.[68] In the first Jesus *prepared* for the foundation. During his lifetime, he did not institute the Church itself but laid its foundations: he assembled a group of believers, he selected apostles, he promised the primacy to Peter, and he even instituted the sacraments of baptism and Eucharist. The second stage, the actual *institution,* took place after the resurrection. Only then did he complete the final establishment of the Church; only then did he actually confer the primacy upon Peter; only then did he give the power to teach, sanctify, and rule to the apostolic college. Only then did the Church come into existence. As expressed by Van Noort, "The Church is clearly a society, and no society has been properly constituted until its authority has been established. Strictly speaking, then the Church was established by Christ after the Resurrection."[69] The final stage was the *promulgation* of the Church's existence which took place on Pentecost. At this time, the Church became necessary for the salvation of humankind.

Historical Demonstration

A fundamental theology that could dissect with such ease the foundation of the Church into various stages could even more confidently affirm that the institution of the Church was a matter of historical demonstration. In response to the issues raised by Loisy, Monsignor Émile-Paul Le Camus, bishop of la Rochelle, triumphantly maintained in *False Exegesis, Bad Theology*:

> The institution of the Church by Jesus Christ is therefore established on a series of absolute relevant historical facts. Consequently, it is historically demonstrable, and not only an object of faith as Loisy thinks. The

will of Christ on this point remains verifiable by the historian. Without much effort one would even be able to recognize that the Church has been constituted with a monarchical form, a form especially propitious for maintaining order. Indeed by a simple analysis of the texts, one can (*pace* Loisy) demonstrate the divine institution of the Roman Pontificate and determine the legitimate conditions of its existence.[70]

What the bishop of la Rochelle so confidently maintained in 1904 was still being maintained fifty years later. In regard to the truth of the Catholic Church, the method of fundamental theology was to be empirical, illative, and historical.[71] The empirical method analyzed what was observable: the rapid spread of the Church, its continued existence, its contributions to society. Such empirical data were taken as signs of God's presence and they suggest that the life and existence of the Church was a moral miracle. The illative method sought to show how the Catholic Church had properties that were appropriate for the Church of Christ and indeed corresponded to those very characteristics intended by Christ for his Church.

The historical method, however, was the most basic method of this fundamental theology for the other two methods depended upon it. It was the task of historical method to demonstrate through strict scientific inquiry, as definitely and as completely as possible, that the historical Jesus had deliberately and intentionally established the Roman Catholic Church with Peter as its primate and with an apostolic college entrusted with a triple mandate that was to be passed on to successive generations of bishops.

Although a basic continuity exists in the historical demonstration of this fundamental theology from the eighteenth to the twentieth century, Loisy's eschatological interpretation does mark a caesura in the argumentation. Prior to Loisy, as the classic fundamental theology of the nineteenth century by Perrone well illustrates, the argument was made that Jesus founded a Church and that this Church existed prior to the Scriptures.[72] The focus was on the priority of the Church over the Scriptures because the fundamental theological demonstration was directed primarily against the Protestant scriptural principle. This focus on the Church's priority over Scripture disappears. Instead, the historical arguments seek first of all to demonstrate that the eschatological interpretation of Jesus' proclamation should be so understood that it does not make the foundation of the Church foreign to Jesus' mind and intention. The primacy of Peter and the hierarchical structure of the Church were the mainstays of the demonstrations in the nineteenth as well as in the twentieth century, except that the twentieth century raised objections to the authenticity of Matt 16:17–19 and to the use of the term "ecclesia" in relation to the historical Jesus.[73]

After the modernist controversy, the historical demonstration adopted three basic arguments: (1) a refutation of the claim that the eschatological meaning of Jesus' proclamation excluded the intention to institute an enduring Church; (2) an interpretation of Jesus' gathering of the disciples as the assembly of an apostolic college in preparation for the foundation of the Church and for the conferral of the threefold power to teach, sanctify, and rule; and (3) a defense not only of the historicity of Jesus' promise to Peter but also of the actual conferral of the primacy on Peter. All three arguments served to demonstrate that Jesus intended, prepared, and de facto established the Church as an enduring and indestructible institution.

The defense of the historicity of Jesus' promise to Peter (Matt 16:17–19) was not only the high-point of the demonstration but also provided the basis by which any doubts about the arguments in (1) and (2) could be resolved. This structure is found with slight variations in almost all recent fundamental theological textbooks, for example, Van Noort (1957), Salverri (1958), Schmaus (1958; with modifications, 1972), and even Rahner (1976).[74] Moreover, contemporary ecclesiologies are based on the same criteria, especially on the promise/investiture category to deal with the Petrine texts—as exemplified most recently by Faynel (1970), Gherardini (1974), and Mondello (1978).[75]

Eschatology and Church
Since the eschatological interpretation of Jesus' proclamation of the kingdom was seen as the main obstacle to the notion of his explicit intention to establish the Church, the argument in fundamental theology sought to develop a conception of the kingdom as "all comprehensive." The kingdom that Jesus preached, it claimed, was "not only eschatological, spiritual, and internal, but also existing on earth, visible, and external."[76] But such a definition simply combined into one concept diverse and even contradictory strains of interpretation. It was comprehensive insofar as it included strains of the nineteenth-century liberal conception of the kingdom as spiritual and internal, just as it incorporated the history-of-religions reference to the eschatological-apocalyptic dimensions as well as the traditional Roman Catholic reference to visible and external society. However, in the end, the argument offered no consistent interpretation.

Its methodic procedure was to amalgamate New Testament texts into one harmonic view. Scriptural references appearing to imply moral perfection (for example, Luke 15:1–32) were interpreted as showing the internal and spiritual nature of the kingdom. Apocalyptic references or parables of the final judgment (for example, Matt 25) were seen as indicating the eschatological dimension. Those references that appeared to imply a present existence, continued activity, and future growth of the kingdom were claimed as proofs that Jesus' proclamation of the kingdom referred to the Church. Consequently, its response to the consistent eschatological interpretation of the kingdom proclamation centered on the parables of growth. In these parables, the emphasis appears to be on the present activity of the coming kingdom. The parable of the mustard seed (Mark 4:30–32) is the classic apologetical example:

> And he said, "With what can we compare the kingdom of God, or what parable shall we use for it? It is like a grain of mustard seed, which, when sown upon the ground, is the smallest of all the seeds on the earth; yet when it is sown it grows up and becomes the greatest of all shrubs, and puts forth large branches, so that the birds of the air can make nests in its shade."

In taking this parable to exemplify the growth of the Church, fundamental theology stood at the end of a long history of interpretation. Gregory the Great saw the parable as an illustration of the coming together of divine grace and human virtue.[77] John Chrysostom interpreted it as a description of the missionary proclamation; the preaching of the disciples leads to the gradual transformation of the whole world.[78] Consequently, Schmaus argues against the consistent eschatological interpretation that the "kingdom of God presents itself and realizes itself in the kingdom of the Son."[79] The kingdom of God that has appeared in Christ has not only the character of a beginning, but it grows as a mustard seed.[80] This interpretation is seen to be confirmed by the selection of the Twelve and by the role given to Peter, especially within Matt 16:17–19 that seems to parallel the Church and the kingdom of heaven. In this way, the next two arguments (from the selection of the Twelve and Peter) were seen as further proofs not only that Jesus intended to institute a Church but also that his proclamation of the kingdom included the Church.

Apostolic College
Since the selecting of the apostles and their commissioning were considered central institutional acts establishing the Church, two Gospel

texts came prominently into consideration: Mark 3:14–19 and Matt 28:18–20. The first reads:

> And he appointed twelve to be with him, and to be sent out to preach and have authority to cast out demons: Simon whom he surnamed Peter; James the son of Zebedee and John the brother of James, whom he surnamed Boanerges, that is, sons of thunder; Andrew, and Philip, and Bartholomew, and Matthew, and Thomas, and James the son of Alphaeus, and Thaddaeus, and Simon the Cananaean, and Judas Iscariot, who betrayed him.

Although this text does not use the term "apostles," it was interpreted as the act of founding the apostolic college. The interpretations simply amalgamated the notions of "apostle" and "twelve" into the conception of an apostolic college.

In view of this distinction between preparation and institution, Matt 28:18–20 was looked upon as the actual institution of the apostolic college. During the lifetime of Jesus, the apostles were prepared for their ministry, but only after the resurrection were they empowered with authority.

> And Jesus came and said to them, "All authority in heaven and on earth has been given to me. Go therefore and make disciples of all nations, baptizing them in the name of the Father and of the Son ad of the Holy Spirit, teaching them to observe all that I have commanded you; and lo I am with you always, to the close of the age."

These concluding verses of Matthew's Gospel appear to express not only the authority and commission of the apostles but also their universal and indestructable mission. They are the disciples of Jesus and are empowered to make others into disciples.

Jesus and Peter

Within fundamental theology, Matt 16:17–19 became the main proof-text of the historical demonstration that Jesus, during his earthly ministry, had indeed intended to institute a Church, had associated that Church with the kingdom of God, has promised primacy to Peter, and had foreseen the Church's future institutional existence. It was used to buttress and confirm the arguments interrelating kingdom and Church. It clearly indicated the purpose of the selection of the apostles. Although Matt 16:17–19 was not understood by many early church fathers nor by Aquinas as referring to the foundation of the Church upon Peter and was never the crucial text, it became now the pivotal Gospel statement of fundamental theology.[81] These versus are:

[17] And Jesus answered him,
"Blessed are you, Simon Bar-Jona:
For flesh and blood has not revealed this to you,
but my Father who is in heaven.
[18] And I tell you, you are Peter,
and on this rock I will build my church,
and the powers of death shall not prevail against it.
[19] I will give you the keys of the kingdom of heaven,
and whatever you bind on earth shall be bound in heaven,
and whatever you loose on earth, shall be loosed in heaven."

These verses are attested in most of the ancient codices and versions. The expressions, vocabulary, and style all point to the antiquity of the text. The expressions, "flesh and blood," "gates of hell," "be bound," "be loosed," "my father in heaven," "lord of heaven," "Bar-Jona," all reflect semitisms that can be best explained by maintaining that the Greek text of Matthew has for these particular verses its source in a spoken tradition or written Aramaic source. The verses therefore stem from Palestine and go back to the historical Jesus. The play on the names Peter/rock also point to an Aramaic background.[82]

In addition to this emphasis upon the semitic character of the verses, certain lines of interpretation were drawn out within fundamental theology. The calling of Simon Peter was interpreted as a change (rather than an addition) of a name, parallel to the change of names in the Hebrew Scriptures when prominent persons assumed new roles, for example, Abram/Abraham (Gen 17:5), Jacob/Israel (Gen 32:28). These persons had their name changed not only at decisive points in their lives but also when they assumed new roles that functioned to mark a turning-point in the history of Israel.

Therefore, when Jesus called Simon by the name of Peter or more precisely *Kephā*, he was giving him a new role and responsibility. This new role was to be the foundation or the rock of the Church. Other texts were drawn upon to confirm this new role: Luke 22:31–32 refers to Peter's role in strengthening the brethren; John 21 has Jesus give Peter the role of feeding Jesus' sheep. In short, two other Gospels appear to confirm Peter's foundational role in the Church.

In addition to the metaphor of rock (= foundation), two other metaphors are involved. Verse 19 gives Peter the keys to the kingdom of heaven and the power of binding and loosing. The metaphor of keys was explained as signifying Peter's supreme jurisdiction so that whatever Peter does on earth will be ratified in heaven. The power was seen as universal because of the term "whatever." The limitation, of course, was to religious and moral matters. It was, however, noted that whoever has the keys of a house or a city has supreme authority and administers the whole house or city. Hence, the power of the keys involves more authority than merely binding or loosing since others without the keys can do that as well. This distinction was important because Matt 18:18 promises the loosing and binding also to the disciples. It was therefore necessary to distinguish their power from Peter's and to place his authority over their authority. In short, the whole verse was interpreted as pointing up Peter's supreme jurisdiction over the whole Church.[83]

Since verse 18 referred to "Church" and verse 19 referred to "kingdom of heaven," the fundamental theological argument equated Church and kingdom. One recent manual confidently asserts: "That the 'kingdom of heaven' is in truth the Church here on earth is obvious. Certainly Peter is not promised authority over the realm of glory; besides, our Lord explicitly adds that whatever Peter binds or looses *on earth* will be ratified."[84] Much more careful and cautious is Schmaus, but the intent is the same: "The power of the keys related to the kingdom of heaven. Peter is the foundation-rock of the Church; kingdom of heaven and Church are not identical but they are most closely connected. . . . The Church is at the same time organ and appearance, instrument and locus of the kingdom of heaven, of God's kingdom."[85]

This interpretation, therefore, both presupposed and asserted the interconnection of Church and kingdom.[86] To the question whether Jesus explicitly and intentionally founded a Church, fundamental theology appeared to have an unshakeable historical answer: Jesus preached the kingdom of God not only as an imminent end but also as a present reality that grew; he established an apostolic college; he promised the primacy to Peter in Matt 16:17–19 and conferred it later. It is no wonder that in 1904 Le Camus could have claimed that a simple analysis of the texts made the foundation of the Church not an object of faith, but one of historical demonstration. And in 1976, almost three-quarters of a century later, Karl Rahner in *Foundations of Christian Faith* produces the same threefold historical argument with its culmination in the Matthean text. Even though he felt it necessary to complement this historical demonstration with a formal fundamental theological approach, he still maintained the same historical arguments to demonstrate that Jesus founded a Church.[87]

Critique of the Historical Demonstration
The conviction within Roman Catholic fundamental theology that Jesus' institution of the Church can be historically demonstrated has

perdured despite criticism of each of the supporting pillars of the argument. Although an almost unanimous exegetical consensus within Protestant theology has gone in a different direction that has even been called a "new consensus" and a "post-new consensus,"[88] Roman Catholic fundamental theology has still advanced the historical demonstration—with some modifications to be discussed in chapter 4.

There are several reasons for these continued attempts at historical demonstration. The increased awareness of the multivalence of eschatological language has weakened the hermeneutical basis of those historical arguments that pointed exclusively to the imminent end-time expectation within the kingdom proclamation.[89] The renewed quest for the historical Jesus has given more confidence to the exploration in systematic theology of the significance of Jesus' historical call to discipleship.[90] Although severely criticized by some Protestant colleagues,[91] Oscar Cullmann's *Peter: Disciple, Apostle, Martyr*[92] was widely read in Catholic theological circles, since as a non-Catholic he acknowledged the primacy of Peter within the New Testament and conceded that the historical Jesus spoke the words of Matt 16:17–19 to Peter (but at the last supper rather than at Caesarea Philippi). Cullmann rejected only the succession of that primacy within the Church. In short, some significant reasons seemed to confirm the traditional historical demonstration.

Therefore, the pros and cons of each historical argument should be weighed. Is it historically demonstrable that Jesus directly intended and explicitly willed to establish a Church? An affirmative answer would support the traditional fundamental theology and its methodic approach. A negative answer would destroy the central assumption of that fundamental theology. But a challenge to the historical demonstrability of the foundation of the Church would at the same be a challenge to a whole conception of fundamental theology as traditionally understood.

A further problem could be raised: to deny that a historical demonstration is probative does not involve eo ipso rejection of the belief that Jesus founded a Church. Not all objects of belief can or even should be historically demonstrable. Such a distinction is indeed important but it can be distorted. The reasons speaking against the probative nature of the historical demonstration will necessarily affect what the de facto relation between Jesus and the Church was or how it is to be conceived. The critique of the historical demonstrability of the Church's foundation therefore challenges theology not only to rethink the nature and function of fundamental theology but also to understand in a new way the relation between Jesus and the Church. Historical and theological issues are not identical, but they do sometimes mesh, and a challenge to the historical will be, at the same time, a challenge to the theological.[93]

Eschatology and Community
The meaning of Jesus' proclamation of God's rule and kingdom remains a controverted issue within contemporary exegesis.[94] Scholarly proposals to reconcile the diverse strains of eschatology within the Gospel materials are legion: imminent, realizing or inaugural, realized eschatology, etc. Many scholars point to clear-cut references to an imminent expectation as definite indications that Jesus expected the end-time in the immediate future.[95] Others suggest the opposite: not Jesus himself, but the early Christian community gave birth to the expectation of the imminent end-time when their Easter experience led them to conclude that soon the dead would rise.[96] It has even been suggested that Jesus himself may not have been clear about the future and could have had both imminent as well as "realized" expectations.[97]

Nevertheless, an assessment of the traditional demonstration of fundamental theology can be made without necessarily resolving all the problems inherent within New Testament eschatology. In its identification of the Church and the kingdom of God, fundamental theology relied heavily upon the parables of growth as foretelling the presence and growth of the Church. Consonant with this interpretation of the parables of growth was its interpretation of Matt 16:17–19 that appeared to identify the Church and the kingdom of God.

Although the parables of growth have received different interpretations not only in the past but also in contemporary exegesis, some points of consensus have emerged.[98] First of all, despite their name, the parables of growth do not emphasize stages of growth or gradual development but rather contrast the beginning with the end. In addition to emphasizing this contrast, the parables underscore the certainty and specificity of the end. The end so relates to the beginning that it results from the beginning with certainty. What has begun in the seed, therefore, not only comes to such a wonderful end but also to an end that is specified by the nature of the seed itself. Finally, the parables do not depict the end-result as the Church on earth, but rather as the kingdom of God in its complete fulfillment.

The parable of the mustard seed was a prime example in fundamental theology. Its text in Mark 4:30–32 has parallels in Matt 13:31–32, Luke 13:18–19, and in the apocryphal Gospel of Thomas.[99] The text does not stress stages of growth nor the gradual process of growth of the mustard seed. Instead, it contrasted the smallest seed and the greatest of all shrubs (Matthew and Luke incorrectly have "trees" rather than "shrubs"). The resulting shrub is already specified in the seed. Moreover, the final image is an image that was used in the Old Testament to describe the messianic kingdom (Ezek 17:23). The final verse is an allusion to a metaphoric image that was commonly present in Jewish expectations of the end-time. Consequently, "the end of the parable is not the worldwide Church, but the fulfilled kingdom of God."[100]

Obviously the question can be raised whether a difference of meaning exists between the parable as told by the earthly Jesus and as retold by Mark's Gospel. Still central to both would be the contrast. The smallness of the mustard seed was proverbial, whereas the grown mustard shrub reached almost three meters high and was larger than other shrubs. The image in Ezekiel is used also in 31:6 to refer to pagan nations coming to Israel at the end-time. Mark elsewhere stresses that the Gospel must be preached to all nations before the end-time comes (see Mark 13:10). The eschatological point of the parable is still present, but the missionary preaching to the nations becomes the condition of the fulfillment of the kingdom.

If an interpretation of the Gospel material does not allow an identification of God's kingdom with the Church either in a reconstruction of the possible meaning of the historical Jesus or in the evangelists' redaction, then the first prong of the historical demonstration is weak. Nevertheless, the issue of the relation between eschatology and Church is not thereby resolved negatively. Recent sociological analyses have shown that the expectation of the imminent end within millenarian groups does not prohibit, but rather furthers the growth of the community.[101] Likewise, historical studies have shown how the Qumran group formed a community with rules— their imminent expectation, in fact, made reason for its formation.[102]

Consequently, if eschatological expectation cannot be equated with the expectation of a Church, neither does eschatological expectation prevent the formation of community. But then, the nature of such a community becomes the crucial issue. How is the emergence of a permanent institutionalized Church justified? A justification of an interim (even if structured) community that awaits an imminent end does not amount to a justification of the Church. The challenge to fundamental theology remains even after the demise of its historical demonstration: how is the identity of Christian ecclesial existence to be justified?

Mission of the Twelve

In arguing that Jesus instituted an apostolic college with authority in the early Church, traditional fundamental theology assumed that the terms "apostles" and the "Twelve" were coextensive and combined them into the specific idea of "apostolic college." Unfortunately, such assumptions are still widespread and popular references to "the twelve apostles" reinforce such convictions.

The New Testament evidence indicates, however, that the apostles and the Twelve are different groups with distinct functions, despite some overlapping.[103] Acts 14:4 and 14 refer to Paul and Barnabas as apostles, but they are not members of the Twelve. Rom 16:7 refers to Andronicus and Junia as apostles, yet neither he nor she belongs to the Twelve. 1 Cor 15:5-7 clearly distinguishes between the Twelve and the apostles. Jesus appeared to Cephas, then to the Twelve, then to 500 brethren, then to James, then to all the apostles. It is therefore important to keep the notion of apostle and that of the Twelve distinct.[104]

The historical texts about the Twelve present a surprising puzzle. All the Gospel writings presuppose the existence of the Twelve. But except for the pre-Pauline formula in 1 Cor 15:5-7 the Pauline writings do not refer to the Twelve. Moreover, there is absolutely no reference to the Twelve in the Catholic and Pastoral Letters. Consequently, one of the most controverted contemporary exegetical and historical questions is whether the earthly Jesus selected the Twelve. Would the Twelve as a historical group have disappeared so quickly if he had instituted them and given them a continued function within the Church. Moreover, 1 Cor 15:5 states, "he appeared to Cephas, then to the twelve." But it should be eleven, for obviously Jesus did not appear to Judas. Is it possible then that the Twelve do not represent a definite group of individuals whom Jesus selected during his earthly ministry, but that the Twelve formed and constituted itself only after the Easter-experience and in expectation of the end-time? This historical hypothesis might explain why Paul can speak of an appearance to the Twelve even though Judas's absence should have made it eleven. It might also explain why after the seven are appointed, the Twelve play no further role in Jerusalem. Several New Testament scholars concur in this historical reconstruction.[105] Its likelihood cannot be easily discounted.

Nevertheless, reasons do exist that make it equally probable, if not more probable, that Jesus did in fact during his earthly ministry select the Twelve.[106] All the Gospel traditions, including Q, refer to the existence of the Twelve. That one of those Twelve betrayed Jesus was a scandal to early Christianity; the existence of the betrayal cannot be attributed to early Church interests. In addition, no evidence exists that the Twelve exercise a continued function of leadership in Jerusalem that could explain their post-Easter origin. Indeed, 1 Cor 15:5 presupposes the Twelve as a group already existing and not as one constituted by the appearance. The reference to "the Twelve" could have become a stereotyped expression referring to the group itself rather than to the actual number of individuals. Although Paul refers to the Twelve, the Gospel accounts clearly indicate that eleven experienced the postresurrection appearances. (The differences in the list of names remains a problem. Judas, son of James, in Luke and Acts, Thaddeus in Mark, and "Lebbaeus" in some Matthean textual witnesses cannot be reconciled, but a postresurrection constitution does not explain away the problem.) The differences in the order of the names can be explained by the Old Testament reference to the twelve tribes of Israel.[107]

In short, the selection of the Twelve by the historical Jesus is not at all susceptible to a firm and conclusive historical demonstration. That they go back to the earthly Jesus is at most a probable opinion, and in my judgment the more probable of the two. But even if we assume this probable judgment as true have we then demonstrated what the traditional fundamental theology sought to demonstrate?

In the Gospel material, there is only one saving attributed to Jesus himself about the purpose and function of the Twelve. In Matt 19:28 and Luke 22:28–30 (a quotation from Q—the source common to Matthew and Luke), the following saying is attributed to Jesus: "Truly I say to you in the new world when the Son of man shall sit on his glorious throne, you who have followed me will also sit on twelve thrones, judging the twelve tribes of Israel." Obviously the twelve have an eschatological function. They shall judge in the eschatological future when the kingdom is established. The Greek verb for "to judge" used here also means "to reign." Did the Twelve have more than this eschatological role? As for a missionary role, only Peter of the Twelve is ever described outside of Palestine in the New Testament texts. "As for exercising supervision," Raymond E. Brown notes, "there is no NT evidence that any of the Twelve ever served as heads of local Churches; and it is several centuries before they begin to be described as 'bishop' of first-century Christian centers, a description which is surely an anachronism."[108] A historical reconstruction should therefore take the statement in Q seriously. The Twelve have at the time of Jesus a symbolic function since the twelve tribes no longer existed, but only two and a half tribes. The Dead Sea

Scrolls, moreover, describe how the community of the New Covenant also adopted the symbolism of the Twelve and had a special group of twelve in its Community Council (IQS 8:1) representing the twelve tribes of Israel.

In conclusion, the second prong of the historical demonstration is also weak. It cannot be historically demonstrated that Jesus instituted an apostolic college as the foundation of the Church. The selection and mission of the Twelve pose several important questions for fundamental theology. Why do the Gospel accounts relate that Jesus had selected the Twelve and why does the group afterwards appear to be so short-lived, so ephemeral? Why is it almost neglected in major portions of the New Testament. Why is it that even for Luke, who has emphasized and equated the Twelve and the apostles, the influence of the Twelve almost disappears in Acts so that the circle of the Twelve basically performs "its only function, after the testimony to Israel on Pentecost to change the community-structure by overseeing the democratic appointment of the seven table-servers."[109] The role and function of the Twelve, their relation to the historical Jesus and to the emergent Church remain a historical puzzle and a fundamental theological issue that a foundational theology as a reconstructive hermeneutics must face squarely.

Jesus and the Petrine Ministry

The historical demonstration, as noted above, focused primarily on Matt 16:17–19. It argued that the expressions, vocabulary, and syntax all point to the semitic coloring of the verses; that these semitisms point to a Palestinian origin or background for the verses and make credible the authenticity of the text as a witness to what the historical Jesus did indeed promise to Peter. But each step should be examined to determine how probative the historical demonstration is.

Expressions, vocabulary, and syntax:[110] The expressions, "flesh and blood" and "gates of hell" are allegedly semitic. Yet "flesh and blood" is found often as an expression within New Testament *koine* Greek, for example, 1 Cor 15:20; Gal 1:15; Eph 6:12; and Heb 2:14. "Gates of hell" appears in Hellenistic writings such as Wis 16:13; Pss Sol 16:2; 3 Macc 5:51; and 2 Enoch 43:1. "My father in heaven" and "lord of heaven" are favorite expressions of Matthew. The expression "my father in heaven" does reflect a rabbinic phrase, but the Greek form is so common in Matthew's Gospel that it has been called a Matthean trait.[111] Consequently, the expressions may exhibit semitic coloring, but it need not be explained by recourse to an Aramaic spoken tradition or written source.

Likewise, the name "Bar-Jona" is allegedly a translation from the Aramaic. Yet such a usage of "bar" is clearly present in other New Testament texts—for example, Bar-Jesus in Acts 13:6, Bar-tholomew in Mark 3:18, and Bar-sabbas in Acts 1:23 and 15:22—where no claim is made for an Aramaic substratum. A semitic coloring is seen in the syntax of "be bound" and "be loosed." But here again such usage is found in other Hellenistic texts (for example, Jos War I, 5:2).[112]

The stylistic form of the macarisms and the construction of the three verses are indeed not common in classical Greek. But for authors influenced by Septuagint such stylistic characteristics are possible without recourse to the Aramaic.[113] Since the verb "has . . . revealed" (*Apokalyptein*) lacks a direct object in Greek, it has been argued that Matthew did compose the verse, borrowing from an Aramaic source. But an affinity between Matt 16:17 and Gal 1:15 (each has the same verb) has led Jacques Dupont to observe that the two passages are attempts to interpret within a standardized form an account of the revelatory experiences of Peter and Paul.[114] Again, there is no need for recourse to an Aramaic source or tradition.

In verse 18 not only is a new name given to Simon but two parallel sentences use the wordplay *petros-petra* to explain it. The second of these parallel sentences must also refer to Peter and he is therefore the rock upon which the Church is founded. The *petros/petra* play is based upon an Aramaic substratum or was perhaps developed within an Aramaic community because of the identity of *Kephā›/kephā›* in Aramaic.[115] It should be noted that Matthew uses here as elsewhere Simon and not the Semitic form Symeon (See Greek of Acts 15:14). Moreover, the use of Peter (Greek, *petros*) after the use of Simon Bar-Jona is surprising, since the name Cephas had widespread currency in the Greek New Testament texts (John 1:42; I Cor 1:12; 3:22; 9:5; 15:5; Gal 1:18; 2:9,11,14). Consequently, if the attempt is made to explain why Cephas was not used but Peter, then instead of going back to an Aramaic substratum, it is indeed possible and even probable that the saying stems from the early Church rather than from Jesus' Aramaic words. The Peter/rock saying may "represent an early interpretative tradition which has been linked to its present context by way of the similarity of *Petros* to its own keyword, *petra*."[116]

This evidence suggests caution in making historical claims of authenticity on the basis of semitisms. However, even if most of the counterarguments stood, it would still seem that Matt 16:17–19 has an unusually high density of semitisms—a fact overlooked when individual claims are singularly rebutted. Moreover, at present no evidence exists for the use of Peter as a name in Greek prior to its use in the Matthean text.[117] But that would not speak against the origin of the text as an "early interpretative tradition."

Palestinian origin and historical Jesus: If the semitisms can be explained without reference to an Aramaic tradition or source, then the argument for the Palestinian origin and the authenticity of the verse is weakened. It is often suggested today that the context and background of the text is Antioch and Syria rather than Palestine. The term "Church" (ecclesia) is scarcely possible in an Aramaic context, but stems from Hellenistic Christianity.[118] The reference to revelation found also in Galatians is a Greek term. The issue of binding and loosing implies debates about law and right teaching. Consequently, neither Palestine nor the historical Jesus, but the Jewish-Christian community of Antioch, is responsible for the formation of the text.

With these alternative interpretations in mind, the text should be examined. Peter's confession of Jesus' messiahship occurs in the synoptic tradition in Mark 8:27–33, Matt 16:13–23, Luke 9:18–22. Whereas Luke does not relate its locale, Mark and Matthew place the episode at Caesarea Philippi. The oldest form is the Markan version which is the basis for Matthew and Luke.

A comparison of the Matthean and Markan versions shows that the Matthean version has additional material. Peter confesses not only that Jesus is the messiah but also that he is the son of the living God. Additional is Jesus' bestowal of the title *petros* (masculine) meaning rock and his promise to build the Church on "this rock" (*petra*, feminine). John 21:15–17 has a similar version, but it takes place at Lake Tiberias. How is the diversity to be understood and how does an interpretation of the diversity resolve the problem of the origin and authenticity of the verses?

Traditional fundamental theology harmonized the accounts: Jesus promised at Caesarea Philippi (Matthew's text) what he conferred at Lake Tiberias (John's text). Such an interpretation jumps over the difficulties. If Jesus had spoken to Simon at Caesarea Philippi what Matthew records, why are no traces of it found in Mark 8 and Luke 9? Does it seem plausible that Luke and Mark would have deliberately deleted such material? Only the Matthean version has the term "Church" (ecclesia). No other Gospel tradition would have omitted Jesus' reference to the Church if he actually did refer to it. The obvious explanation is that the Matthean account of Jesus' promise to Peter at Caesarea Philippi is not a historical report, but an account permeated with Matthean redaction.

As is often Matthew's custom, he adds material to Mark's presentation in order to draw out the theological lines of his Gospel. It is most likely, therefore, that Jesus did not promise the primacy to Peter at Caesarea Philippi. The Matthean text does not record an historical event at Caesarea Philippi during the earthly ministry of Jesus. Does this mean that the theological account reflects only Matthean theological creativity; or is there a *fundamentum in re*? Some have suggested that perhaps the event took place at the last supper[119] and others have suggested a postresurrection appearance.[120] The combination of historical description and theological interpretation is so intertwined that the interpretation of it is indeed complex. Much of the theological affirmations in the text reflect not the time during Jesus' ministry but the community's subsequent situation.[121] The relationship between history and theology needs further specification as the discussion of other solutions and my own proposals will show. Nevertheless, what is certain is that the third and final prong of the traditional fundamental theology has not achieved its goal: to provide a historical demonstration independent of faith that Jesus has established the Church.

In conclusion, the analysis of the three proofs of the classic historical demonstrations shows that they lack the apodictic character that has been claimed for them. The question remains: how does fundamental theology deal with the foundation of the Church by the historical Jesus. Is it unascertainable as a historical demonstration and therefore merely an object of faith or is it possible to develop a fundamental theological approach to the foundation of the Church? How can the consideration of the foundation of the Church remain a task of fundamental theology and not be relegated to dogmatic theology as an object of faith?

These questions have challenged contemporary theology. An existential and transcendental fundamental theology seeks to complement the historical demonstration by showing the transcendental and existential necessity of a Church—given faith in Jesus as the Christ. Recent historical-critical approaches to fundamental theology have suggested new ways of viewing the christological foundation of the Church, or have proposed that the Church be considered a creation of God's Spirit. Each of these approaches needs to be analyzed, sympathetically but critically, before it can be shown how foundational theology as a reconstructive hermeneutics provides an approach to the foundation of the Church whereby this foundation is both an object and ground of faith.

Chapter 4

Contemporary Fundamental Theology and the Foundation of the Church

Despite criticisms, several major fundamental theologies published in the last decade still appeal to the historical demonstration as a proof that the earthly Jesus founded a Church,[122] and in popular writings it is still taken as a common presupposition of Christian faith. Nevertheless, also within the last decade new approaches to the problem of the foundation of the Church have been made. Although the traditional historical demonstration is still very much alive and although some new approaches have developed only as complements to the traditional demonstration, one characteristic is decisive for most of these contemporary approaches: they seek to take seriously the criticisms and weaknesses of the historical demonstration, to acknowledge the eschatological dimension of Jesus' proclamation of God's reign, and to reject an oversimplified harmonization of diverse historical data about the origin of the Church.

Transcendental Fundamental Theology

Existential phenomenology and transcendental philosophy have provided contemporary theology with categories to "bracket" or to "complement" the historical issues. Within Roman Catholic theology the indirect method of Karl Rahner is an outstanding illustration.[123]

Conflict between Eschatology and Intention

In Rahner's own words,

> The problems inherent in this [the classic fundamental theology's] un-
> derstanding of the foundation of the Church by Jesus, were, however,
> raised sixty or seventy years ago by the Modernists. It is not surprising
> that the initial reaction to these problems in the Church was sharp,
> conservative and defensive and that it took some time, perhaps too
> long, before they were really seriously considered, discussed and dealt
> with. At a very modest and cautious estimate, we can, I think, say that it
> has taken the Catholic Church fully sixty or seventy years to deal to
> some extent with the ecclesiological problems raised by fundamental
> theology within the Catholic sphere . . . and brought sharply into focus
> by the Modernist movement.[124]

In formulating the issue, Rahner situates it in the tension between two poles: Jesus' intentionality and the eschatological meaning
of his proclamation of God's reign. He asks pointed questions about
Jesus' intention and will. Had Jesus "himself intended and founded"
or "could he think in terms of a 'period of the Church'"? Is its foundation "within the horizon of Jesus' proclamation" or did Jesus "evidently will a church as his own church"?[125] All these questions underscore the intentionality of Jesus as the one pole. The other pole is the
expectation of the imminent arrival of a transcendent reign brought
about by God. How can the expectation of the kingdom and the
conscious intention to establish a Church be reconciled? This problem
has, as Rahner emphasizes, "in Catholic ecclesiology (especially in its
struggle with Modernism) either not been seen or has been re-
pressed."[126]

The contrast between eschatological consciousness and explicit
intention to establish a Church represents an acute challenge especially to Rahner's christology which seeks to integrate the shift from
being to consciousness that has taken place within modern christology. It is characteristic of this modern christology, as Fitzmyer notes,
that "the most crucial question in this whole area of christology will
always remain that about the consciousness of the historical Jesus of
Nazareth."[127] Although this consciousness was understood as ontological and not merely psychological in most major christological formulations from Schleiermacher to Rahner, the modern emphasis
upon consciousness as the expression of the being of Christ represents a new foundationalism that seeks to ground christological affirmations in the consciousness of Jesus.[128] The foundation of the
Church as a problem of the conflict of two intentionalities is therefore

not only a problem arising out of the discovery of the eschatological dimension of Jesus' proclamation of God's coming reign but also a problem resulting from the modern emphasis upon the consciousness of Jesus as the focal point of christology.

Transcendental Deduction of Church

The need for an indirect method that uses transcendental reflection and phenomenological analysis rather than historical analysis stems, in Rahner's opinion, from the complexity of the historical and exegetical issues. Just as a decision about the historicity of the resurrection in the New Testament texts demands a highly specialized background in linguistics, history, and exegesis, so too does the issue of the foundation of the Church. The complexities of the text of Matt 16:17–19, of the selection of the Twelve, and of the eschatological interpretation of the kingdom presuppose a degree of learning that make it possible only for a trained scholar to deal adequately with such questions. Indeed, they are beyond the competence of the average systematic theologian—not to mention the average Christian.

The complexities are such that pros and cons can be given for each side. Consequently, an indirect method of fundamental theology must be employed that uses transcendental arguments and phenomenological analyses to provide an existential foundation for belief in the Church. In *Foundations of Christian Faith* this indirect transcendental approach does not replace the historical demonstration, but is a precondition or concomitant of acceptance of the historical argument. In fact, Rahner gives all the traditional elements of the historical demonstration to justify founding acts by the historical Jesus, especially that founding act of the promise of the primacy to Peter in Matt 16:17–19.[129] In *A New Christology*, however, the inadequacy of the recourse to the earthly Jesus is readily admitted and the transcendental argument is developed independently of any appeal to specific foundational acts of the earthly Jesus that can be historically demonstrated.[130]

This indirect approach argues for the foundation of the Church in three distinct steps:[131] first, Christians believe Jesus to be the absolute savior. They see in Jesus God's historically tangible and irreversible offer to humankind. For such a salvific offer to be absolute and irrevocable, it is necessary that a continued and abiding faith in Jesus exist. God's offer of salvation in Jesus is such that it necessarily includes the abiding faith in Jesus. Second, such an enduring faith cannot be simply a private faith or an individualistic belief; it must be public and communal if God's offer is to be continued. Third, this public and communal faith must have a history if there is to be in the world a history of salvation with continuity and identity.

The above arguments deduce the necessity of the Church from the Christian presupposition and belief in Jesus as absolute savior. The belief in Jesus as God's unsurpassable offer of grace in history has validity only if this historically unsurpassable offer has a continued permanence and tangible presence in history. Thus, the nature of faith in Jesus demands the historical permanence of the Church.

This argument from the nature of faith in Jesus is complemented by a transcendental reflection on human nature. If human beings are interpersonal by nature and not accidentally so, if human beings have a religious dimension to their existence, then the Church as the institutional mediation of religion is not accidental but essential. For Rahner, the interpersonal constitution of human nature "implies that the reality of interpersonal relationship belongs to the religion of Christianity," and it "follows from this perspective too that in the Christian understanding religion is necessarily ecclesial religion."[132]

Such an argument appears at first glance to be similar to Loisy's proposal that the Church is necessary so that the gospel of God's reign can continue to be preached. Indeed, the argument that the Church is necessary so that God's presence of grace in Jesus can continue historically and with external tangibility is structurally similar to Loisy's. But what is new and decisive is that the necessity for the Church is placed within the context of the divine-human relation and its necessity is deduced from each side of that relation.[133] Such an approach to justify the Church's existence is possible only because of a completely new view of it—different from that of traditional fundamental theology.

Foundation of Church and Symbolization of Grace

Theological assumptions about grace, Christ, and the Church underlie this existential and transcendental justification of the Church.[134] The institutional Church is primarily the unambiguous symbolization and the explicit manifestation of God's grace. Consequently, the Church does not primarily bring salvation to human beings because it continues Jesus' preaching of the kingdom as a future event, but rather because it continues to symbolize God's grace and salvation present in Jesus. To "say that the Church is the persisting presence of the incarnate Word in space and time," is to "imply that it continues the symbolic function of the Logos in the world."[135]

A structural and functional equation exists between Christ and the Church. Jesus is the real symbol of God's self-communication to the world. The Church has the function of making historically present and tangible within the world this symbolization of God's self-communication. Hence the relation between Jesus and the Church is much more profound than his specific acts of institution. A structural similarity exists because Jesus and the Church have the same function. Indeed, the Church must be Church if Christ is to be Christ—an enigmatic affirmation at first glance, yet profoundly true. Only if the symbolization of God's self-communication in Jesus continues historically can Christ continue to be a real symbol of God's presence for humanity. A symbol symbolizes to the extent that it is perceived and taken as a symbol. Moreover, the symbol must continue to be present qua symbol for it to symbolize. The Church not only proclaims Jesus as the real symbol of God's presence, but the Church in its relation to Jesus continues itself as the symbolization of grace.

Such a theological conception of Christ and the Church contrasts starkly with previous fundamental theology. Whereas the latter used Aristotelian categories of causality to explain the foundation of the Church, this existential and transcendental fundamental theology uses categories drawn from the anthropology of German Idealism.[137] Its basic model is the self-actualization of the human person in space and time. Matter is not a limitation of transcendence but the locus of the realization of transcendence. Human persons by expressing themselves in time and space actualize and realize themselves. God's graceful self-communication comes to expression and realization in the spatial-temporal dimension of human history and existence.

Therefore, just as the humanity of Christ is the symbol of God's self-communication, so too the Church continues this symbolization. A functional identity exists but with an important difference. Because of the personal unity of the divine self-communication and the successful human acceptance in Jesus, Christ is the real symbol and sacrament of God's presence. The Church, however, is a symbol only insofar as it refers back to Christ and continues the symbolization that has come to expression in him. Consequently, the Church is founded upon Christ or, more precisely, the Church belongs to the provenance of Christ.

This relation between Christ and the Church, however, can be understood adquately only in relation to the double conception of the Church.[138] The Church in its broader conception includes all of humanity insofar as all humanity is offered God's grace and is thereby constituted as the People of God. When human persons standing under God's offer of salvation make a decision for the absolute good, God, they affirm their membership in the People of God and bring that membership to expression in the dimensions of space and time.

The Church in this conception makes visible through its institutional office, sacraments, and proclamation the salvation offered by God. The relationship between the Church and humanity is not one of salvation and nonsalvation, but one of sign and signed reality. The Church as an institution, moreover, is the further intensification, symbolization, and explication of the grace affirmed by all belonging to the People of God. The grace offered to all human beings to affect the total human dimension, especially the communal dimension of human existence, must necessarily become actually expressed in time and space as an ecclesial structure, as Church.

This conception of the Church provides a new view of church office and or its divine institution.[139] Office and ministry are fundamentally actualizations and intensifications of the Church as the continuation of the real symbol of Christ. Although office and the notion of divine institution were originally conceived in relation to individual founding actions by the historical Jesus, they are in this conception basically expressions of the nature of the Church. What is considered divine law in the Church is now seen as an expression of the essence of the Church in a way analogous to that of positive and natural law. All of this involves a significant shift and a further drawing out of the consequences of the Church as a real symbol.[140]

Since the Church's foundation is rooted in Jesus' function as a real symbol of the presence of God, then how this symbolic function is understood affects how the foundation of the Church is understood. Two significant shifts take place: at first, for Rahner, the real symbol was located in the incarnation and cross so that the historical Jesus and his death on the cross were considered the foundational events constituting the Church.[141] Not only were the actions of the historical Jesus significant, but his human acceptance of God's will in dying expresses the divine human unity. Later the resurrection as God's confirmation of Jesus' life is seen as the real symbol of God's presence because it manifests the victory of divine grace.

In this changed conception, a shift from language about "foundation" to language about "provenance" takes place.[142] Within the ontology of grace the relation between Christ and the Church is so conceived that the traditional term "foundation" loses its significance. Those "instituting acts" and "foundational acts," that were previously maintained alongside of the conception of the Church as a sacrament, now fade into the background. The Church is considered to be the result of Jesus and within the provenance of Jesus. Such a shift from foundation to provenance, from historical Jesus and his death on the cross to resurrection, results not only from a further awareness of historical-critical exegesis but also stems from a further explication of Church as a foundational sacrament that continues the symbolic function of Jesus.

Historical Event and Transcendental Theology

The transcendental deduction of Church from a phenomenological analysis of Christian faith and human existence elicits several new insights. It shows the inner connection not only between faith in Christ and the communal expression of that faith but also between ecclesial existence and human existence. It relates the Church to Jesus not merely juridically and volitionally through a set of instituting or founding actions, but rather intrinsically through the salvation present in Jesus. Moreover, it exhibits the Church's existence not as accidental to the religious dimension of human existence, but as essential to the communal and interpersonal nature of human personhood.

Such a procedure, however, partly reverses the approach of traditional fundamental theology to the Church. That fundamental theology sought through an impartial historical demonstration to secure the truth of the Church as an ascertainable fact prior to faith and accessible to all undertaking a similar such investigation. The transcendental deduction of the Church starts out in part with the givenness of faith in Jesus as the unsurpassable savior and moves from that belief to the necessity of an enduring Church. At the same time, it argues that the religious and interpersonal nature of human existence demands a form of religion that is not only historical but also communal.

Despite such advantages a phenomenological and transcendental approach is not entirely unambiguous about the historical issue of the foundation of the Church. The transcendental deduction of the necessity of the Church could be applied to almost any religion or faith that has come into existence and has formed a community. Any religious belief with a claim to unconditioned truth would express iteself in a community of faith in order to have public, communal, and historical existence. To argue that the continued existence of a community of believers is a necessary condition for the continued belief in the presence of an unsurpassable offer of salvation does underscore the transcendental necessity of the Church given the absoluteness of

Christian claims about Jesus, but it does not resolve eo ipso the historical and fundamental theological issue as to whether Jesus founded a Church or whether the Roman Catholic Church stands in direct relation to the historical Jesus. Such theological questions are historical issues; they cannot be resolved by transcendental arguments or phenomenological arguments.

A starting-point from the faith of contemporary Christianity or from the intersubjective and religious dimension of human nature does not enable one to establish a historical connection between the meaning of the historical Jesus and the emergence of the Church. The very formulation of the issue in terms of the contrast between the consciousness of imminent end-time and the foundation is not thereby resolved. Even the attempt to resolve the issue of the relation to one's own Church with reference to the experience of such a Church as Christian or containing Christian substance[143] raises historical questions. What is Christian? What is Christian substance? Can an appeal to experience answer these questions without reference to the historical origin, emergence, and development of what is Christian?

Finally, a significant shift appears in the conception of eschatology so that the resolution of the problem of the foundation of the Church bypasses the initial formulation.[144] The problem is: how could Jesus have intended to institute a Church in view of his eschatological expectation of an imminent end? So formulated eschatological refers to the coming of God's reign in the immediate future as an apocalyptic event. However, insofar as Jesus is interpreted as the real symbol and the self-manifestation of God's grace, a realized eschatology is surreptitiously slipped in. The problem of the foundation of the Church is posed in terms of the apocalyptic expectation of the end-time, but the resolution is posed in terms of a realized eschatology. Jesus Christ is the sacrament of God in his humanity. The Church is in the provenance of Jesus because it continues to exercise this symbolic and sacramental function.

Historical and Theological Justifications
of a Post-Easter Church

The increased application of historical criticism to the New Testament led to greater awareness not only of the eschatological significance of Jesus' proclamation but also of the post-Easter emergence of the Church's universal mission and the gradual development of diverse church orders. In contrast to the transcendental deduction of the Church from Christian faith in Jesus and the intersubjective religious dimension of human existence, fundamental theology and systematic theology sought in the post-Vatican II period to develop a new historical and theological justification of the Church. They sought neither to bypass the historical issues—as did, for the most part, the indirect method—nor to rehash the traditional demonstration. Instead, taking seriously the insights of form and redaction criticism into the post-Easter nature of the Gospel traditions and their theological, rather than historical, interests, fundamental theology sought to open up new paths for a theological *and* historical justification of the Church.

Despite considerable diversity, this theological and historical justification took two basic paths or, more precisely, two different directions on the same path: one approach moves *from* the historical Jesus *to* the emergence of the Church after Easter. It concedes that Jesus did not institute the Church, but still tries to relate the origin of the Church to Jesus' intention and will on the grounds that Jesus, while he may not have instituted the Church, did lay the foundations for it. The other approach starts out from the emergence of the Church after Easter. It views the Church primarily as God's new creation through the activity of the Holy Spirit and emphasizes Peter's role.

Christological

At the time of Vatican II a new theory of the relation between Jesus and the Church was proposed by Anton Vögtle.[145] It soon came to be adopted by other Roman Catholic exegetes, for example, Rudolf Schnackenburg (though with modifications).[146] It has since become the standard "moderate" Roman Catholic explanation in more recent Catholic textbooks, and has become widespread due to the influence of Küng (1967), Schmaus (1972), and McBrien (1980).[147] It has absorbed elements of the conservative Protestant exegetical consensus that had been forged by Oepke, Kümmel, and Cullmann,[148] and it has modified suggestions already made by Eric Peterson and Heinrich Schlier, two well-known scholars of early Christianity and converts to Catholicism.[149] Although since abandoned by Vögtle and Küng, it still can be considered a dominant Catholic opinion alongside of the traditional historical demonstration.[150]

This theory places the relation between Jesus and the Church within the framework of a theology of salvation history as dialogic. God's initiative calls for a human reaction so much so that God's plan depends in part upon the human response. Jesus' message and mission was directed exclusively to Israel. After Israel's religious leaders grew hostile to Jesus and rejected him, God "changed" the salvific plan. In other words, at first Jesus did not intend to establish the Church as a separate community within Israel. He preached—according to God's will—conversion to all Israel. For that reason, he selected disciples and sent them out to preach. Jesus expected God's future reign in Israel. He did not think of or plan for a Church when he began his public ministry.

During his ministry, Jesus became increasingly aware of growing opposition, and the execution of John the baptizer might have made him aware of the possibility of his own rejection and death. Only after this point in time would Jesus have begun to think of an organization or community that was not identical with all of Israel. However, such a community or organization should not immediately be identified with the Church. In view of this growing awareness of his rejection, Jesus most probably, at the last supper, initiated his disciples into the meaning of his pending death[151] and urged the commemoration of this last meal.[152] The promise to Peter (Matt 16:17–19) was most probably spoken at this meal and without the Matthean redactional elements. Luke 23:31 refers to Jesus having prayed for Peter to strengthen his brethren, and this could have a historical kernel in what Jesus actually said at the last supper.

Did Jesus establish the Church at the last supper? Here opinions divide, but the basic position maintains that at that time Jesus neither founded nor instituted the Church. Instead, he expected a short "interim period" between his death and the Parousia.[153] In view of this expectation of an "interim period," Jesus encouraged his disciples to commemorate the last supper. It is this expectation of an interim period that provides the link between Jesus' eschatological expectation and the foundation of the Church. Jesus did not found the Church, but laid the foundation for the Church insofar as he willed and intended that, during the time between his death and the Parousia, his disciples would celebrate common meals, would remain united in their belief, and would await the Parousia.

This historical and theological hypothesis has several distinct advantages. It faces squarely the New Testament evidence that the historical Jesus most probably understood his mission to be directed to Israel. It refuses to explain away by harmonization Jesus' expectation of the imminent arrival of God's reign. It acknowledges that Jesus did not institute a Church during his earthly ministry. Yet it also links the Church implicitly with Jesus' intention insofar as it claims that, toward the end of his life, Jesus saw the need for a special community within Israel. Moreover, its category of a dialogic salvation history is much more adequate to explain the relation between Jesus and the Church than any nineteenth-century romantic theory of organic development. The movement from Jesus' proclamation to the establishment of the Church is not the development of an acorn to an oak tree; it involves negations and new affirmations.

Nevertheless, it leaves several questions open: even if the hypothetical historical reconstruction of the last supper is granted, the question remains what did Jesus intend by the commemorative meals? Did he lay the foundation for a special group within Israel or for the Church? The problem of Jesus' eschatological expectation and that of the first Christian communities still remains. How did the transition from the community's self-understanding as an eschatological community within Israel to the understanding of it as an enduring institution take place?

These questions shift the focus from the earthly Jesus and the last supper to the post-Easter situation. Moreover, they challenge whether a christological foundation can be given for the emergence of the Church after Easter. In claiming that Jesus laid the foundation for the Church, but did not institute the Church during his earthly ministry, this position maintains, at the most, that the Church is implicit in Jesus' understanding of his death and in his command to celebrate common meals. Is there then no pre-Easter foundation of the Church?

The transition from the pre-Easter earthly ministry to the post-Easter emergence of the Church is, within this approach, sometimes made by an appeal to the appearances of the Risen One. For example, Gerald O'Collins argues that the appearance of Jesus to Peter not only constitutes the foundation of the Church but also establishes the primacy of Peter, for Peter was the first person that Jesus appeared to.[154] Nevertheless, such a historical foundation for the Church and primacy has several problems. Jesus did not appear first to Peter according to two of the Gospels. Matthew's Gospel actually excludes a first appearance to Peter.[155] More significantly, however, if the statements of the Risen Lord are taken as exact historical statements and not later theological explanations, then significant problems of interpretation arise. For example, the command of the Risen Lord to undertake a universal mission in Matt 28:18–20 makes inexplicable the problems of the early Church described in Acts about whether to engage in a mission to the Gentiles.[156] Consequently, the foundation of the Church and its universal mission cannot be based upon an appearance of Jesus. Instead, a further development must take place. The dialogic salvation history must be continued even into the post-Easter period. It is this conclusion that has led even proponents of this position to move to a post-Easter and a pneumatological foundation of the Church.[157]

Such a bridge is attempted by Hans Urs von Balthasar. On the one hand, he emphasizes that at the last supper Jesus laid the foundations for the Church through the establishment of the Eucharist in relation to his impending death.[158] On the other hand, the Church is founded only after Easter through the appearances of the Risen Jesus.[159] It is these appearances that reveal the meaning of Jesus' words and deeds. The New Testament texts relating to Peter symbolize the Church as an institution, whereas those in reference to John symbolize the Church as love. In a very speculative synthesis, the fundamental root of the Church, indeed its foundation, is traced back to Mary as the symbol of human receptivity and faith. However, the Church as an institution emerges only after Easter even though its foundations were laid previously. But such an interpretation, with its combination of realistic and symbolic elements, fails to take into account how much of the interpretation of the last supper and the Easter appearances reflects the situation and theology of a second and third generation Church.[160]

Pneumatological

The historical judgment that the Church de facto emerged only after Easter has been combined with a different theological justification. Instead of a christological foundation for the Church, a pneumatological justification has been developed. It is not so much the activity of Jesus, but the activity of the Holy Spirit that is the foundation of the Church. Such a combination of historical judgment and theological speculation needs to be carefully analyzed since historical issues should not be too readily submerged within theological rationales. Even though the appeal to the Spirit enjoys great popularity today because of the increasing awareness of pneumatology with ecclesiology, anthropology, and fundamental theology, such an appeal cannot burke the historical issues of continuity and identity.

The justification of the Church through an appeal to the Holy Spirit rather than to the ministry of the earthly Jesus has been developed in various ways. In the essay "The Church as Sacrament of the Spirit," Walter Kasper proposes that the Church be understood as the sacrament of the Spirit in contrast to the previous emphasis, especially within Rahnerian theology, upon the Church as the sacrament of Christ. His starting-point is the absence of an intention by Jesus to institute the Church: "As is well known, it is scarcely possible to prove an expressed foundation of the Church by the earthly Jesus. There was no place for it within Jesus' message of the imminent coming of the reign of God."[161] Moreover, the Church is possible only after Israel through its leaders had rejected Jesus.

The salvation-history approach, initiated by Peterson and Schlier, developed and adapted by Kasper and Ratzinger, proposes not only that the Church was founded after Easter and after Jesus' rejection by Israel but also that the origin of the Church was only possible after Jesus' rejection and death.[162] Only after Jesus' disciples—called by Jesus to be representatives of the new Israel—and only after Israel in its leaders had rejected Jesus could a new stage in salvation history begin. Only after the end of his life does the possibility for a new life emerge.[163]

Therefore, it is concluded that "the Church as a Church composed of Jews and Pagans came into life at the moment that the disciples of Jesus decided 'in the Spirit' to inaugurate the eschatological assembly of all people. The disciples then proclaimed the death and resurrection of Jesus and the sending of the Spirit as the breaking in of a new age that they made present through the proclamation and the sacramental celebration in Spirit."[164] The problem of the relation between Jesus and the Church is resolved through reference to the Spirit. The continuity between Jesus and the Church is therefore not based on an existential continuity or on a political or social continuity, but rather on a continuity given by the activity of God's Spirit. Within this approach, the gulf separating Jesus and the Christian community is overcome through the experience of the Spirit. Not the religious dimension of human subjectivity, but the experience of Christ in the Spirit makes possible Christian ecclesial existence as Church. As the sacrament of the Spirit, the Church is the experience of Christ in the Spirit.[165]

This approach emphasizes the necessity of Israel's rejection of Jesus to the point of death as a precondition for the foundation of the Church as a sacrament of the Spirit. Hans Küng also refers to the significance of the death of Jesus and the role of the Spirit, but with a quite different theological conception. "The Church owes to the Spirit its origin, existence and continued life, and in this sense the Church is a *creation of the Spirit*."[166] The Spirit, as God's Spirit and not as a human spirit, creates the Church by creating the possibility of a human response in freedom. The Spirit gives to believers the possibility of affirming God's action in the death and resurrection of Jesus. The decision of believers and the free gathering together to form the Church results from the summons to faith given by God in the power of God's Spirit.[167]

Likewise the death of Jesus is necessary for the post-Easter emergence of the Church. However, what is emphasized is not the salvation-history role of the death of Jesus as the expression of Israel's rejection of Jesus, but rather the death of Jesus as the personification in an event of who Jesus is. During his earthly ministry Jesus called human beings to believe, but to decide for or against the rule of God was to decide for or against Jesus. The event of the death and resurrection became the symbolic abridgement and concrete core of the message of the kingdom so that the "Christian message is essentially the message of the Crucified and this crucified Jesus the concretation—so to speak—of the earthly Jesus as a whole."[168] Significant for Küng (in his reliance on Pauline theology) is "not man (anthropology), nor Church (ecclesiology), nor even salvation history in general, but the crucified and risen Christ."[169]

This description of the Church's foundation as a post-Easter creation by the Spirit interprets the relation of the Church to the life and death of Jesus quite differently from salvation-history and existential transcendental approaches. The death of Jesus is not an event within one stage of salvation history that opens up to the new stage of the Church. Nor is the death and resurrection of Jesus the foundation of the Church as the "real symbolic" expression of the ultimacy of human existential hopes. Nor is the Church implicit within Jesus' activity of gathering disciples, proclaiming the kingdom, and celebrating common meals. Instead, since the death of Jesus sums up what and who Jesus is, the death of Jesus lies at the foundation of the post-Easter Church. Because the crucifixion of Jesus brings to the fore what Jesus is, it is necessary that Jesus be crucified and rise before the Church can come into existence and can believe in the Risen One as the crucified One.[170]

A significant shift has taken place from the previous hypothesis that Jesus did not found, but laid the foundations for the Church—a position, as noted earlier, maintained by Küng in the *Church*, but abandoned in *On Being a Christian*.[171] This shift follows certain directions of contemporary exegesis that have even more strongly emphasized the eschatological and symbolic function of the Twelve and have questioned the historicity of Jesus' predictive interpretation at the last supper of his death as atoning. Therefore, these actions are now not put forward as laying the foundation for the Church. Instead of affirming that the foundation for the Church is laid through what Jesus said, did, and preached, it is now asserted that the foundation exists in what happened to Jesus, in his death and resurrection, and in the Spirit's summons for belief in the crucified Jesus. In this view, Jesus cannot be considered the founder of a Church.[172]

This switch from the foundational significance of Jesus' actions preparing for an "interim Church" to the foundational significance of faith in Jesus as the crucified points to a basic change in the conception of the Church. For now the Church is the congregation of believers who stand under the cross. The Pauline doctrine of justification becomes increasingly the central key within this conception of the Church.[173] God's Spirit creates the Church because the Spirit calls believers who are both sinners and justified to trust in God's saving act in the crucifixion and resurrection of Jesus. The Church is therefore not so much a visible society or a sacrament of Christ or of the Spirit as it is the congregation of believers who are both sinners and justified.

A third theological approach also makes the death of Jesus into a condition for the foundation of the Church, but within a different theological framework. Whereas the salvation-history approach emphasized the death of Jesus as the event expressing a stage of salvation history and whereas Küng's conception affirms the centrality of the crucifixion of Jesus in order to apply the Pauline doctrine of justification to the Church, Edward Schillebeeckx has focused on the necessity of the death of Jesus in order to highlight the totality of the life of Jesus. During the time of Jesus' earthly life a christological confession was not possible, since such a confession should have as its object the totality of Jesus' life and not just one particular aspect or one specific event. Moreover, since Jesus in his person was constitutive for the coming of God's reign, only when his life was at an end could it manifest who he was. The acknowledgment and confession of Jesus can take place as a christological affirmation, therefore, only after his life is complete, because only then does the confession have as its object the constitutive totality of Jesus' life.[174]

The foundation of the Church, therefore, not only took place after the death of Jesus, but is related to the Easter experience.[175] A correlation exists between the Easter experience as the confession of Jesus and the emergence of the Church. Since the disciples confess Jesus in the Easter experience as the definitive revelation of God, only after it can they come together as a Christian community. Several conclusions are drawn from this interpretation of the Easter experience. Only after Easter, therefore, is it possible to speak of the origin or the foundation of the Church. In fact, Schillebeeckx maintains that the Church did not exist even implicitly before Easter since no christo-logical confession was possible before then. Only after Jesus' life was over, and only after the Easter belief in the meaning of his whole life, is it even possible for the Church to begin.

This conclusion leads, however, to the further question: how then did the Church emerge after the death of Jesus if during his life not even an implicit christology was possible? The answer given is that only after Jesus' death "does he become epiphaneous, that is transparent; it is through faith that we grasp who he is."[176] Despite the admittedly sparse New Testament data, the origin of the Church is therefore described as follows: at the arrest and death of Jesus there was a failure on the part of his disciples. But Peter undergoes a "conversion experience" in which he grasps the meaning of the person of Jesus as constitutive for the revelation of God. Taking the historical initiative, Peter assembles the band of disciples. Therefore, the Church is not only founded after Easter, but Peter is the founder of the Church.[177] In no way, therefore, did the early Christian communities "receive any kind of church order from the hands of Jesus when he still shared our earthly history," for the first Christians as the Christian community "developed spontaneously from below."[178]

These three interpretations of the Church's origin after Easter have the advantage that they take very seriously the discontinuity between the pre-Easter and post-Easter situation. Moreover, they bring Roman Catholic fundamental theology and ecclesiology into line with much contemporary critical Protestant exegetical scholar-ship. Whereas the position that Jesus laid the foundations for the Church, especially at the last supper, rested on a more conservative exegesis, this position takes into account the contemporary critique of that exegesis and the new consensus, especially among Protestant exegetes.[179]

Nevertheless, these new positions do have several significant weaknesses. The dialogic salvation-history view of the relation between Jesus and the Church uses the category of new beginnings and their repeated frustration. First, Jesus preaches to all Israel, he is rejected. Then the disciples preach to only Israel; they are rejected. Then they go to all nations and the Church begins. Three distinct new beginnings in the history of salvation. Such a view does not suffi-ciently elaborate the relation between Jesus and the Church insofar as the definitive emergence of the Church in its universality and distinc-tiveness is not simply a new beginning, but is intrinsically related to Jesus. The historical points of identity between the earthly Jesus and the post-Easter Church are not sufficiently elaborated. The bridges of continuity between Jesus and the Church are not constructed.

Moreover, as a fundamental theological approach it is inadequate to both Scripture and to contemporary experience. It is selective in its interpretation of Scripture, for the dialogic salvation-history position passes off as a universal law of development what can be described as a Lukan interpretation of salvation history. It does not take into account contemporary experience because the line of continuity is theologically placed within God's changing plan of salvation. It postulates a knowledge of God's original plan and assumes a change in the divine plan so that the foundation of the Church is divinely legitimated by the change in God's plan. The fundamental theological problem of showing the points of continuity between Jesus and the Church and of elaborating a foundation within human history of our faith in the Church is not resolved; it is skipped over.

Similar criticisms can be advanced against the positions of Küng and Schillebeeckx. Insofar as Schillebeeckx argues that there is no implicit christology during the lifetime of Jesus and therefore no implicit Church, he does not draw out the lines of continuity between the disciples' commitment to Jesus prior to his death and their belief in Jesus after his death. Fundamental theology has to raise the question: what was it about Jesus, his proclamation, his actions, etc., that led to his execution and that ultimately led to the breaking of the horizons of Jewish expectations? What emerged after Easter had indeed elements that transcend the pre-Easter experience of Jesus, but these must be seen in relation to who and what Jesus was. How the belief in Jesus as the Christ is ultimately a decision about the significance of the historical Jesus and how the emergence of the Church is a spelling out, a making explicit, and even a further interpretation and realization of the meaning of Jesus is what fundamental theology must explore in order to show the foundation of the Church in Jesus.

Chapter 5

A Reconstructive Hermeneutic of the Church's Foundation

Hermeneutical Issues

The discussions about the foundation of the Church have formulated the issue as the tension between two poles: *explicit intention* and *founding*. The traditional and modern apologetic answered that Jesus deliberately, freely, and knowingly intended to found a Church. The more contemporary historical and exegetical approaches have argued: *one*, that whereas Jesus did not intend to found a Church, he explicitly intended the foundations of the Church insofar as he planned for a community during an interim period; or *two*, that the Church arose after Easter and could be founded only after Jesus has died. The existential approach sought to complement the historical issue by considerations that would make the historical affirmation more credible. Implied therefore in all these discussions are notions of "intention" and "foundation," each of which needs to be examined.

Critique of Traditional Presuppositions

Critique of Reduction of Meaning to Intentionality
Since the nineteenth century and the romantic conception of both hermeneutics and institutions, the meaning of a text, an action, and even an institution lies in the intent of its author or agent.[180] The interpretation of a literary text, a human action, and a social institution must grasp this intention. The experience of empathy with the author, agent, or founder enables interpreters to get to the roots of

the individual's psychological experience that gave birth to the work. It makes understanding possible. The psychological process whereby the interpreter grasps the intention or purpose of the other's subjectivity lies at the basis of interpretation.

Contemporary discussions of the foundation of the Church have focused almost exclusively on the intention of Jesus. As we have noted, his expectation of an imminent end appears to speak against the intention to found a Church. Such a line of argument, however, demands not only that the words and deeds of the historical Jesus be reconstructed from the Gospel texts but also that Jesus' intention and volition be extracted from them. The meaning of the gathering of the disciples would lie, then, in what precisely Jesus *intended* when he gathered disciples. The meaning of his celebration of common meals would lie in what Jesus definitely *intended* by celebrating such meals. The theological and historical formulation of the problem has linked meaning and intentionality, foundation and intention.

Recent hermeneutical theory, however, has strongly criticized such an emphasis upon intentionality and subjectivity in approaching the meaning of a work, event, or institution. Hans Georg Gadamer's *Truth and Method* argues forcefully for the independence of meaning from intentionality.[181] Paul Ricoeur has explicated the noematic and ideal characteristics of texts and events once they have come into existence.[182] The meaning should be derived primarily from the text, act, event, institution, rather than from the intention of the author, agent, or inaugurator.

Applied to the foundation of the Church, the meaning of Jesus' words and deeds should not be explicated by attempting to specify his explicit intention and deliberate volition. Not only do words and deeds have a meaning independent of intention and volition; the situation is also different with regard to Jesus. We know about Jesus only through the Gospel texts which have a meaning independent of the historical Jesus because they were not written by him. The words and deeds narrated within them do not lie primarily in Jesus' intention. To the extent that meaning crisscrosses with intentionality, the meaning will lie within the ambit of the relation among the text, contemporary recipient, and the evangelist. We have no direct access to Jesus' words and deeds but only as handed down, interpreted, and reinterpreted by the evangelists and the early Christian communities. Therefore, the recourse to the intention of Jesus in the formulation of the issue of the foundation of the Church overlooks not only how meaning and intentionality are distinct but also neglects the very nature of the Gospel texts themselves.

Critique of the Category Foundation

In addition to the identification of meaning and intentionality, during the nineteenth century there developed under the influence of romanticism a view of the origin of institutions that strongly emphasized the personality of founders.[183] Although romanticism acknowledged the independent force of social customs and legal institutions, it tended to interpret them from their origins as creations of the genius of great personalities. The spirit of an institution and the laws of a society were attributed to the impact of the personality standing behind that institution. The founders of institutions imprinted their spirits and personalities upon the institutions.

This view of institutions strongly influenced nineteenth-century religious historiography. Just as historians referred to the founding fathers of a nation, so too did they speak of the founding religious personalities behind the origin of religious institutions. Theories of the origin of religions were even influenced by it. For example, Friedrich Creuzer's *Symbolik und Mythologie der alten Völker* traces the origin of mythology back to the intellectual creativity of priests.[184] A century of research on Moses sought to interpret the Mosaic law and the Jewish religion primarily as products of his personality.[185] The history of early Christianity was often interpreted with respect to the different impact that the personality of Jesus and that of Paul had upon the development of the Christian religion.

Such a view of the origin of institutions, and even religious institutions, ignores the overall logic of the emergence and development of institutions. Social and environmental factors influence their character; ideas and ideals have practical implications. Adaptations to new situations and different environments similarly influence institutional structure. Institutions develop a spirit that cannot be reduced to the personality or the intention of the "founder." The complex background of the origin of institutions and the multiple factors of their developments speaks against any romantic conception that traces the spirit of an institution and its structures to the personality and intention of a founder.

Such an overemphasis has long been criticized in the history of religions. Joachim Wach wrote, "As is well known, none of the great founders intended to 'found a religion.'"[186] Such a claim indicates that caution should be used in resolving the question whether Jesus founded a Church—a caution applicable not only to affirmative but also to negative responses. Hans Küng has boldly asserted, "Jesus is not what is generally understood as a founder of a religion or a Church."[187] Such an assertion, however, makes sense only if it is readily known or specifiable what meaning the phrase has "what is generally understood as a founder." Can the category of "founder" be applied to Buddha, Confucius, Lao Tzu, Moses, etc.? The historical distances and the religious development between the period of these "founders" and the emergent religious institutions are in several cases much greater than with regard to Jesus. Even less than Jesus, they can be called founders of their religions. An examination, therefore, of the concept of founder indicates that it is indeed very questionable to deny that Jesus was a founder of a Church or was "what is generally understood as a founder," when the very concept of founder cannot be applied to the other great world religions.

The ambiguities of the category founder, and the flaws in identifying meaning with intention, suggest that the fundamental theological problem of whether the historical Jesus founded a Church deserves an answer that does not reduce foundation totally to explicit foundation and does not operate with an overly simplified notion of founder. With these qualifications, I will sketch a more adequate approach to the issue of the foundation of the Church.

Hermeneutical Principles of Christian Origins

Recent developments within the philosophy of action, linguistic theory, and hermeneutics can contribute to an understanding of the methodological issues that should be brought to the interpretation of the relation between Jesus and the foundation of the Church. All these developments point in the direction of refusing to identify the meaning of a historical action with an agent's intention. Notions of consequences, rules, pragmatics, and reception that have been worked out in these theoretical developments broaden the framework of the interpretation of every significant historical action and should be applied to the foundation of the Church.

Meaning as Retrospective

How meaning goes beyond an agent's intention readily illustrates the degree to which the meaning of an act or event can only be understood when what goes beyond the agent's intention is also taken into account. How the consequences of an action belong to its meaning becomes evident in the distinction between chronicle and narrative. To write meaningful history as a narrative of actions, the act must be seen in relation to future actions. Historical narratives do not simply itemize individual discrete actions, but are the narrative constructions of the meaning of an act in its interrelation with antecedent and subsequent events. For example, the murder of the Austrian Arch-duke Ferdinand in Sarajevo on 28 June 1914, the War Council of William II on 5 July 1915, Chancellor Bethmann Hollweg's blank check to the Austrian ambassador, the Versailles Treaty in 1919, etc.—the narrative construction of history weaves together all these events as a part of the story of World War I. The agents of the initial events did not understand them as the beginning of World War I. The meaning of the individual events is available only retrospectively when each event can be grasped as a part of a continuous narrative.

The experiment of a recording computer able to note in detail every action and event in history has been proposed to illustrate the meaning of history.[188] Such a computer would record events with the utmost accuracy, but it would only provide a chronicle rather than a historical narrative. The computer would not be able to anticipate future events and so it could not perceive the meaning of a present event as part of a continuum that extends to the future. It could chronicle, but not narrate.

Staying with the example of World War I, we can imagine a historian questioning the meaning of the 1919 Treaty of Versailles. If she were to ask the signers of the treaty, they would respond that they were ending the war of 1914–1918. They would see the treaty as the end of a set of events that had begun several years earlier. Today, a historian looking back upon the treaty would have to show how the meaning of that event is much more than the signers intended. At that time, they were not only ending what has since come to be known as World War I, they were sowing the seeds for World War II through the harsh reparations imposed on Germany. The meaning of the Treaty of Versailles is as much determined by future events as by the intention of the agents.

Since history is not an itemized succession of events, but involves continuity, the crucial question becomes what are the criteria of continuity, especially when meaning is not reduced to intentionality. It is not sufficient to have mere temporal sequence or chronological sequence in order to have narrative continuity. It is not sufficient to determine the relation between Jesus and the Church as a temporal or chronological continuum; and it is necessary to elaborate criteria of continuity that are not reduced to intentionality.

Meaning and Rule-governed Behavior
To establish criteria of continuity, it is necessary to consider the relation between meaning and rule-governed behavior, pragmatic truth claims, and reception. In linguistic philosophy the relation between

intention and meaning, as well as between meaning and praxis, has been further developed in the theory of speech-acts. Developing the insight that all speaking involves an action, John L. Austin distinguished between locutionary actions (the saying of something), illocutionary acts (informing, ordering, and undertaking, etc.), and perlocutionary acts (bringing about something, achieving something, e.g., convincing, deterring, etc.).[189]

This theory of speech-acts has been developed in several ways.[190] One of these is John R. Searle's proposal that speaking a language involves performing actions according to rules and presupposes certain background material and contextual information.[191] The distinction between regulative and constitutive rules is important to an understanding of speaking as a rule-governed behavior. A rule is regulative insofar as it antedates behavior, exists independently of behavior, and regulates behavior as an imperative. The rules of etiquette are regulative. They regulate interpersonal behavior that exists independently of these rules and is not constituted by them. Constitutive rules, however, do not just regulate but, as analytic rules, create the possibility of action. For example, chess rules constitute the game of chess. They do not just regulate the game, for to go against them is not simply to go against etiquette but is to fail to play chess.

Speaking a language entails conventions and constitutive rules just as does human action. "Sometimes in order to explain adequately a piece of human behavior we have to suppose that it was done in accordance with a rule, even though the agent himself may not be able to state the rule and may not even be conscious of the fact that he is acting in accordance with the rule."[192] Or again, the ability to speak and the ability to do something depend upon a mastery of rules and conventions, even though in an important sense a person "may not know that he knows the rule or that he does what he does in part because of the rule."[193] Consequently, a distinction exists between "to have a meaning," and "to mean something." Speaking and acting involve both "intentional" and "conventional" aspects. To understand and to know the meaning of an utterance entail knowing the conditions and rules of the utterance. Understanding a set of sentences, therefore, is not simply equated with knowing the intention, but it involves a knowledge of the context and background as well as the implicit rules of language and behavior according to which such sentences were spoken.

This correlation between language and human behavior in the theory of speech-acts has been extended by Paul Ricoeur to human actions.[194] The paradigm of speech-acts makes possible a typology of actions and such a typology would also imply a criteriology since a type entails constitutive rules and allows the construction of "ideal models."[195] Moreover, since actions like speech-acts can be characterized not only according to their propositional content but also according to their illocutionary force, the propositional content, as well as the illocutionary force, belongs to the "sense-content" of action. Human actions, like speech-acts, have a temporal and a logical status. An event as a human action appears and disappears—its temporal sense. But actions have also a logical status that enables them to make their impression on time. Actions can therefore become fixed in time and open to future interpretations because they have more than a mere temporal status.

These analyses show how actions are open to future interpretations insofar as "to have a meaning" is distinct from "to mean something." Moreover, insofar as human action takes place against specific historical backgrounds and in relation to specific rules of human interaction, an action is not open to an unlimited range of interpretation, as Ricoeur sometimes suggests, but rather is limited. The meaning of human actions is limited in that human actions can be classified according to patterns of behavior, specific contexts, and historical locus. Consequently, historical interpretations must presuppose not only that actions have a meaning beyond that which might have been intended but also that they can be classified and limited within a system of rules and patterns. Future horizons, consequences, and events may discover a meaning not made explicit by the agent, but this meaning is not unlimited for the typology of action also restricts its meaning. Consequently, in interpreting Jesus' proclamation and actions, the significant question is not what did Jesus intend, or whether he intended a Church or to lay the foundation for the Church or whether he intended an interim community for an interim period.[196] Instead, the question should be whether his proclamation and actions have a meaning that legitimates the emergence of a Church. Do they have a meaning so that the Church does not simply stand after Jesus in time, but that its existence and meaning are entailed in the meaning that Jesus' proclamation and actions can have?

Comparing Jesus with other religious figures makes possible the location of Jesus within a typology of meaning and action. Buddha established a monastic community, Muhammad set up a religious-political city-state, Confucius established an educational institution. Whether Muhammad, Confucius, Buddha intended any further development is less appropriate as a question than the inquiry whether the ensuing social and religious traditions can be seen as a typification of the meaning and praxis initiated by the religious figure.

Likewise, Jesus' preaching and action, as presented in the Gospel material, provides the basis for a typology of action and meaning. Jesus' proclamation, his gathering of disciples, his celebrating of meals, his performing of exorcisms and healings all enable a typification of Jesus as a prophet, wise man, miracle worker, etc.[197] Such characterizations do not exhaust the significance of Jesus, but they both set up the possibilities for future interpretation of Jesus' meaning; at the same time, they delineate and demarcate the limits of possible interpretations. They open up possibilities of some interpretations and exclude others. The typology of meaning and action provides, therefore, a way of marking out the possibilities and limitations of interpretation when the explicit intention is not historically ascertainable. It also sets up criteria by which continuity and discontinuity can be legitimated without recourse to intentionality.[198] These possibilities have to be further specified with regard to the pragmatics and reception of the meaning of Jesus within early Christianity.

Meaning and Interactive Truth Claims
The development of the theory of speech-acts in the direction of a universal pragmatic highlights the interactive nature of language. Its emphasis upon interactive truth claims has implications for any consideration of the meaning of Jesus' proclamation. The theory of speech-acts as developed into a universal pragmatic is not only concerned with the syntactic and semantic aspects of sentences but also with the pragmatic features of utterances. Not language alone, but speech, not linguistic competence alone, but communicative competence and speech-acts are the objects of a pragmatics of language.

It has been suggested that utterances relate to the realm of language, external reality, internal reality, and normative social reality.[199] Utterances taking place in the medium of language should meet the criteria of intelligibility and comprehensibility. Utterances relate to external reality and the world of objects and events about which true or false statements are made. They relate to society with its normative reality, that is, to a social life of shared values and norms. And they also relate to internal reality as the expression of individual intentional experience. Each relation implies a validity proper to it. The relation to language entails claims of intelligibility, of cognitive relation to external reality (propositional truth), of the interactive (rightness), and of the expressive (truthfulness).

The distinction between the cognitive and the interactive is central to Jürgen Habermas's development of the interactive and pragmatic dimension of speech-acts.[200] Linguistic communication takes place when individuals simultaneously enter into communication on two distinct levels: the level of intersubjectivity and of propositional content. In speaking, either the intersubjective or the propositional dominates. The intersubjective dominates in the interactive use of language where the relations between the speakers is established, for example, warnings, promises, commands, imperatives, etc. In the propositional, the content of the language, its cognitive content is thematized and the interactive is only indirectly present. For example, I assert (to you) that there is a chair in the room. The content of the assertion is underscored whereas the fact that an interactive assertion is made (to you) is only indirectly present. But when I say, "I recommend that you move the chair," then the interactive aspect dominates.

This distinction between the interactive and the cognitive implies a distinction also on the level of validity claims. The interactive use refers to validity claims and is dependent upon recognized norms and actions, whereas the cognitive speech-act relates to objects of external reality. The truth reference of the propositional content of the interactive use of language is merely implicit, whereas the validity claims of the social normativity is explicitly invoked. Hence in regulative and interactive speech (e.g., commands, admonitions, etc.), it becomes important to see their validity claims primarily against the background of social norms and expectations and only indirectly in regard to propositional statements. The validity claim of interactive speech-acts is only indirectly propositional even if the claim is made that the truth of its propositional assertion rationally grounds it—a claim not applicable to all religious statements.[201]

This shift from a focus on language to the interactive dimension of speaking has important consequences for interpretation in general and for the theological issue of the relation between Jesus' proclamation and the Church.[202] The interpretation of speaking should, therefore, in general not be limited to the semantic dimension of what is said, but must take into account the pragmatic and interactive dimension with its respective truth claims. Thus, any interpretation of Jesus' preaching that takes into account the semantic dimension but not the interactive dimension does not explicate adequately the meaning and truth claim of Jesus' proclamation.

If the meaning of the proclamation about God's reign is isolated and is interpreted primarily as statements about external reality (when the end-time will arrive) or as expressions of the intentional beliefs of Jesus (what he did anticipate), but not in its interactive force with societal norms and expectations, then the full meaning of his preaching is missed. The pragmatic and interactive dimensions of Jesus' preaching must be considered if the significance of his proclamation is to be ascertained.

Moreover, against the background of Habermas's grid of speech-acts with their various reality domains and truth claims, the proclamation of the imminence of God's reign relates primarily to society and its normative reality, that is, to the social life of shared values and norms. Jesus' proclamation does not so much consist of utterances providing propositional information about external reality or expressing his internal convictions as it consists of an interactive use of language whereby the intersubjective level, with its relation to societal norms, dominates and the propositional content is present only implicitly. The language about the kingdom is a part of regulative and interactive speech with its admonitions, commands, recommendations, warnings, and so on.

Consequently, my suggestion that Jesus' proclamation of God's reign should be interpreted not primarily in terms of its propositional content, but rather in relation to its intersubjective force and interactive pragmatic, does not dispense with the issue of its truth; it emphasizes it and gives it a different locus. My suggestion differs from Norman Perrin's emphasis upon kingdom language as a tensive symbol and Paul Ricoeur's development of the metaphorical twist involved in kingdom language.[203] In these cases, the metaphorical and symbolic content of kingdom language is so much underscored that the truth claim of the proclamation is interpreted in relation to its propositional multivalence or to its expressive disclosure possibilities. Ultimately, such an interpretation of the kingdom proclamation does not go far beyond an existential interpretation of the expressive self-disclosure that has occurred in Jesus' proclamation.[204]

The focus on the interactive dimension of the kingdom proclamation singles out how that proclamation challenges the normative values of society and entails commitments from its hearers so that its proclamation necessarily establishes and constitutes community. Moreover, because the content of the kingdom proclamation is not rationally verifiable, the truth claim of the proclamation's interactive imperatives is not established in rational discourse, but is established through a commitment to the person and praxis of the proclaimer. Its meaning, therefore, cannot be ascertained independently and separately from an analysis of the reception of this proclamation and its interpretation within the community of disciples. For this reason, a hermeneutics of reception is essential to an understanding of the pragmatic dimensions of the kingdom proclamation.

Meaning and Reception
Recently, a significant advance has been made in the field of hermeneutics.[205] Known as "reception hermeneutics" or as the hermeneutics of the "Konstanz School," it has been developed by Hans Robert Jauss and has sought to overcome the formalistic method of literary criticism which abstracts from history and society, the orthodox marxist interpretation of literature as a mirror of society, and, above all, the hermeneutics of Gadamer with its dogmatic overevaluation and universalization of the classic without reference to the cultural and historic limitations of its origins. Although this "reception hermeneutics" has received scant attention within theology,[206] and has been primarily applied to literary works, its hermeneutical insights are very useful for the interpretation of the meaning and reception of Jesus within early Christianity.

Several concepts are basic to reception hermeneutics. One is the "expectation horizon" of a work. The reconstruction of the expectation horizon of a work is important to determine the effect of a work upon its contemporaries. In being "received" a work often negates set expectations. Differences often exist between the expectation horizon and the novelty of the work that has appeared. A new work in making conscious certain experiences often effects a radical change of horizons; it often creates a new consciousness. This distance between the horizon of expectation and the horizon created by the new work can often be measured in the broad spectrum of public reaction and of critical judgment. In looking back at the contemporary reception of a work, it can often be ascertained that the degree to which the work only mirrors the expectations of the public, to that degree the work is mere entertainment literature. But to the degree that a work challenges the horizons of the audience, creates new horizons, forms new expectations, to that degree the work manifests its originality and its creative status.[207]

The original distance between the work and its audience disappears for later generations in the measure that the transformation of horizons has already taken place. The transcendence of the original work that led to negative reactions to it has been replaced by an awareness of the work as a standard work. What was new and strange has now become traditional and familiar. The originality of classics has been lost; they have become so acceptable that they must almost be read against the grain of their present-day acceptance in order to grasp their originally provocative and transcendent character.

A reception hermeneutic, therefore, starkly contrasts with Gadamer's use of Hegel's conception of the classic as the prototype of the historical mediation between past and present. In Gadamer's conception, the classic as a classic transcends its past and has relevance for the present. The horizon of the present must be merged with the horizon of the classic in order to grasp the truth represented in the work.[208] What Gadamer's model overlooks is the original negativity of the classic. Because it broke the expectation horizons of its time, it was often negatively received and its original audience often reacted against it. What is in the classic today taken as a matter of course may have in the original situation been the most provocative. Consequently, as we have said above, a classic should be read against its value for the present so that the original horizon and the reversal and transformation of horizons that took place under its impact can be perceived. A hermeneutic should go beyond asking what the classic has to say to the contemporary situation to asking how did the classic go against the expectations of its time, how did it transform these expectations, and how does this transformation have significance for the contemporary situation.

This reception hermeneutic can be condensed to the following technical thesis: "a syntagmatic displacement within a synchronic structure becomes, in its reception, a paradigmatic condensation within a diachrony."[209] An individual work stands often in contrast to prevailing conventions. It is often misunderstood, unintelligible, or disallowed by those prevailing conventions. It may be contemporaneous or synchronic with these conventions, but its relation is often contingent and contrasting. Only through the history of a work's reception does one discover what is creative and paradigmatic. This insight leads to the development of the notion of "concretization." In comprehending the meaning of a work that goes beyond or contrary to its expected horizon, persons must attempt to understand it also diachronically in the history of the "concretizations" of its reception. The concept of "concretization," developed by Jan Mukarovksy and Felix V. Vodicka within Prague structuralism, has been taken over and has become a central component of reception hermeneutics.[210] The interpretation of a work must also proceed to analyze the various "concretizations" of the work within its reception. The meaning of a work lies not simply in its auctorial intention or in its initial reception, but rather and also in relation to the history of its reception. A dynamic tension often exists between a work and the normative expectations of a work, so that the history of its interpretation of the work must constantly elaborate its meaning by showing the historical sequence of its reception amid changing norms and changing anticipations.

Although developed primarily within literary criticism, this hermeneutics of reception has distinct points of applicability for the problem of the relation between Jesus and the Church. It points first of all to the tension between the meaning and horizon of expectation. To grasp the meaning of Jesus is to comprehend the degree to which Jesus goes beyond the canons of expectation of his contemporaries and surpasses the immediate horizon not only of his disciples but also of his own immediate explicit self-consciousness. Attempts, therefore, to interpret Jesus primarily from the category of the "history-of-religions background" or from the perspective of indigenous religious traditions tend to reduce the meaning of Jesus to that of the horizon of his background and to limit his significance to the normative expectations of his time. Such a procedure minimizes, indeed overlooks, the extent to which the meaning of Jesus consists precisely in his changing of the horizons of expectation and his creation of new horizons.

Benedetto Croce has observed, "Every true work of art has violated an established genre, and in this way confounded the ideas of critics who thus found themselves compelled to broaden the genre."[211] In a similar fashion, it can be said that Jesus has violated the established genres and in this way confounds those critics that interpret him according to a preconceived genre. In interpreting the historical Jesus, the genres of rabbi, prophet, wise man, magician, and others are used. Yet an adequate interpretation must ask to what extent are we compelled to broaden the genre according to which we interpret Jesus. Only through the concretizations of Jesus in his diverse receptions does the extent to which Jesus transcends these genres become evident.[212]

The tension between originality and the horizon of expectation highlights the dimension of negativity. What transcends an environment or a horizon necessarily involves a challenge to that environment and a critique of its horizons. This dimension of negativity is often overlooked in the romantic hermeneutics that inspires much modern christology. Where the meaning of Jesus is located primarily in Jesus' intentionality and consciousness or in the impact of his personality, then the contrast between the horizon of expectation and the newness of reception is diminished. Instead, a continuum of spreading influence is postulated and what follows belongs simply to the provenance of Jesus. Thereby, the transcending of horizons is neglected and the challenge to the recipients' horizons and expectations is minimized.

The application of this reception hermeneutics, therefore, goes strongly against a consciousness christology. Attempts to locate the meaning of Jesus precisely in regard to the consciousness of Jesus seek to establish a foundation that is anterior to the tension between the horizon of expectation and the reception of the newness of Jesus. The insights of form and redaction criticism showing the practical impossibility of going back to the consciousness of Jesus, even where some reconstruction of his proclamation and praxis is possible, are based on the awareness that all such reconstructions are reconstructions of reception. Such a limitation is not a hermeneutical loss, but rather a strength, for it is in the reception of Jesus that the full meaning and significance of Jesus can emerge in its power to overturn the expected genres.

This emphasis on the transcending of the horizons of expectations points to the significance of the notion of concretizations and of a diachronic over a synchronic reception. The point of christology, therefore, is not simply that reception reflected in one normative testimony which may be the earliest reception and thereby most synchronic, as Schubert Ogden has recently emphasized.[213] Instead, the meaning of christology is grasped only diachronically through a series of concretizations. The relation between Jesus and the Church is such that a synchronic relation does not take precedence over the diachronic reception. Instead, it is only through a series of diachronic receptions that one can grasp what is paradigmatic about Jesus and what is not; what transcends the immediate horizons of expectation and what does not. Only through the history of successive receptions with their overturning of previous conceptions does the meaning of Jesus and his relation to the Church become more fully disclosed. The concretization of the creative tension between successive expectations and receptions makes manifest how the relation between Jesus and the Church is not one of simple contiguity, but rather one of a foundation based upon the breaking through of the horizons of expectation.

Although theoretically such a hermeneutic of reception demands not just a survey of the New Testament receptions of Jesus, but rather an analysis of diverse concretizations throughout the history of Christianity, obvious limitations prevent such a study. Instead, it will be necessary to elaborate the fundamental theological problem of the foundation of the Church by Jesus in the light of its successive receptions within the New Testament testimonies.

Communities and Church within the New Testament

On the basis of these hermeneutical principles, the foundational issue of the relation between Jesus and the Church can be approached with a foundational theology as a reconstructive hermeneutics. Such an approach seeks to avoid some basic tendencies within traditional and contemporary fundamental theology. By harmonizing the various texts, fundamental theology failed to perceive the diverse conceptions present within the New Testament writings themselves. In addition, the New Testament texts were interpreted from the specific modern question: did Jesus found the Church or did Jesus found a particular church order? Although aware of the dangers of proof-texting, of neglecting diversity, and of approaching with inadequate pre-understandings, contemporary fundamental theology has also neglected the diversity within the New Testament writings insofar as it has not sought to sketch out the "concretizations" and receptions within the New Testament and has sought to go beyond the text and establish the foundation in a clear-cut picture of the "historical" origin of the Church.

Both the traditional and the contemporary fundamental theology, therefore, share the common presupposition of searching for a uniform foundation independent of the diverse New Testament concretizations and receptive testimonies. The interpretations of Matt 16:17–19 easily illustrate what I call their "category mistake." For traditional fundamental theology these verses report a historical event at Caesarea Philippi where Jesus promised the primacy to Peter. Contemporary fundamental theology, more aware of the redactional elements in the Matthean text, proposed that Matt 16:17–19 probably referred to an event at the last supper (as the Lukan text seems to indicate) where Jesus encourages Peter and refers to his impending death. Moreover, as contemporary fundamental theology began to take into account the postresurrectional perspective of all the New Testament accounts, it interpreted all of them as referring to a singular event of foundation after the resurrection.[214] The foundation of the Church and the primacy of Peter was based on this event. Therefore, even the most recent approaches within fundamental theology failed to elaborate the diversity of meanings disclosed by the New Testament texts and failed to explore how this diversity entailed a reception with a transcending of horizons and expectations; rather, these approaches sought to unify the diversity into a single historical account that would provide a firm historical basis for the Christian faith.

In proposing foundational theology as a reconstructive hermeneutics, I am suggesting that the fundamental theological issue of the Church's foundation be resolved neither by a historical demonstration independent of faith nor by a transcendental deduction of ecclesial existence nor by a historiography of post-Easter origins, but by a sketch of how the reception of Jesus' foundational significance is concretized in the diverse New Testament texts themselves. To the extent that the problem whether Jesus founded a Church is a modern formulation, it cannot alone be the guiding heuristic for reading the New Testament texts. Therefore, methods of correlation that bring our modern questions to the text often fail to perceive how the vision and praxis disclosed in the New Testament texts themselves reveal a horizon that transcends and even critiques our own horizons. Methods of correlation, therefore, need to be complemented by a reconstructive hermeneutics that seeks to uncover the concretizations of the tensions between horizons of expectation and transformed horizons of reception. To raise the foundational theological question of the Church within such a reconstructive hermeneutics also means that the New Testament texts cannot be read within the limit of the classic problems of fundamental theology: eschatology and community, selection and mission of the disciples, and the relation between Peter and Jesus. Instead, a distinct set of concretizations of the relation between Jesus and the Church emerge.

The Community Called Church

The first set of questions for a reconstructive hermeneutics should be: how did the early Christian communities express their reception of Jesus? How did they express their self-understanding as communities grounded in Jesus? And how did such expressions change and even effect transformations of their horizons of expectation? Such an approach, therefore, does not search the New Testament for proof-texts that could provide a historical demonstration that the historical Jesus intended to found a Church. It does not, as the transcendental fundamental theology does, argue for a general justification of the Church's necessity as the continuation of the unsurpassable salvation present in Jesus. Instead, it starts concretely from the New Testament testimonies themselves in order to ask: how was this continuation expressed in the diverse concretizations of early Christian faith? Consequently, it also does not seek to provide a historical explanation of the origins of Christianity. Instead, it seeks to show how the first Christian communities expressed their self-understanding in relation to Jesus and how they thereby brought forth a reality and a vision exhibiting the ground of their meaning and praxis in the meaning and praxis of Jesus.

Church and Church of God
The Greek-speaking early Christians used the term "ecclesia" as their self-designation. Their use of the term is, however, so complex that several major points are still debated. According to one hypothesis, the choice of "ecclesia" indicates a certain anti-Judaism and antinomianism; another sees a link between ecclesia and the Old Testament concept of the People of God. And still another hypothesis maintains that only at the end of the New Testament period does the notion of ecclesia as a universal and distinctive concept emerge. These hypotheses need to be examined.

Since the term "synagogue" is consistently avoided as a form of Christian self-designation (the single exception being Ja 2:2), the argument has been made that the use of ecclesia, rather than suggesting that the Church continues as God's chosen people, indicates a contrast between the early Christian community and Israel.[215] Unfortunately, the evidence is not sufficient to claim that ecclesia was chosen instead of synagogue because the latter represented a community of law, whereas the former indicated an assembly based on the gospel.

Much more serious is the claim that the early Christians first used the term ecclesia to designate the concrete community of a particular city or an actual assembly of that community. Only afterwards did the early Christians use ecclesia to refer to the whole Church. Paul's use of the term ecclesia was therefore interpreted as limited to the local assembly. Only the later deutero-Pauline writings were regarded as having a more universalistic sense of Church. Such observations seek to demonstrate that the very notion of Church is a late development. Only after a considerable period of time did the early Christian communities even begin to understand themselves as a Church in a sense that goes beyond that of a particular assembly or a specific community.

This same point has been much more forcefully put by Rudolf Bultmann in his classic essay outlining the changes within the self-understanding of early Christianity.[216] He proposed *three decisive changes*. In the beginning, the early Christians did not understand themselves as the adherents of a new religion over against Judaism. Even the Twelve were not an institution in competition with the Jewish Sanhedrin. The *first* change, however, took place within the Pauline conception of the Church and the admission of pagan Christians without the requirement of the law. Although such a change was significant, the Pauline conception still retained its continuity with the history of Israel. Here, too, no new religion was present and the early Christians still understood themselves as the People of God within the history of God's plan of salvation. The *second* change took place with the Pauline notion of the Body of Christ. Here the eschatological conception of the Church as the People of the end-time was complemented by the notion of the Church as the Body of Christ. Since the notions Body of Christ and People of God do not immediately stand in contrast to each other, this change did not eo ipso entail a fundamental opposition to the previous view. But with time a conflict emerged. The delay of the parousia made Christians accustomed to the tasks of the world. Practical necessities led to the establishment of regulations and order; the needs of ministry to the development of office. A *third* change took place when the Church began to understand itself as the present institution of salvation. Now office and institution are of the essence of the Church. They are constitutive of Church. Only at this last and final stage, Bultmann maintains, did the Christian faith become a new religion, and the Church emerge as a distinctive world-historical institution.

Such an interpretation of early Christian self-understanding not only undercuts any claim that Jesus founded the Church or intended to lay the foundations for an interim community, but presents a challenge to any attempt to uncover the foundational relation between Jesus and the Church. The complexity of the question whether the first Christians understood themselves as a distinct religious community and when they began to see themselves as a Church is, in no small measure, due to the difficulty of reconstructing the diverse levels of the New Testament texts. In beginning with the earliest texts, namely, the Pauline writings, the problem of differentiating Pauline and the pre-Pauline layers comes immediately to the fore.

It is obvious that 85 percent of the time Paul uses the term ecclesia in reference to the specific group,[217] particular assembly, or local community. The use of the term ecclesia for the local community is quite often applied to the house community.[218] In addition, Church in the singular refers to the concrete community of a particular city, for example, the Church of Rome, or in the plural, it refers to the communities of an area, for example, the Churches of Judea.

The meaning of the term ecclesia has recently been illuminated through its use in contemporary Hellenistic writings—not as previously through classical Greek or the Septuagint, but from those Hellenistic and Jewish Hellenistic writings contemporary to Christianity.[219] The term ecclesia referred in Hellenism to political assemblies. Jewish Hellenistic literature uses ecclesia not only for political but also for cultic assemblies—these cultic assemblies, however, are not purely religious but have political significance. In the diaspora, the assembling ensured the Jews of their political as well as religious identity. The Jewish Hellenistic ecclesia functioned to praise God *and* to regulate itself as a political-religious community. Members of the diaspora community were often censured or excluded in the eccelsia; speeches were given; persons exercised positions of authority in the assembly; and the letters of the prophets were read aloud. The Christian Churches had structural similarities to the Jewish Hellenistic assemblies. They assembled to praise God; their assembly was a place for speaking, hearing, and preaching. As it was a cultic assembly the speeches were considered to express the presence of God's spirit or wisdom. In the assemblies, the apostles and elders exercised leadership roles, and the assembly made decisions affecting the membership.

Therefore, the Christian use of the term ecclesia directly takes up the widespread Jewish Hellenistic terminology at the time. The consistent use of ecclesia and the avoidance of the term synagogue is, therefore, not opposed to Jewish contemporary usage and should not be explained as expressing a deliberate opposition to Jewish law. Instead, the early Christians were using the term most commonly used by Hellenistic Jews to designate their assemblies. At the same time, this interpretation of ecclesia from contemporary Hellenistic usage modifies the proposal that the Old Testament notion of the People of God was the primary analogue for understanding the meaning of ecclesia.[221] The choice of the term ecclesia was not primarily for eschatological reasons. As in contemporary Hellenistic literature so too in early Christian literature, the reference to ecclesia as an assembly refers to a cultic assembly, its spirit-filled praise of God, its prophetic utterances, and its self-regulation. The immediate elements dominate the meaning of ecclesia when the Christians use the term for their actual assemblies.

Although predominantly used for the individual assembly, ecclesia has a different connotation in its syntagmatic use, that is, in its combination with other expressions and terms.[222] An analysis of the Pauline texts exhibits this use not only for Paul's theological statements but also in the pre-Pauline traditions present within his writings. The first syntagmatic use is the phrase the "Church of God" or the "Church of God in Jesus." The second are the references to the "Church in Jesus." And finally, it is important to see how the New Testament usage reflects a reception of Deut 23 that modifies its horizon. Such a usage correlates with other designations of the first Christians as "holy," "elect," "poor," and a "koinonia." In short, it is only when this complex of crisscrossing meanings and connotations is taken into account does the meaning of the early Christian self-appellation as Church come to the fore.

The expression "Church of God" characterizes not just the actual assembly and not only a particular Church, the Church of Jerusalem; it also has a universalistic sense.[223] Its use does not stand at the end of the development of New Testament ecclesiology, but rather at the very beginning. It is therefore incorrect to assume that only as late as Ephesians does the notion of Church have a universalistic, and even cosmic, meaning,[224] for such a usage can be found in the earlier texts and in the connotations associated with the expression the "Church of God."

In three cases, 1 Cor 15:9, Gal 1:13; and Phil 3:6, Paul refers to his persecution of the Church of God.[225] He most probably refers to the Church of Jerusalem and to the Christians in Jerusalem. In referring to the Church of Jerusalem as "the Church of God," Paul has most probably taken over an expression that had its origin in the community of Jerusalem and that expressed its very self-designation. It does not primarily refer to the community as an individual community, but rather to the community as *the* Christian community.

The Church of God should not be understood as referring exclusively either to the individual community, on the one hand, or to the eschatological community, on the other. In Gal 1:22, it is used in the plural to refer to the Churches of Judea.[226] In Gal 2:5, it is not identified with the local Jerusalem community, but includes Judea. Yet the linguistic evidence also shows that the Church of God does not simply refer to the Church as an ideal eschatological community. The syntagma "the Church of God" refers to a concrete historical community even though it transcends the individual local community—as an examination of its use in the interpretation of Deuteronomy shows.[227]

In Hellenistic Judaism, Deut 23 is interpreted to show the national or religious groups that are excluded from the ecclesia of God. The conditions of membership are spelled out as conditions of holiness and justice. These conditions relate to actual membership and de facto exclusion. The Church of God, therefore, does not simply refer to an eschatological community, but rather to a historical religious community for whom justice and holiness are conditions of admission.

Election to Holiness and Justice in Christ

Against the background of the religious and political interpretation of Deut 23 within Jewish history, the early Christian understanding of itself as the Church of God becomes clearer. When the notion of People of God was applied to all of Israel, the question arose of the admission of others to this status. The interpretation of Deut 23:2–9 was important because it was seen as setting out the conditions of membership in the People of God. Although the term ecclesia was used with reference to individual assemblies, the admission conditions are conditions of belonging not just to an individual assembly, but to a whole group. Deut 23:2–9 is interpreted in relation to holiness and righteousness or justice. Philo, for example, applies the text to the proselytes called into the Church of God. He places this Church of God in relation to God's reign, participation in immortality, and possession of faith. Those proselytes coming into the Church of God also enter into the political community of the Jews.

This tradition is apparently continued within early Christianity. Just as the expression "saints" was a group-designation in Jewish literature,[228] so too it describes the Christian communities within the New Testament. Just as Philo interpreted Deut 23 in terms of holiness and righteousness or justice to describe the proselytes who have been called to convert to God and to become members of the Church of God, so too does early Christianity describe its converts as those called to holiness and righteousness or justice. These are not from nature holy, righteous or just, but have their holiness and justice from Christ Jesus. The two conditions—righteousness (better, justice) and having been made righteous—by Jesus—need to be explicated in order to understand the conditions of membership in the Church of God within early Christianity.

Within contemporary Judaism radical justice is a condition of admission, and external criteria are already considered to be irrelevant (see Philo, Questions on Exodus 2:2). The circumcision of the flesh finds it universalization and radicalization in the circumcision of the heart. "The universalism of this ecclesia is, therefore, founded in the strictness of its admission conditions (especially in the existence of a measure of justice and holiness that only God can give)."[229]

This conception of righteousness as the criterion of admission to the People of God correlates with the communal understanding of justice. The righteous or the just are such not in an individualistic sense, but rather in a relational sense, insofar as they are in a "justice-relation" to society and to God. As Ferdinand Hahn has noted, "Justice, especially as the 'justice of God,' has a constitutive meaning as well for the foundation as for the preservation of the community."[230] Therefore, justice is more than mercy. Whereas mercy and compassion express solidarity, loyality, and readiness to help, justice is fundamentally a community-establishing behavior. Moreover, a relation exists between faith and the justice of God. Whereas the justice of God is the turning of God to creation to establish the saving order for all, faith is trust and reliance on God. Faith is the corresponding attitude to God's revelation of justice. Since justice and faith imply a new life in Christ and since justice is a community concept, then the practice of justice manifests the truth of the community.

In view of this emphasis upon the necessity for holiness and justice as requirements for admission to the Church of God, it is no wonder that the formula "called to be saints"[231] is the designation of the Christian community in the prescripts of Romans, 1 Corinthians, and 1 Clement. In 1 Corinthians the expression is parallel to that of "Church of God." The holiness of the People of God and the Church of God was emphasized under priestly influence in Jewish circles. In early Christianity the "saints" came to be a name designating the Christians. However, this holiness referred to the existence of the Church in Christ—a reference to the saving effect of Christ, but it need not involve a reference to the atoning death of Christ.

Ernst Käsemann has, however, constantly pointed out how the holiness and the righteousness of the Church of God can be understood as a question of justice.[232] This justice of God is understood not so much as a property of God but as the comprehensive reality that pervades human history. It refers to God's reign that affects history and the life of the community. "The Spirit is life in view of justice" (Rom 8:10).[233] "Just as sin reigned in death so too grace should reign by the justice for everlasting life" (Rom 5:21). The life of the Christian community is described as a life in justice.

A connection exists between justice and the universalistic dimension of the Church of God. Although the meaning of the term ecclesia stems from the Hellenistic community and refers to the empirical community and to the house-church,[234] when it is used syntagmatically as the Church of God it has a much more universal meaning as is evident within its apocalyptic context.[235] The ecclesia of God has a universal character in the Jewish conception of the community of salvation of all the just. The Book of Enoch, for example, describes how the community of the just will appear and how sinners will be judged (53:6). Then the just and elect will be allowed to appear in the house of assembly and will no longer be hindered. This notion of the eschatological community of the just stands as the link to the New Testament conception of the Church of God with its quality of holiness and justice. As Windisch has shown, the sayings about the entering of the kingdom of God reflect this connection, since the conditions for entering the kingdom of God are similar to those for entering the People of God.[236]

The formula "in Christ" shows both the basis of this holiness and justice of the Church of God and the distinctiveness of this early Christian self-designation. "In Christ" may simply refer to Christian existence. Gal 3:28, for example, states, "For you are all one in Christ Jesus." Individual members of the Christian communities are described as "in Christ" (Rom 16:7, 11) or "in the Lord" (1 Cor 1:3); Christian communities themselves are also said to be "in Christ" (Gal 1:22 and 1 Thess 2:14). Consequently "in Christ" is not just an expression of individual piety, but is an ecclesiological formula. Nevertheless, the meaning of the formula and its expression of the distinctive self-understanding of the Christian communities is somewhat controverted.[237] In its most general sense, "in Christ" refers to the condition of being specified by Christ. "It often expresses in a quite general way the state of being determined by Christ whereby it supplies the lack of the not yet coined adjective 'Christian' or a corresponding adverb."[238]

Attempts to explain the meaning of the formula have ranged from the mystical and local to the more instrumental and spatial. In 1892 Adolf Deissmann suggested that the "in" has a local meaning and should be interpreted mystically as union with the exalted Christ. The history-of-religions concept of mystical union was seen as the background from which this formula should be interpreted. More recently, its Hebrew background has been emphasized, and the formula has been interpreted as the incorporation of the Christian into the Christ-event. Faith becomes primarily the acceptance of the events of salvation history. Most often and most properly "in Christ" expresses a relation, a relation between Christ and what has happened to the Christian community. Moreover, it indicates that Christ is present and has power in the community through the Spirit just as the community is incorporated into Christ through the Spirit. The formula, therefore, also designates the new creation that has taken place through God's action in Christ (2 Cor 5:17).[239]

In short, the formula "in Christ" expresses the newness of the Christian reality established by Christ's action that has taken place in the past and is now taking place in the Spirit. God's saving action has taken place in Christ; the Christian community now lives in Christ in the power of that saving action and in the likeness of Christ. The "in Christ," therefore, relates the Christian community to Christ as the source and origin of the community's power and strength; at the same time, it expresses how that power effects a likeness between Christ and the community. Thus, "in Christ" means Christ both as source of the community's power and as source of the community's becoming like him in holiness and justice.[240] Such an interpretation of "in Christ" points to the significance that the term "koinonia" had for the early Christians.

The early Christian communities understood themselves and designated themselves as "koinonia" or "fellowship."[241] Nevertheless, the direct translation of koinonia into the modern term "fellowship" is somewhat misleading. Fellowship does not primarily mean in the New Testament coming together or associating for a specific goal. Instead, it includes the notion of participating and sharing in something. This difference in meaning is so pronounced that it has been suggested that the Greek *koinōnia* should be translated into English or Latin not by "society" or *societas* but by "participation" or *participatio*. The notion of association or society does not suffice to explain what Church is. The Church as koinonia does not consist simply, therefore, of those associating to confess their belief in Jesus as the Risen Lord, but rather they share in a communion and participation with the Risen Lord that grounds their unity with him. This unity is established in the baptism —also in the Eucharist—of Christians.[242] The personal presence of the exalted Lord in the community is decisive for the understanding of early Christian use of koinonia. Paul's expression "The grace of the Lord Jesus Christ and the love of God and the fellowship of [and participation in] the Holy Spirit be with you" (2 Cor 13:14) and Paul's development of the Body of Christ notion for the individual community are expressions and further explications of this conception. The relation to the Risen Lord is so strongly emphasized that "the belonging to the Lord does not only found the earthly community of believers, but the belonging to the

Lord and the community with him can be placed in question when the concrete koinonia with brother [and sister] is not realized (1 Cor 11:17ff; 1 John 1:6ff).''[243]

Several conclusions can be drawn from this survey of the early Christians' understanding of themselves as the Church of God in Christ. First, the earliest New Testament writings show no trace of the modern fundamental theological problem of whether the earthly Jesus explicitly willed to found a Church. Yet these very same writings contain formulas and conceptions that express strongly that the Church is founded in Christ and is based upon a relation between Christ and the Church. He is not only the source of the Church's holiness and justice, but its holiness and justice is in the likeness of his and is the new reality of Christian life. Even the Church's understanding of itself as a koinonia expresses strongly this union with Christ.

Second, modern studies have emphasized very strongly the use of the term ecclesia for the local community; most recent studies have shown to what degree ecclesia was used in association with house-churches.[244] However, it is another matter to claim that the first Christian communities understood themselves in the beginning solely as local assemblies or communities and only gradually and after a long period of development understood themselves as Church. Against this opinion, it was argued that the earliest notion of the Church as the Church of God, most probably first associated with the Jerusalem community, had a universal connotation in the very beginning. This idea of Church of God was broadened by Paul—some would claim modified—insofar as he applied it to other Churches. In this complex question, the judgment of Raymond Brown best sums up the results: "in tracing how Christians understood themselves as a church, one could argue for a logical progression from original unity to regional or ideological diversity and finally to universality."[245]

Third, the first Christian communities had a self-understanding that could be described as both actual and eschatological. They did understand their assemblies as actualizations of the presence of the Spirit and as anticipations of the eschatological future. And they also understood themselves as having been made holy and just through God's saving act in Christ Jesus. The holiness and justice that in diaspora Judaism was a condition of admission to the Jewish political and religious community was, with a christological foundation, also a condition of membership in the Christian Church of God.

The relation between their existence in Christ and God's saving act in Christ Jesus is not further spelled out. It is this task that the Gospels perform. Insofar as they show the identity between Christ and Jesus, so too they spell out, each in its distinctive way, the relation between the Christian community and the earthly Jesus.

Gospel Testimonies to Jesus and the Foundation of Christian Identity

The Gospels are narratives about Jesus *and* stories of Christian identity. They do not just relate the story of Jesus, they also spell out the beginning of the Christian story of discipleship. Although they narrate the life, deeds, and praxis of Jesus, they are not earlier than the pre-Pauline formula or the Pauline writings, but represent a later stage of theological reflection that goes back to the earthly Jesus and attempts to draw the lines of continuity between the earthly Jesus and the heavenly Christ, between the disciples of the earthly Jesus and the post-Easter Christian communities.

In examining the Gospels as testimonies to Jesus, a hermeneutics of reception requires one to observe how their receptions and their interpretations of the Jesus traditions differ from both the modern and the contemporary fundamental theological problem.[246] This caution is even more important with the Gospels than with respect to the Pauline traditions and writings. Since the Gospel traditions describe Christian identity in relation to the earthly Jesus, their dominant interest can much more easily be interpreted as a historical and apologetic one. Nevertheless, this interest is not historical in the sense of modern historiography but is closely intertwined with theological and kerygmatic concerns. The apologetic interests present are not those of anti-Enlightenment fundamental theology, but of the struggles within early Christianity for self-identity.

The Kingdom and the New Family

As the first and earliest Gospel, that of Mark provides a theological interpretation of the community of disciples in their relation to Jesus, of his proclamation of the kingdom, and of his praxis of healing and miracles. It has been noted that Mark's Gospel does not use such traditional terms as "ecclesia," "Body of Christ," "Community of Faith," "Fellowship," and "People of God." As a result Siegfried Schulz concludes, "About one thing, Mark leaves no one in doubt: the earthly Jesus had during his lifetime not founded any community. Mark had decisively refused to anticipate the Matthean construction of history."[247] Although Mark describes the disciples and crowds as following Jesus, it is not permissible, according to Schulz, to claim that Jesus established a community during his lifetime.

In my opinion, this interpretation of Mark's Gospel is inadequate. Jesus' proclamation of God's reign should be seen in the context of how Mark interprets it and places it within his overall theological vision. Moreover, Mark's Gospel with its eschatological texts should not be interpreted in terms of forms without taking into account the social context of Mark's theological vision and its function within the community, for Mark's interpretation of the kingdom proclamation is a function of his understanding of the Christian community and its relation to Jesus.[248] If the eschatological vision is viewed exclusively as expectation of an imminent end without taking into account the intention, context, and function of such a vision, then it might be legitimate, as some have concluded, to claim that Jesus gathered the disciples in order to prepare for an interim community, but that Jesus did not establish a new community. The new community is only a post-Easter creation of the Spirit.

Recently sociological studies of millenarian groups have shown that a community's self-understanding and its eschatological vision are correlative.[249] Eschatological vision and self-constitution do not contrast with each other, but are intrinsically bound together and specify each other. The eschatological vision determines the constitution of the community, forms its concrete existence, and determines its social praxis. The social praxis and the self-constitution likewise both express and contribute to the eschatological vision.

How then is early Christianity to be understood? Mark describes Jesus as constituting a new and radical family for which he is the model.[250] Two passages in Mark's Gospel are especially noteworthy: Mark 3:31–35 and Mark 10:29–30.[251] The first passage is at the end of chapter 3, a significant chapter because it lists the names and describes the calling and appointing of the Twelve. Verses 32–35 read:

> "Who are my mother and my brothers?" And looking around on those who sat about him, he said, "Here are my mother and my brother! Whoever does the will of God is my brother, and sister, and mother."

Doing the will of God is what is decisive for becoming a brother, sister, and mother of Jesus. Doing the will of God is what is decisive for becoming a member of the family of Jesus. Those called by Jesus form with Jesus a new family. According to Mark 10:29–31:

Jesus said, "Truly, I say to you, there is no one who has left house or brothers or sisters or mother or father or children or lands, for my sake and for the gospel, who will not receive a hundredfold now in this time, houses and brothers and sisters and mothers and children and lands, with persecution, and in the age to come eternal life. But many that are first will be last, and the last first."

In this statement, the old family is exchanged for a new family based on following Jesus and the gospel. Mark spells out quite consistently in his Gospel what it means to become a member of Jesus' family and to do the will of God: not only following Jesus even unto the suffering of the cross but also radically reversing one's values, standards, and order of life.

The central section of the Gospel, Mark 8:27–10:52, illustrates with reference to Peter that the disciples must learn to suffer as Jesus suffered.[252] Jesus corrects Peter's confession of faith and his understanding of discipleship. It is not enough to follow Jesus; it is also necessary to follow in the way of the cross. At the same time, Mark also emphasizes the reversal of values involved in the new family. Mark 10:17–28 underscores that it is not sufficient to follow the commandments: one must sell what one has and give to the poor. Riches and possessions are an obstacle to entry into the kingdom of God (vv. 23 and 25). The disciples must also reverse the roles: "But it shall not be so among you; but whoever would be great among you must be your servant, and whoever would be first among you must be the slave of all" (10:42–44). The disciples are not to be first but to be last and are to receive children in their midst (9:35–37), for children are to be admitted into God's kingdom and the disciples are "to receive the kingdom of God like a child" (10:15). Mark's Gospel proclaims that the new family of Jesus is constituted by a reversal of values: poverty, not riches; servantship, nor lordship, last and not first, children and not just adults.

All these images are important for they set the conditions of discipleship and the requirements for membership in Jesus' new family. Too often, Jesus is viewed in the light of previous models. He is depicted as a rabbi whose disciples are like a rabbi's disciples. He is a prophet whose disciples are like a prophet's school. The insight of reception hermeneutics that every genre breaks through its categories needs to be applied. Mark's Gospel employs the imagery of a new family with a radical reversal of power relations: not the power of money but the power of poverty, not the power of lordship but the power to serve. The order of power within society is overturned in the new family of Jesus.

Modern questions have been posed to Mark's Gospel. Did Jesus intend to found a Church or at least an interim community to prepare for the kingdom? Did the Church arise only after Easter as a creation and sacrament of the Spirit? Mark's Gospel provides an answer not to modern theological questions about founding a Church. Instead, Mark's Gospel proclaims that Jesus called persons into a new family of disciples and into a new community with a new set of values. Within this context, Mark's statements about the Twelve and Peter should be interpreted. The primary task of the Twelve is to be with Jesus and Peter must learn that to be a disciple is to suffer.

Mark's description of the new family of Jesus provides the context for his conception of the Twelve and their role. In taking over the Twelve from a pre-Marcan tradition in which they were understood as the representative group of the new People of God, Mark retains but modifies this eschatological function insofar as he translates it into a concrete historical task.[253] The Twelve have as their function to be with Jesus and to continue the saving work of Jesus. They receive from Jesus a share in his authority and therefore are able to perform exorcisms. These exorcisms are for Mark the characteristic sign of the eschatological event of Jesus' ministry. Since these exorcisms heal and liberate human beings, they are eschatological signs of the definitive victory of God in Jesus over the power of evil.

The Twelve, therefore, do the very same work that Jesus did. They exorcise, heal, and call people to conversion. They have the responsibility of performing the work of Jesus. Too often, fundamental theology has read the Markan scene about the Twelve as the institution of the twelve apostles and equated the Twelve with the apostolic college. Thereby, it has overlooked several important points of Mark's presentation. The Twelve have as a primary purpose to be with Jesus. This task or role of "being with Jesus" is not a role that is passed on to successive generations, but represents a unique and special role of the Twelve.[254] In addition, healing by exorcism is placed parallel with preaching as a primary task of the Twelve. And more importantly, Mark has, in addition to the group of the Twelve, the group of the "four" and the group of the "three"—classifications overlooked in traditional fundamental theology.

Mark does not insist on the Twelve as the narrow circle around Jesus, but quite often has the narrower circle of three (5:37; 9:2; 14:33).[255] Moreover, four persons are called in the very beginning of the public work of Jesus (1:16–20). They are named in 1:29 as Peter, Andrew, James, and John. They are singled out in Mark's editorial addition to the eschatological discourse in Mark 13 (see 13:3). Insofar as Mark has limited the instruction of the eschatological discourse to the four that were called first, Mark appears to point to the eschatological discourse as the "final revelation" of Jesus or as the "final testimony" of Jesus that will later be entrusted to all.

The group of three witnesses the miracle of the resurrection of the dead (5:37), the glorification of Jesus (9:2–8), and the scene in Gethsemane (14:32–32). In the scene in which the Twelve are named, not Peter's alone, but other names are also changed. So Mark 3:16–17: "Simon whom he surnamed Peter; James the son of Zebedee and John the brother of James, whom he surnamed Boanerges, that is, sons of thunder." Karl G. Reploh has suggested that the especial emphasis upon the three indicates the structure and order of Mark's community[256] whereas Günther Schmahl believes that the singling out of three indicates a theological motif, often encountered in the Old Testament, to emphasize their witness to the history and gospel of Jesus.[257]

Consequently, Mark's description presents the three and the four as the primary witnesses to the revelation of Jesus, whereas the Twelve have as their primary task to be with Jesus and to carry out his work. If the Church is to see its historical foundation in the Twelve, then this foundation is a foundation of those who receive their identity from being with Jesus and carrying out his praxis. The eschatological function of the Twelve in the tradition is modified to a historical task; this historical task provides the point of continuity for the Church's identity with Jesus.

The Way of the Church: Stages Not Institution

The same questions concerning Jesus and the origin of the Church are equally foreign to Luke's Gospel or the Acts. For as Gerhard Lohfink has observed: "One simply does not discover in Luke's Gospel any text that is constructed as referring to an *act of institution or an act of foundation.* Neither the choice of the Apostles nor their being Sent Out nor the Institution of the Last Supper nor the death on the cross, nor even the words of the Risen One after Easter have this function according to Luke."[258]

Instead of locating the institution or foundation of the Church in one act or at one time, Luke describes a process in which the Church emerged. According to Luke's description of this process, Jesus "had not founded a Church but played the decisive role in the process that led to the Church."[259] This process can according to one interpretation be divided into six stages, that is, six stages on the way to the emergence of Church. The first stage begins in the Old Testament as the history of the assembly in Israel—a history of the just as well as the unjust. In view of this history, Luke 1:5–2:40 points to Israel's expectation of redemption. The second stage is the preaching of John the baptizer and his assembly of disciples. John preaches to all of Israel, but is rejected by the leaders of Israel (Luke 7:29f.).

The third stage begins with Jesus. Just as John the baptizer called all of Israel to conversion, so too does Jesus now seek to assemble all of Israel. Luke locates Jesus in relation to his disciples, the people of Israel, and the leaders of Israel. During his earthly life, he instructs his disciples before the people of Israel. However, just as the leaders of Israel have rejected the prophets, so too do they reject Jesus (Luke 13:33–34). His disciples are loyal to Jesus; they even remain in Jerusalem during the time of his death and resurrection. His community represents the true Israel. When Jesus selected the Twelve from the disciples and sent them out, he sent them out not to establish a new Church or a special group, but to convert all of Israel.

The fourth stage entails the appearances of the Risen One and the new understanding of the apostles. Consequently, what constitutes apostleship now is the witness of the resurrection as well as the accompaniment of Jesus during his earthly ministry. The apostles proclaim not only the coming reign of God but also Jesus' life, death, and resurrection. At Pentecost the community of disciples receive the Holy Spirit and the fifth stage begins. The apostles preach to Israel and there is a great response until the story of Stephen. It is after his execution that the sixth stage begins: the acceptance of pagans. Now the other nations are admitted and they are preached to. After this acceptance Luke begins to use regularly the term Church that he had previously used only twice previously in Acts (Acts 5:11 and Acts 8:1–3).[260]

Luke's description of the emergence of the Church in stages and as a part of the ongoing process of salvation history sharply challenges the diverse systematic approaches within fundamental theology. Taking Matt 16:17–19 as a historical event of foundation at Caesarea Philippi, the traditional fundamental theology overlooked totally that Luke had a completely different version of the foundation of the Church. Contemporary approaches that stress the last supper or the appearance of Jesus to Peter as the foundational event also disregard Luke, for they fail to take into account the extent to which Luke describes the emergence of the Church after Easter as part of a gradual realization and reception of the meaning of Jesus. Luke's salvation-history approach shows that the Church's continuity with Jesus should not be understood as taking place once and for all, but as being a gradual process. The conclusion to be drawn from Luke is that the reception of the meaning and significance of Jesus should not be isolated to one moment in time, not even to a single point of the experience of Easter, but rather regarded as a process. Such a view would imply that the continuity between Jesus and the Church involves several elements—some present prior to Easter, others present only gradually after Easter.

If the continuity between the earthly Jesus and the Church is not drawn by Luke with the image of a single act of foundation, it is, however, explicated in Luke's conception of discipleship as the following of Jesus.[261] Although the notion of following Jesus is present already in Mark, it receives its special emphasis and distinctive interpretation in Luke. To be a disciple of Jesus is to follow Jesus on his path toward Jerusalem and to the Father. The sayings of Jesus on the need to follow him are sharpened in the Lukan redaction.

Luke's conception of discipleship is consonant with his understanding that God's revelation in Jesus does not take place in isolated acts, be they exorcisms and resuscitations or Jesus' own suffering and death, but rather takes place as parts of a pattern depicted as a way. In fact, Luke describes the primitive Palestinian community as "the Way" (*hē hodos*). He alone uses the term in an absolute sense. In addition, "way" is used syntagmatically in the phrases "a way of salvation" (Acts 16:17) and "the way of the Lord" (Acts 18:25) or "the way of God" (Acts 18:26). Although Luke most probably did not create the term "the Way" but took it over from pre-Lukan sources—as its use in the Qumran literature to designate the community indicates—his use of it does illustrate the Lukan ecclesiological motif of discipleship as the following of Jesus.

"Thus for Luke Christian discipleship is portrayed not only as the acceptance of a master's teaching, but as the identification of oneself with the master's way of life and destiny in an intimate, personal following of him."[262] The disciple is one who walks in the footsteps of Jesus and follows him. In this respect, it is the primary duty of the disciples to give testimony (*martyria*) to Jesus: they are to give testimony to all that Jesus did "in the country of the Jews and in Jerusalem" and to what God did in raising Jesus from the dead (Acts 10:39–41). The disciples' own way of life is described with a strong emphasis on the correct use of material possession and wealth.[263] No other evangelist preserves Jesus' sayings about the rich and the poor as strongly as Luke does. No one emphasizes as strongly as Luke the selling of "all they have" (Luke 18:22) and "leaving everything" to follow Jesus (Luke 5:11). In addition, Luke's presentation of John the baptizer's preaching has him urge people to share food and tunics with those needing them (3:11), and Luke gives an ideal description of the Jerusalem community as sharing its wealth in order to provide a model for others.

Further, Luke's view of the Twelve is distinctive.[264] He identifies the Twelve and the apostles. The criteria for membership in the Twelve (Acts 1:21–22) are also criteria for membership among the apostles (Luke 6:13). It is necessary to have accompanied Jesus throughout his life and it is necessary to give witness to his resurrection. The Twelve, therefore, provide the link between the earthly Jesus and the early Church. Nevertheless, after their symbolic function in relation to the community on Pentecost, their function is limited to supervising the appointment of the seven table-servers. After this, their role is no longer mentioned in Acts. Even for Luke, therefore, the Twelve do not serve as an apostolic college that has successors, but as a foundational link between the early Church and the earthly Jesus.

Luke's concretization of the relation between the earthly Jesus and the Church presents several elements of fundamental theological significance. The foundation of the Church is not the result of a single act of institution, but takes place through the gradual revelation of God. A continuity exists between the Church and Jesus insofar as it is the Church's task to give testimony to Jesus by following his way—a way involving the sharing of wealth and possessions. The Twelve (apostles) function as witnesses of Jesus' earthly way and his resurrection. Beyond their foundational function, they are given no concrete historical task that is to be passed on to others.

The Preeminent Disciple in the Community of Justice

Since Matt 16:17–19 has played such a significant role within controversial theology and fundamental theology, it is important to distinguish the ways the text can be approached.[265] The text can be approached from the perspective of current dogmatic and controversial debates. It can also be used to uncover biographical data about Peter and his possible role during Jesus' earthly ministry in order to secure a historical foundation for his role within the life of the early Church. Or the text can be viewed in the light of a reconstructive hermeneutics that asks just what does Matthew's portrayal of Peter reveal about Jesus and the early Christian community. Does it exhibit a reception of Jesus providing a vision and praxis that can ground the Christian faith not only in Jesus but also in the community of disciples?

Matthew's Gospel is indeed distinctive among the Gospels in that, as Jack Dean Kingsbury observes, "in contradistinction to both Mark and Luke, it is within Jesus' earthly ministry that Matthew locates the foundation of the 'church' (16:18, 18:17)."[266] Matthew alone of the four Gospels uses the term ecclesia. Moreover, it is in Matthew that the "special pre-eminence of Peter then is not founded upon a special manifestation of the exalted—who originally and supposedly from heaven—gives a special commission, but rather upon the fact of Peter's witness to the earthly activity of Jesus and indeed especially to Jesus' ethical instructions."[267] The foundation of the Church during the earthly life of Jesus and the promise of the keys to Peter is contained only in Matthew's Gospel.

Therefore, when foundational theology takes a reconstructive hermeneutical approach, its primary questions are not the dogmatic or the historical but rather the hermeneutical questions. What vision of the Christian community and its relation to Jesus does the Matthean text disclose? Why is the promise to Peter and the foundation of the Church by the earthly Jesus central to Matthew's Gospel? Why is the term ecclesia taken over from the pre-Pauline traditions and from the Pauline writings and inserted within this central "Petrine pericope"? Why does Matthew's Gospel offer a vision of continuity between the Church and the earthly Jesus that differs from the Markan and Lukan conceptions? Does Matthew's Gospel offer a vision that grounds our faith in the Matthean community's reception of the meaning and praxis of Jesus?

Matthew's guiding purpose, it has been suggested, is precisely to show how his community has an unbroken continuity of praxis with the earthly Jesus. For the sake of this continuity, he portrays Jesus as founding the Church during his earthly ministry. Moreover, it is Jesus as God's revelation who teaches the community his Father's will and who is thereby the source of the community's doctrine and praxis. The key to Matthew is the teaching and praxis that he seeks to articulate in his portrayal of the continuity between the Church and the earthly ministry of Jesus.

This key can be found in 5:17–48 that contains Matthew's programmatic statements about law and morality: the Sermon on the Mount and the six conclusions or applications expressed in the antitheses.[268] In 5:20 Matthew proclaims outright: "Unless your righteousness [justice] exceeds that of the scribes and Pharisees, you will not enter the kingdom of God." Although commonly translated as "righteousness," justice is the more accurate reading, as John Meier notes.[269] In Matthew it has two basic meanings. It refers to God's saving activity (5:6 and 6:33) and it also describes the Christian praxis of doing God's will, the authentic Christian life-activity. True discipleship in justice is to overflow in doing God's will so the orthopraxis of the Christian disciples exhibits the orthodoxy of the better justice taught by Jesus as God's will. Günther Bornkamm observes that how consistently Matthew "orientates everything he has to say about the essence of discipleship around the law and righteousness is shown, finally, by the concepts *dikaios* and *dikaiosune*."[270] Jesus is justice (27:19) and he fulfills all justice (3:15). Justice is the comprehensive characteristic of the piety of the disciples (6:1) whose persecution for Jesus' sake is equivalent to persecution for justice's sake (5:10f.).

Matthew's emphasis on justice stands out in relation to the Gospels of Mark and Luke.[271] The concept is already present in the Old Testament (Deut 33:21) and in late Judaism (T. Dan. 6:10)—and especially in wisdom literature (Pss 33 and 36).[272] Although the notion of hungering after justice stems from wisdom literature, its presence within Matthew's Gospel along with the emphasis on justice stems from Matthean redaction. All references in Matthew (3:15; 5:6, 10, 20; 6:1, 33; 21:32) are editorial additions.[273] This justice, however, is not simply ethical behavior; as in the Hebrew Scriptures and the wisdom literature, it is a doing of the will of God. The better justice demanded reflects a life-praxis that expresses God's law and corresponds to God's kingdom. Hence, the doing of justice as the will of God is the criterion for the new community (7:21; 12:50; 21:31). Admission into the kingdom of Heaven depends upon justice toward the least of the brothers and sisters.

Matthew's emphasis upon justice as doing the will of God is correlated with his christology and ecclesiology. Jesus' earthly function is to interpret the law. He appears as a second Moses not in antithesis but in correspondence.[274] He is seen as the royal Son of God who perfectly knows God's will and, therefore, not only fulfills justice but also teaches it. Indeed, his principal activity during his earthly ministry is seen as the teaching of God's will and justice. When, therefore, Matt 16:17–19 puts the saying about the revelation of Jesus as God's Son to Peter in the context of the promise of the keys, the text is to be interpreted in the light of the whole Gospel's emphasis upon God's justice and will. This context likewise explains why Matthew does not relate Peter primarily to the heavenly and Risen Christ, but to the earthly activity of Jesus.

Therefore, Peter's role in relation to the rest of the disciples and to the power of the keys must be seen in the light of Matthew's basic motif that Jesus is the revelation of God's justice.[275] In the Gospel

Peter is evidently depicted as the exemplary disciple—with all of a disciple's distinctive characteristics, both positive and negative. He is called with the others to become a disciple of Jesus (cf. 4:18–20 with 4:20–22 and 9:9); he exhibits "little faith" in crying out to be saved (cf. 14:30–31 to 8:25–26). Both Peter and the disciples make known their faith, receive divine revelation, and have the power of binding and loosing (i.e., especially in regard to right teaching of God's will and justice). Yet both also fail to watch in time of trial and temptation.

But Peter also appears as a spokesperson for the rest of the disciples. He speaks out. He asks about the temple taxes (17:28–29); he asks how often one must forgive (18:21); he requests an explanation of a parable (15:55); he complains of having left everything for the sake of Jesus (19:27); and on the Mount of Transfiguration he speaks out for James and John (17:1, 4). But in addition to his role as spokesperson, Peter is preeminent and is called the first of the apostles (10:2). This preeminence is based, according to Matthew, upon the earthly ministry of Jesus and not upon the resurrection appearances.[276] Where Paul lists Peter as the first witness of the resurrection in 1 Cor 15:5, Matthew has Jesus appear not first to Peter, but to the eleven apostles together—he even eliminates the weak reference in Mark 16:7. Peter's status as "the first" of the disciples stems from having been the first disciple to be called. In his lists of the apostles, Matthew makes sure that they follow the order of his description of the successive call of the first four.

When Peter confesses his faith in Jesus as "Son of the living God," he is acting as spokesperson *and* as preeminent disciple. His preeminent role as the first disciple should not be played off against his role as spokesperson and exemplary disciple. The confession that Peter makes to Jesus in Matt 16:15–16 is the same confession that had already been made by the disciples. In 14:33 the disciples in the boat have already confessed him as the Son of God and have worshiped him.[277] Therefore, Peter's faith is not given to him, for the others have been described as having that faith. His faith does not stand out in contrast to that of the other disciples, but exemplifies it.

Yet Peter does indeed appear to be distinctive insofar as he is not only promised the power of binding and loosing (16:19bc), as the other disciples are (18:18), but he is also promised the keys of the kingdom of heaven (19a) and is called the rock on which the Church will be built (16:18). Both verses are difficult to interpret. Nevertheless, within the overall emphasis in Matthew upon Jesus' teaching of God's will and justice, the meaning becomes evident. Two other verses are best brought to bear on the interpretation of the promise of the keys.[278] In Matt 23:13 ("But woe to you, scribes and Pharisees, hypocrites! Because you shut the kingdom of heaven against humans; for you neither enter yourselves, nor allow those who enter to go in") the images of locking (*kleiō*) and of the kingdom of heaven are brought together. Matt 23:13f goes against the Pharisaic interpretation of justice as is clear from the reference to their false use of teaching authority (Matt 23:1–4) and the emphasis upon a better justice (Matt 5:20). Peter's power of the keys, therefore, refers to teaching authority. It is Peter's task to teach Jesus' interpretation of God's will and justice so that others, for whom the praxis of this will and justice is a condition, can enter into the kingdom of heaven.

Likewise, the verses on binding and loosing (Matt 16:19bc) most probably refer to teaching authority.[279] They are therefore to be considered a parallel explication of the verse on the keys. Consequently, the power of teaching reflected in 16:19 is also present in 18:18 where not just Peter, but all have the power of loosing and binding. The authority of teaching and the faith of the community is exemplarily present in Peter, the first apostle and the spokesperson for the others.

The verse describing Peter as the rock upon which the Church will be built should also not be interpreted in a way that unduly separates Peter from the rest of the disciples. The image of foundation stone is a common image in the later writings of the New Testament.[280] Its use by second or third generation Christians, however, was not limited to Peter. Ephesians refers to the Church as the household of God that is "built upon the foundation of the apostles and prophets, Christ Jesus himself being the cornerstone" (2:20). Revelation describes the wall of the New Jerusalem as having "twelve foundations, and on them the twelve names of the twelve apostles of the Lamb" (21:14). Gal 2:9 points to James and Cephas and John as the pillars. In 1 Tim 3:15 the Church itself is the pillar and foundation of truth. In view of this usage of the foundation in reference to other apostles and to the Church itself, it seems best to interpret Peter as the rock upon which the Church will be built not in isolation from the other apostles, but precisely in his function as the exemplary apostle and as the spokesperson for them.[281]

Several conclusions can be drawn from this interpretation of Matthew's vision of the relation between Jesus and the Church and, in particular, of the crucial verses of chapter 16. First, it appears as if the apologetical reading of the passage has tended, on the one hand, to overemphasize the singularity of Peter or, on the other, to eliminate it. For example, the authors of *Peter in the New Testament* maintain that Peter cannot be seen "simply as the spokesman of a common opinion"; whereas Kingsbury, denying exactly such a view, argues for Peter as a "typical" disciple in Matt 16:13–20.[282] Obviously, the faith that Peter expresses had been confessed by others. But yet as the "first apostle," the first called, the exemplary disciple and the spokesperson for others, he was not simply one among many. Instead, he has a preeminence to teach God's will and justice, revealed in Christ and at the center of the community's life-praxis.[283] His preeminence as a spokesperson and as the first to be called does give him a "primacy," but it is a primacy to speak out of his faith and the community's faith that God's will and justice have been made known to Christ.[284]

Second, my interpretation focused upon the Matthean vision rather than upon a historical demonstration. As such it differs not only from the traditional but also from contemporary fundamental theological approaches insofar as they seek to go behind the text to uncover a historical core as the foundational element. Instead of inquiring how the vision and praxis disclosed in the text provides the foundation for faith linking the Church to Jesus, these historical approaches get lost in a labyrinth of speculative historical questions. For instance, how does one balance out the high number of semitisms that are perhaps indices of antiquity against the Hellenistic concepts that possibly reflect the theological issues of third-generation Jewish Hellenistic Christians at Antioch?[285] Questions like this can be hypothetically and imaginatively answered at best, but never with definitive certainty.

Moreover, these historical approaches contradict the Matthean text. If they follow the exegesis of Rudolf Bultmann and argue from the literary form of the text as an Easter appearance narrative that the foundation of the Church is based on a conversion experience of Peter (Schillebeeckx) or the appearance to Peter (O'Collins), they overlook the fact that the Matthean text excludes such a first appearance to Peter. If they follow the exegesis of Oscar Cullmann and see Jesus laying the foundations for an interim community at the last supper (Schmaus, Küng in *The Church*, McBrien), they overlook the theological vision of Matthew that seeks to link Peter and the Church to the earthly ministry of Jesus.[286]

Third, Matthew struggles to present a vision that draws the lines of continuity between the earthly Jesus and the Church amid contemporary conflict over the life-praxis of the community. He most probably argues against a double front: Hellenistic Christianity and Pharisaic Judaism.[287] Where Hellenistic Christianity viewed the law as being without validity and saving significance, Pharisaic Judaism upheld it. Matthew uses theological categories from Hellenistic Christianity to criticize Pharisaic Judaism and uses the theological tradition of Pharisaic Judaism to criticize the Hellenistic abrogation of the law. The community of Matthew is caught in the tension between its continuity with Israel and its separation from it.[288] Within this tension, Matthew explicates the justice of the Christian community as a "better justice," and yet shows that Christ is the fulfillment, not the abrogation of the Torah. He describes a difference within the identity and an identity within the difference.

In the context of this encounter of Hellenistic Christianity and Pharisaic Judaism, Matthew selects the pre-Pauline and Pauline term ecclesia, with its political and religious associations, to emphasize that the Church is to be a community overflowing with a better justice based on Jesus who came to fulfill and perfect. The notions associating the justice of God's community with the conditions for admission into the kingdom come to expression in Matthew's Gospel, and their full theological development is his vision of how the meaning of Christianity relates to the meaning of Jesus.[289]

Matthew's Gospel provides us with a vision of his community and its self-understanding in relation to the earthly Jesus.[290] This vision crisscrosses but does not totally correlate with the questions of modern fundamental theology. The question whether at Caesarea Philippi Jesus promised the papal primacy to Peter is, in that form, manifestly anachronistic; hence, not answered. Nevertheless, Matthew does strongly stress that Peter was the "first" of the apostles and had an exemplary authority in regard to teaching, an authority associated with his faith, but not separated from the rest of the community. If modern fundamental theology asks whether Jesus with his eschatological consciousness could have instituted a Church, Matthew's Gospel does not address that question. Yet in his struggle against the eschatological and apocalyptic emphasis of the false prophets and teachers within his community,[291] Matthew answers, in his Gospel, that God's will and justice, not apocalypticism, constitute the essence of Jesus' message.

Although historical-critical research wavers between assigning the traditions behind Matt 16:17–19 to an early Palestinian tradition of a christophany narrative or to an Antiochian theological interpretation of such a narrative, what does remain evident is that Matthew draws clearly the lines of continuity between the earthly Jesus and the community. It is not apocalypticism, but rather the law and the better justice that provides this continuity. A community facing major dangers from within, from false teachers and false prophets, is forced to deal with right teaching and the foundation of this right teaching. It therefore displays a view of Jesus that emphasizes his teaching of God's will and justice and Peter's role in expressing the faith of the community in this teaching and in guaranteeing its continuance. Matthew's Gospel, therefore, offers us a concretization of the relation between Jesus and the Church that provides a vision of Christian and ecclesial existence, and this vision is a foundation for faith in Jesus and for the life-praxis of Christian community.

Calling to the Discipleship of Faith

John's Gospel especially stands in the crossfire between modern historical scholarship and traditional fundamental theology. Whereas the latter argued from John 21 that the actual conferral of the primacy took place after Easter and the more contemporary fundamental theology saw the Johannine accounts as the more "historical version," historical criticism has pointed out that John 21 is a later editorial addition by an ecclesiastical editor. One line of interpretation even maintains that the Gospel itself has little room for the Church and is indeed individualistic, even antiecclesial in its theological affirmations. To search John's Gospel for a concretization of the relation between Jesus and the Church is to enter a battleground already strewn with the corpses of fallen hypotheses. Questions regarding sacraments, church office, Peter, and so on in John's Gospel are all highly controversial. For the purposes of the relation between Jesus and the Church, it suffices to focus on John's interpretation of Jesus' call to discipleship and the meaning of discipleship.

No other event seems more historically secure than Jesus calling the disciples. Critics have denied the resurrection of Jesus, the promise of primacy to Peter, and the institution of the Eucharist, but none has denied that Jesus assembled disciples. An examination of the Gospel accounts, however, shows that this "historical foundation" does not exist independently of interpretation, but only as mirrored in and through diverse interpretations. The calling of disciples is depicted within the Gospel traditions not merely as a bare historical fact, but as an event with theological significance. Jesus' assembling of disciples is, therefore, foundational, not insofar as the calling is an incontestable historical event, but rather insofar as the de facto historical calling is displayed as a theological vision of the relation between the disciples and Jesus.

The Johannine description of the calling of the disciples differs considerably from the synoptic accounts.[292] The Fourth Gospel describes the first disciples as former followers of John the baptizer and has the calling take place in Jordan rather than in Galilee. In addition, Andrew, and not Peter, is the first disciple called. Moreover, where the synoptics have a direct calling of the disciples by the earthly Jesus, the Johannine account relates an indirect calling alongside of the direct calling. Although his double calling is in line with the Johannine technique of double narration, it also brings to the fore a theological point. John's account describes first of all the testimony of John the baptizer to Jesus, and he places it parallel to Jesus' own calling. By making both accounts parallel, John underscores the contemporaneity of the baptizer to Jesus while, at the same time, stressing that he is inferior to Jesus. The newly won disciples of Jesus confess Jesus as the Messiah and call other persons to discipleship.

This indirect calling leads to an encounter with Jesus and to the confession of faith in him. In John's account, Andrew, Simon Peter's brother, goes to Simon Peter and tells him that they have found Christ (v. 42). Only then does Simon Peter go to Jesus and confess Jesus as the Christ. Peter's confession takes place after Andrew's and at this time—not later in the ministry—is his name changed to Peter. An analysis of the text indicates that whereas in verse 43 Jesus takes the initiative and calls his disciples, in verses 41, 42a, and 45f. it is one of the disciples who calls. Although scholars might debate in which verses lies the tradition and in which the editorial redaction,[293] it is obvious that the existent text combines the motifs of the calling by others and the calling by Jesus. The result of both is a direct encounter with Jesus and a confession of faith.

The Fourth Gospel mirrors a situation in which a direct discipleship has been replaced by a calling through others. Similarly, a discipleship based on the community between the disciples and the earthly Jesus has been replaced by a community of discipleship based upon the call of others. It is this situation that provides the Gospel with the opportunity to theologically elaborate the relation between faith in Jesus and discipleship. John's Gospel does not describe discipleship in terms of Mark's new family with its new values or in terms of Matthew's Sermon on the Mount with its radical justice or in terms of Luke's following in the footsteps of Jesus.

In addition, the Gospel does not even use the term apostle as a title—except for one nontechnical use to mean "messenger." Even though it presupposes the existence of the Twelve (6:67, 70), John's Gospel has nothing about the constituting and sending out of the Twelve. These differences do not mean that John has no sense of discipleship and of community. Instead, he develops the notion of discipleship within the horizon of faith in Jesus. Discipleship itself is thereby given an ecclesial significance insofar as "the notion itself is broken open, expanded, and adapted for a new application."[294]

This expansion of the concept of discipleship becomes evident if one examines how John not only interrelates discipleship and faith, but also uses the images of the model shepherd and the vine with its branches to illustrate the disciple's unity and community with Jesus. In addition, he applies the concept of discipleship within the particular post-Easter situation of the community through his use and interpretation of the Paraclete, the Beloved Disciple, and Peter.

The relation between faith and discipleship is central not only in major passages but also in key images. Whereas the synoptic Gospels mainly refer faith to miracles, John relates faith to discipleship. Faith is the fundamental decision toward Jesus as God's revealer. Faith is associated with seeing, knowing, and following Jesus. "The believing in Jesus is in the Fourth Gospel identified with discipleship; the notion of discipleship and the christologically conceived formula 'to believe' mutually explain each other."[295] The story of the Samaritan woman illustrates this mutuality. On the basis of her testimony, the Samaritans begin to believe in Jesus and come to him (John 4:30, 39–42).

The image of the model shepherd and the flock of sheep (John 10:1–18, 26–30) likewise displays the intertwining of discipleship and faith. The central statement: "I am the good shepherd; I know my own and my own know me, as the Father knows me and I know the father; and I lay down my life for the sheep." The mutual knowledge of the Father and the Son is parallel to the mutual knowledge between flock and shepherd. The shepherd knows his sheep and calls them by name; they know him and follow him. Although this mutual knowledge and calling by name is sometimes taken as an indication of the individualism of John's Gospel—even for some Catholic scholars[296]—the overall image and connotation is clearly communal. The reference in 10:16 to other sheep designates not only the community established by the shepherd but, as Ferdinand Hahn suggests, points to a future unity that should prevail.[297] The reference in 11:52 "to gather into one the children of God who are scattered abroad" likewise underscores the gathering leading to unification.[298]

The image of the vine and the branches in John 15:1–17 is also open to an ecclesial interpretation.[299] Verses 1–8 describe the Father's relation to the vine and its branches, whereas verses 9–17 explain Christ as the vine and the believers as the branches. Insofar as the believers are one with Christ, they bear fruit. This imagery has also been interpreted as a form of individualism or personal mysticism that contrasts with an authentic notion of the Church. But such inter-pretations amount to a "reading into" the text. Why should Paul's notion of the Church with its diverse individual charisms be less individualistic than John's emphasis upon the oneness of the branches with the vine? To argue that the symbol of the vine excludes church office because all the branches are directly united with Christ is a speculative deduction. The evangelist has depicted and illustrated the relation between Jesus and his disciples with a metaphor that discloses how the disciples are not just related to Jesus, but are re-lated to him as the very source and root of their new life.

The oneness between Jesus and the disciples is based upon the oneness of Jesus with the Father.[300] Yet Jesus' oneness with the Father is the basis of his mission or of his "being sent." "The Father who sent me" runs through the discourse of Jesus. Because Jesus is one with the Father, he is sent into the world and he performs the work of the Father in the world. Oneness and mission are in John two sides of the same coin. Consequently, although John does not have the ex-plicit sending out of the apostles as do the synoptic Gospels, it would be false to conclude that he has no sense of mission. Just as the branches bear fruit (especially love) because they are one with the vine, so too do they continue the work of Jesus, suffer persecution, and give testimony. Even considering the differences among the syn-optic accounts, one can concur with Hahn's observation: "From the thought of the mission of Jesus, it is then possible in the Fourth Gospel to speak of the participation of the disciples in Jesus' task as we know it from the Synoptic tradition. Objectively speaking, genu-ine Jesus tradition is preserved that has been made christologically and ecclesiologically significant."[301]

John's conception of the relation between discipleship and faith is further elaborated in his theological interpretation of the situation of his community, not only as a post-Easter situation but also as that of a later generation. The time of seeing and believing is over.[302] After Jesus' death, the time of believing without seeing has begun. A dis-continuity exists between the present time of the community and the time of Jesus and the first disciples. Nevertheless, despite this discon-tinuity, an even more fundamental and basic continuity exists. Al-though faith in the earthly Jesus was associated with a seeing, faith in Jesus was not based upon sight alone because his divine sonship was inaccessible to sight alone. Faith was necessary to see the true mean-ing of Jesus as the Son of God. The miraculous works and words are not so much proofs as they are signs of Jesus' unity with God. If the tradition and sources were interested in their wondrous nature, the

Johannine redaction underscores the necessity of faith to see the meaning of these signs.

This deeper insight into the unity between Jesus and God communicated by the Spirit is necessary not only during the earthly ministry but also after Easter.[303] What the Spirit communicated during the life and ministry of Jesus, the Paraclete does after Jesus is gone. The Paraclete has the same function after Jesus' death as the Spirit had before.[304] The Paraclete functions as the presence of Jesus when Jesus is absent. John's theological conception of the Paraclete is his affirmation that "with the departure of the earthly Jesus from this world the witness to Christ is not at an end but that the response to this ongoing witness to Christ is just as decisive for the ultimate destiny of those who hear it as the relation to the message Jesus was for the contemporaries of Jesus."[305]

John uses the Paraclete to legitimate the Johannine message.[306] The pre-Easter tradition is accessible only through the Paraclete. Even though he does not have Luke's salvation-history approach, for John the time of the Church is—even much more than for Luke—the time of the Spirit or the Paraclete. Jesus returns as present in the Spirit. Since the Paraclete does not teach anything new but interprets Jesus, the earthly tradition is declared normative but mediated through the interpretation of the Spirit. This function of mediating between the present and the past is performed not only by the Paraclete but also by the Beloved Disciple.[307] So much do they have the same function that the suggestion has been made—but generally not accepted— that the Beloved Disciple and the Paraclete are the same.[308] The Beloved Disciple, appearing in the second part of John's Gospel, may be a historical person and the source of the community's tradition, but he nevertheless has a symbolic function as the ideal disciple.[309] The Beloved Disciple is present during all the crucial events: last supper, trial, passion, crucifixion, and resurrection.

In John's Gospel proper (excluding chap. 21), the Beloved Disciple and Peter are contrasted. At the last supper, the Beloved Disciple rests on Jesus' breast, whereas Peter is at a distance. Therefore, Peter does not address Jesus, but has to request the Beloved Disciple to do so. During the arrest and passion, where Peter denies Jesus, the Beloved Disciple stands beneath the cross. On Easter morning the Beloved Disciple wins the race with Peter to the grave, but he allows Peter to enter first. Yet nothing is said about Peter's belief, whereas the Beloved Disciple sees the empty grave and believes. The Beloved Disciple therefore represents the ideal disciple: he is close to Jesus, he is faithful to Jesus, and upon seeing the empty grave, he believes.

Perhaps the Beloved Disciple symbolizes the ideal post-Easter disciple who manifests love, fidelity, and belief. In contrast, Peter has all the frailty of the disciples during the earthly ministry, their questioning, denials, and seeing but not believing.[310]

This contrast between Peter and the Beloved Disciple within the Gospel provides a background to the interpretation of chapter 21—the chapter that alongside of Matt 16:17–19 formed the crux of the historical demonstration within traditional fundamental theology and which has been even more emphasized within those contemporary fundamental theological approaches stressing a post-Easter foundation of the Church. Because of stylistic differences—not to mention theological differences—this chapter is almost universally considered a supplement to the completed Gospel. It describes a scene in which six disciples go fishing along with Simon Peter, and at his invitation. They have caught nothing that night. In the morning Jesus standing on the beach urges them to cast their nets. No one recognizes Jesus but the Beloved Disciple. After catching the fish, they share the bread and fish with Jesus, who passes it out to them, and they recognize him as the Risen One. After breakfast, Simon Peter is asked by Jesus to confess his love three times. And Jesus each time asks him to feed or to tend his sheep. The Beloved Disciple is not asked to confess his love—for he has not denied Jesus, but he is also not given the commission to feed the sheep. Jesus predicted the martrydom of Peter, but states that the Beloved Disciple will remain until he comes—an ambiguous statement that is given the clarification that it does not mean he will not die. It is therefore assumed that the Beloved Disciple has also died at the time of the writing of chapter 21.

The seven disciples (including Peter) are described as fishing and as having success only after the appearance of Jesus. Most probably, this story reflects their roles as founders of Christian communities.[311] Although the chapter still emphasizes the special role of the Beloved Disciple (he first recognizes Jesus; and his future is foretold), Peter's pastoral role over all of Christianity appears to be acknowledged in that he alone is given the commission to feed and tend Jesus' sheep. The chapter, therefore, acknowledges the Petrine pastoral role; at the same time, underscores the significance of the Beloved Disciple. Since this chapter portrays Peter in a more favorable light than the rest of the Gospel, and since it acknowledges Peter's role as shepherd of Jesus' sheep, it is probable that this chapter seeks to modify the image of Peter portrayed in the rest of the Gospel by acknowledging and underscoring his pastoral role. At the same time, it points out the special position of the Beloved Disciple; thereby, it makes an appeal to the communities more directly under the influence of Petrine traditions to acknowledge the Johannine interpretation of the significance of Jesus.

If, therefore, the fundamental theological question whether Jesus founded the Church is put to John's Gospel, an answer is given that crisscrosses but does not correlate with the question. Jesus is seen as the foundation of the Church, but the foundation is given a theological rather than historical treatment. The synoptics described Jesus as establishing the Twelve, sending them out, instituting baptism and the Eucharist. John's Gospel has none of these explicit foundational actions. Jesus does call disciples, but the call of others to discipleship also leads to an encounter with Jesus. Discipleship and faith are interrelated and the historical scenes are replaced by the metaphors of the model shepherd with his flock and the vine with its branches. Even the historical account of calling disciples is placed within the theological framework of John's conception of faith and discipleship.

Although there is no evidence for an explicit institution of apostolic foundation, sacramental practice, and church offices in John's Gospel, they should not necessarily be excluded from the Johannine community. It is not just that the argument from silence should not be allowed to carry too much weight; rather, it is important to perceive the uniqueness of the Johannine conception. "The image of Jesus instituting sacraments as a final action tends to identify them with the sphere of church life, while for John the sacraments are continuations of the power that Jesus manifested *during his ministry* when he opened the eyes of the blind (baptism as enlightenment) and fed the hungry (eucharist as food)."[312] Likewise, John's imagery and theological emphasis should not be interpreted as antiecclesial as is often done,[313] but should be seen as reflecting his emphasis on what is foundational: the living presence of Jesus through the Paraclete.

It is this foundational conception that makes John's Gospel so challenging for present as well as for past Christianity. The Gospel challenges modern Catholic ecclesiology because it does not underscore the special presence of the Spirit to the office of apostles or their successors. Instead, Jesus promises the Spirit directly to all the disciples. The Gospel also challenges modern Protestant theology because John does not bind the Spirit to the present word—as the exegetes Ernst Käsemann and Eduard Schweizer maintain—but the testimony of the Spirit is a testimony to the tradition.[314] The Gospel also challenges traditional Christianity for, as contemporary scholarship has shown, the Johannine Christians were defining themselves over against several different groups, among them Jewish Christians, apostolic Christians, Johannine secessionists—so much so that it has been necessary to show that the Johannine community was not an exclusive sect,[315] but sought to remain in continuity with other Christian groups, and even with those communities rooted in the Petrine tradition—as chapter 21 shows.

If traditional and modern fundamental theology found in John's Gospel the confirmation after Easter of the promise recorded in Matt 16:17–19, the crucial contemporary exegetical issue is whether John's Gospel contradicts the institutional primacy of Peter, undercuts the charism of office, and precludes a communal understanding of Christianity. Although my interpretation of John's concretization of the relation between Jesus and the Church has sought to counter such views, obviously the way John's Gospel draws the lines of continuity between Jesus and the community of disciples differs from other concretizations of that relationship. Whereas this difference theologically relates faith in Jesus and discipleship, it offers at the same time a challenge—a challenge well formulated by Raymond E. Brown:

> The presence in our scriptures of a disciple whom Jesus loved more than he loved Peter is an eloquent commentary on the relative value of the church office. The authoritative office is necessary because of a task to be done and unity to be preserved, but the scale of power in various offices is not necessarily the scale of Jesus' esteem and love. . . . The greatest dignity to be striven for is neither papal, episcopal, nor priestly; the greatest dignity is that of belonging to the community of the beloved disciple of Jesus.[316]

This is the challenge of John's vision, but this vision does not stand alone. It must be placed alongside other New Testament testimonies of the relation between Jesus and the Church in a foundational theology that elaborates the diversity of its foundations.

Chapter 6

The Church and the Task of Foundational Theology

The above sketch of the diverse concretizations of the relation between the Church and Jesus shows how the diverse interpretative receptions of the meaning of Jesus portray this relation as an issue of identity. The increased temporal distance to Jesus led to the need not only to draw the lines of continuity between the earthly Jesus and the Church but to draw these lines of continuity as a problem of ecclesial religious identity.

In the pre-Pauline traditions and in the Pauline writings, the early Christian communities understood themselves as the "Church of God." Although their self-understanding as the Church of God stood in continuity with Jewish traditions, they also understood the distinctiveness of their existence, for their foundation was in Christ by whom they were made holy and just. The Pauline writings draw out this distinctiveness by describing the individual community as the Body of Christ. The Gospels, written later than the Pauline letters, also draw out the lines of continuity, but they do so not in the form of a historical demonstration, but rather in the form of a historical theological description of Christian identity. Mark's Gospel shows that the Twelve had the function to be with Jesus and to perform his healings. Jesus' call to discipleship is the call to a new family with a new set of values. Luke describes discipleship as following in the way of Jesus. The Church, therefore, was not founded in a single institutional act, but gradually begins to discover its own way as it understands through the Spirit the implications of its calling. In the face of the tensions between the life-praxis of its justice and the traditional expectations, Matthew's Gospel points back to the teaching of the earthly Jesus and to Peter as the first and exemplary apostle possessing teaching authority concerning the right understanding of justice. John's Gospel shows the interrelationship between faith and discipleship within the context of the tradition coming from the Beloved Disciple and its interpretation of Jesus.

The reconstruction of diverse New Testament testimonies showed that the Gospels depicted the relation between Jesus and the Church in the categories of religious identity and historical continuity. The questions of modern fundamental theology were found to crisscross but not to correlate with the theological interests of these writings. Questions of the institution of the Church, the existence of an apostolic college, and the role of Peter, if applied to the Gospel writings, received not only diverse answers, but answers not completely correlative to the question asked. Likewise, the modern fundamental theological attempts to demonstrate historically that Jesus instituted a Church at Caesarea Philippi, at the last supper, at a post-Easter appearance or only laid the foundations for a post-Easter creation of the Church by God's Spirit, when confronted with the Gospel traditions, discovers that these traditions do not give a single unified answer to the historical issue, but provide diverse conceptions of the interrelation between historical continuity and theological identity. Any one of the proposed solutions in modern fundamental theology, if isolated and taken as a single definite answer, stands in opposition to certain New Testament traditions.

This diversity within the New Testament writings and this difference between the modern fundamental theological problem and that of the New Testament writings themselves makes more acute the three reasons why fundamental theology has concentrated on the relation between Jesus and the Church. Fundamental theology sought to show that the Church was not merely an object of faith but that its divine institution could ground Christian faith; it attempted to legitimate a particular church order; and it sought to specify the religious identity of ecclesial Christianity. From the perspective of our previous hermeneutical principles and analysis, each of these problems needs to be taken up, but in the reverse order and under the titles of continuity and identity, divine institution, and ground of faith.

Continuity and Identity

It is incontestable that after the death of Jesus a community emerged that, through its confession of him, gradually and with increasing clarity distinguished itself from Judaism. Historically, the Church followed the life and death of Jesus, so that a chronological continuity between Jesus and the Church exists. Thus, the emergence of the Church as a social institution can be viewed according to sociological principles. Daniel Harrington suggests that Max Weber's "routinization of charisma" provides an apt category, and argues that "in the instance of early Christianity the charismatic personality, teaching, and activity of Jesus formed the impulse that led to 'routinization' by the early church over a fairly long period of time."[317] Others would cite the categories of social discontent, economic deprival, and cognitive dissonance applied to millenarian movements to show how disappointment of initial expectations leads to the formation of community.[318] Still others would suggest that Jesus' calling of disciples provides the necessary historical continuity for the existence of the Church.[319] But neither historical nor social continuity constitutes a continuity of identity. The theological identity and continuity between Jesus and the Church is more than mere historical or sociological continuity based upon chronological contiguity or social development.

Ultimately, fundamental theology must resolve the nature of this continuity. Traditional fundamental theology sought to base it upon the explicit intention and will of Jesus as founder. Existential fundamental theology established a functional existential equivalence between Christ and the Church. Contemporary fundamental theology uses the categories of foundation or creation to underscore the continuity or to point to the discontinuity.

The problem of the continuity between the Church and Jesus remains acute because the general exegetical consensus is still often summed up in traditional terminology of intentionality. Aelred Cody expresses this consensus by concluding, "one cannot prove, with critical methods that he [Jesus] did found the Church, or that he did intend to found the Church," so that "the question whether or not Jesus before his death and exaltation founded the Church as we know it . . . cannot be given an affirmative answer."[320] Likewise, Wolfgang Trilling concludes, "Let us summarize: the historical probability that Jesus 'thought,' 'willed,' or 'founded' a Church is extremely small."[321] How then can continuity be construed from the approach of a foundational theology that does not fall into the weaknesses of the previous fundamental theological positions and avoids the hermeneutical pitfalls sketched above.

One widespread approach in christology entails the use of the "implicit-explicit" schema. Jesus did not proclaim an explicit chris-

tology, but his proclamation and actions contained an implicit christology. Transferred to ecclesiology this approach maintains that Jesus
did not explicitly found the Church, but that the Church is implicitly
founded in his proclamation and action.[322] However, the use of this
schema, even for christology, is not without ambiguity, both historical and conceptual. *Historically:* whereas Raymond E. Brown suggests
that the implicit-explicit schema constitutes the basic category of post-
Bultmannians (precisely in its reaction to Bultmann's existentialism)
and of moderate Roman Catholic scholars,[323] others view the implicit-
explicit schema to be Rudolf Bultmann's major contribution to the
resolution of the relation.[324] *Conceptually:* it is not clear according to
which criteria an implicit-explicit relation is established and affirmed,
especially since such criteria entail a definite knowledge of both the
implicit and explicit.

Four types of implicit-explicit relation can be distinguished: logical-relevant, developmental-organic, existential-functional, and her-
meneutical-practical.[325] Each of these can be applied to the theological
problem of the relation between Jesus and christology or between
Jesus and the Church.

The logical-relevant type relies on the classic syllogism. The conclusion not only results logically from the premise, but there is a
connection of meanings between the premises.[326] Although logical
conceptions of the development of doctrine had been prevalent
within the manualist tradition, its applicability to the relation between Jesus and the Church has never been taken seriously in critical
scholarship. Much more seriously employed is the developmental-
organic schema. An acorn develops into an oak tree, but not into a
maple tree. Therefore, an oak tree is implicit within the acorn,
whereas the maple tree is not. The explicit develops out of the implicit, but in the developmental-organic schema whereas what is explicit is much more than what is implicit, this "more" has in some
way been already predetermined in the implicit. Loisy's appeal to the
division between the apostles and the rest of the disciples as the seeds
for the development of the hierarchy fits into this pattern.

The existential-functional schema does not designate logical
equivalency or developmental determinacy, but equivalency of function. Jesus' preaching of the kingdom implied an existential decision.
This decision was existentially equivalent to the post-Easter decision
in faith. A decision for Jesus as the Christ is existentially and functionally equivalent to a decision in the face of Jesus' proclamation of
God's reign.

Preferable to the logical, existential, and developmental schemas is a hermeneutical schema. Based on the relation between a work of art and its interpretation, it provides the best model for understanding how the foundation of the Church is implicit in the life and activity of Jesus.[327] The example of a novel permeated with Christian symbols can illustrate this type of implication. These symbols have been made the basis of an interpretation of the novel as a Christian novel. Yet a critic can ask whether such an interpretation is correct. The critic can doubt whether the author explicitly intended to use such symbols or whether the author wanted to produce a "Christian" novel. But assume that the author's intention is unknown. No personal biographical data is available. The novel itself exists and stands in its own right. It can be justifiably given a Christian interpretation because de facto it contains Christian symbols. In fact, it could have had Hindu symbols, but it does not. Irrespective of the author's intention, interpreters are warranted in giving the novel a Christian interpretation, even as they would not be warranted in giving it a Hindu interpretation because the novel itself contains Christian symbols.

The issue of the implicit foundation of the Church in the ministry of Jesus is, of course, much more complex than this example of a novel suggests. Jesus' words and deeds do not exist as a narrative that can be read independently, but they are found almost exclusively within the New Testament writings or other Christian documents. Nevertheless, the hermeneutical schema appears more adequate to the complexities of the problem than do the other models. The logical schema has no room for development because it basically presupposes a simple identity. The developmental-organic model presupposes the goal from the very beginning. External factors may influence the degree of development but not the basic type and final end. The existential-functional model has no criteria to delineate what is in fact functionally equivalent.

Moreover, a hermeneutical model has the advantage of allowing for an openness to future diversity much more than a logical or developmental model does. At the same time, it has more objectivity than the existential model, for it can place limits on such openness. The symbols, actions, and words provide the objective basis for the interpretation of any work; nevertheless, a work is open to diverse interpretations that go beyond the logical or the organic. In determining identity and continuity in relation to a work or action, a hermeneutical and practical model implies that historical continuity is not given a priori or existentially, but rather is itself a hermeneutical and a practical construction.[328] What constitutes continuity is determined by a judgment as to what is essential or accidental and what is primary or secondary. Such judgments cannot be a priori predetermined, but can only be made retrospectively and through practical decisions.

A nontheological example can illustrate the hermeneutical and practical nature of historical continuity and identity. The question can be asked whether American foreign policy since World War II has identity and continuity. Republicans and Democrats looking at American foreign policy will argue that significant discontinuities took place exactly at the change of administrations from Democratic to Republican and vice versa. A Russian might argue that no discontinuity exists because the policy has constantly had the same practical goal of increasing America's global influence and diminishing Russia's. Even a judgment about recent decisions in regard to mainland China is open to such diverse judgments. A Formosan would see American foreign policy as radically discontinuous and even as entailing a total reversal. But a Russian would judge it to be basically continuous for it is just another step in the United States's policy to isolate Russia and to establish ties with Russia's enemies. In these cases the concrete data, political decisions, and governmental actions are not controverted. What is controverted is whether the policy has a fundamental identity and continuity. Obviously, what one group regards as primary and essential, another group does not. Since the practical consequences differ for each group, their interpretative judgments of identity and continuity differ.

This example illustrates the retrospective and constructive nature of judgments about identity and continuity. Such judgments are not simply theoretical judgments, but also approximate the prudential judgments of practical reason.[329] They are not limited to the theoretical consideration of the data, but they have the task of interpreting and judging what are the more significant overarching factors and what are the primary elements that influence practice. The data are basically the same, but how they are interpreted and evaluated differs. Judgments about identity and continuity, therefore, entail an interplay of theoretical and practical judgments. They are decisions that cannot be a priori predicted and logically deduced, but can only be evaluated retrospectively in relation to their theoretical selectivity and practical evaluation.

This insight into the hermeneutical and practical nature of continuity affects conceptions of the relation between Jesus and the Church. At stake is not only whether what Jesus said and did is open to an interpretation that shows the legitimacy of the Church's continuity with Jesus but also entails a judgment about Jesus. How is the meaning and significance of his words and actions interpreted? How are judgments made as to what constitutes the primary over against the secondary within Jesus' proclamation and action. Should Jesus' apocalyptic expectation be taken as much more primary than his wisdom sayings or vice versa?[330] Should his exorcisms be understood primarily in relation to eschatology as imminent expectation or to eschatology and presently operative reality? Should his miracles of healing be understood only within the context of his proclamation of God's coming reign or should they be seen in the context of the double commandment of love? Reconstructions of Jesus' proclamation and action from the Gospel traditions entails decisions involving evaluation, selection, and discrimination of the diverse data. These decisions concern not only which traditions are the earliest and the most probably historical but also the relative significance of the various traditions for the meaning of Jesus. Just as perception does not take place without some *Gestalt* by which certain lines and structures come to the fore and others recede into the background, so too any reconstruction of the historical Jesus necessitates not only the reconstruction of historical data but also the formation of a *Gestalt*. Such a formation takes place only when some of the historical data come to the forefront as decisive for the *Gestalt* and other data recede into the background—historical but less significant.[331]

Consequently, theological interpretations of how the Christ-kerygma or the Church relates to Jesus should be classified according to how the lines of continuity and discontinuity are drawn rather than according to the implicit-explicit schema.[332] This schema can be applied to Bultmann, to post-Bultmannians, to Catholic exegetes aware of historical criticism, and even to conservative exegetical positions that are not fundamentalistic. Each of these maintains that an implicit-explicit relation exists, but each draws the line differently and thereby displays how differently they understand not only Jesus but also Christ and the Church.

Bultmann, for example, maintains that Jesus' proclamation of the kingdom entails an existential decision. The existential self-understanding called for by Jesus' proclamation correlates with the existential self-understanding entailed in faith in God's eschatological act in Jesus. The Christian community exists in the everyday world of time and space, but it is constituted in and through the existential decision of faith and obedience to the kerygma proclaiming Jesus' death as the eschatological event par excellence. In this respect, the Church as an eschatological community of believers is implicit within Jesus' proclamation of the kingdom.[333]

The post-Bultmannians explicate further and differently how the

Church and the Christ-kerygma is implicit in the historical Jesus. Basically, they seek to establish a continuity between Jesus and the Church's proclamation of Jesus with reference to his sovereignity and authority. Bornkamm stresses the directness of Jesus' authority that sets him apart from Jewish leaders.[334] Käsemann stresses Jesus' unparalleled sovereign freedom;[335] Ebeling and Fuchs stress Jesus' faith in the nearness of God;[336] Herbert Braun and James Robinson stress Jesus' self-understanding before God, entailing an inner freedom from the world;[337] and Norman Perrin stresses Jesus' proclamation of the forgiveness of sin and the offer of a new relationship expressed in table-fellowship.[338]

In all these positions, the existence of the Christian community finds its implicit legitimation. But it is an understanding of the Christian community or Church that is equally as specified as that of the historical Jesus—so much so that the actual discontinuity comes not with the Church but with early Catholicism. If Jesus' sovereign freedom and authority over the law is the heart of his message, then his message implies a Church that is sovereignly free and does not stand under the law. If Jesus' faith in the nearness of God is the key to understanding the earthly Jesus, then a similarly structured faith becomes the key to ecclesial existence. If forgiveness of sin and table-fellowship are the core of Jesus' message, then the Church's essence consists in table-fellowship and forgiveness. If an inner freedom from the world expresses Jesus' self-understanding and his new existential understanding, then freedom from the world is what constitutes the Church—a conclusion that would lead more to Gnosticism than to Catholicism as the legitimate explication of Jesus' meaning and significance (a conclusion now drawn by James Robinson).[339]

This survey of the use of the implicit-explicit schema indicates that both the Bultmannian as well as the post-Bultmannian position use this schema to describe the relation between Jesus and the Church. More significantly, it shows how continuity between Jesus and the Church is established on the basis of distinctive correlations. And finally, it indicates how continuity between the earthly Jesus and the post-Easter Church is established on the basis of a conception of Jesus and the Church that places the caesura not between Jesus and the Church, but between the Church and the development of early Catholicism. In sum, although it is important to argue that the Church is implicitly founded in the proclamation and activity of Jesus, it is more important to raise the issue of the foundation of the criteria of continuity. The post-Bultmannian new quest sought to legitimate the relation between the Church and Jesus by an appeal to the historical Jesus as the object and ground of faith. In contrast, both the hermeneutical principles and the concretization outlined in the previous section suggest that the historical Jesus is the object but not the ground of faith in the Church. This ground of faith can be provided only by the way the Gospel materials draw the lines of continuity between Jesus and Church.

I would like to illustrate this methodic principle by an example from music. The first movement of a concerto often begins with a long orchestral *ritornello* that contains the main subjects, and when the solo instrument enters these subjects are restated and expanded, developed and recapitulated. Apart from the fact that this rule has many exceptions, it presents the problem to the listeners: which of the many themes of the opening *tutti* will belong to the first subject and which will belong to the second subject? Take, for example, Mozart's Concerto in C Minor (K. 491). Anyone listening to this concerto immediately realizes that what one would expect to be the first and second subjects are not so, and it becomes clear not in the *tutti* or the exposition but only in the recapitulation what the first and second subjects are.[340]

Applying this principle to the implicit-explicit schema, I suggest that the relation between the Church and Jesus should be described as an implicit relation—indeed can so be described—only if one takes the Gospel material as normative for how the lines of continuity are drawn. The foundation of the Christian faith rests not on the earthly Jesus as its ground, but rather in the interaction between the earthly Jesus and his reception by the earthly Christian communities as disclosed within the New Testament. This does not mean that the earthly Jesus is theologically irrelevant as has been claimed.[341] But rather the earthly Jesus is to be compared to the subject of a concerto. The full meaning and significance is not from the very beginning perceptible, but it is only at the end that its meaning and significance comes fully to the fore, only after its meaning has been developed and recapitulated. The earthly Jesus is theologically relevant, but he becomes a *Gestalt* only through the combination of historical reconstruction and a reconstructive hermeneutics, that is, through the interaction between reconstructions of the earthly Jesus and reconstructions of the reception of Jesus within early Christianity. Since the vision of Jesus presented by early Christians has as its object the earthly Jesus, it is possible for historical reconstructions to challenge details of the early Christian reception of Jesus. However, judgments about the continuity between the early Christian reception of Jesus and the earthly Jesus as historically reconstructed should take as normative those criteria of continuity that were elaborated within the testimony of the early Christian communities.

Looking back again, at the concretizations of the relation between Jesus and the Church in the Gospel writings, we can ascertain that Mark presented Jesus as forming a new family, with a new set of values, and with an understanding of discipleship as sharing in Jesus' suffering. Insofar as historical research shows Jesus as a wandering charismatic prophet and assumes wandering prophets behind the Gospel of Mark, it does not invalidate the vision of Mark. However, Mark's Gospel does indeed go beyond the historical reconstruction and presents a foundational vision of a new community. Luke emphasized following in the footsteps of Jesus, sharing of wealth, and the gradual emergence of the Church. He offers a vision (going beyond any historical reconstruction) that grounds faith in its surplus of meaning, vision going beyond but not contradicted by the earthly life of Jesus. Likewise, Matthew's Gospel underscores Jesus' teaching of a new justice both in fulfillment of and in tension with Judaism. Matthew's vision may go beyond the earthly Jesus and deal with problems of his own community. Since historical research shows an earthly Jesus both within and in tension with the Judaism of his time, it does not invalidate Matthew's vision even though Matthew's Gospel develops the significance and meaning of this tension in terms of his own community's life. John's connection of faith and love with discipleship formalizes in a highly theological conception a vision of the Church and Jesus that goes beyond Jesus but is not contradicted by historical reconstructions of Jesus.

Each of these concretizations of the relation between the Church and Jesus presents a vision of that relation. Historical reconstructions do not so much establish the continuity of that relation as serve as limit conceptions. They set the limits for the possibility of hermeneutical reconstructions. The actual vision that establishes the continuity is given in the Gospel testimonies themselves. Since they are visions that go beyond the earthly Jesus and his intention, they have their foundation in the earthly Jesus to the extent that his proclamation and action would be open to such an interpretation. The selection and *Gestalt* that ground the Christian faith is provided by the early Christian reception and interpretation of the meaning of Jesus.

On the basis of this hermeneutical principle, it can be affirmed that the Church, indeed, does have its foundation in the earthly Jesus and in the attempts of the early Christian communities to elaborate the significance and meaning of Jesus. The individual Gospels drew quite distinctive lines of continuity. These lines of continuity differ from modern fundamental theological attempts at a historical reconstruction as well as from the new quest's attempt at a psychological or existential reconstruction of the consciousness of Jesus. In the conception of foundational theology as a reconstructive hermeneutics, it is *how* the Gospel testimonies offer a vision and praxis of both the Church and Jesus that provides a foundation for Christian faith—a foundation not provided by the historical demonstration alone because what comes to the fore in the Gospels is an interpretation and vision that extends the horizon of history and moves the past into the present.

Reception and Divine Institution

Traditional fundamental theology sought within its historical demonstration not only to prove that Jesus founded a Church but also to show that he instituted specific sacraments, various ministries, and a concrete church order. The theological shift in regard to the institution of the Church by the earthly Jesus has made it necessary for a reconceptualization of the notions of divine institution and of *de jure divino*.[342] The traditional appeal to explicit volitional and intentional institution by the earthly Jesus and to an ahistorical permanence of institutional structure has given way to two distinct contemporary theological options: functionalism and developmentalism. Each of these, however, has deficiencies that my proposal for a hermeneutical model and my appeal to a reception hermeneutics avoids.

The functional approach rejects the very notion of divine institution and divine law, arguing that neither the Church itself nor any of its sacraments can be traced back definitively to the explicit intention of the earthly Jesus.[343] Moreover, since church order gradually evolved only in the postapostolic period, the notion of divine institution should be totally abandoned for Church structures and be replaced by functional considerations. Church order should be determined by concrete societal situations and by practical needs. Functional criteria rather than theological appeals to divine institution should be decisive for church order. Moreover, since the criteria and goal of church structures are functional, it is sometimes maintained that ministry and service should replace the concept of "office" in any discussion of church order.[344]

The developmental approach tends to maintain that some elements are to be considered as divine institutions, whereas other elements are not. For example, it is suggested that in view of the sacramental nature of the Church, ordination, Eucharist, baptism, and penance are *de jure divino*.[345] They not only express the essence of the Church, but they are also "divinely instituted by Christ."[346] Other elements that enable the Church to perform its sacramental function, especially its institutional features, are also to be considered *de jure divino*. The institutional features can be considered divinely instituted because they not only help the Church to perform its primary function but also develop out of its primary function. Just as a chicken tells us what an egg is so too do these show us what apostolicity and catholicity means.[347] There may also be temporary developments inspired by the Spirit that are to be considered divinely instituted though not apostolic, and there may be developments that are merely the result of ecclesiastical law.

The weakness of the functional approach lies in its insufficient reflection upon the religious identity of the Church. Granted that the Church like any social institution is subject to historical conditions, social factors, and cultural contingencies; nevertheless, the Church has a historical religious identity. In its diverse structures and activities, it must reflect this. The conceptions of divine law and divine right have, therefore, a legitimacy insofar as a Church that would fail to bring its religious identity to the fore in its activity and structures would fail in its religious mission and purpose. All functional and strategic considerations, as important and necessary as they are, must be related to the Church's divinely given religious historical identity.

The developmental approach strives to hold fast to the Church's historical origins and its religious identity and to make origins and identity more decisive than functional needs for church order, ministerial structures, and sacramental system. Yet at the same time, this approach strives to account for historical change and to allow for further growth to a degree not possible within traditional fundamental theology with its stress on a permanency based on divine institution by the earthly Jesus. Nevertheless, the developmental approach has several weaknesses implicit in how it specifies continuity, irreversibility, and identity.

Developmental theories often use the organic model of growth as their root metaphor[348] in order to explain continuity. The episcopal supervision of the Church has grown out of the apostolic as a chicken grows out of an egg—as some have put it. Unfortunately, the organic analogy does not sufficiently explain the differences between episcopal supervision and either apostolicity or the Twelve. Bishops are not simply the outgrowth of either apostles or the Twelve. Not only did the Twelve have a unique foundational role as the link between the earthly Jesus/Risen Lord and the early Church, but they apparently did not have any supervisory function over individual local Church communities.[349] Likewise, the role of the wide-ranging missionary apostle was quite distinct from that of the local bishop.[350] The emergence, development, and background of the episcopacy comes from quite a different context and role than that of apostle.[351] To describe the episcopacy as the organic development of apostolicity overlooks these differences; indeed it fails to see that other trajectories were inherently possible. The relation between episcopacy and apostolicity can therefore be viewed as continuous only on the basis of a hermeneutical model allowing for greater discontinuity, diversity, and transformation than the organic developmental model.

The developmental theory has substituted "irreversibility" for "permanency" as its basic category. It acknowledges historical change and recognizes that all church structures and sacraments were not present in the time of origins. Nevertheless, the dynamics of the developmental model force the conclusion that divine institution entails an irreversible development. Mature adults do not seek to return to childhood. Therefore, once a sacramental system and a church order has reached its stage of maturity, it is irreversible. For example, Dulles suggests that, in addition to ordination, baptism, Eucharist, and penance (considered to be instituted by Christ as attested by the Scriptures or of apostolic origin), other elements that have only developed subsequently should be considered of divine institution and irreversible. These are the three previously unmentioned sacraments, of confirmation, marriage, and the anointing of the sick, the papal office as a development of Petrine ministry, and the episcopacy as a ministry of local supervision.[352]

Here the developmental approach can go astray. A hermeneutical model might be more helpful, for it can explain the possibility of diverse interpretations that are still valid even though diverse. They find their legitimation not so much in their successive development as in the validity of their interpretations. In the natural sciences, Maxwell's electromagnetic field theory and the action-at-a-distance theory are incompatible yet equally valid interpretations of electrodynamics. If the additional sacraments are considered not so much as a further development, but rather as diverse and legitimate interpretations of the relation between Jesus and the Church, these diversities between confessions can be acknowledged as diverse interpretations claiming divine right.

The developmental conception must deal with the identity of the divinely instituted. How does it distinguish between the primary and the secondary, between the essential and the nonessential? Neither the traditional approach (tracing identity back to the instituting will of the earthly Jesus) nor the functional approach (using criteria of utility and adaptability) had to face the problem. But since the developmental conception seeks fidelity to religious origin and appropriateness to changing situations, it needs to develop criteria of identity and continuity. Therefore, it often makes an appeal to Christ and to the theological conception of the essence of the Church. Karl Rahner makes the understanding of the Church as a sacrament central to his specification of divine institution, and Avery Dulles argues that ordination, baptism, Eucharist, and penance are divinely instituted because they correspond to what represents "Christ's irrevocable gift to his Church" and they express the true nature of the Church as a sacrament of salvation.[54]

The description of the Church as a sacrament often includes viewing some sacraments as divinely instituted insofar as they express the essence of the Church. Yet such a conclusion is historically and systematically questionable. Even if allowance is made for the development of the notion of sacrament, the description of four sacraments as divinely instituted by Christ does not sufficiently emphasize that Jesus himself did not baptize and that the baptismal commission articulates the theology of a second- or third-generation Christian community. The reference to penance that the Council of Trent saw in John's Gospel is historically questionable and open to reinterpretation.[355] Moreover, the notion of the Church itself as a sacrament—despite some roots in patristic and medieval traditions[356]—is basically a nineteenth- and twentieth-century conception. Moreover it is systematically questionable because the stress on the Church as a sacrament posits only one view of the Church as essential and overlooks other elements of religious and historical identity.

My proposal is that a hermeneutical model and the concretizations in the New Testament of the relation between Jesus and the Church provide a twofold basis for understanding divine institution. Divine institution should not be taken as a legal concept based on a founding will or as a dogmatic concept reflecting some abstract essence of the Church. Instead, divine institution is a hermeneutical concept. Something is divinely instituted to the degree that it mirrors the relation between Jesus and the Church as normatively described in the New Testament.

This proposal has several advantages over the functional and developmental approaches in that it elicits the criteria of identity and change. Something is divinely instituted to the degree that it mirrors the relation between Jesus and the Church as normatively described in the historical concretization of religious identity in the New Testament. The papacy is, therefore, not simply the developmental growth of Peter's role; nor is the papacy simply the managerial center of unity necessary for any organization. Rather, to the extent the papacy seeks to be a historical concretization and interpretation of Petrine ministry, to that extent it has its legitimation. Likewise, episcopacy is not the organizational development of the roles of the apostles or the Twelve, but expresses how the original relation between Jesus and the disciples came to be structured in the postapostolic period. Consequently, its points of identity are in how this structure mirrors that relation. The tripartite division (episcopacy, presbyterate, and diaconate) can scarcely be considered of divine institution, for in its earliest structure the distinction between the episcopate and the presbyterate was at times nonexistent. Although in the post-Tridentine period the presbyterate and diaconate were received as distinct orders, yet in concrete practice they were not distinct ministeries in Roman Catholicism until Vatican II.

The concretization of the relation between Jesus and the Church generates images that are much more comprehensive than does the systematic construction of the Church as a sacrament. They display how religious identity is a historical identity, entailing a relation not only to Jesus but also to the world, to other human beings, and to God. In Mark's Gospel the disciples are called not only to give up all to follow Jesus in a discipleship of suffering but also to become members of Jesus' family. The Twelve not only have the function of being with Jesus and of proclamation, they are also to heal and to exorcise. Matthew's Gospel not only stresses the preeminence of Peter's faith and teaching authority, it also shows that this teaching authority concerns the right teaching of God's will and the right praxis of God's justice. Luke's Gospel not only traces the developing stages of the Church but also teaches that discipleship consists in following in the footsteps of Jesus and following a way of life involving the sharing of wealth. John's Gospel in chapter 21 balances the Petrine ministry of the institutional Church with the Beloved Disciples's rule of faith and love. In all these concretizations the normative criteria of the Gospels come to the fore: pastoral ministry as well as love and faith; Petrine teaching authority as well as the praxis of God's justice; proclamation as well as healing. Since both dimensions of the Church are concretized, both should be considered as divinely instituted. A code of canon law or a basic constitution of the Church should therefore express as equally divinely instituted not only regulations of hierarchical order, conditions for the performance of the sacraments, but also the praxis of justice, faith, and healing. The criteria are provided in the New Testament concretizations of the relation between Jesus and the Church, and all Christian Churches are called to show how their legal codes can be seen as further concretizations, reflections, and interpretations of these original images.

Church: Object and Ground of Faith

The traditional fundamental theology often complemented its historical demonstration and its move from Christ to the Church by beginning with the Church and moving back to Christ. Cardinal Victor Dechamps (1810–1883) exemplifies the fundamental theological argument that the Church with its marvelous and extraordinary qualities was a divine sign and a ground of faith. Vatican Council I (1861–1870) sought to complement its historical demonstration by an emphasis on the Church as sign.[357] Not only do biblical miracles and prophecies demonstrate Christ's authority, but the extraordinary qualities of the Church are an indication of its divine origin. "The Church itself, because of its marvelous propagation, its exalted sanctity, and its inexhaustible fruitfulness in all that is good, because of its catholic unity and its unshaken stability, is a great and perpetual motive of credibility and an irrefutable proof of its own divine mission."[358]

Although this Vatican I statement is strikingly overconfident—and not shared by many today—it does represent a conviction with deep roots in the history of Catholic theology. In his anti-Manichean writings, Augustine avows, "I would truly not have believed the Gospel, unless the authority of the Catholic Church had moved me."[359] The foundation for his trust in the authority of the Church rested on the "supernatural phenomena" displayed by the Church. In response to the question how members of the Church would be convinced of the Church's authority, Augustine answered that it was through the Church's miracles and wisdom. His theology sought to integrate the wisdom mediated through the Church with the existence of miracles within that Church. Moreover, against the Manicheans, he especially stressed the significance of apostolic succession and the enduring antiquity of the Church.

The empirical ambiguity of the Church as a historical phenomenon and religious institution makes this empirical apologetical approach somewhat ineffectual. Its validity, however, consists in its attempt to provide a foundation for faith beyond mere historical demonstration. Since the gospel is mediated to the present through the Church, the fundamental theological move from the Church to the gospel can be extended one step further from the gospel to Jesus. The Augustinian claim that there is no faith in the gospel without the authority of the Church can be complemented with the claim that there is no faith in Jesus without the authority of the gospel.

Therefore, fundamental theological attempts to legitimate the Church, either through a historical demonstration of the intention of the earthly Jesus or through a historical demonstration of a post-Easter foundation, fail to take adequately into account how the gospel grounds faith in Jesus, just as the Church grounds faith in the gospel. The meaning and significance of Jesus has endured in history because of the Christian Church's faith in Jesus and because of the Gospel accounts expressing this faith. Insofar as the Gospels offer interpretations of Jesus concretizing his significance and meaning for the Church, they offer a vision and a praxis that illuminate historical as well as contemporary values. The grounding of this vision does not occur by going beyond the Gospel texts through historical demonstration, but rather by showing how the sense and reference of the Gospel texts open up a vision that, through its illuminative power and praxis, grounds faith. It is not that our deepest hopes find their correlation in the Gospels and are thereby grounded—as the transcendental existential approach has argued—but rather that a vision and a praxis are displayed in the Gospels that show us what our vision and praxis should be. Historical demonstrations seeking to go behind the Gospel's vision to bare facticity do not produce a greater foundation but subtract from the foundation presented in the Gospels, just as the attempt to ground the Gospels in the transcendental experience of the need for salvation provides a foundation that subtracts rather than adds to the fullness of the vision and praxis displayed in the Gospels. This conclusion does not obviate the Augustinian claim that Christians believe in the gospel because of the authority of the Church, but makes possible a new view of this authority. It becomes necessary to examine how the Church in its present reality and praxis mediates to the present the concretizations of the relation between Jesus and the Church displayed in the Gospels. This question needs to be raised in the next two chapters on the relation between the Church's social mission and its religious identity. For such a question is not simply an issue of social ethics, but rather a fundamental theological issue: how does the Church's mission display its religious identity and thereby show its truth?

Church of Disciples

Each fundamental theological approach presupposes a distinct conception of the Church. Traditional fundamental theology, viewing the Church as a society, emphasized the formal unity given by the papacy and the hierarchy. It equated the Church's foundation with the institution of the papacy and the apostolic college. Transcendental fundamental theology, interpreting the Church as a sacrament, emphasizes that the Church has the same "sacramental" function as Jesus. Just as Jesus symbolized the grace of God in concrete history so too the Church continues that symbolization. Other approaches transfer the category of sacrament from the provenance of Christ to that of the Spirit and refer to the Church as the sacrament of the Spirit. Less sacramental approaches refer to the Church as the community under God's Spirit or as the sinful and justified Church.

The principles of a hermeneutics of reception affect not only the foundation of the Church but also the conception of the Church. The element of reception needs to be incorporated into the theological understanding of the Church's nature. The major weakness of the institutional, and especially the sacramental, model of the Church consists in failure to take into account the notion of reception. Underlying the sacramental understanding of the Church is an emphasis upon an identity of function and role. The distance between Jesus and the Church is downplayed and the role of reception in linking Jesus and the Church is overlooked.

A conception of the Church based upon a hermeneutics of reception would make discipleship the basic model of the Church. Discipleship, however, within a hermeneutic of reception is not simply imitation or an immediate following of the historical Jesus. But rather such a discipleship presupposes distance and mediation. It presupposes a distance between the context of the historical Jesus and the context of present experience and praxis. Moreover, it presupposes that, given this distance, all discipleship is mediated through previous testimonies to the meaning of Jesus and through previous receptions. For these reasons, discipleship is not imitation, but a new reception and interpretation of Jesus' meaning and significance.

A common assumption has been that the notion of discipleship changed radically after Easter. Contemporary studies of the New Testament show that two diverse conceptions of discipleship existed: the more wandering charismatic disciple and the more local and sedentary discipleship. It has even been suggested that a continuity exists between the wandering of Jesus' life and the wandering missionary after Jesus' death, but not between the former and the understanding of discipleship in the local sedentary community. But discipleship should not be reduced to a notion of continuity as sameness; it must be open to radically new forms of discipleship based upon new receptions. This potentiality for new receptions made it possible for the Church to grow and develop. It also began to raise in a new fashion the question of the Church's mission.

NOTES

1. Hermann Samuel Reimarus, *The Goal of Jesus and His Disciples*, introd. and trans. George Wesley Buchanan (Leiden: Brill, 1970). *Reimarus Fragments*, trans. Ralph S. Fraser and ed. Charles H. Talbert (Philadelphia: Fortress, 1970), contains Reimarus's "Concerning the Intention of Jesus and His Teaching" and David Friedrich Strauss's "Hermann Samuel Reimarus and His Apology."

2. Giorgio Jossa surveys the political interpretations of Jesus since Reimarus in *Gesù e i movimenti di liberazione della Palestina* (Biblioteca di cultura religiosa 37; Brescia: Paideia, 1980). In contrast to Martin Hengel, Jossa distinguishes clearly between the Zealots and the Sicarii and sees a relation between the political implications of Jesus' preaching and the possible misunderstanding by Roman and Jewish authorities.

3. Elisabeth Schüssler Fiorenza sketches diverse contemporary interpretations of eschatology and offers a view that takes redaction criticism seriously in "Eschatology of the New Testament," *Interpreter's Dictionary of the Bible, Supplementary Volume*, ed. Keith R. Crim et al. (Nashville: Abingdon, 1976), pp. 271–77. See also Norman Perrin, *Rediscovering the Teaching of Jesus* (New York: Harper and Row, 1967), esp. pp. 154–206.

4. Introd. Rudolf Bultmann, trans. Thomas Saunders (New York: Harper and Row, 1957).

5. For a Roman Catholic appraisal of Harnack's theology, see Karl H. Neufeld, *Adolf von Harnack. Theologie als Suche nach der Kirche* (Paderborn: Bonafacius, 1978).

6. *What Is Christianity?*, p. 191.

7. Trans. Christopher Home (Philadelphia: Fortress, 1976; original ed. London: Isbister, 1903).

8. For the relation between Loisy and Harnack, see Dieter Hoffmann-Axthelem, "Loisy 'L'Evangile et l'Église'. Besichtigung eines zeitgenössischen Schlachtfeldes," *ZThK* 65 (1968) 291–328; and Bernard B. Scott's introduction to Loisy, *Gospel*, pp. xi–lxxiii, especially xlii–lxiii.

9. Trans. John Bowden (New York: Harper and Row, 1969), pp. 33–34. In my opinion, Conzelmann does, however, very perceptively and significantly poses the problem when he asks: "But what does it mean? The pertinent theological question is whether and to what extent Jesus and his work were rightly understood and carried on after his death, through the formation of the church" (p. 34).

10. *Dogmatik des christlichen Glaubens*, vol. 3 (Tübingen, J. C. B. Mohr, 1979), p. 29.

11. Johannes Weiss, *Jesus' Proclamation of the Kingdom*, trans. Richard H. Hiers and D. Larrimore Holland (Philadelphia: Fortress, 1971).

12. E. S. Fiorenza, "Eschatology," pp. 271–77.

13. See Emile Poulat, *Histoire, dogme et critique dans la crise moderniste* (Paris: Castermann, 1979, 2nd ed.), pp. 43–189, who maintains: "Il faut d'abord oublier Harnack pour comprender Loisy" (p. 61). Gabriel Daly suggests that "Loisy contrived a deliberately ambiguous method of approach in several respects" (*Transcendence and Immanence: A Study in Catholic Modernism and Integralism* [Oxford: Clarendon, 1980], pp. 56f.).

14. See the analysis of the similarities and differences between Harnack and Loisy by Poulat, *Histoire*, pp. 89–102; and by Bernard Scott, in Loisy, *Gospel*, pp. xliii–lxvii.

15. Loisy, *Gospel*, pp. 15–22 and 170–72. See Loisy's article under the name Fermin, "Le dévelopment chrétien d'après le cardinal Newman," *Revue du Clergé français* (1898), pp. 5–20.

16. Loisy, *Gospel*, pp. 146–64.

17. Ibid., pp. 146–47.

18. Ibid., p. 147. Loisy refers more to the risen Christ in *Autour d'un petit Livre* (Paris: Alphonse Picard et Fils, 1903), pp. 170–72. See also his *Les Évangiles synoptiques*, 2 vols. (Paris: Ceffonds, 1907/8), 1:883–84.

19. *Gospel.*, p. 166.

20. See Poulat, *Histoire*, pp. 124–61, for a discussion of the initial reactions and criticisms, and pp. 103–12 for the Roman condemnations.

21. *Gospel*, p. 166.

22. Loisy, *Autour*, p. 171.

23. Ibid., p. 161.

24. Rudolf Bultmann, "Die Frage nach der Echtheit von Mt 16, 17–19," *ThBl* 20 (1941) 265–79, reprinted in *Exegetica* (Tübingen: J. C. B. Mohr, 1967), pp. 255–77, esp. 255–57.

25. See, Loisy, *Les Évangiles synoptiques*, 2:8ff.

26. Among the primacy statements of Vatican I is: "If anyone says that the blessed Apostle Peter was not constituted by Christ the Lord as the Prince of all the Apostles and the visible head of the whole Church militant, or that he received immediately and directly from Jesus Christ our Lord only a primacy of honor and not a primacy of true and proper jurisdiction, let him be anathema" (DS 3055). The planned preamble did, however, affirm: "The eternal Shepherd and Bishop of our souls . . . determined to build a holy Church" (DS 3050).

27. Washington, D.C.: United States Catholic Conference, 1973.

28. Latin text originally in *ASS* 40 (1907) 470–78; DS 3401–66. On the French context of the decrees, see Roger Aubert, "Aux origines de la réaction antimoderniste: Deux documents inédits," *EThL* 37 (1961) 557–78.

29. No. 52 of *Lamentabili* (DS 3452).

30. After *Pascendi* and *Lamentabili* were issued, George Tyrrell wrote *Christianity at the Cross-roads* (London: Longmans, 1910) in which he contrasts Loisy's eschatological interpretation with Harnack's liberalism (see pp. 46–104 and 114–222).

31. For Ernesto Buonaiuti's conception of the relation between Jesus' eschatological proclamation and the foundation of the Church, see Bernardino Greco, *Ketzer oder Propet? Evangelium und Kirche bei dem Modernisten Ernesto Buonaiuti (1881–1946)* (Zurich: Benziger, 1979).

32. See the commentary on *Lamentabili* by Poulat, *Histoire*, pp. 103–12. Loisy had himself responded in *Simples réflexions sur le décret du Saint-Office "Lamentabili sane exitu" et sur l'encyclique "Pascendi dominici gregis"* (Paris: Ceffonds, 1908; the 2nd ed., also 1908, was expanded by 30 pages).

33. For the influence of Carl Braig, Heidegger's theology teacher, upon Pius X's conception of Modernism, see Richard Schaeffler, "Der 'Modernismus-Streit' als Herausforderung an das philosophisch-theologische Gespräche heute," *ThPh* 55 (1980) 514–34. For the influence of Joseph Lemius, possibly the drafter of *Pascendi*, see Daly, *Transcendence*, pp. 232–34.

34. DS 3537-50; translation here from *The Church Teaches: Documents of the Church in English Translation*, trans. John F. Clarkson et al. (St. Louis: B. Herder, 1955), p. 37.

35. "I accept and freely acknowledge the external proofs of revelation, that is, the divine facts, first of all, miracles and prophecies, as most certain signs of the divine origin of the Christian religion" (ibid., my translation).

36. See Thomas Aquinas Collins and Raymond E. Brown, "Church Pronouncements," in *The Jerome Biblical Commentary, Volume II, The New Testament and Topical*

Articles, ed. Raymond E. Brown, Joseph A. Fitzmyer, and Roland E. Murphy (Englewood-Cliffs, N.J.: Prentice-Hall, 1968), pp. 624–33: ". . . many of these decrees now have little more than historic interest, being implicitly revoked by later decrees, by *Divino Afflante Spiritu*, and by Vatican II" (72:25). See especially the commentary of Joseph A. Fitzmyer, *The Historical Truth of the Gospels* (Glen Rock, N.J.: Paulist, 1965).

37. For a description of the measures taken against theologians, see Norbert Trippen, *Theologie und kirchliches Lehramt im Konflikt. Die kirchlichen Massnahmen gegen den Modernismus im Jahre 1907 und ihre Auswirkungen in Deutschland* (Freiburg: Herder, 1977).

38. See Part IV of this volume, where the history and structure of fundamental theology is discussed.

39. See Joseph Schumacher, *Der apostolische Abschluss der Offenbarung Gottes* (FThS 114; Freiburg: Herder, 1979).

40. For recent discussions of the notion of divine right and its interrelation with the issue of the foundation of the Church or with the differences in church order, see Karl Rahner, "Reflection on the Concept of 'Ius Divinium' in Catholic Thought," in *Theological Investigations* 5 (Baltimore: Helicon, 1960), pp. 219–43; Carl J. Peter, "Dimensions of Ius Divinum in Roman Catholic Theology," *TS* 34 (1973) 227–50; and Avery Dulles, "'Ius Divinum' as an Ecumenical Problem," *TS* 38 (1977) 681–708; reprinted in Dulles, *A Church to Believe In* (New York: Crossroad, 1982), pp. 80–102.

41. Josef Finkenzeller, "Die Zählung und die Zahl der Sakramente. Eine dogmengeschichtliche Untersuchung," in *Wahrheit und Verkündigung*, ed. Leo Scheffzyk (Munich: Kösel, 1967), 2:1005–33. For the Tridentine text itself, see Sess. 7, canon 1 (DS 1601). The diversity of the medieval opinions about the number of the sacraments has unfortunately received insufficient attention until recently.

42. See, for example, how cautious Trent was in regard to auricular confession: so Karl-Josef Becker, "Die Notwendigkeit des vollständigen Bekenntnisses in der Beichte nach dem Konzil von Trient," *ThPh* 47 (1972) 161–228; and Carl J. Peter, "Auricular Confession and the Council of Trent," *Proceedings CTSA* 22 (1967) 185–200.

43. Sess. 22, cap. 1 (DS 1739–42).

44. DS 1776; see also DS 1773.

45. DS 3056–58.

46. See *Lumen gentium*, nos. 20, 23, and 32.

47. See Johannes Heckel, *Lex caritatis, Eine juristische Untersuchung über das Recht in der Theologie Martin Luthers* (Munich: Abhandlungen der Akademie der Wissenschafter, Philosophisch-historische Klasse, N.F. 36, 1953); A. C. Piepkorn, "Ius Divinium and Adiaphoron in Relation to Structural Problems in the Church: The Position of the Lutheran Symbolical Books," in *Papal Primacy and the Universal Church* (Minneapolis: Augsburg, 1974), pp. 119–26; Edmund Schlink, "Zur Unterschiedung von *Jus divinum* und *Jus humanum*," in *Begegnung. Festschrift Heinrich Fries*, ed. Max Seckler (Graz: Styria, 1972), pp. 233–50.

48. See Jan Weerda, "Ordnung zur Lehre. Zur Theologie der Kirchenordnung bei Calvin," in *Calvin-Studien 1959*, ed. Jürgen Moltmann (Neukirchen-Vluyn: Neukirchener Verlag, 1960).

49. It is important to keep in mind that the Council of Trent was much more cautious than is generally recognized in the manual tradition in its understanding of divine institution, as the essays of Peter and Dulles (cited n. 40 above) point out.

50. The current debate on the ordination of women has led to the Vatican's "Declaration on the Question of the Admission of Women to the Ministerial Priesthood," which argues from the "attitude of Jesus." See Leonard Swidler and Arlene Swidler, eds., *Women Priests: A Catholic Commentary on the Vatican Declaration* (New York: Paulist, 1977).

51. See the collection of classic essays by Hatch, Harnack, Sohm, Batiffol, and Lietzmann, in Karl Kertelge, ed., *Das kirchliche Amt in Neuen Testament* (Wege der Forschung 439; Darmstadt: Wissenschaftliche Buchgesellschaft, 1977).

52. For a survey of the debate, see James M. Robinson, *A New Quest of the Historical*

Jesus (SBT 25; London: SCM Press, 1959). For the often overlooked difference between historical continuity and objective continuity, see Rudolf Bultmann's response to the New Quest, "The Primitive Christian Kerygma and the Historical Jesus," in *The Historical Jesus and the Kerygmatic Christ*, ed. Carl E. Braaten and Roy A. Harrisville (New York: Abingdon, 1964), pp. 15–42; also in the same volume the important essay by Schubert M. Ogden and Van A. Harvey, "How New is the 'New Quest of the Historical Jesus'?" pp. 197–242.

53. See how chapter 9 of this volume links the development of the social and political ministry of the church with the development of christology.

54. Loisy, *Autour*, p. 171; see also pp. vii–ix and 161.

55. Joachim Salaverri, *De ecclesia Christi*, in *Sacrae Theologiae Summa*, vol. 1, ed. Patres Societatis Jesu (Madrid: BAC, 1958, 4th ed.), p. 532: "voluntate libera, auctoritate et expressa aliquid determinate et stabiliter in ordine morali vel juridico."

56. Francis A. Sullivan, *De ecclesia*, vol. 1 (Rome: Gregorian Univ. Press, 1965, 2nd ed.), p. 130.

57. Medard Kehl, *Kirche als Institution* (FTS 22; Frankfurt: Josef Knecht, 1976), pp. 69–74; Thomas Franklin O'Meara, "Philosophical Models in Ecclesiology," *TS* 39 (1978) 3–21; T. Howard Sanks, *Authority in the Church: A Study in Changing Paradigms* (AAR Dissertation Series 2; Missoula, Mont.: Scholars, 1974).

58. Ad. Tanquerey, *Synopsis Theologiae Dogmaticae Fundamentalis* (Tournai: Desclée, 1959), p. 419; Joannes Perrone, *Praelectiones theologicae*, vol. 1 (Prima editio Tusca; Prati, Raynerus Guatus, 1844), pp. 253–59.

59. Perrone, *Praelectiones*, pp. 150–72.

60. T. Zapalena, *De ecclesia Christi*, vol. 1 (Rome: Gregorian Univ. Press, 1955, 2nd ed.), p. 233.

61. For the distinction between *causa seconda* and *causa instrumentalis*, see Hermann J. Pottmeyer, "Theologie der synodalen Strukturen," in Adolf Exeler, ed., *Fragen der Kirche heute* (Würzburg: Echter, 1971), pp. 164–82.

62. G. Paris, *De vera Christi ecclesia* (Malta: Muscat, 1949). The first volume of Journet's work appeared in English under the title *The Church of the Word Incarnate: The Apostolic Hierarchy* (New York: Sheed and Ward, 1955). See also R. M. Schultes, *De ecclesia catholica* (Paris: Lethielleux, 1925).

63. Roger Aubert, "Die ekklesiologische Geographie im 19. Jahrhundert," in Jean Danielou and Herbert Vorgrimler, eds., *Sentire Ecclesiam* (Festschrfit für Hugo Rahner; Freiburg: Herder, 1961), pp. 430–71; also Felix Malmberg, *Ein Leib–Ein Geist* (Freiburg: Herder, 1960).

64. See Michael Schmaus, *Katholische Dogmatik*, vol. III/1, *Die Lehre von der Kirche* (Munich: Max Hueber, 1958), pp. 113–201.

65. Sullivan, *De ecclesia*, pp. 28ff.

66. See Robert Bellarmine, *Opera Omnia*, vol. 1, edited J. Fevre (Paris, 1870), controv. III, bk. 1, cap. 9ff; Perrone, *Praelectiones*, 1:150–55; John Baptist Franzelin, *De ecclesia Christi* (Rome: S. C. de Propaganda Fide, 1887), pp. 121ff. and 159ff.

67. See Salaverri's survey of the five distinct positions concerning the time when Jesus founded the Church, in *De ecclesia*, pp. 554–55.

68. Gerhard G. Van Noort, *Dogmatic Theology*, vol. 2, *Christ's Church*, trans. and rev. John J. Castelot and William R. Murphy (Westminster, Md.: Newman, 1957), p. 11; Tanquerey, *Synopsis*, 1:421–23.

69. Van Noort, *Christ's Church*, p. 11.

70. *Fausse exégèse, mauvaise théologie. Lettre aux directeurs de mon séminair, à propos des idées exposées par M. Loisy dans "Autour d'un petit libre"* (Paris: Oudin, 1904), p. 98 (my translation).

71. Salaverri, *De ecclesia*, pp. 501–6.

72. Perrone, *Praelectiones*, 1:259–68. Proposition II: "Ecclesia a Christo instituta anterior est quavis Scriptura."

73. For a history of the interpretation, including the issue of authenticity, see

James Burgess, *A History of the Exegesis of Matthew 16:17–19 from 1781 to 1965* (Ann Arbor, Mich.: Edwards Bro., 1976).

74. See n. 68 above for Van Noort, n. 55 for Salaverri, and n. 64 for Schmaus (later modified in his *Dogma 4: The Church: Its Origin and Structure* [New York: Sheed and Ward, 1972]); for Rahner see n. 87 below.

75. Vittorio Mondello, *La Chiesa del Dio Trino* (Naples: Dehoniane 1978), pp. 245–81; P. Faynel, *L'Église*, vol. 1 (Paris: Desclée, 1970), pp. 262–66; Brunero Gherardini, *La Chiesa. Oggi e sempre* (Milan: Ares, 1974), pp. 117–32.

76. Salaverri, *De ecclesia*, p. 509.

77. Homily on Ezechiel, bk. 2, homily 3; *PL* 76, 960.

78. John Chrysostom, Homily on Matthew 3, 46; *PG* 58, 476.

79. Schmaus, *Die Lehre von der Kirche*, p. 105.

80. Ibid., p. 105.

81. See Joseph Ludwig, *Die Primatsworte Mt XVI, 18–19 in der altkirchlichen Exegese* (NTAbh XIV, 4; Münster: Aschendorff, 1952); Karl Froehlich, *Formen der Auslegung von Mt 16, 13–18 in lateinischen Mittelalter* (Tübingen: Präzis, 1963).

82. Today, the medieval speculation on the relation between *kephā*› and the latin *caput* has been abandoned; see the survey of Yves M. Congar, "Cephas–Céphalè–Caput," *Revue du moyen âge latin* 8 (1952) 5–42.

83. Examples of this exegesis can be found in Van Noort, *Christ's Church*, pp. 63–64; Salaverri, *De ecclesia Christi*, pp. 562–76; and Albert Lang, *Fundamentaltheologie* vol. 2 (Munich: Max Hueber, 1962), pp. 58–90. The binding and loosing has often been interpreted in this tradition as referring to the power of excommunication and the sacramental forgiveness of sins—some texts with an anti-Protestant polemic even argue that it is not only the declaration of foregiveness but the real forgiveness that is here promised. However, since the nineteenth century, the rabbinic parallels have been taken into account in Roman Catholic exegesis, See Herbert Vorgrimler, "Binden und Lösen" in der Exegese nach dem Tridentinum bis zu Begin des 20. Jahrhunderts," *ZKTh* 85 (1963) 460–77.

84. Van Noort, *Christ's Church*, p. 62.

85. Schmaus, *Die Lehre von der Kirche*, pp. 168–69.

86. See Salaverri, *De ecclesia*, pp. 555–57, who speaks of an "inadequate coincidence of Church and kingdom of God."

87. Karl Rahner, *Foundations of the Christian Faith* (New York: Crossroad, 1978), pp. 332–35. See also Rahner's "Zur Ekklesiologie," in *Diskussion über Hans Kungs 'Christsein,'* ed. Hans Urs von Balthasar et al. (Mainz: Matthias Gur̈newald, 1976), pp. 105–11. For criticisms of Rahner's exegesis and his reference to founding acts by the historical Jesus, see "Seminar on Rahner's Ecclesiology: Jesus and the Foundation of the Church—An Analysis of the Hermeneutical Issues," *Proceedings CTSA* 33 (1978) 229–54. Rahner has modified the position taken in *Foundations;* his modifications and development will be discussed in the section on the foundation of the Church in transcendental fundamental theology.

88. Gerhard Heinz, *Das Problem der Kirchenenstehung in der deutschen Protestantischen Theologie des 20. Jahrhunderts* (TTS 4; Mainz: Matthias Grünewald, 1974), pp. 213–20, surveys diverse Protestant positions and elaborates the "new consensus" and its critique.

89. See Norman Perrin, *Jesus and the Language of the Kingdom* (Philadelphia: Fortress, 1976).

90. Martin Hengel, *The Charismatic Leader and His Followers* (New York: Crossroad, 1981).

91. Ernst Haenchen, "Petrus-Probleme," *NTS* 7 (1960/61), pp. 187–97; reprinted in *Gott und Mensch. Gesammelte Aufsätze*, vol. 1 (Tübingen: J. C. B. Mohr, 1965), pp. 55–67: and Rudolf Bultmann, "Die Frage nach der Echtheit von Mt 16, 17–19" (cited in n. 24 above), who argues against Cullmann's earlier volume on Christ's kingship that anticipated some of the theses.

92. Philadelphia: Westminster, 1962, 2nd ed.

93. Still important, even though he minimizes the effects of the historical, is Maurice Blondel's "History and Dogma," in *The Letter on Apologetics and History and Dogma* (New York: Holt, Rinehart and Winston, 1964), pp. 221–87.

94. For the terminological differences between "rule" or "reign" and "kingdom of God," see Rudolf Schnackenburg, *God's Rule and Kingdom* (New York: Herder and Herder, 1963), pp. 354–57. Schnackenburg indicates the reasons why it is preferable to refer to God's reign or rule rather than kingdom of God.

95. Erich Grässer, *Das Problem der Parusieverzögerung in den synoptischen Evangelien und in der Apostelgeschichte* (Berlin: Alfred Töpelmann, 1957); Thomas W. Manson, *The Teaching of Jesus* (Cambridge: Cambridge Univ. Press, 1935); and Werner G. Kümmel, *Promise and Fulfillment* (SBT 23; London: SCM Press, 1957).

96. Ernst Käsemann, *New Testament Questions Today* (Philadelphia: Fortress 1969), esp. chap. 4 and 5.

97. Raymond E. Brown, *Jesus God and Man* (New York: Macmillan, 1967), p. 77.

98. The literature on the parables is immense, for a good treatment with excellent bibliography, see Hans-Joseph Klauck, *Allegorie und Allegorese in synoptischen Gleichnis Texten* (NTAbh 13: Münster: Aschendorff, 1978).

99. The Gospel of Thomas, no. 20: "The disciples said to Jesus: 'Tell us what the Kingdom of Heaven is like.' He said to them: 'It is like a mustard seed, smaller than all seeds. But when it falls on the tilled earth, it produces a large branch and becomes shelter for the birds of heaven.' "

100. Joachim Gnilka, *Das Evangelium nach Markus* (EKK II/1; Einsiedeln: Benzinger/ Neukirchen-Vluyn: Neukirchener Verlag, 1978), p. 100.

101. See John G. Gager, *Kingdom and Community: The Social World of Early Christianity* (Englewood Cliffs, N.J.: Prentice-Hall, 1975), pp. 20–65; Peter Worsely, *The Trumphet Shall Sound: A Study of "Cargo" Cults in Melanesia* (New York: Schocken, 1968); Kenelm Burridge, *New Heaven, New Earth* (New York: Schocken, 1969).

102. Elisabeth Schüssler Fiorenza, "Cultic Language in Qumran and in the New Testament," *CBQ* 38 (1976) 159–77; Gerhard Klinzing, *Die Umdeutung des Kultus in der Qumrangemeinde und im NT* (Böttingen: Vandenhoeck, und Ruprecht, 1971).

103. See Beda Rigaux, "The Twelve Apostles," *Concilium* 34 (1968) 5–15, and "Die 'Zwölf' in Geschichte und Kerygma," in Karl Kertelge, ed., *Das kirchliche Amt im Neuen Testament* (Darmstadt: Wissenschaftliche Buchgesellschaft, 1977), pp. 279–304; Elisabeth Schüssler Fiorenza, "The Twelve," in Leonard and Arene Swidler, eds., *Women Priests: A Catholic Commentary on the Vatican Declaration* (New York: Paulist, 1977), pp. 114–39.

104. Hans von Campenhausen, "Der urchristliche Apostelbegriff," now in Kertelge, *Das kirchliche Amt*, pp. 237–78; Jürgen Roloff, *Apostolat–Verkündigung–Kirche. Ursprung, Inhalt und Funktion des kirchlichen Apostelamtes nach Paulus, Lukas, und den Pastoralenbriefen* (Gütersloh: Gerd Mohn, 1965); C. K. Barrett, *The Signs of an Apostle* (Philadelphia: Fortress, 1972); Ferdinand Hahn, "Der Apostolat im Urchristentum. Seine Eigenart und seine Voraussetzungen," 20 (1974) 54–77.

105. Mostly defended by Helmut Köster, *Einführung in das Neue Testament im Rahmen der Religionsgeschichte und Kulturgeschichte der hellenistischen und römischen Zeit* (New York/Berlin: Walter de Gruyter, 1980), pp. 756–60. The arguments against the historicity of the "Twelve Apostles" and for its basis in Lukan theology were first developed by Günter Klein, *Die Zwölf Apostel. Ursprung und Gehalt einer Idee* (FRLANT 77, Göttingen: Vandenhoeck, und Ruprecht, 1961). Klein claims: "That the Twelve as institution do not belong in the life of Jesus can be demonstrated with a probability bordering on certainty" (p. 37, my translation). For a rather speculative view of the relation between the notion of apostle and the gnostic model, see W. Schmithals, *The Office of Apostle in the Early Church* (Nashville: Abingdon, 1969).

106. See Joseph A. Fitzmyer, *The Gospel According to Luke I-IX* (Anchor Bible 28;

Garden City, N.Y.: Doubleday, 1981), pp. 253–57. While noting that Luke seems to identify the Twelve with the "apostles," Fitzmyer summarizes the standard reasons for tracing the origin of the group to the ministry of Jesus. For Mark's Gospel and the Twelve, see Günther Schmahl, *Die Zwölf im Markusevangelium. Eine redaktionsgeschichtliche Untersuchung* (TThSt 30; Trier: Paulinus, 1974); and Konrad Stock, *Boten aus dem Mit-Ihm Sein. Das Verhältnis zwischen Jesus und den Zwölf nach Markus* (AnBib 70; Rome: Biblical Institute, 1975).

107. Fitzmyer, *Luke*, pp. 613–21. He notes that "the fluctuation in the names reveals that they were not all precisely remembered as time wore on" (p. 614). A similar fluctuation in the order of the names takes place with the twelve tribes of Israel in Gen 49, Deut 33, and Judg 5. The differences in names, however, still remains a problem, even for those postulating a post-Easter constitution of the Twelve.

108. Raymond E. Brown, *The Critical Meaning of the Bible* (New York: Paulist, 1981), p. 129.

109. Fitzmyer, *Luke*, p. 254.

110. For an important defense of this position based on the Aramaic background, see Joachim Jeremias, "Golgotha und der heilige Felsen. Eine Untersuchung zur Symbolsprache des Neuen Testaments," *Angelos* 2 (1926) 74–128; for his most recent views on Peter, see *New Testament Theology, Part One* (New York: Scribners, 1971).

111. J. C. Hawkins, *Horae Synopticae* (Oxford: Oxford Univ. Press, 1909).

112. Christoph Kähler, "Zur Form- und Traditionsgeschicht von Matth. XVI. 19," *NTS* 23 (1977) 36–58, here pp. 38–39.

113. Ibid., p. 44.

114. "La révélation du Fils de Dieu en faveur de Pierre (Mt 16, 17) et de Paul (Gal 1, 16)," *RechSR* 52 (1964) 411–20. Matt 16:17, moreover, is very close to what is known as the Johannine logion; see Matt 11:25–27 and Luke 10:21–22.

115. "On that level, precisely because of the Aramaic identity of *Kephā*/*kephā*, there can be no doubt that the rock on which the church was to be built was Peter" (Raymond E. Brown et al., *Peter in the New Testament* [New York: Paulist/Minneapolis: Augsburg, 1973], p. 92).

116. Max Wilcox, "Peter and the Rock: A Fresh Look at Matthew XVI. 17–19," *NTS* 22 (1976) 73–88, here p. 79.

117. See Joseph Fitzmyer, "Aramaic *Kephā* and Peter's Name in the New Testament," in *To Advance the Gospel* (New York: Crossroad, 1981), pp. 112–24, and his earlier "The Name Simon," in *Essays on the Semitic Background of the New Testament* (Missoula, Mont.: Scholars, 1974), pp. 105–12. See also J. K. Elliot, "Kēphas: Simon Petros: ho Petros: An Examination of New Testament Usage," *NovT* 14 (1972) 241–56.

118. The response to the inappropriateness of "ecclesia" in a Palestinian context is usually that the Hebrew term *qāhāl* stood in its place in the tradition or source. For the problems with ecclesia in this context see Philip Vielhauer's essay on "Oikodome," now in *Oikodome. Aufsätze zum Neuen Testament*, vol. 2 (Munich: Chr. Kaiser, 1979).

119. See Collmann, *Peter.*

120. Reginald H. Fuller, " The 'Thou Art Peter' Pericope and the Easter Appearances," *McCQ* 20 (1967) 309–15.

121. Hartwig Thyen, *Studien zur Sündenvergebung* (FRLANT 96; Göttingen: Vandenhoeck und Ruprecht, 1979), pp. 218–36.

122. See nn. 74 and 75 above.

123. For a phenomenological approach more indebted to Husserl and less to Kantian transcendental philosophy than Rahner, see the two brilliant works by Edward Farley, *Ecclesial Man: A Social Phenomenology of Faith and Reality* (Philadelphia: Fortress, 1975) and *Ecclesial Reflection: An Anatomy of Theological Method* (Philadelphia: Fortress, 1982).

124. Karl Rahner, *A New Christology* (New York: Seabury, 1980), p. 21.

125. See Rahner, *Foundations*, pp. 326, 329, 327, and 335 respectively.

126. Karl Rahner, "Zur Ekklesiologie," p. 106 (cited in n. 87 above).

127. Joseph A. Fitzmyer, *A Christological Catechism: New Testament Answers* (New York: Paulist, 1981), p. 3.

128. See Schubert Ogden, *The Point of Christology* (New York: Harper and Row, 1982); and Francis Schüssler Fiorenza, "Reflective Christology," *Cross Currents* 32 (1982).

129. *Foundations*, pp. 332–35.

130. *New Christology*, pp. 18–31.

131. *Foundations*, pp. 329–32.

132. *Foundations*, pp. 322–23.

133. Within Rahner's theology, the God-world relation is a concrete historical relation involving God's offer of salvation and human response. The theory of the "supernatural existential" is a condition for the transcendental deduction of Church.

134. For an excellent exposition of Rahner's ecclesiology in *Foundations*, see Michael A. Fahey, "On Being Christian—Together," in Leo J. O'Donovan, ed., *A World of Grace* (New York: Seabury, 1980), pp. 120–37.

135. Rahner, *Theological Investigations*, 4:423.

136. See Karl Rahner, "The Church and the Sacraments," in his *Inquiries* (New York: Herder and Herder, 1964), pp. 191–299.

137. A brilliant exposition of the role of self in German Idealism is Mark C. Taylor, *Journeys to Selfhood: Hegel and Kierkegaard* (Berkeley: Univ. of California Press, 1980).

138. See James J. Buckley, "On Being a Symbol: An Appraisal of Karl Rahner," *TS* 40 (1979) 453–73.

139. Medard Kehl, *Kirche als Institution* (FTS 22; Frankfurt: Josef Knecht, 1976), pp. 171–238, esp. 204–13.

140. See the essays by John Galvin and Michael A. Fahey in "A Changing Ecclesiology in a Changing Church: A Symposium on Development in the Ecclesiology of Karl Rahner," ed. Leo J. O'Donovan, *TS* 38 (1977) 736–62. For Rahner's latest conception of divine institution and divine law in the Church, see his *Vorfragen zu einem ökumenischen Amtsverständnis* (QD 65, Freiburg: Herder, 1974), esp. pp. 32–39.

141. For earlier emphasis on the death of Jesus and the foundation of the Church, see his theological doctoral dissertation, *"E latere Christi". Der Ursprung der Kirche als Zweiter Eva aus der Seite Christi des Zweiten Adam. Eine Untersuchung über den typologischen Sinn von Jo 19, 34* (Th.D. dissertation, Innsbruck, 1936; microfilm in Center for Research Libraries, University of Chicago).

142. Rahner, *New Christology*, pp. 18–31.

143. Rahner, *Foundations*, pp. 346–69.

144. This problem is not limited to Rahner, but to every phenomenological justification of communal and ecclesial existence based on the perception of the reality of salvation; see, for example, Farley's discussion of ecclesial reality in *Ecclesial Man* and *Ecclesial Reflections*.

145. Articles by Anton Vögtle: "Messiasbekenntnis und Petrusverheissung. Zur Komposition von Mt 16, 12–23," *BZ* 1 (1957) 252–72 and 2 (1958) 85–103; "Jesus und die Kirche," in *Begegnung der Christen. Studien evangelischer und katholischer Theologen*, ed. Martin Roesle and Oscar Cullmann (Stuttgart: J. Knecht, 1959), pp. 54–81; "Ekklesiologische Auftragsworte des Auferstandenen," *Sacra Pagina*, vol. 2, ed. Joseph Coppens et al. (BEThL 12/13; Paris/Gembloux: J. Duculot, 1959), pp. 280–94; "Der Einzelne und die Gemeinschaft in der Stufenfolge der Christusoffenbarung," in *Sentire Ecclesiam*, ed. Jean Daniélou and Herbert Vorgrimler (Freiburg: Herder, 1961), pp. 50–91; "Das christologische und ekklesiologische Anliegen von Mt 28, 18–20," *SE* II/1, ed., Frank L. Cross (TU 87; Berlin: Akademie Verlag, 1964), pp. 266–94; and "Exegetische Erwägungen über das Wissen und Selbstbewusstsein Jesu," *Gott in Welt*, vol. 1, ed. Johann B. Metz (Freiburg: Herder, 1964), pp. 608–67.

146. Rudolf Schnackenburg is much more cautious than Anton Vöglte about the change or break in Jesus' ministry and his dawning awareness of the possibility of

rejection; see his "Kirche," *LThK* 6 (Freiburg: Herder, 1962), pp. 167–72; also his *The Church in the New Testament* (New York: Seabury, 1965), pp. 12–17, where the post-resurrection origin of the Church is emphasized.

147. Hans Küng, *The Church* (New York: Sheed and Ward, 1967), p. 108: "In the *pre-Easter period*, Jesus by his preaching and ministry *laid the foundations* for the emergence of a post-resurrection Church" (Küng's emphasis). See also Michael Schmaus, *The Church* (cited in n. 74 above), pp. 21–26; and Richard McBrien, *Catholicism* (Minneapolis: Winston, 1980), pp. 575–77.

148. Albrecht Oepke, "Der Herrnspruch über die Kirche. Mt 16, 17–19 in der neuesten Forschung," *StTh* 2 (1948) 110–65; Werner G. Kümmel, *Promise and Fulfillment* (SBT 23; London: SCM, 1861, 2nd ed.); id., *Kirchenbegriff und Geschichtsbewusstsein in der Urgemeinde und bei Jesus* (Göttingen: Vandenhoeck, und Ruprecht, 1968, 2nd ed.); id., "Jesus und die Anfänge der Kirche," *StTh* 7 (1953) 1–27, now in *Heilsgeschehen und Geschichte. Gesammelte Aufsätze 1933–1964* (Marburg: N. C. Elwert, 1965), pp. 289–309; and Cullmann, *Peter*.

149. Eric Peterson, "Die Kirche," in *Theologische Traktate* (Munich: Kösel, 1951), pp. 409–29; Heinrich Schlier, "Die Entscheidung für die Heidenmission in der Urchristenheit," in *Die Zeit der Kirche* (Freiburg: Herder, 1966, 4th ed.), pp. 90–107. Both emphasize much more strongly the post-Easter origin of the Church and the role of the Spirit in the turn toward the universal mission.

150. In *On Being a Christian* (Garden City, N.Y.: Doubleday, 1976), pp. 283–86 and 478, Hans Küng rejects his earlier position. For Vögtle's later position, see "Zum Problem der Herkunft von Mt 16, 17–19," in *Orientierung an Jesus. Zur Theologie der Synoptiker*, ed. Paul Hoffmann et al. (Freiburg: Herder, 1973), pp. 373–93, where he has been influenced by Hartwig Thyen's interpretation of Matt 16 as a protophany narrative. Vögtle's "Die hermeneutische Relevanz des geschichtlichen Charakters der Christusoffenbarung," *EThL* 43 (1967) 470–87, acknowledges the interpretive nature of the post-resurrectional words of Jesus that are not *ipsissima verba*. See also his sections on Jesus and the early community in *Ökumenische Kirchengeschichte*, vol. 1, *Alte Kirche und Ostkirche*, ed. R. Kottje (Mainz: Matthias Grünewald/Munich: Chr. Kaiser, 1970), pp. 3–36. This position is still defended by Heinz Schürmann and by Rudolf Pesch, Vögtle's student and successor. Since Pesch locates the foundation of belief in the resurrection in the earthly ministry of Jesus and the disciples' response, it is therefore consistent to locate the foundation of the Church in the pre-Easter period.

151. According to Küng, the idea of an atoning death would then lead to and "explain the idea of the founding of a Church" (*Church*, p. 77). For a survey of those maintaining Jesus' interpretation of his death at the last supper and its relation to "atoning death," see John Galvin, "Jesus' Approach to Death: An Examination of Some Recent Studies, *TS* 41 (1980) 713–44. However, the historigraphy of this article is interesting because the authors discussed in the text refer to Jesus' interpretation of his death, whereas those in the footnotes—Vögtle, Gnilka, etc.—are all much more cautious.

152. It is in respect to both the impending death and the interpretation of the last meal that Küng has radically changed his position in *On Being a Christian*.

153. Kümmel, *Promise and Fulfillment*, pp. 64–82.

154. Gerald O'Collins, "Peter as Easter Witness," *HeyJ* 22 (1981) 1–18.

155. Against O'Collins is the exegetical consensus in Brown et al., *Peter in the New Testament*, p. 106: "Matthew does not hint (as some would interpret Mark 16:7 to do) that Peter was the first among the Twelve to see the risen Jesus; and indeed his account of the appearances of the risen Jesus to the Eleven on the mountain in Galilee (28:16–17) leaves no room for an earlier appearance to Peter." For the historical role of Mary Magdalene, see Elisabeth Schüssler Fiorenza, *In Memory of Her* (New York: Crossroad, 1983). pp. 304–7, 321–23, 332–33.

156. Brown, *Critical Meaning*, p. 13: "Moreover, although theoretically these words were spoken in the early 30s, often there is little evidence that they influenced

church life in the next few decades." This statement is corroborated by an analysis of Matt 28:18–20 in relation to Matthean theology; see the important essay by Günther Bornkamm, "The Risen Lord and the Earthly Jesus: Matthew 28:16–20," in *The Future of Our Religious Past*, ed. James Robinson (New York: Harper, 1971), pp. 202–29. For a different view, see Benjamin J. Hubbard, *The Matthean Redaction of a Primitive Apostolic Commissioning: An Exegesis of Matthew 28:16–20* (Missoula, Mont.: Scholars, 1973).

157. See Vögtle's later essays: especially "Zum Problem der Herkunft von Mt 16, 17–19," "Die hermeneutische Relevanz des geschichtlichen Charakters der Christusoffenbarung," and *Ökumenische Kirchengeschichte*, 1:3–36 (all cited in n. 150 above).

158. See *Herrlichkeit*, vol III/2, pt. 2 (Einsiedeln: Johannes, 1959), pp. 150–86, where von Balthasar carefully differentiates between the time of Jesus and that of the Church. In response to the problem whether Jesus foresaw a Church for an interim period, he refers to the establishment of the Eucharist (p. 170, n. 14).

159. *Mysterium Salutis*, vol. III/2, p. 133, develops the post-Easter foundation of the Church in the resurrection appearances, combining historical and symbolic elements; see also *Theodramatik*, vol. II/2 (Einsiedeln: Johannes, 1978), pp. 241–410, and his collection *Pneuma und Institution* (Einsiedeln: Johannes, 1974), pp. 202–35. On office and discipleship, see *Sponsa Verbi* (Einsiedeln: Johannes, 1961), pp. 80–147. The best treatment of von Balthasar's ecclesiology is Kehl's section in *Kirche als Institution*, pp. 239–311. Although extremely partial to von Balthasar's position, he concedes that it is a problem how the Church stems from Christ and yet exists prior to Christ because of the mariological foundation of the Church (p. 289, n. 284).

160. See Raymond Brown, *Critical Meaning*, p. 40, on the words at the last supper and its relation to the Tridentine statement that Christ instituted seven sacraments (DS 1601 and 1752). For a defense of the traditional interpretation of Jesus' prediction of his death at the last supper, see Rudolf Pesch, *Das Abendmahl und Jesu Todesverständnis* (Freiburg: Herder, 1979). See also the criticism by Ferdinand Hahn, "Das Abendmahl und Jesu Todesverständnis," *TRev* 76 (1980) 265–72.

161. Walter Kasper and Gerhard Sauter, *Kirche—Ort des Geistes* (Herder: Freiburg, 1976), pp. 12–55, here p. 38.

162. Walter Kasper, "Elements zu einer Theologie der Gemeinde," in *Virtus Politica*, ed. Joseph Möller and Hans Kohlenberger (Stuttgart: F. Frommann, 1974), pp. 33–50. For Ratzinger's development of the post-Easter foundation of the Church based on the work of Peterson and Schlier, see "Kirche, III. Systematisch," *LThK*, 2nd ed., 6:173–83, and *Das Volk Gottes* (Düsseldorf: Patmos, 1969), pp. 75–89.

163. Kasper, *Kirche—Ort des Geistes*, pp. 39–40.

164. Ibid., p. 40.

165. Ibid., pp. 41–43.

166. Küng, *Church*, p. 228.

167. Ibid., pp. 221–22.

168. Küng, *On Being a Christian*, p. 399, see also p. 383.

169. Ibid., p. 403.

170. Ibid., pp. 396–410.

171. Cf. Küng, *Church*, pp. 108–12, with *On Being a Christian*, pp. 283–86 and 318–25. Unfortunately, the English translation of *Church*, p. 111, distorts Küng's text when it says, "Vögtle himself . . . goes beyond Kümmel in assuming, without sufficiently weighty grounds, that Jesus. . . ." The German reads "*nicht* ohne schwerwiegende Grunde" (*Die Kirche* [Freiburg: Herder, 1967], p. 96).

172. *On Being a Christian*, p. 286.

173. Ibid., pp. 399–410. For a description of the role that the doctrine of justification plays in Küng's ecclesiology, see Kehl, *Kirche als Institution*, pp. 123–70, esp. 133–50.

174. Edward Schillebeeckx, *Jesus*, pp. 385–97.

175. Ibid., 385–90.

176. Ibid., 387.

177. Ibid., 389.

178. Edward Schillebeeckx, *Ministry: Leadership in the Community of Jesus Christ* (New York: Crossroad, 1981), pp. 1–37, here p. 5, and *Christ: The Experience of Jesus as Lord* (New York: Crossroad, 1980), pp. 463–627.

179. See Heinz, *Das Problem der Kirchenenstehung*, pp. 316–409, for Bultmannian and post-Bultmannian interpretations of the foundation of the Church.

180. See Richard Palmer, *Hermeneutics* (Evanston: Northwestern Univ. Press, 1969), pp. 84–97; Friedrich Schleiermacher, *Hermeneutics: The Handwritten Manuscripts* (Missoula, Mont.: Scholars, 1977).

181. New York: Seabury, 1975.

182. For Ricoeur's basic theory, see his *Interpretation Theory: Discourse and the Surplus of Meaning* (Forth Worth: Texas Christian Univ. Press, 1976); and for an excellent collection of his more recent publications, see *Hermeneutics and the Human Sciences*, ed. John B. Thompson (New York: Cambridge Univ. Press, 1981).

183. See Leo Dullaart, *Kirche und Ekklesiologie. Die Institutionslehre Anrold Gehlens als Frage an den Kirchenbegriff in der gegenwärtigen systematischen Theologie* (Mainz: Matthias Grünewald, 1975), esp. pp. 52–96. Romanticism emphasized not only individuality but also the common spirit within institutions.

184. Leipzig and Darmstadt: Heyer und Leske, 1819.

185. Klaus Koch, "Der Tod des Religionsstifters," *KD* 8 (1962) 100–23; and the response of Ferdinand Baumgartel, "Der Tod des Religionsstifters," *KD* 9 (1963), 223–33.

186. *The Sociology of Religion* (Chicago: Univ. of Chicago Press, 1944), p. 342.

187. *On Being a Christian*, p. 286.

188. Arthur C. Danto, *Analytical Philosophy of History* (New York: Cambridge Univ. Press, 1965), pp. 112–42. See, however, the critical analyses of the inadequacy of Danto's position: Jürgen Habermas, *Zur Logik der Sozialwissenschaften* (Philosophische Rundschau, Beiheft 5; Tübingen: J. C. B. Mohr, 1967), pp. 161–67; and Hans Martin Baumgartner, *Kontinuität und Geschichte* (Frankfurt: Suhrkamp, 1972), pp. 269–94.

189. J. L. Austin, *Philosophical Papers*, ed. J. O. Urmson and G. J. Warnock (London: Oxford Univ. Press, 1970). See his "Performative-Constantive," in *Philosophy and Ordinary Language*, ed. C. E. Caton (Urbana: Univ. of Illinois Press, 1963), pp. 22–23. At first he had distinguished between "constantive" (that affirms something as true or false) and "performative" (that is successful or not). In his posthumous work, *How to Do Things with Words*, ed. J. O. Urmson (London: Oxford Univ. Press, 1962), he saw that all speaking is action. His previous distinction is more an analytical division of one and the same statement.

190. Peter Strawson, "Intention and Convention in Speech Acts," *PhRev* 73 (1964) 439–60; John R. Searle, *Speech Acts* (New York: Cambridge Univ. Press, 1969), pp. 22–71; id., "Austin on Locutionary and Illocutionary Acts," *PhRev* 77 (1968); and Jürgen Habermas, "What Is Universal Pragmatics?" in his *Communication and the Evolution of Society* (Boston: Beacon, 1979), pp. 1–68.

191. In addition to Searle's *Speech Acts*, see his *Expression and Meaning: Studies in the Theory of Speech Acts* (New York: Cambridge Univ. Press, 1979).

192. *Speech Acts*, p. 42.

193. Ibid., p. 42. Note Searle's modification of H. P. Grice, "Meaning," *PhRev* (1957) 377–88.

194. Paul Ricoeur, "The Model of the Text: Meaningful Action Considered as a Text," *Social Research* 38 (1971) 529–55.

195. See also Wolfgang Mommsen, "Verstehen und Idealtypus. Zur Methodologie einer historischen Sozialwissenschaft," in *Max Weber. Gesellschaft. Politik und Geschichte* (Frankfurt: Suhrkamp, 1974). Also important is J. W. N. Watkins, "Ideal Types and Historical Explanation," in *Readings in the Philosophy of Science*, ed. H. Feigl and M. Brodbeck (New York: Appleton-Century Crofts, 1953), pp. 723–44.

196. Obviously implied in this de-emphasis of intentionality are the recent discus-

sions about the limitations of Jesus' knowledge; see especially Joseph Ratzinger's essay "Bewusstsein und Wissen Christi," *MThZ* 12 (1961) 78–81. Philipp Kaiser, *Das Wissen Jesu Christi in der lateinischen (westlichen) Theologie* (Rosensburg: Pustet, 1981), gives a thorough survey of the issue from medieval to contemporary times. His interpretation of church documents (pp. 266–70) suggests that the *Pastoral Constitution on the Church in the Modern World*, no. 22, has modified both *Lamentabili's* condemnation of Loisy on the issue and the decrees of 1918.

197. Cf. Martin Hengel, *The Charismatic Leader and His Followers* (New York: Crossroad, 1981), and Helmut Koester, *Introduction to the New Testament*, vol. 2 (Philadelphia: Fortress, 1982), pp. 73–85.

198. For the different meanings of continuity, see Hans Michael Baumgartner, *Kontinuität und Geschichte* (Frankfurt: Suhrkamp, 1972).

199. See Jürgen Habermas: "What Is Universal Pragmatics?" in *Communication and the Evolution of Society* (Boston: Beacon, 1979), pp. 1–68; "Wahrheitstheorien," in *Wirklichkeit und Reflexion. Walter Schulz zum 60. Geburtstag*, ed. Hans Fahrenbach (Pfullingen: Neske, 1973), pp. 211–65; and *Theorie des kommunikativen Handelns*, 2 vols. (Frankfurt: Suhrkamp, 1981).

200. For a critical discussion of Habermas's universal pragmatics, see David Held, *Introduction to Critical Theory: Horkheimer to Habermas* (Berkeley: Univ. of California Press, 1980), pp. 330–78; and *Habermas: Critical Debates*, ed. John B. Thompson and David Held (Cambridge, Mass.: MIT Press, 1982), especially the essay by Thompson, "Universal Pragmatics," pp. 116–33, and Habermas's "A Reply to My Critics," pp. 219–83.

201. Habermas, "What Is Universal Pragmatics?" pp. 50–68. His attempt to give a completely rational foundation for illocutionary validity claims overlooks the importance of limit concepts, especially the significance of religious language. The inadequacy of his attempt at a total rational foundation has been raised by several of his critics and cannot be discussed here. See, however, Habermas's response to his critics, especially to Peukert, in "A Reply," pp. 245–47.

202. The significance of the interactive dimension of communicative competence has been elaborated for the understanding of redemption in my essay "Critical Social Theory and Christology," *Proceedings CTSA* 30 (1975) 63–110.

203. Norman Perrin, *Jesus and the Language of the Kingdom* (Philadelphia: Fortress, 1976); and Paul Ricoeur, "Biblical Hermeneutics," *Semeia* 4 (1975) 27–148.

204. "Preface to Bultmann" by Paul Ricoeur, in his *Essays on Biblical Interpretation*, pp. 49–72.

205. See Hans Robert Jauss, *Literaturgeschichte als Provokation* (Frankfurt: Suhrkamp, 1970) and *Ästhetische Erfahrung und literarische Hermeneutik* (Munich: Fink, 1977). A translation of several of Jauss's important essays has been edited by Paul de Man. *Toward an Aesthetic of Reception* (Minneapolis: Univ. of Minnesota Press, 1982). Several important collections of essays discussing this hermeneutical approach have appeared: Rainer Warning, *Rezeptionsästhetik* (Munich: Fink, 1979, 2nd ed.); Gerhard Köpf, *Rezeptionspragmatik* (Munich: Fink, 1981); and Gunter Grimm, *Rezeptionsgeschichte* (Munich: Fink, 1977).

206. See Ralph P. Crimmann, *Karl Barths frühe Publikationen und ihre Rezeption* (Bern: Peter Lang, 1981), who applies the notion of reception of Barth's early theology.

207. See Jauss's essay "Literary History as a Challenge to Literary Theology," in *Toward an Aesthetic*, pp. 3–45.

208. See Jauss's criticism of Gadamer's concept of the classic for its inability to provide a foundation for a reception beyond the period of its origination (ibid., pp. 29–32).

209. Paul de Man, "Introduction," in Jauss, *Toward an Aesthetic*, p. xiv.

210. See Roman Ingarden, "Konkretisation und Rekonstruktion," and Felix Vodicka, "Die Rezeptionsgeschichte Literarischer Werke" and "Konkretisation des li-

terarischen Werkes," for the notion of "concretization." All three essays are in Warning, *Rezeptionsästhetik*, pp. 42–112.

211. *Estetica* (Bari, 1902, 2nd ed.), p. 40; quoted from Jauss, *Toward an Aesthetic*, p. 78.

212. Here a parallel exists between the foundation of the Church and the resurrection of Jesus. The interpretation of the resurrection of Jesus within the Pesch-hypothesis makes the horizon of expectation the criterion of the interpretation of the resurrection rather than the reception as expressed in the New Testament texts the criterion of the interpretation.

213. See Francis Fiorenza, "Reflective Christology," *Cross Currents* 32 (1982).

214. See Gerald O'Collins, "Peter as Easter Witness," pp. 1–18.

215. For example, Wolfgang Schrage, " 'Ekklesia' und 'Synagoge.' Zum Ursprung des urchristlichen Kirchenbegriffs," *ZThK* 60 (1963) 178–202. For a criticism of Schrage, see Hartwig Thyen, "Zur Problematik einer neutestamentlichen Ekklesiologie," in *Frieden–Bibel–Kirche*, ed. Gerhard Liedke (Stuttgart: Klett, 1973), pp. 96–173, esp. 142.

216. "Die Wandlung des Selbstverständnisses der Kirche in der Geschichte des Urchristentums," *Glauben und Verstehen*, vol. 3 (Tübingen: J. C. B. Mohr, 1960), pp. 131–42. See also his *Theology of the New Testament*, 2 vols. (New York: Scribners, 1951 and 1955).

217. Josef Hainz, *Ekklesia. Strukturen Paulinischer Gemeinde-Theologie und Gemeinde-Ordnung* (Biblische Untersuchungen 9; Regensburg: Pustet, 1972).

218. See Roberts Banks, *Paul's Idea of Community: The Early House Churches in Their Historical Setting* (Grand Rapids: Eerdmans, 1980).

219. Klaus Berger, "Volksversammlung und Gemeinde Gottes. Zu den Anfängen der christilichen Verwendung von 'ekklesia,' " *ZThK* 73 (1976) 167–207. See also J. Y. Campbell, "The Origin and Meaning of the Christian Use of the Word Ekklesia," *JTS* 49 (1948) 130–42. Still very useful, especially for its references to Greek classical usage, is C. G. Brandis, "Ekklesia" in *PW* 5 (1905 ed.) 2163–200.

220. Against Schrage ("Ekklesia") who held that the choice of "ecclesia" was made without any reference to the LXX and solely on the basis of the profane Greek political assembly, Bornkamm argues that the profane use of "ecclesia" does not explain its universal and theological significance. It is, however, definite that this self-designation took place in the geographic area of Hellenistic Jewish Christianity. See Günther Bornkamm, "Die Binde- und Lösegewalt in der Kirche des Matthäus," in *Geschichte und Glaube*, vol. 2 (Munich: Kaiser, 1971), pp. 37–50.

221. See Lucien Cerfaux, *The Church in the Theology of St. Paul* (New York: Herder and Herder, 1959). For the notion of People of God, see the classic work by Nils Alstrup Dahl, *Das Volk Gottes. Eine Untersuchung zum Kirchenbewusstsein des Urchristentums* (Darmstadt: Wissenschaftliche Buchgesellschaft, 1963; reprint of 1941 ed.).

222. Helmut Merklein, "Die Ekklesia Gottes. Der Kirchenbegriff bei Paulus und in Jerusalem," *BZ* 23 (1979) 48–70.

223. Karl Holl, "Der Kirchenbegriff des Paulus in seinem Verhältnis zu dem der Urgemeinde," in *Gesammelte Aufsätze zur Kirchengeschichte*, vol. 2 (Tübingen: J. C. B. Mohr, 1928), pp. 44–67. See the observations in response to Holl by Wilhelm Mundle, "Das Kirchenbewusstsein der ältesten Christenheit," *ZNW* 22 (1923) 20–42. Mundle recognizes as an implication of Holl's thesis that "the leap from early Christianity to Catholicism is not as great as it had appeared in Sohm's conception" (p. 20). For a defense of the Catholic interpretation, see Paul-Gerhard Müller, *Der Traditionsprozess im Neuen Testaments* (Freiburg: Herder, 1981).

224. For the specific characteristic of the conception of the Church in Ephesians, see Joachim Gnilka, *Der Epheserbrief* (Freiburg: Herder, 1971), especially "Die Ekklesiologie," pp. 99–111. See also Helmut Merklein, *Das kirchliche Amt nach dem Epheserbrief* (SANT 33; Munich: Kösel, 1973).

225. See Rudolf Schnackenburg, "Ortsgemeinde und 'Kirche Gottes' im ersten

Korintherbrief," in *Ortskirche–Weltkirche. Festgabe für Julius Kardinal Döpfner*, ed. Heinz Fleckenstein (Würzburg: Echter, 1973), pp. 32–47. See also Heinz, *Ekklesia*, pp. 229–66, with Merklein's modifications in "Die Ekklesia Gottes," pp. 48–72.

226. 1 Thess 2:14 refers to the "churches of God in Christ Jesus which are in Judea." See also 1 Thess 1:1; 2 Thess 1:1; Acts 9:31; 10:37; 11:1, 29.

227. Berger, "Volksversammlung," pp. 167–207.

228. Gerhard Delling, "Merkmale der Kirche nach dem Neuen Testament," *NTS* 13 (1966/1967) 297–316.

229. Berger, "Volksversammlung," pp. 199.

230. "Einheit der Kirche und Kirchengemeinschaft in neutestamentlichen Sicht," in *Einheit der Kirche Grundlegung im Neuen Testament*, ed. Ferdinand Hahn et al. (QD 84; Freiburg: Herder, 1979), pp. 9–51, here p. 43.

231. P. Jovino, "L'Église communauté des Saints dans les Actes des Apôtres et dans les Épîtres aux Thessaloniciens," *RevistB* 16 (1968) 495–526. See Delling, "Merkmale," pp. 303–6.

232. See especially "The Righteousness of God in Paul," in *New Testament Questions of Today* (Philadelphia: Fortress, 1969), pp. 168–82. A good survey of opinions is present by Käsemann's student Peter Stuhlmacher, *Gerechtigkeit Gottes bei Paulus* (FRLANT 876; Göttingen: Vandenhoeck und Ruprecht, 1964).

233. Ernst Käsemann, *Commentary on Romans* (Grand Rapids: Eerdmans 1980), pp. 214–52, esp. 214–17, where he develops the notion of justification as the fashioning of a new creature; see also pp. 21–32 for a general exposition of justification.

234. See, Käsemann, *Romans*, pp. 411–16.

235. Berger, "Volksversammlung," pp. 196–201; Bornkamm, "Binde," pp. 37–50.

236. Hans Windisch, "Die Sprüche vom Eingehen in das Reich Gottes, *ZNW* 27 (1928) 163–92.

237. For "in Christ" see Franz Neugebauer, *In Christus. Eine Untersuchung zum Paulinischen Glaubensverständnis* (Göttingen: Vandenhoeck und Ruprecht, 1961); Kramer, *Christ, Lord*, pp. 139–44; Conzelmann, *An Outline*, pp. 208–12; Werner George Kümmel, *The Theology of the New Testament* (Nashville: Abingdon, 1973); pp. 217–20; and Käsemann, *Romans*, pp. 220–25.

238. Bultmann, *Theology*, 1:311.

239. Käsemann, *Romans*, pp. 220–25.

240. Berger, "Volksversammlung," 186–87.

241. For a word study see J. Y. Campbell, "*Koinonia* and Its Cognates in the New Testament" *JBL* 51 (1932) 352–80; for an emphasis on the spirit of communion fostering community, Schuyler Brown, "Koinonia as the Basis of the New Testament Ecclesiology," *One in Christ* 12 (1976) 157–67; for the relation between Christology and Ecclesiology, Rudolf Schnackenburg, "Die Einheit der Kirche unter dem Koinonia-Gedanken," in Hahn, ed., *Einheit*, pp. 52ff.

242. Ferdinand Hahn, "Taufe und Rechtfertigung. Ein Beitrag zur paulinischen Theologie in ihrer Vor- und Nachgeschichte," *Rechtfertigung* (Göttingen: Vandenhoeck und Ruprecht, 1976), pp. 95–124.

243. Hahn, "Einheit der Kirche," p. 16.

244. For literature, see Hans-Joachim Klauck, *Hausgemeinde und Hauskirche im fruhen Christentum* (Stuttgart: KBW, 1981).

245. Raymond E. Brown, "New Testament Background for the Concept of Local Church," *Proceedings CTSA* 36 (1981) 4.

246. James M. Robinson, "On the *Gattung* of Mark (and John)," in *Jesus and Man's Hope*, vol. 1 (Perspective 11; Pittsburgh: Pittsburgh Theological Seminary, 1970), pp. 99–129.

247. *Die Stunde der Botschaft* (Hamburg: Furche, 1970), p. 143.

248. Howard Clark Kee, *Community of the New Age: Studies in Mark's Gospel* (Philadelphia: Westminster, 1977), pp. 77–105.

249. See the works cited in n. 101 above.

250. Kee, *Community of the New Age*, pp. 145–75.

251. Gnilka, *Das Evangelium nach Markus*, 1:143–55 and 2:91–95.

252. Maria Horstmann, *Studien zur markinischen Christologie. Markus 8, 27–9, 13 als Zugang zum Christusbild des zweiten Evangeliums* (NTAbh 6; Münster: Aschendorff, 1973, 2nd ed.).

253. Schmahl, *Die Zwölf*, pp. 43–110; Kertelge, "Die Funktion," pp. 193–206.

254. See also Gnilka, *Das Evangelium nach Markus*, pp. 136–43.

255. Schmahl, *Die Zwölf*, pp, 128–40.

256. *Markus—Lehrer der Gemeinde* (SBM 9: Stuttgart: KBW, 1969).

257. Schmahl, *Die Zwölf*, pp. 111–27.

258. Gerhard Lohfink, "Hat Jesus eine Kirche gestiftet?" *ThQ* 161 (1981) 81–97, here p. 92. See also his dissertation, *Die Sammlung Israels. Eine Untersuchung zur lukanischen Ekklesiologie* (SANT 39; Munich: Kösel, 1975).

259. Lohfink, "Hat Jesus," p. 92.

260. Fitzmyer, *Luke*, pp. 251–52.

261. Fitzmyer, *Luke*, p. 258. See also Mark Sheridan, "Disciples and Discipleship in Matthew and Luke," *BTB* 3 (1973) 235–55.

262. Fitzmyer, *Luke*, p. 241.

263. H. J. Degenhardt, *Lukas Evangelist der Armen: Bestiz und Besitzverzicht in den lukanischen Schriften: Eine traditions- und redaktionsgeschichtliche Untersuchung* (Stuttgart: KBW, 1965); Jacques Dupont, "Les pauvres et la pauvreté dans les évangiles et les Actes," *La pauvreté évangeliqué* (Lire la Bible 27; Paris: Cerf, 1971), pp. 37–63; and Luke T. Johnson, *The Literary Function of Possessions in Luke-Acts* (SBLDS 9; Missoula, Mont.: Scholars, 1977).

264. Gerhard Schneider, "Die zwölf Apostel als 'Zeugen'. Wesen, Ursprung und Funktion einer lukanischen Konzeption," in *Christuszeugnis in der Kirche. Festschrift für F. Hengsbach*, ed. Paul Werner Scheel and Gerhard Schneider (Essen: Fredebeul und Koenen, 1970), pp. 39–65.

265. Jack Dean Kingsbury, "The Figure of Peter in Matthew's Gospel as a Theological Problem," *JBL* 98 (1979) 67–83.

266. *Jesus Christ in Matthew, Mark, and Luke* (Proclamation Commentaries; Philadelphia: Fortress, 1981), p. 87.

267. Edward Schweizer, *Matthäus und seine Gemeinde* (SBS 71; Stuttgart, 1974), p. 151.

268. John P. Meier, *Law and History in Matthew's Gospel: A Redactional Study of Mt. 5:17–48* (Rome: Biblical Institute Press, 1976).

269. *The Vision of Matthew* (New York: Paulist, 1979), pp. 237–39. See also Raymond Thysman, *Communauté et directives éthiques. La catéchèse de Matthieu* (Gembloux: J. Duculot, 1974), pp. 36–47.

270. "End-Expectation and Church in Matthew," in *Tradition and Interpretation in Matthew*, by Günther Bornkamm, Gerhard Barth, and Heinz Held (Philadelphia: Westminster, 1963), pp. 15–51, here p. 30.

271. See Albert Descamps, *Les justes et la justice dans les évangiles et le christianisme primitif* (Gembloux: J. Duculot, 1950).

272. Hubert Frankemölle, "Die Makarismen (Mt 5, 1–12; Lk 6, 20–23). Motive und Umfang der redaktionellen Komposition," *BZ* 15 (1971) 52–75; M. J. Suggs, *Wisdom, Christology and Law in Matthew's Gospel* (Cambridge: Harvard Univ. Press, 1970).

273. Hubert Frankemölle, *Jahwebund und Kirche Christi* (NTA 10; Münster: Aschendorff, 1974), 273–307.

274. Bornkamm, "End-Expectation," pp. 35–36.

275. Ulrich Luz, "Die Jünger im Matthäusevangelium," *ZNW* 62 (1971) 141–71.

276. Paul Hoffmann, "Der Petrus-Primat im Matthäusevangelium," in *Neues Testament und Kirche*, pp., 94–114, and with slight modifications his "Die Bedeutung des Petrus für die Kirche des Matthäus," in *Dienst an der Einheit. Zum Wesen und Auftrag des Petrusamts*, ed. Joseph Ratzinger (Düsseldorf: Patmos, 1978), pp. 9–26.

277. Kingsbury, "The Figure of Peter," esp. p. 74 and n. 25, where he argues against Brown, Donfried, and Reumann, *Peter in the New Testament*, pp. 87, 106–7.

278. Hoffmann, "Die Bedeutung des Petrus," pp. 16–17. See his *Studien zur Theologie der Logienquelle*, pp. 302–4.

279. See Hartwig Thyen, *Studien zur Sündenvergebung* (FRLANT 96; Göttingen: Vandenhoeck und Ruprecht, 1970), pp. 218–59, esp. 233–35.

280. See Peter Lampe, "Das Spiel mit dem Petrusnamen—Matt. XVI, 18," *NTS* 25 (1978/79) 227–45; Philip Vielhauer, *Oikodome. Aufsätze zum Neuen Testament* (Munich: Kaiser, 1979), especially *"Oikodome."*

281. Hoffmann, "Die Bedeutung des Petrus," pp. 21–25.

282. *Peter in the New Testament*, p. 106; Kingsbury, "The Figure of Peter," p. 74.

283. See J. Kahnmann, "Die Verheissung an Petrus: Mt. XVI, 18–19 im Zusammanhang des Matthäusevangeliums," *L'Évangile selon Matthieu*, ed. M. Didier (BETL 99; Gembloux: J. Duculot, 1972), pp. 261–80.

284. Wolfgang Trilling contends that the content of the teaching is not the preaching of the cross and resurrection nor Mary's "good news" nor Luke's conversion but rather the command (*Gebot*) of Jesus Christ (*Das wahre Israel* [SANT X; Munich Kösel, 1964], p. 38).

285. An example of changing historical judgments is Anton Vögtle. Influenced by the recent studies of Hoffmann, Thyen, and Hahn, he now locates the Matthean primacy text in Antioch and among third generation Christians. See his, "Zum Problem der Herkunft von Mt 16, 17–19" (cited in n. 150 above).

286. See Reinhard Hümmel, *Die Auseinandersetzung zwischen Kirche und Judentum im Matthäusevangelium* (Munich: Chr. Kaiser, 1963).

287. Bornkamm, "The Risen Lord," pp. 213–16.

288. This tension has made it possible for authors today to offer two fundamentally contrasting interpretations of Matthew; cf. Georg Strecker, *Der Weg der Gerechtigkeit* (FRLANT 82; Göttingen: Vandenhoeck und Ruprecht, 1966, 2nd ed.), with Hümmel, *Die Auseinandersetzung.*

289. Paul Hoffmann and Volker Eid, *Jesus von Nazareth und eine christliche Moral* (QD 66; Herder: Freiburg, 1975), pp. 27–108.

290. See Kenzo Tagawa, "People and Community in the Gospel of Matthew," *NTS* (1969/70) 149–62; also the survey by Daniel J. Harrington, "Matthean Studies since Joachim Rohde," *HeyJ* 16 (1975) 375–88; and the analysis of the situation of the Matthean community by William G. Thompson, "An Historical Perspective in the Gospel of Matthew," *JBL* 93 (1974) 243–62.

291. Alexander Sand, "Propheten, Weise und Schriftkundige in der Gemeinde des Matthäusevangeliums," in Josef Hainz, ed., *Kirche im Werden. Studien zum Thema Amt und Gemeinde im Neuen Testament* (Paderborn: Schöningh, 1976), pp. 167–84; Eduard Schweizer, "Gesetz und Enthusiasmus bei Matthäus," in his *Beiträge zur Theologie des Neuen Testaments* (Zürich: Zwingli, 1970), pp. 49–70; and Wolfgang Trilling, "Amt und Amtsverständnis bei Matthäus," in K. Kertelge, ed., *Das kirchliche Amt*, pp. 524–42.

292. See Raymond Brown, *The Gospel According to John*, vol. 1, *I–XII* (Garden City, N.Y.: Doubleday, 1966); and Rudolf Schnackenburg, *The Gospel According to St. John*, vol. 1 (New York: Herder, 1967), for the interpretation of John 1:35–51.

293. Cf. Ferdinand Hahn, "Die Jüngerberufung Joh 1, 35–51," in *Neues Testament und Kirche*, pp. 172–90, with J. Louis Martyn, *The Gospel of John in Christian History* (New York: Paulist, 1978), pp. 33–42.

294. Rudolf Schnackenburg, *Das Johannesevangelium*, vol. 3 (Freiburg: Herder, 1975), "Excurse 17. Jünger, Gemeinde, Kirche im Johannesevangelium," pp. 231–45; E.T. *The Gospel According to St John*, vol. 3 (New York: Crossroad, 1982), "Excursus 17: The Disciples, the Community, and the Church in the Gospel of John, pp. 203–17. My translation follows more closely the German text on p. 236.

295. Hahn, "Einheit der Kirche," p. 20.

296. John F. O'Grady, "Individualism and Johannine Ecclesiology," *BTB* 5 (1975) 227–61, and "Johannine Ecclesiology: A Critical Evaluation," *BTB* 7 (1977) 36–44.

297. Ferdinand Hahn, "Die Hirtenrede in Joh. 10," in *Theologia—Signum Crucis. Festschrift E. Dinkler* (Tübingen: J. C. B. Mohr, 1979), pp. 185–200.

298. Many scholars (e.g., Bultmann, Barrett, Schnackenburg, and Brown) interpret the other sheep in the parable as the Gentiles who will be converted as a result of the Gentile mission. John 11:52 is also interpreted in this direction. To interpret this in the history of the Johannine community, see Raymond E. Brown, "'Other Sheep Not of This Fold': The Johannine Perspective on Christian Diversity in the Late First Century," *JBL* 97 (1978) 5–22. For an interpretation of the reference in terms of Jewish Christians belonging to conventicles separate from the Johannine community, see Martyn, *Gospel of John*, pp. 115–21.

299. R. Borig, *Der wahre Weinstock. Untersuchung zu Jo 15, 1–10* (SANT 16; Munich: Kösel, 1967).

300. See Juan Peter Miranda, *Der Vater, der mich gesandt—religionsgeschichtliche Untersuchungen zu den johanneischen Sendungsformeln* (Bern: Herbert Lang, 1972); M. L. Appold *The Oneness Motif in the Fourth Gospel* (WUNT II/1; Tübingen: J. C. B. Mohn, 1976); and A. Correll, *Consummatum est. Eschatology Eschatology and Church in the Gospel of St. John* (London: SPCK, 1958).

301. Hahn argues against Ernst Käsemann's position (*The Testament of Jesus* [Philadelphia: Fortress, 1968]) that John does not really have an ecclesiology but only thinks of the individual believer (Hahn, "Einheit der Kirche," p. 32).

302. Ferdinand Hahn, "Sehen und Glauben im Johannesevangelium," *Neues Testament und Geschichte. Festschrift Oscar Cullmann* (Zurich: Zwingli, 1972), pp. 125–41. See Schnackenburg's excursus on "faith" in *Gospel According to St John*, 1:558–75.

303. Ulrich Wilckens, "Der Paraklet und die Kirche," in *Kirche. Festschrift für Günther Bornkmann* (Tübingen: J. C. B. Mohr, 1980), pp. 185–204.

304. On the relation between Jesus and the Paraclete, see Raymond E. Brown, "The Paraclete in the Fourth Gospel," *NTS* (1966/67) 113–32.

305. Werner G. Kümmel, *The Theology of the New Testament* (New York: Abingdon, 1973), p. 316.

306. "John uses the concept of the Paraclete to justify the audacity of the Johannine proclamation. If there are insights in the Fourth Gospel that go beyond the ministry, Jesus foretold this and sent the Paraclete, the Spirit of Truth, to guide the community precisely in this direction (16:12–13). Yet the Paraclete is portrayed not as speaking anything new but as simply interpreting what came from Jesus (16:13–15)" (Raymond E. Brown, *The Community of the Beloved Disciple* [New York: Paulist, 1979], pp. 28–29).

307. Wilckens, "Der Paraklet," pp. 199–203. See also Ulrich B. Müller's discussion of the Paraclete in relation to the authorization of tradition, "Die Parakletenvorstellung im Johannesevangelium," *ZThK* 71 (1974) 31–77.

308. The thesis of A. Kragerud, *Der Lieblingsjünger im Johannesevangelium* (Oslo, 1959), that is generally not accepted.

309. Both Peter and the Beloved Disciple are used as paradigmatic figures in the Fourth Gospel. See D. J. Hawkin, "The Function of the Beloved Disciple Motif in the Johannine Redaction," *LThPh* 33 (1977) 135–50. For contrasting descriptions, see Brown, *Peter in the New Testament*, pp. 133–39 for the Gospel, and pp. 139–47 for chap. 21.

310. Wilckens, "Der Paraklet," pp. 201–3.

311. See Rudolf Pesch, *Der reiche Fischfang* (Düsseldorf: Patmos, 1969); and Ernst Ruckstuhl, "Zur Aussage und Botschaft von Johannes 21," *Kirche des Anfangs. Heinz Schürmann Festschrift*, ed. R. Schnackenburg et al. (Leipzig: St. Benno, 1977) pp. 339–62.

312. Brown, *The Community*, p. 88. See also Harold Hegermann, "Er kam in sein Eigentum. Zur Bedeutung des Erdenwirkens Jesu im vierten Evangelium," in *Der Ruf Jesu und die Antwort der Gemeinde. Festschrift Jeremias* (Gütersloh: Gerd Mohn, 1970), pp.

112–31; and Ferdinand Hahn "Der Prozess Jesu nach dem Johannesevangelium," *Evangelisch-Katholischer Kommentar zum Neuen Testament,* vol. 2 (Neukirchen-Vluyn: Neukirchener Verlag, 1970), pp. 23–96, esp. 94–96.

313. In addition to Käsemann, *The Testament of Jesus,* see Eduard Schweizer, "Der Kirchenbegriff im Evangelium und den Briefen des Johannes," in *Neotestamentica* (Zurich: Zwingli, 1963), pp. 254–71, and *Church Order in the New Testament* (SBT 32; London: SCM, 1961), pp. 117–24.

314. Klaus Haacker, "Jesus und die Kirche nach Johannes," *ThZ* 29 (1973) 179–200; S. Pancaro, " 'People of God' in St. John's Gospel's Gospel," *NTS* 16 (1969/70) 114–29; and H. T. Wrege, "Jesusgeschichte und Jüngerschaft nach Joh. 12, 20–33 und Hebr. 5, 7–10," in *Der Ruf Jesu,* pp. 259–88.

315. Wayne A. Meeks, "The Man from Heaven in Johannine Sectarianism," *JBL* 91 (1972) 44–72. See D. Moody Smith, Jr., "Johannine Christianity: Some Reflections on Its Character and Delineation," *NTS* 21 (1974/75) 222–48. For the diverse communities, see Brown, *The Community,* esp. pp. 59–91 and 166–69.

316. Brown, *The Community,* p. 164.

317. *God's People in Christ: New Testament Perspectives on the Church and Judaism* (Philadelphia: Fortress, 1980), p. 29.

318. See Gager, *Kingdom and Community* (cited in n. 101 above).

319. See Avery Dulles, "Imaging the Church for the 1980's," *Thought* 56 (1981) 121–38, esp. p. 128; reprinted in *A Church to Believe In* (New York: Crossroad, 1982), pp. 1–18.

320. "The Foundation of the Church: Biblical Criticism for Ecumenical Discussion," *TS* 34 (1973) 3–18.

321. Wolfgang Trilling, " 'Implizite Ekklesiologie.' Ein Vorschlag zu thema: Jesus und Kirche," *Dienst der Vermittlung,* ed. Wilhelm Ernst and Konrad Feiereis (Leipzig: St. Benno, 1977), pp. 149–64, here p. 160. See also his *Die Botschaft Jesu.*

322. Fiorenza, "Rahner's Ecclesiology," pp. 250–54.

323. Raymond E. Brown, *Biblical Reflections on Crises Facing the Church* (New York: Paulist, 1975), pp. 20–37, esp. 31–33.

324. Kasper, *Jesus,* p. 111, n. 3: "This concept [implicit or indirect Christology] was introduced by Bultmann." See also Conzelmann, *Jesus,* pp. 87–96; and for Bultmann himself, *Theology,* 1:43.

325. For a discussion of implication from a logical perspective and within the context of analytical philosophy, see the article "Implication," in *Encyclopedia of Philosophy,* ed. Paul Edwards (New York: Macmillan, 1967).

326. See A. R. Anderson and N. D. Belnap, *Entailment* (Princeton: Princeton Univ. Press, 1975), for the relation between relevance and implication.

327. Fiorenza, "Rahner's Ecclesiology," pp. 153ff.

328. Hans Michael Baumgartner, in *Kontinuität und Geschichte. Zur Kritik und Metakritik der historischen Vernunft* (Frankfurt: Suhrkamp, 1972), gives an excellent survey of diverse theories of historical continuity. Although his own appeal to a transcendental conception and to totality remains unsatisfactory, his division of theories into views of continuity as an extant of history and as a hermeneutical narrative construction is quite illuminating.

329. See Gadamer, *Truth and Method,* pp. 278–89, for the hermeneutical significance of Aristotle's conception of practical philosophy.

330. Helmut Koester, *Introduction* (cited in n. 197 above), pp. 147–59.

331. E. H. Gombrich, *Art and Illusion* (Princeton: Princeton Univ. Press, 1960).

332. The inadequacy of this schema for ecclesiology is much more evident than for christology. In the former instance, it is scarcely possible to group together Roman Catholics and post-Bultmannians.

333. For a discussion of the relation between the Church, Jesus, and the kerygma in Bultmann and the Bultmannian school, see Hermann Häring, *Kirche und Kerygma. Das Kirchenbild in der Bultmannschule* (Herder: Freiburg, 1972).

334. See the analysis of this common trait by Van A. Harvey, *The Historian and the Believer* (New York: Macmillan, 1966), pp. 164–203; also Günther Bornkamm, *Jesus of Nazareth* (New York: Harper, 1960), pp. 53–63.

335. Ernst Käsemann, *Jesus Means Freedom* (Philadelphia: Fortress, 1969), *Essays on New Testament Themes* (SBT 41; London, SCM 1964), and *New Testament Questions of Today* (Philadelphia: Fortress, 1969). See the excellent survey of his ecclesiology by Daniel J. Harrington, "Ernst Käsemann on the Church in the New Testament, *HeyJ* 12 (1971) 246–57 and 365–76.

336. Gerhard Ebeling, *Word and Faith* (Philadelphia: Fortress, 1963) and more recently his *Dogmatik des christlichen Glaubens,* 2:369–408; Emil Fuchs, *Studies of the Historical Jesus* (SBT 42; London: SCM 1964).

337. Herbert Braun, "Der Sinn der neutestamentilichen Christologie," *Gesammelte Studien zum Neuen Testament und seiner Umwelt* (Tübingen: J. C. B. Mohr, 1962), pp. 243–82; Robinson, *A New Quest,* pp. 93–125.

338. Norman Perrin, *Rediscovering the Teaching of Jesus* (New York: Harper, 1976), pp. 102–8 and 207–48.

339. James M. Robinson, "Jesus: From Easter to Valentinus (or to the Apostles' Creed)," *JBL* 101 (1982) 5–37.

340. See Donald Francis Tovey, *Essays in Musical Analysis,* vol. 3, *Concertos* (London: Oxford Univ. Press, 1935), pp. 1–27 and 42–46; and Charles Rosen, *The Classical Style* (New York: Norton, 1972), pp. 245–50.

341. Schubert Ogden and Van A. Harvey, "How New is the 'New Quest' of the Historical Jesus?" (cited in n. 52 above).

342. For general historical surveys of the concept, see Uvo Andreas Wolf, *Jus Divinum. Erwägungen zur Rechtsgeschichte und Rechtsgestaltung* (Jus Ecclesiasticum 11; Munich: Claudius, 1970), a good survey but unfortunately there is no reference to St. Augustine. For the patristic period, see Ernst Rössler, *Göttliches und menschliches, unveränderliches und veränderliches Kirchenrecht von der Entstehung der Kirche bis zur Mitte des neunten Jahrhunderts* (Paderborn: Schöningh, 1934). Rössler's detail on information is marred by his tracing of divine law from Matt 28:19 and his one-sided confrontation with Sohm. For a focus on the relation between divine law and the papacy, see the excellent survey of conciliar and ecumenical documents in J. Michael Miller, *The Divine Right of the Papacy in Recent Ecumenical Theology* (An Greg 218; Rome: Gregorian Univ., 1980).

343. Johannes Neumann, "Das 'Jus Divinum' im Kirchenrecht," *Orientierung* 31 (1967) 5–8; id., "Erwägungen zur Revision des kirchlichen Gesetzbuches," *ThQ* 146 (1966) 285–304; id., "Das Kirchenrecht im Spannungsfeld der wissenschaftlichen Disziplinen," *ThQ* 152 (1972) 317–325; Edward Schillebeeckx, "The Catholic Understanding of Office in the Church," *TS* 30 (1969) 467–87.

344. Küng, *On Being a Christian,* pp. 490–92.

345. Edmund Schlink, "Zur Unterscheidung von *Ius divinum* und *Ius humanum*" (cited in n. 47 above).

346. In "Reflection on the Concept of '*Ius Divinum*' in Catholic Thought" (cited in n. 40 above), Karl Rahner has developed the relation between divine institution and the essence of the Church. In addition to the essence of the Church, Avery Dulles appeals to "Christ's gift" (" '*Ius Divinum*' as an Ecumenical Problem," pp. 701 and 706 [cited in n. 40 above]).

347. Dulles, "Ius Divinum," pp. 701–2.

348. J. Stöhr, "Modellvorstellungen im Verständnis der Dogmenentwicklung," *Reformata reformanda. Festgabe Hubert Jedin,* vol. 2 (Münster: Aschendorff, 1965), pp. 595–630.

349. See Raymond E. Brown, "Episcopē and Episkopos: The New Testament Evidence," *TS* 41 (1980) 322–38; also in *Critical Meaning,* pp. 124–46. See also Karl Kertelge, *Gemeinde und Amt im Neuen Testament* (Munich: Kösel, 1972), pp. 77–152.

350. Ferdinand Hahn, "Der Apostolat im Urchristenum. Seine Eigenart und seine

Voraussetzung," *KD* 20 (1974) 54–77; Anton Vögtle, "Exegetische Reflexionen zur Apostolizität des Amtes und zur Amtssukzession," *Kirche des Anfangs*, pp. 529–82; Joseph Hainz, "Die Anfänge des Bischofs- und Diakonenamtes," in *Kirche im Werden*, pp. 91–107; see also the survey by Rudolf Schnackenburg, "Apostolizität. Stand der Forschung," *Katholizität und Apostolizität*, Beiheft 2 of *KD* (1971), pp. 51–73.

351. See, for example, the excursus on deacons and bishops in Joachim Gnilka, *Der Philipperbrief* (HThKNT X/3; Freiburg: Herder, 1968).

352. Dulles, "Ius Divinum," pp. 698–701.

353. The complexity and diversity of the theories about the number of the sacraments is well known to all medievalists. In this respect, post-Tridentine sacramental theology represents an impoverishment in comparison with medieval theology; see, for example, Josef Finkenzeller, *Die Lehre von den Sakramenten im allgemeinen. Von der Schrift bis zur Scholastik* (*Handbuch der Dogmengeschichte* IV/1a; Freiburg: Herder, 1980) pp. 62–224.

354. Dulles, "Ius Divinum," pp. 700f. and 706.

355. See Brown, *The Critical Meaning*, pp. 40–41, on the relation between sacraments, the Council of Trent, and historical-critical study of the Bible.

356. See Leonardo Boff's history of the notion of the Church as a sacrament, *Die Kirche als Sakrament im Horizont der Welterfahrung* (Paderborn: Schöningh, 1972).

357. See Harald Wagner, *Einführung in die Fundamentaltheologie* (Darmstadt: Wissenschaftliche Buchgesellschaft, 1981), pp. 23–24.

358. DS 3013.

359. See Cornelius Mayer, "Garanten der Offenbarung. Probleme der Tradition in den antimanischäischen Schriften Augustins," *Augustinianum* 12 (1972) 51–78, esp. 73–77; Pierre T. Camelot, "Autorité de L'Écriture, autorité l'Église. À propos d'un texte de saint Augustin," *Mélanges offerts à m. D. Chenu* (Paris: J. Vrin, 1967), pp. 127–33.

PART III

THE
MISSION
OF THE CHURCH

Introduction

The mission of the Church, a central issue within traditional fundamental theology, was not an especially controverted issue. Basic unanimity existed about the Church's distinctive nature, purpose and mission. Yet today, the Church's mission has become an increasingly debated topic.[1] Missiologists debate about evangelization, its specific role and its applicability, and about the dangers of cultural colonialism.[2] Social ethicists question the legitimacy of the Church's social and political mission in view of the distinction between morality and legality and the necessary pluralism of modern society. Ecclesiologists focus on the relation between mission and ministry,[3] on the role of ordained and nonordained ministries, on the diversity of ministries, and even on the nature of ministry itself.[4] The new Roman Catholic code of canon law raises the problem entailed in the ecclesiastical empowerment known as "canonical mission."[5] The mission of the Church is central to pastoral theology. The practice of ministry is seen within practical and pastoral theology not simply as an application of the Church's teaching to concrete situations but as a source of theological insight. In short, the mission of the Church has increasingly been subject to analysis within systematic, ethical, and pastoral theology.

Nevertheless, a fundamental theological issue underlies all these specific debates and particular controversies, namely, the relation between the Church's religious identity and its understanding of mission. No matter what activity or ministry of the Church is under discussion, the basic question remains: how does this activity or ministry relate to the Church's religious identity? Unless theological reflection and analysis focus on this very question, they are off center; indeed they have not articulated the religious issues and they have not raised the fundamental theological problem underlying the contemporary situation. Such a failure is true not only of theology but also of the Churches themselves. The recent loss of membership within some American Churches has been attributed precisely to this failure.[6] Discussions of the relation between morality and legality,[7] proper form of evangelization, the role of priests, ministers, and of religious women and men in politics—all relate to the fundamental theological problem of the Church's religious identity. And as with our previous analyses, this identity can be ascertained neither from the traditional approach of a historical fundamental theology nor of a transcendental and existential analysis. Again, it is necessary to take up the methodology of foundational theology as a reconstructive hermeneutic and to apply it to the issue of the Church's mission, purpose, and identity.

Chapter 7

The Mission of the Church and Fundamental Theology

Before analyzing the fundamental theological issues surrounding the mission of the Church, this chapter will outline how the Church's mission was viewed and discussed within traditional fundamental theology. Then it will sketch the diverse contemporary theological positions on the Church's mission through a typology of theological options and an analysis of papal statements. The point of these descriptive analyses will be to show that underlying the issue is the fundamental theological question of religious identity.

Mission of the Church in Traditional Fundamental Theology

Traditional fundamental theology linked the mission of the Church with the issue of its foundation by the historical Jesus. It established a correlation between the Church's mission and Jesus' mission on an intentional and ontological level. Jesus instituted the Church for a specific purpose and with a definite mission. The Church continues Jesus' own purpose and mission. The Church, therefore, not only carries out Jesus' intention, but it is also rooted ontologically in the grace and salvation present in Jesus. Just as Jesus' origin and goal is transcendent, so too is the Church's origin and goal.

The historical and theological problems of the foundation of the Church also affect the Church's mission. Whatever objections speak against the possibility that Jesus instituted a Church also speak against any permanent institutionalization of the Church and its mission. To the extent that Jesus' eschatological consciousness excludes the direct legitimation of the Church, so too does it militate against a social, political, or sacramental mission.[8] Consequently, the resolution of the historical and theological problems of the Church's foundation applies to the mission of the Church. The issue of the Church's foundation is not fully resolved until that of its purpose and mission is resolved.

Proper Supernatural Purpose

For its analysis of the Church's purpose, traditional fundamental theology did not take as its starting-point the eschatological and apocalyptic proclamation of Jesus but rather the distinction between nature and supernature. Whereas other human institutions had particular natural goals, the Church has as its own distinctive supernatural goal sanctification and salvation. Not only did this goal determine the purpose and activity of the Church, but it was also the reason that God sent Jesus into the world. Consequently, the demonstration that Jesus founded a Church culminated in the argument that this Church had the same supernatural goal as Jesus.

Viewing the Church primarily as a society with goals and ends like every other society, traditional fundamental theology argued that the Church was a "perfect society," not in order to express its holiness or moral perfection, but rather to underscore its completeness and autonomy.[9] The attribution "perfect society" served to emphasize the independence of the Church from every civil and political system. This overall framework limited the points of theological controversy. Did the Church have a threefold or a twofold end?[10] Some theologians distinguished between a proximate goal (the exercise of the Christian religion), a remote goal (the sanctification of souls), and an ultimate goal (the beatific vision). Contesting this threefold division, others proposed a twofold goal: sanctification and beatific vision. The exercise of the Christian religion was viewed more as a means to an end than as the end itself. In the framework of this controversy, the practice of the Christian life, the preaching and teaching of Christian doctrine, the celebration of Christian rites, and even the participation in the sacraments constituted only the proximate goal of the Church according to one opinion, whereas it was only a means according to the other opinion.

Despite this controversy, a basic consensus existed: the Church's mission was ordered directly and primarily to a supernatural goal, the beatific vision. And, as in the questions of Jesus' resurrection and the

foundation of the Church, the Enlightenment with its deism, naturalism, and rationalism was viewed as the major opponent. Since the
Enlightenment rejected a supernatural revelation at the foundation of
Christianity, it also rejected a supernatural goal. It was against this
position that fundamental theology drew up its battle lines. It appealed to miracles, prophecies, and the resurrection of Jesus to produce a historical argument not only for the foundation of the Church
but also for its specific goal and mission. If the Enlightenment reduced the Church to an institution among others, the fundamental
theology of the period responded by arguing that the Church existed
as a "perfect society" that was independent from the state and had its
own goal and purpose: one that was supernatural in distinction and
in contrast to any natural goal or purpose.

This anti-Enlightenment polemic led to important shifts within
theology. A change took place with regard to the very notion of
"supernatural," which Thomas Aquinas had first used.[12] He taught
that God so created nature and so ordered nature to the supernatural
that, even though the supernatural goal is what nature cannot
achieve by itself, the supernatural is still that to which the natural
tends. In the post-Enlightenment period, nature no longer remained
a relational conception, but became an absolute category. It now referred to the world, especially to the world of nature as a closed
system.

A parallel change took place within theological anthropology.[13]
As a result of controversies within Spanish scholasticism, theological
anthropology began to posit a double finality for human nature: a
purely natural goal with its correlative natural fulfillment and an
added supernatural goal with its supernatural fulfillment. The notion
of nature as a closed system and the religious conception of a double
finality for human nature had its effects on fundamental theology.

Within classic scholastic theology, the nature-supernature distinction was discussed within anthropology, for the supernatural was
the goal of human nature and divine creation. In the post-Enlightenment period, the nature-supernature distinction became increasingly
important for fundamental theology and its development of its conceptions of religion, revelation, and the Church.[14] To counter the
naturalism of the Enlightenment, fundamental theology contrasted
nature and supernature much more sharply than previously. Since
the Enlightenment had pointed to a natural religion underlying all
positive religions, fundamental theology pointed to the necessity of
an extrinsic supernatural revelation as the ground of all positive religion. It did not, as in the romantic apologetic of Schleiermacher and

Lamennais, argue that only positive historical religions and not natural religions existed. Instead, it posited a second reality above and in addition to natural religion, namely, a supernaturally revealed religion.

Improper Social and Political Mission

The more nature and supernature came to be seen as two distinct levels and as two separate goals, the more the Church's mission was related to the supernatural and the more a social and political mission became an improper goal. In the wake of the Enlightenment and the increased interpretation of the natural as a closed sphere, the Church's religious mission was contrasted with a political and social mission. Papal statements reflect this theological viewpoint. Pope Pius XI wrote to Father M. D. Roland-Gosselin that the "the objective of the church is to evangelize, not to civilize. If it civilizes, it is for the sake of evangelization."[15] Pope Pius XII referred to the Church's "strictly religious, supernatural goal."[16] And linking the issue of foundation and mission, Vatican II's *Gaudium et spes* affirmed that Christ gave his Church "no proper mission in the political, economic, or social order. The purpose which He set before her is a religious one."[17] Although these papal statements have been since modified, they reflect and continue theological interpretation of the Church's mission in relation to the twofold goals elaborated by traditional fundamental theology.

The critics of political and liberation theology today take a similar position. They fear that the Church's social and political involvement is reductionistic because it equates a religious mission with a social or political mission. The advocacy of a specific social and political agenda, they argue, surrenders the Church's agenda to that of the world. The Church substitutes natural concerns for supernatural responsibilities.

A dichotomous model of the relation between the religious and the social underlies these criticisms. Evangelization and civilization, transcendence and immanence, supernatural and natural, gospel and law are clearly distinct and separate. When Churches, especially priests and ministers, focus on the mundane rather on the religious, they are to be thought of as "pagans in the pulpit,"[18] for they have forgotten their distinctively religious purpose and have neglected their essential responsibility to evangelize.

This model has its distinct advantages as well as disadvantages.

The neoscholastic emphasis upon the distinctiveness of the natural and the supernatural, each with its own separate teleological orientation, clearly distinguished the different roles of the Church and state in the modern age.[19] In many ways it corresponds to the modern liberal conception of the relation between religion and society, morality and legality, Church and state. Each represents distinct, independent, and autonomous realms. The neoscholastic development also parallels the trend in neo-Lutheranism of the nineteenth century with its emphasis on the distinction between the gospel and law.[20] Whereas the gospel is related to individual grace, personal conversion, and private faith, the law affects the institutional, social, and political. Such an emphasis upon two realms, nature and supernature, gospel and law, leaves no ambiguity about the Church's religious mission.

Challenges have been brought against such a theological dichotomy. Recent historical studies have shown that the classical Thomist distinction between nature and grace was not intended as the separation of two planes or spheres.[21] The emergence of *La nouvelle théologie* after World War II was based upon a retrieval of authentic Thomistic teaching, with de Lubac, Bouillard, Rahner, and Lonergan in the vanguard. Over against the dualistic misinterpretation of Thomas within baroque scholasticism and nineteenth-century neoscholasticism, they sought to show the significance of the integral relation between nature and grace. Although this movement of retrieval concentrated on theological anthropology and the relation between nature and grace, it laid the foundations for the development of political and liberation theology. Similar historical studies have shown that the neo-Lutheran interpretation of the gospel and law distinction involved a distortion of Luther's position.

Not only historically but also systematically, the division of the Church's mission into a properly religious and an improperly social or political mission raised the fundamental theological problem of the nature of that which is religious. The practical question of the Church's mission is at the root a fundamental theological question about the nature and specificity of the religious dimension of life. Is what is religious a separate and isolated experience; or is it a dimension of human experience so that religious identity is best understood not in contrast to other forms of identity, but precisely in and through its relation with them. Various attempts to address the mission of the Church often fail to overcome the dichotomy of traditional fundamental theology because they consider the mission of the Church primarily as an ecclesiological rather than as a fundamental theological question.

Mission of the Church in Contemporary Theology

Three Options of Relating Religious Identity and Church's Mission

In reaction to the dichotomous model, theologians have sought to work out a much more unified vision by introducing the categories of "substitutive mission," "unofficial mission," and "partial mission." Each of these categories goes beyond the traditional approach in a significant fashion; nevertheless, each only inadequately comes to terms with the problem because of a failure to explore the fundamental theological issue of the nature of religious identity. Each, therefore, remains caught up in the presuppositions of the dichotomous model which it had sought to overcome.

Substitutive Mission

Wolfhart Pannenberg maintains that the Church's mission is concerned with the impact of God's kingdom upon all dimensions of human life. But he adds the specific reservation that the "specifically social activities of the Church (its welfare organizations, child care centers, nursing and hospital establishments, schools, etc.) are subsidiary and temporary. The Church engages in these activities as a substitute for the political structure of society."[22] Richard P. McBrien and Juan Luis Segundo have also argued for the notion of substitutive service. McBrien has contended that "only when there is a lack of personnel or institutions to handle imperative needs" and "only where it is clearly a matter of supplying for the deficiences of other responsible agencies" can formal institutional social action be justified.[23] Those attributing a permanent proper social mission to the Church, he suggests, are "theologically conservative" and "argue reductively," for "they are the ones who see no need at all to justify the existence, for example, of Catholic schools, hospitals, counseling agencies, and the like."[24] The Church does have a social mission, but it should formally and institutionally so engage itself only where secular agencies do not.

This proposal appears reasonable at first. If, for example, in a previous century a missionary might have organized sanitation facilities for a village to prevent disease, the Church's mission is not the sanitation business. Moreover, the Church should avoid "patronizing" the world and should allow for the autonomy of human social organization. Where secular authorities do not perform such services, only then can the Church's social involvement be interpreted as the spelling out of the impact of God's kingdom upon all dimensions of life.

Yet the very category of substitutional activity appears inadequate to describe the relation between Church and society, since it seems to imply immaturity and a lack of autonomy. A child of seven needs parental guidance. If its parents should die or are incapable of exercising that guidance, society has some instrumentality for taking care of the deficiency. What society or the parents provide is a substitutional guidance that takes the place of a capacity that the child potentially has and will acquire in maturity. Such substitutional guidance seeks the good of the child and not that of the guardian. Whenever the category of substitution is used, it therefore implies two distinct subjects, one having sufficient maturity, wisdom, judgment, and the like; the other temporarily lacking these qualities. Can the relation between Church and society be so described? Is the Church even acting as Church where such a substitutional activity is claimed to be legitimate?

Traditional practice and history say no. Catholics did not establish universities and schools only as substitute institutions until the state could take them over. They never doubted that schools and hospitals were integral to the Church's mission. Moreover, if taken to its ultimate consequences, a substitutional theory would result in the Church's removal from welfare activities, hospitals, hospices, and educational institutions, and would limit it to liturgical celebration, proclamation, and catechesis. Some indeed have concluded that the Church should not run hospitals but have chaplaincies within hospitals, should not run schools but stress catechetical instruction—legitimate deductions from a substitutional theory.

A substitutional theory clearly splits religious and secular tasks so that a social mission is improper and inauthentic save in exceptional cases. It supports the same dichotomy it purported to overcome. The intuitive insight is that the case of sanitation and that of schools or hospitals should not be equated. Moreover, we need a theory of the relation between Church and state, religion and society, that is not based upon the notion of deficiency, to justify even the temporary social activity of the Church. An adequate theology of the relation between religious identity and social mission would have to show why care for the sick and poor and why education have always been integral to the Church's mission, and why today the same reasons demand a social and political mission that is permanent and not substitutional.

Unofficial Mission

A second proposal uses the category of "unofficial" mission as the means of overcoming the dichotomy between religious identity and social mission. Karl Rahner advocates that "the church as an official church, however, is not the immediate or the proper subject for realizing the concrete humanization of the world."[25] Not only does the official Church lack the qualifications to do so, but the world has the right to exercise its own responsibility for its development. To make the humanization of the world the Church's proper task would be to reintroduce clericalism and integralism.[26]

Rahner suggests an alternative: the Church can inspire, motivate, and move groups of Christians within it. They can organize in the service of the world. Their service can be inspired by Christian motives. Their exemplary lifestyle can serve as a critique of society. Yet as an official institution, the Church has no proper mission for the humanization of the world. Rahner's proposal articulates much of the theology that was at the basis of the Catholic Action movement in Europe. In its beginning, this movement, inspired by the hierarchy, sought to involve laypersons explicitly in a social mission; a direct political mission was often forbidden, but the Catholic Action movement gained momentum, its lay leaders gained a certain autonomy and their leadership flowed over to the Christian democratic parties.[27] In the United States, similar proposals have advocated an unofficial lay involvement in the social mission. These proposals have sought to incorporate into the Catholic Church the American voluntarism exemplified by town-hall democracy and religious congregationalism. Such proposals argued that the emphasis upon voluntary and unofficial social engagement would avoid the excesses of ecclesiastical influence in politics that has characterized some European situations.[28]

In emphasizing unofficial and voluntary service, this alternative acknowledges that every Christian has a social and political mission. Social initiatives need not and should not be the obligation of the hierarchy alone. Nevertheless, this position transfers the previous dichotomy between the religious and the social to the interior of the Church. Its mission is split into an official religious mission and an unofficial social mission. The hierarchy (bishop and priest) has the religious mission, whereas the layperson has the secular mission. If laypersons exercise religious functions, then they should receive orders (e.g., the diaconate). If priests are engaged in secular work, then they perform the proper task of laypersons.[29]

This division into official and unofficial intensifies rather than resolves the problem of the relation between religious identity and social mission.[30] It does not really answer the question how a social and political mission of the Church relates to its religious identity, but simply relegates the social mission to one segment of the Church. It avoids the hard questions: do not the bishops as Christians also have social and political responsibilities? Should they not as overseers also fulfill leadership responsibilities? If the Church is the sign of God's presence and kingdom within the world, must not the whole Church exhibit this presence? Should not the religious identity of the Church, on all its levels and in all its members, be related to its social and political mission? What does the religious identity of the Church, precisely as a religious identity, contribute to a social and political mission?

Partial Mission

A third position argues that it is inadequate to understand the Church's mission as if mission were a singular, monolithic function. Michael Fahey suggests that talk about the mission of the Church should not be inflated to cover all areas. Instead, one should preferably speak about the various tasks of the Church.[31] Likewise, Avery Dulles argues against reducing the Church to one model or image. Since various models can be appropriated for understanding the Church, it is necessary to uphold the fact that the Church is just as much herald as it is mystical community, institution as well as sacrament. A servant model outlines the importance of the "categories of love and service" but it should not be made into the sole or exclusive model of the Church's self-understanding.[32]

This analytical approach integrates as much as possible the social and political mission because it does not eo ipso relegate this mission to an improper, substitutive, or unofficial service. Since service is *one* of the Church's many tasks, a social mission is an integral and legitimate function of the Church. The social mission becomes illegitimate to the extent that it either isolates itself from the Church's religious purpose or makes itself into the primary function. Such an understanding of the social presents, however, a different perspective from contemporary political or liberation theology. Whereas the latter primarily seeks to link the distinct elements of Christian faith, utopian vision, sociological analysis, and political action, this analytical approach seeks, by distinguishing various models, to raise the question of how the Church's distinctive mission and identity can be preserved in its mission of service.[33]

Such a question, however, implies that the Church has a religious mission and identity that can be distinguished from its social mission but can, at the same time, come to the fore in a social mission. Moreover, although the distinction between the sacramental or kerygmatic and the servant role does not relegate the social mission to a proper but secondary role,[34] it does in fact leave such a possibility open. Some indeed have claimed that the sacramental and kerygmatic are the Church's primary function, whereas the social is secondary.[35] Others stress the essential role of social mission, but view it as a precondition or as a consequence of the Church's evangelization.[36]

Because this approach divides up the Church's many tasks, it does not sufficiently explore how they are interconnected. How should the sacramental relate to the social mission and vice versa? How should the social mission relate to the task of proclaiming the word and of being a mystical *communio*? These questions are at the center of the problem. Further, whereas the appeal to models represents an analytic approach, the Church as a concrete phenomenon is holistic. The approach, therefore, divides in theory what is not distinguished in practice. It constructs an abstract and analytical model of distinct tasks that are in fact necessarily interrelated. Finally, this approach runs the risk of giving priority to one task as much more specifically related to the Church's mission. Service can be easily reduced to a secondary function.[37]

Nevertheless, the emphasis upon plurality of tasks does point to the significance of all tasks while raising the question of how the distinctive nature of the Church is exercised in its social mission. It sharply articulates an issue raised by political and liberation theologies, but it does not resolve the issue.

Both political and liberation theology have sought to provide further clarification.[38] They have attempted to link evangelization and a social or political mission through eschatology. In reacting to individual existential interpretation of God's reign, they have emphasized that the proclamation of this reign must draw out the social and political implications.[39] This eschatological message should guide the Church's political mission primarily to negative criticism. On the basis of the transcendent images of Christian eschatology, the Church should critique political ideologies, but should not offer concrete, positive political proposals.[40]

Liberation theology also develops the implications of eschatology for christology, ecclesiology, spirituality, and theological methodology.[41] By stressing the unity of salvation history and world history, it links eschatology and liberation. The Church not only uses eschatology as a source of critique but also strives for authentic anticipations and partial realizations within history of the eschatological reality. If political theology tends to emphasize the transcendence of eschatological hope over and against social and political planning, liberation theology tends to underscore how each realization of love, justice, and peace is not just a shadow of God's eschatological reign, but is a partial anticipation and incomplete realization of that reign.[42]

The critics of both political and liberation theology allege that they are reductionistic in that they reduce the Christian message to social and political reform.[43] Insofar as political and liberation theology have based their proposals primarily upon eschatology, they have only tangentially raised the question of how the Church's religious identity is related to its social and political mission. To defend political and liberation theology against its critics and to root the problem of the Church's mission within the fundamental theological problem of the Church's identity, it is necessary to analyze the nature of religious identity.

The Challenge of Religious Identity

The Catholic Church has a long tradition of social teaching. Since Vatican II, official Church documents have especially grappled with the relation between the Church's religious identity and its social and political mission.[44] If previous to Vatican II these documents contrasted religious identity and social mission, since Vatican II they have sought to interrelate them. This development has been described as a kind of zigzagging. I do not agree. It seems to me that the Church's official documents seek to hold fast to two elements without reducing one to the other: religious identity and social-political mission. In nuancing the traditional contrast between evangelization and civilization, between religious purpose and social mission, they challenge theologians to reflect more deeply on the Church's religious identity and its relation to a social and political mission.

The document *Justice in the World*, issued by the International Synod of Bishops (1971), is crucial, for it proclaimed: "Action on behalf of justice and participation in the transformation of the world appear to us as a constitutive dimension of the preaching of the gospel or, in other words, of the Church's mission for the redemption of the human race and its liberation from every oppressive situation."[45] The mission to transform the world is not secondary, improper, or derivative; it is constitutive of gospel proclamation. The document goes beyond previous affirmations, beyond viewing justice and liberation as only prerequisites or consequences of the Church's mission.

Church documents, especially papal statements, have since quoted this text, but they have not used the expression "constitutive" independently of the quoted text. The International Theological Commission's *Human Development and Christian Salvation* suggests that "constitutive" does not mean "essential" but "integral."[46] However, the formulations of *Justice in the World* are carefully nuanced. The document states that transformation of the world is, in some way, constitutive of the proclamation of the gospel. It does not make it the sole or exclusive element of that proclamation; but if the transformation toward justice is missing, then a distortion of the gospel occurs. Insofar as the gospel message calls human beings away from sin, it calls them to love and to practice justice.

Subsequent papal statements wrestle with the issue. Paul VI opened the Third Assembly of the Synod of Bishops on 27 September 1974 with the challenge: "It will be necessary to define more accurately the relationship between evangelization properly so called and the human effort towards development for which the Church's help is rightly expected, even though this is not her specific task."[47] The Church has a specific task, not identified or contrasted with human development. Instead, the pope challenges the synod to work out the relation between evangelization and development.

The synod itself produced two documents. The first, *On Human Rights and Reconciliation*, affirmed that "the promotion of human rights is required by the gospel and is central to her ministry."[48] The second, *Evangelization of the Modern World*, not only asserts "the intimate connection between evangelization and liberation," but it explains that the "Church, in more faithfully fulfilling the work of evangelization, will announce the total salvation of humans or rather their complete liberation, and from now on will start to bring this about."[49] Furthermore, it explains that evangelization is interrelated with liberation, but salvation is much more than the present liberation that it now begins to bring about. Such an approach is dialectical in that it avoids a simple affirmation of identity or nonidentity.

A similar but different dialectic appears in the statements of Paul VI and John Paul II. In his closing address to the 1974 synod, Pope Paul VI drew up a balance sheet of the work and urged that further study should show how human liberation is to be emphasized without detriment to the essential meaning of evangelization.[50] Paul VI's document, *Evangelization in the Modern World* (to be distinguished from the synod's), both links and distinguishes evangelization and human liberation. They are linked in two basic ways. First, the gospel is not complete unless it is interrelated with social human life. Second, specific bonds exist on the level of anthropology, theology, and the gospel. Anthropology: the human subject of evangelization is a concrete person living in social and political structures. Theology: redemption affects creation; to restore justice requires the combating of injustice. Gospel: to proclaim love for humans includes proclaiming justice and peace for them.[51]

Paul VI, therefore, carefully distinguished. Evangelization is not identical with human liberation because some forms of liberation are not consistent with the gospel and because evangelization entails more than liberation. This "more" is developed in two ways. It is more encompassing insofar as the establishment of God's kingdom is much more universal than any improved social or political order. It is much more profound insofar as it reaches the personal depths of human life and strikes at sin, the root of social and political injustice within human nature.[52] In Paul VI's dialectical view, the gospel is incomplete without liberation, just as liberation is incomplete without the gospel. When the Pope emphasizes the primacy of evangelization, he is pointing to an evangelization that includes liberation, transforms liberation, and is more than liberation. He does not retract the thesis that justice is a constitutive element of evangelization, but explains the profound interrelation between them.[53]

A different vision, but similar dialectic, is present in John Paul II's address to the Third General Assembly of Latin American bishops at Puebla and in his encyclical letters *Redemptor hominis* and *Laborem exercens*,[54] even though his position on the relation between the Church's religious identity and its social mission is not always easy to interpret. He affirms that "evangelization is the essential mission, the distinctive vocation, and the deepest identity of the Church"; and, at the same time, quotes the synod's affirmation that action for justice is a constitutive dimension of the Church's mission.[55] When he declares that the Church's mission is "religious and not social or political," he affirms in the very same sentence that the religious mission must touch upon all the dimension of concrete human life.[56] Such dialectical affirmations might make it possible to classify his theological position under various options: social mission as improper; social mission as unofficial; and social mission as partial but secondary.

A closer examination is necessary. The differences between John

Paul II and his predecessors have been noted. Joachim Giers, for example, argues that he does not develop *Mater et magistra*'s correlation between economic and social progress, but warns against overpowering economic progress. Moreover, he does not pick up the 1971 reference to the relation between the kingdom and earthly progress.[57] But such criticisms rest on a partial selection of his writings. *Laborem exercens*, for example, does relate human work to earthly progress and to the development of the kingdom.[58]

John Paul II's contribution lies in his focus on the personalistic and the christological dimensions of the social mission.[59] First, he especially develops Paul VI's anthropological link between evangelization and human liberation. He not only affirms that evangelization deals with concrete human subjects living in specific sociopolitical situations; he also affirms that at the heart of political and social distortion is a false image of human nature. Against it evangelization offers an image of human personhood rooted in Christ. Consequently, he does not offer so much a natural law or a natural ethic as the basis of the social mission as he offers a theological—indeed a christological foundation—though his tendency to separate lay and priestly functions goes somewhat against this christological foundation. Second, the originality of Christian liberation consists not only in its agreement with the gospel message but also in its disclosure of concrete personal attitudes: concern for the unity of the People of God, for the poor and needy, for the inviolability of the individual. The theme of the option for the poor, developed so strongly in liberation theology, repeatedly occurs in his various addresses and encyclicals. Third, personal individual consciences must be formed and sensitized to social and political justice. Not just structural change and institutional improvement, but personal conscientization and individual transformation must be accomplished.

John Paul II's difference from Paul VI should be explained not as a retreat but as a shift of emphasis and perspective in relating evangelization and social justice. Within the context of the individualism of modern European liberalism, Paul VI underscored the significance of power and political structures.[60] In linking evangelization with human liberation through theology and anthropology, he emphasized that redemption affects creation and therefore the Church must combat structures of injustice. In the context of Eastern European state communism,[61] John Paul II emphasizes the conversion of the heart. Both describe redemption as a renewal of creation and both view this new creation as the overcoming of sin. Paul VI used the image of new creation as a contrasting image to concrete situations of injustice, whereas John Paul II refers more to the new creation in the hearts of people.[62] *Dives in misericordia*, consequently, underscores much more what charity and mercy contribute to justice than what justice contributes to charity. Each Pontiff affirms the truths emphasized by each other even though their perspective is quite different. And each wrestles with the relation between religious identity and the Church's social and political mission.

Two conclusions can be drawn from this survey of recent papal teaching. First, all documents affirm that the commitment to social justice is integral to the Church's mission. All grapple with the interrelation between religious identity and social mission. I suggest that a basic continuity runs through the various documents which becomes apparent in their resolution of the problem. Human dignity and love for people is the link between evangelization and liberation. The documents refer to eschatology, especially the transcendence of eschatology, to show that evangelization should not be identified totally and exclusively with human progress. The post-Vatican II teaching stands in a long tradition of social doctrine. Ever since Leo XIII's *Rerum novarum*, the Church's social teaching has stressed that mutual rights and duties in political relationships should take into account the dignity of the human person and the significance of love within justice.[63] When, therefore, the post-Vatican II documents appeal to human dignity and Christian love to interrelate evangelization and social mission, they develop this tradition.[64] At the same time, their emphasis on eschatology to differentiate human liberation and salvation contrasts with much recent political and liberation theology. Political theology appeals to eschatology to justify the Church's critical political function, whereas liberation theology argues that, if eschatological salvation perfects human liberation, then it is intrinsic to liberation. The magisterium, however, follows the line of *Lumen gentium* more than of *Gaudium et spes* on the function of Christian eschatology.[65]

Second, the magisterial statements all point to an unresolved issue and raise the same challenge. John Paul II, for example, challenges theologians and bishops "to carry out serious reflection on the relationships and implications between evangelization and human advancement or liberation, taking into consideration in such a vast and important field, what is specific about the Church's presence."[66] This challenge is framed by J. Bryan Hehir: "To determine precisely how justice can be described as properly belonging to the work of the Church and to describe precisely what is the style of a religiously-based social political ministry is one of the question of the *Gaudium et spes* decade."[67] Furthermore, to relate religious identity and social-political mission is not merely to search for a religious justification of the Church's involvement in social justice, but is also to search for the very meaning of the Church.

This issue was well put by Paul Tillich when he observed that the Church has, in fact, contributed much to Western civilization. It has advanced culture, furthered peace, promoted social justice. Each benefit can be countered with a deficit. But both pros and cons would miss the point, "for a church that is nothing more than a benevolent socially useful group can be replaced by other groups not claiming to be churches: such a church has no justification for its existence."[68] The Church is more than a lobbying group, more than an agent of social welfare. It has a distinctive religious identity, and if it is to be church, its religious identity must come to the fore in its style of commitment to social justice and in its commitment to human liberation.

Chapter 8

The Foundational Problem of Religious Identity and Social Mission

Foundational theology, as developed and articulated in this volume, consists of several elements: a hermeneutical reconstruction of the religious vision, warrants for the illuminative significance of the vision in theory and practice, and articulation of the vision's relation to relevant background theories. In the issue of the relation between mission and religious identity all these elements come into play. It will be necessary to analyze the methodological presuppositions involved in specifying the Church's religious identity. The hermeneutical reconstruction of the Christian tradition will focus neither on eschatology nor on anthropology, but on the nature of religion itself, specifically as manifested in the development of the Christian tradition in its development of a social mission and a political ministry in theory and in practice. The warrants for this development come not only from the nature of the religious vision but also from the nature of the political one. Finally, considerations drawn from theories of societal and political evolution form the relevant background theories to any consideration of the Church's mission. This chapter will, therefore, begin by discussing the hermeneutical reconstruction of religious identity and go on to deal with the problems of warrants and the background theories of social evolution.

Hermeneutical Reconstruction of Religious Identity

Methodological Presuppositions

As a religious institution, the Church has a religious identity and a religious purpose. That is obvious. But what is religious? What is distinctively, specifically, or properly religious? The answers to these questions are not obvious. Indeed, these questions have given rise to much debate not only in regard to the contemporary issue of the legitimacy of the Church's social and political mission but also, and more particularly, in regard to the validity of modern theology itself.

In the wake of the Enlightenment and its ethical versions of Christianity, Schleiermacher protested against the reduction of religion to metaphysics or morality and argued for its distinctive, independent status. Nevertheless, in the twentieth century, Karl Barth polemicized against all of the previous century from Schleiermacher to Ritschl because it culminated in what he considered to be Ritschl's reduction of faith to ethical practice.[69] Today, the critics of liberation as well as political theology claim that, in the end result, these theologies reduce religion and faith to social or political practice. Consequently, the scene of modern theology has been well described by David Tracy, when he states that its constant concern has been "to describe certain basic factors which characterize a religious as distinct from a moral, an aesthetic, a scientific, or a political perspective."[70]

Inadequacy of Specific Difference

Influenced by the Kantian critique of the knowability of what transcends experience, many theologians have suggested that the notion of "limit" points to the religious.[71] Features that express the limits of ordinary experience (e.g., experiences of finitude and contingency) or that point to what lies beyond experience are religious. From this vantage, not only the Social Gospel and Ritschlianism but also liberation theology have been criticized. Their alleged reduction of faith to ethics and religion to political and social reform reflects their neglect of the "limit" character of religion.[72] However, the notion of a "limit" is problematic. On the one hand it presupposes the otherness and the unknowability of that which transcends; on the other hand, insofar as the "limit" points to that which transcends, it presupposes some knowledge of the transcendent. Unless what is religious intersects with what is known, a limit-experience cannot be experienced as such or as pointing to the transcendent.

Moreover, when the concept of limit is combined with the methodological approach of searching for the specific difference, it leads to a distortion rather than to a grasp of what is distinctive. Although the search for the essence or distinctive purpose often defines that purpose in terms of a "specific difference," such a focus on the specific difference often posits a partial element as the total meaning and so fails to describe adequately a reality's true meaning or identity. For example, if Catholicism and Protestantism were defined primarily in terms of their specific differences, the number of sacraments or belief in the papacy would be essential points; the common commitment to Christ would be overlooked. Or if Christianity were defined in terms of its specific difference vis-à-vis other religions, the love of God would be secondary because other religions also preach the love of God. If, taking Aristotle's definition of the human person as a rational animal, one were to describe human identity by the specific difference between human beings and animals, then the focus would be on rationality alone. But if human nature is viewed exclusively or primarily as rationality, the meaning of human identity is distorted.

Similarly, if religious identity is defined precisely in its specific difference from the ethical, social, or political, then the religious is distorted. As human nature is not pure rationality but an incarnate rationality, so religiosity is not pure religiosity, but manifests itself within the ethical, social, and political. If the religious is viewed in its specific difference from the ethical, social, and political, then what is religious will cease to be a dimension of life. Likewise, if the mission of the Church is defined precisely and exclusively in its specific difference from other groups, what is shared in common is overlooked. It could be stated that love of neighbor is only accidental to Christianity because other groups preach it. The Church's religious mission should be seen, therefore, in the way its specificity comes to the fore precisely in its interrelation with other dimensions of human life.

My methodic suggestion to avoid the inadequacies of the categories of limit and specific difference goes against certain strains of contemporary theology, especially Protestant neo-orthodoxy which has been influenced by Kierkegaard's distinction of the religious from the aesthetic and the ethical, a distinction that views the religious as the suspension of the ethical.[73] Recently, Hans Urs von Balthasar's theological aesthetic has criticized such a theological separation and has argued for the intersection of the beautiful and transcendent.[74] Likewise, Justus George Lawler has brilliantly shown the relation between the aesthetic and the religious in regard to literature, and especially literary form.[75] The same task needs to be done for the relation between religious identity and social mission. It demands a methodology based on intersecting patterns more than on the specific differences of limit-experiences.

Intersecting Patterns

In his analysis of language, Ludwig Wittgenstein advanced important reflections on the nature of essential definitions. Although I do not concur with all his criticisms of essentialism and all his objections to theoretical conceptions of the nature of language, I do think that his arguments about the fallacy of assuming a common denominator for a phenomenon are important for theology. A game illustrates the point. We all know what a game is, but if asked to explain a game, we might be tempted to assume that there is one common denominator to all games, otherwise they would not be called games. He asks: Are games amusing? Think of chess and ticktacktoe. Competition? Think of patience. Winning and losing? In ball games yes, but not in throwing a ball against a wall. Skill? Compare tennis and ring-around-a-rosy. These examples show that a game cannot be defined by a simple common denominator, a specific difference, or a single particular characteristic. A complicated network of similarities overlaps and crisscrosses. At times there are overall similarities, at times similarities only in detail. What is present at one time is not present at another.[76]

Such an analysis can illumine the complex phenomenon of religion. An analysis of religious actions shows that there is neither a common denominator nor a specific difference but rather a complex set of crisscrossings and intersecting patterns that makes religious actions religious. Persons can fast to lose weight or from religious motivation; the same act, but the motivation or purpose differs. Persons can accept invitations to a gourmet restaurant or to a Seder; here not so much the motivation as the context, tradition, and spirit determine the action. The crisscrossing between religion and work is another example.[77] Benedictines can understand manual labor as religious and as constituting along with prayer their existence as monks. Here a religious tradition of Christianity and a particular spirituality affirms the meaning of work and gives it a religious dimension. But in the case of a workaholic, the religious tradition should bring out the relativity of all work. The action, work, is the same, but in one case religion affirms it, in another religion relativizes it. In medieval times caring for the sick and poor was viewed both as an act of charity and as an act of religion. Responding to the objection that almsgiving was not an act of charity but of religion, Aquinas argued that it could be considered both because of the crisscrossing of virtues and the interrelating of formal and material aspects.[78]

Such crisscrossing takes place on a much more basic level than motivation, context, and direction. It also takes place historically within a religious tradition, and it is the historical intersection of the religious and the secular that becomes determinative for the meaning of the act. A meal can be secular or sacred. Washing can be a secular action or a sacrament. How the action is understood today depends upon how the religious tradition has incorporated it along with other actions within its religious symbol systems and how it views the action in relation to God's transcendent presence and purpose within history. Individuals today stand within a religious history that determines how certain actions are to be understood. An action is therefore understood as religious not simply by a specific difference but by a complex intersection of motivation and purpose, context and meaning, religious history and tradition. All come together to constitute the religious identity of human activity.

"Appresentation" of Religious Identity

"Appresentation" is a technical category used in Husserl's phenomenology to describe how a human subject can perceive the ego of another subject when only the body of the other is perceived, not the ego in its otherness as an ego.[79] Referring to how the transcendent other is indirectly perceived, appresentation involves several elements. (1) An apperceptive transfer or analogizing apperception takes place because the body of the other resembles my own body. (2) Indices reveal a unique pattern of changing but concordant or harmonious behavior. (3) Through an imaginative and associative presentation the other is appresented precisely as other.

The category of "appresentation" has been broadened from its narrow use by Husserl and has been used to describe the process of human communication and to refer to religious meaning.[80] In all communicative action more is appresented than is directly perceived. Human action takes place within a broad horizon of possible meanings and diverse interpretations. If a particular meaning is to be communicated, a certain limitation of possible meanings must take place, just as every action is also interpreted in a broader context than is immediately evident.

The specification and the communication of the meaning of

actions entails several elements. In every action I implicitly identify myself as a subject. Whenever I act, I understand myself as a subject. Whenever I act, I understand myself in relation to the act in a variety of ways: as a friend, a teacher, a professional. The subject acting is one person, but there is a plurality of possible self-identifications, one or more of which is made in carrying out the particular activity. Likewise, the action itself can be represented in a specific way. Although it might be quite simply described, it is at the same time open to more horizons of interpretation and understanding than are explicitly exhibited. In every action, therefore, there is not only a specific self-referential identification but also a specific representation by which the act is understood in a specific way.

Such an analysis helps us understand the religious dimension in a variety of ways. Quite often it is claimed that the difference between social help as a secular or religious act lies in the motivation. Quite often religious actions are identified through some specific manifest characteristic. The phenomenological description above indicates that human actions are much more complex than motivation or what is manifest. I suggest that an analogy can be drawn between appresentation and the perception of the religious identity of actions.[81] Just as we do not immediately and directly intuit the ego of another, but grasp the presence of the other through an association of concordant and similar behavior and through a grasp of all that is copresent in action, so we grasp acts to be religious to the extent that they are concordant with what we understand to be religion and to the extent that we grasp religious elements to be copresent in action, even though these are not directly ostensible. Yet this suggestion makes it even more imperative to take up the fundamental theological task of defining what is religious and how it is to be understood in the Christian tradition.

Religious Identity and the Historical Quest for Meaning

The challenge to relate the Church's social-political mission to its religious identity raises the fundamental theological issue of the nature of religion and of Christian identity. Unfortunately, a dichotomy has emerged within contemporary theology insofar as analysis of the nature of religion and of the Church's mission have been separated and isolated from each other. The shift of treatments on the mission of the Church to ecclesiology has led to a neglect of the fundamental theological problem of the relation between the Church's mission and the Christian religion. I shall therefore attempt to link the fundamental theological and the hermeneutical issues surrounding the nature of religion with those of the Church's mission.

Unfortunately, definitions of religion are notoriously controversial.[82] Inadequate are substantial definitions that identify religion solely with particular beliefs, since religion is much more than the affirmation of a certain belief.[83] Equally inadequate is a definition of religion without any reference to beliefs.[84] Likewise, an experiential definition, as Rudolf Otto's definition of religion as the experience of the numinous or mysterious, is inadequate because it fails to cover the wide range of religions and to encompass all that is entailed within religion.[85]

Although many today combine a functional and an interpretative analysis of religion, it is important to bring the historical dimension to the fore. A functional theory explains religion through its role in integrating society: religion is the glue that bonds society. Religious beliefs, basic values, and civil religion can exemplify this function. Historical religions, however, have not merely integrated societies but challenged them.[86] An interpretative theory explains how religion provides a set of symbols that establishes moods and motivations by formulating conceptions of a general interpretation of existence.[87] Such a definition appears too broad. Is any general interpretation of reality thereby religious? It would seem not for there can be general world views that do not make the claim to be religious and yet offer interpretations of reality. Therefore, it is important not simply to follow a functional or an interpretative approach, but rather to combine both with reference to the articulation of meaning as religious within historical religions.[88]

Since only concrete historical religions exist, the function and meaning of a religion should be determined not by excluding but by taking into account the historical self-reflection and praxis of the religion itself—for us, the Christian religion. An adequate methodological approach to religion, therefore, should not define it exclusively as a specific difference in isolation from other dimensions in life. Instead, it should investigate how what is religious comes to the fore in a complex series of overlappings that determine a person's self-identification and interpretation of reality within the history of a religious tradition. Likewise, to describe the function and meaning of religion from the starting-point of a historical religion is to show the impact of particular religious beliefs upon a particular historical community, its self-understanding and its interpretation of reality. To illustrate the meaning and function of Christian religious identity, two particular beliefs will be examined in relation to religious identity and social mission.

Correlation between Belief in the Transcendent
and in Human Personhood

To see the interrelation between religious identity and social mission, it is necessary to see how the belief in a transcendent God correlates with the emergence of the belief in the inviolability of human personhood. A phenomenology of religion shows that the category of personhood originates with the religious experience of transcendence. Although the inviolable dignity of human beings is often viewed as a humanist heritage or a moral imperative independent of religion, its roots lie historically within religious experience. The inviolability of persons is neither empirically demonstrable nor factually necessary. Individuals can be treated as objects and things. Relying upon the phenomenology of religion, Pannenberg argues that the experience of the ultimacy or "nonmanipulatableness" of power that makes a concrete claim upon human beings is the basis of the human personification of reality and of the human self. Therefore, "the concept of the personal is originally based on a religiously determined experience of reality, or of the powers governing it."[89] From a different perspective, Karl Rahner's transcendental analysis also shows how the experience of transcendence entails for human beings the experience of themselves as persons.[90]

This correction between the religious experience of transcendence and the awareness of self as a person illustrates our above-mentioned methodological principle that the interpretation of reality and self-identification go hand in hand.[91] Belief in God and belief in the self as a unique, irreplaceable individual are not only correlative beliefs; they have common historical roots with the experience of reality as religious. Although many attempt today to establish the dignity of the human person not on a religious but on a humanistic or purely rationally ethical basis, the historical religious roots of this dignity should not be forgotten. In regard to human dignity, religious beliefs and nonreligious attitudes crisscross. The religious belief in God as the ultimate power of the universe does not negate human personhood, as is claimed in a humanistic critique of religion, but radically affirms this personhood and historically grounds its emergence within Western religious tradition.

Therefore, to proclaim belief in a personal God is not the same as teaching that Dione is a moon of Saturn. Instead, the proclamation of

God entails a vision of reality; this vision has a function, for it determines how human and social life is understood and often structured.[92] The religious belief that a personal power grounds all power and force within the universe grounds the transcendence of the human person not only in the face of nature but also over and against society. All societal and political organization of power should, therefore, be so structured that it mirrors the personal ground of the universe and safeguards the transcendence of the individual person.

Since belief in God provides a vision of human reality, belief in God cannot be proclaimed without, at the same time, spelling out how this vision of ultimacy affects reality. Likewise, an interpretation of reality entails an interpretation of ultimacy. The images and language used to express the belief in God have profound effects on how the human self and human society is understood. For this reason, feminist theology has become so important and central to Christian theology, the revision of the image of God as patriarchal goes hand in hand with the revision of patriarchal structures of society. Liberation theologians have likewise shown how contemporary experiences of oppression and injustice can provide a key for uncovering distorted visions of God and ideological uses made of those images. Consequently, there is not only an interrelation between belief in God and the interpretation of reality, but the interpretation and praxis of reality also affects the concept and image of God.

Identification of Jesus with Wisdom, Logos, and Power
The proclamation of Jesus as wisdom, logos, and power correlates with the development of the Church's social and political mission. Christians proclaim not only the transcendence of a personal God but also the presence of the divine power and wisdom in Jesus as a saving presence. Indeed, they identify Jesus with the ultimate divine power and wisdom. Recent scholarship has shown how early Christians used diverse traditions to interpret Jesus: final eschatological prophet, crucified and Risen Lord, divine man, logos (John's prologue), and "power and wisdom" (1 Cor 1:25).[93] Yet amid this diversity an important development takes place. On the one hand the historical Jesus preaches the coming kingdom of God. His exorcisms, healings, and miracles are signs of the breaking-in of the power of the kingdom. The eschatological wholeness of the kingdom is proleptically anticipated. At the same time, Jesus is interpreted with diverse strains of the wisdom tradition. Q views Jesus as an eschatological prophet who is wisdom's envoy. In the Pauline tradition, a wisdom christology links God's plan of creation with Jesus; in Matthew, Jesus'

life activity and wisdom are linked; in John's prologue, Jesus is understood as the incarnation of the logos.[94]

Wisdom christology became the most developed trajectory in the postbibilical period. Although susceptible to isolation in schools, it was linked with strains of Stoic thought and with the universalism of the logos speculation. Nicaea defined Christ to be more than an intermediary wisdom figure, power, or demiurge; he is consubstantial with the ultimate power and wisdom of the universe. That ultimate power and wisdom is present in Jesus and Jesus is identical with it.

This decision was a "de-Hellenization" because it went against the Hellenistic dualism between the world and the transcendent God.[95] The identification of Jesus as logos and wisdom with the ultimate power of the universe was significant in how it was used to bridge creation and redemption. In the Old Testament, wisdom was the personification of God and of God's activity in the world. God's creation has a purpose. Proverbial wisdom saw the world of appearances as pervaded with divine order that made human existence meaningful.[96] In Stoic thought, wisdom and logos pervaded all of creation; truth, righteousness and justice were the incorporations of universal wisdom.[97] Because this christology bridged creation and redemption, the development of this christological trajectory in the postbiblical period provided the theological foundation of a social mission of the Church and supplied the basis for a theology of creation.

Here lies the profundity of the Christian vision. If the Church has as its task to evangelize and to proclaim Christ, then it proclaims that Christ "reveals the character of the power behind the world."[98] In proclaiming the meaning and power behind the world, the Church is concerned with the manifestation of that meaning and power in the world. The identification of Jesus as logos and wisdom with ultimate power and justice of the universe is of significance for the meaning of wisdom and justice. For in the Christian vision the Jesus identified with wisdom, justice, and logos is the historical Jesus with his preaching of the kingdom and with his miracles and healings. Such a vision radically revises traditional Hellenistic dualism and alters an understanding of the universe as a structured order. The meaning of the wisdom and logos underlying the universe now becomes manifest in the saving actions and proclamation of Jesus. This linkage of the meaning of the historical Jesus with the meaning of the universe connects the Church's proclamation of Jesus with its political and social mission.

My proposal about the meaning of the Christian vision should be understood within the context of post-Enlightenment discussions about the nature of rationality. What has come to the forefront in the contemporary understanding of rationality is the inadequacy of the Enlightenment's conviction that rationality consists in universal a priori structures or in a scientific empirical methodology—and the realization that rationality is also dependent upon concrete historical paradigms. Consequently, in pointing to the significance of the link between the historical Jesus and both the distinct wisdom and logos traditions, I am suggesting that a twofold movement constitutes the development of Christian belief in Jesus. On the one hand the historical Jesus becomes the paradigm for what is rational. His concrete life-praxis becomes the historical and concrete paradigm for wisdom and justice. On the other hand the attempt to link the historical Jesus with these traditions sought to underscore the public meaning and universal significance of Jesus. What took place involved an attempt to link (and yet not without tension) the historical Jesus and the public conceptuality of rationality. What took place led to a new understanding of the historical Jesus and a revision of Hellenistic rationality. This pattern of the interrelation between the historically concrete Jesus and the categories of public rationality becomes a task for successive generations of Christians seeking to show the meaning and significance of Jesus for their own time and coming to new understandings both of Jesus and of their own public rationality and endeavors.[99]

Vision and Praxis: A Guideline
A question remains: does my reference to the interpretative and functional nature of religion and to the combination of the historical Jesus and the logos and wisdom traditions in Christianity provide some resolution to the issue of the relation between the Church's identity and its social or political ministry? Does it help resolve the alternatives proposed: is a political or social ministry proper or improper, permanent or substitutional, official or unofficial, constitutive and essential or partial and secondary? A basic rule can be proposed: the more the social or political ministry of the Church is related to Christianity's interpretative and practical function as a religion to exhibit and to proclaim Jesus as the power and wisdom of the universe, the more constitutive, essential, and distinctive this ministry is.

This guideline is proposed in the context of the previous methodological considerations. The religious does not exist in isolation from other dimensions of reality; it transects them through its interpretative and practical function of specifying the action, reality, and the self. The more an action can be integrated within a Christian's consciousness of God; the more specifically that action can be integrated with the Christian's proclamation of the identity of God's logos with Jesus in his life-activity, the more an action or ministry properly and distinctively belongs to the Church. This guideline offers a criterion. Not every action can be so integrated. Some actions can be more integrated than others. The history of Christianity is loaded with examples not only of social and political action exhibiting the meaning of Jesus but also of actions distorting that meaning. The criterion of the relation between social and political involvement and religious identity is, therefore, not simply the meaningfulness, or even the ultimacy of an action, but the possibility of its integration within that meaning present in the Church's understanding of the significance of Jesus and his life-praxis.

Two examples of social ministry can illustrate my proposal before the more complex issue of political ministry and mission is raised. Why has education been understood as central to the Church's mission?[100] Because education is more than professional training. It deals with the meaning of human life and as such raises questions of ultimacy and value. A crisscrossing takes place between a holistic education and the interpretative function of Christian proclamation. Although it might be possible to distinguish formally between education and religion, they are concretely and intimately interrelated in praxis. If education deals with the meaning of life, it must raise questions about the religious dimensions of life. If Christianity proclaims Christ as logos and wisdom, it must spell out this wisdom for all dimensions of life. The Church's ministry in education is therefore not substitution. Because a crisscrossing exists among religion, meaning, and education, more can be appresented in education than the merely technical or the acquisition of skills. This crisscrossing takes place not only in humanistic courses open very explicitly to such an intertwinement but also in more professional or technical courses. The action or course in itself might appear purely technical; yet because it is a part of an overall ministry, it participates in the religious dimension of the overall educational endeavor.

Yet my guideline also provides criteria for the evaluating of the success or failure of an educational ministry. A Catholic college or medical school that was unable to communicate a sense of the sacredness of life to its students would be a failure. It would be a travesty to concentrate exclusively on the professionalism of the vocation without linking it and modifying it in view of the values and ideals embodied in the Christian tradition that takes seriously the meaning of Jesus' life.

Does the Church have a proper mission in maintaining hospitals?[101] Although sin and disease are no longer considered interrelated as in antiquity, persons in serious illness do confront the limits of human existence. Today the hospital is the context for the experience of birth, serious illness, and often death. These experiences entail a religious dimension. The Church, therefore, does have a proper mission, not only because the healing that takes place in hospitals can exhibit the love and healing of Jesus but also because it can offer a comprehensiveness of health care. It can deal with the interrelationship of the medical, existential, and religious dimensions of serious illness. The Church's mission is, therefore, based on the interpretative function of religion and its explication in practice of the meaning of Jesus' life-praxis in the context of modern health care.[102]

Education and health care, therefore, belong intrinsically to the Church's mission, not simply because, as social ministries, they are presuppositions of the Church's evangelization or consequences of the Church's charity, but because their proper and fullest execution engages the religious dimension of life. According to our guideline, the more a form of education and of health care does that, the more the Church has a proper mission in that area. But what of the Church's action on behalf of justice or its concern for the poor and oppressed? Does my proposed guideline help us to understand political ministry? Does my guideline—the more the Church's ministry to the world involves dimensions of life in which questions of ultimacy, meaning, and transcendence as historically articulated in Christianity emerge and intersect, the more intrinsic that action is to the Church's religious identity—help us to understand how social and political action on behalf of justice belongs to the proper mission of the Church? Does it help us to understand religious identity within a political ministry?

The Church's Mission: Reconstructive and Foundational Warrants

The proposed guideline links the mission of the Church with a hermeneutical retrieval of the Church's religious identity. For a foundational theology such a linkage in itself is insufficient unless, at the same time, it considers contemporary and historical warrants and it relates its retrieval to background theories of social development and political evolution. Foundational theology therefore must take into account and reconstruct the relation between the religious and the political as well as between social ministry and political praxis. These reconstructions, however, should be joined to an analysis of the Church's function and goal in order to demonstrate that the execution of the Church's mission provides a warrant for the truth and meaning of Christianity and is, therefore, at the center of foundational theology.

Reconstructions of the Relation between the Religious and the Political

Secularization is a common label to describe contemporary society. Many assume that contemporary society is secularized because political authority does not rest upon explicit religious legitimations, but is founded upon democratic institutions and procedures that are independent of the churches. Theologians like Harvey Cox and Johann B. Metz have even lauded this secularization as a genuine consequence of Christianity, for it allowed the world to be world and the Church to be Church. Quite often, theologians have taken over Max Weber's interpretation of modern society insofar as religion is seen as having been relegated to the private and personal sphere, whereas the public, bureaucratic, and the political spheres have become technocratic and secular.

The Religious Dimension of the Political

The assumption that society is secularized because religion has become privatized or because political authority is not based upon explicit religious legitimations simplifies the relation between the religious and the political.[103] Societies do not operate in a vacuum. Beneath social and institutional interaction, there are substantial and latent aspects of social reality. Common symbols, widely shared commitments, similar values, and generalized world views are the binding forces of social reality. Without such shared commitments and symbols a society would not exist, for it would lack cohesiveness. Modern societies are consequently much less secular than they appear. The recently developed notions of civil religion, public religion, and even the more individualized "invisible religion," all point to the latent quasi-religious forces underlying much of contemporary society's political cohesiveness and decision making. A positivistic interpretation of political legislation based upon the liberal conception of the separation of Church and state or the distinction between religion and society overlooks some fundamental interrelationships.

The discussion that has developed around the concept of "civil religion" and its applicability to the United States has significance for foundational theology. In applying the traditional concept of civil religion to the United States, Robert Bellah was somewhat ambiguous. On the one hand civil religion seems to be a separate and differentiated religion alongside of other positive religious cults in society and in contrast to them. On the other hand civil religion seems to be a dimension or aspect of society comparable to the religious dimension of other societies that have just, in fact, evolved according to different patterns.[104]

One can avoid some of the ambiguity surrounding the concept of civil religion by distinguishing its diverse elements and various presuppositions.[105] Four such elements can be discerned: symbols, values, civic piety, and mythic belief systems. The symbolic element underscores that every society and collectivity has a set of symbols and rituals by which it defines itself and sets itself apart from other groups. The life of the group or society is interpreted and understood through these symbols that give it identity. In addition to the symbolic and ritual expression of societal unity, common and generally accepted cultural values are essential to the functioning of a coherent society. These common value orientations serve to support social solidarity and a particular social-political order. Civic piety, expressed by Rousseau's term "civil religion," is not concerned with symbols, rituals, and general value orientations so much as it is with duties, obligations, and rights that are addressed to the civil ordering of the society's government. Finally, there are belief systems or mythic frameworks by which a society identifies its origin or destiny. For the American republic such a belief would be its conviction of being God's chosen people with a manifest destiny of liberating itself and others from the shackles of political domination.[106]

Consequently, civil or political religion does not so much represent a clearly differentiated public religion, but rather a much more diffused and latent form of religious legitimation. Its symbols, values, mythic belief systems are latent—as such, much more operative and effective than any manifest public religion. This state of affairs shows that the issues of political theology and of the Church's mission are not simply questions of the application of theory to practice, but are foundational issues of the Church's self-understanding and self-discovery.

The Church's mission has, as its first task, in its political and social ministry the development of a political theology.[107] Such theology would have as its primary function to uncover the latent symbols, values, and belief systems that undergird the particular society in which the Church exists. This uncovering can be critical; it can also be affirmative of aspects of society. Moreover, it is not merely an analysis of society, but also a self-analysis.

Civil religion has a basic ambiguity. On the one hand, insofar as a political society tends to absolutize certain national symbols, values, and beliefs into a political ideology, it tends to absolutize itself as a political religion and thereby to stand in opposition to the Christian eschatological vision. On the other hand, insofar as a society's particular beliefs and values are part of a cultural, religious, and Christian heritage with a positive value, they can serve as standards by which the de facto practice of a society and a nation is either fostered or criticized. They can provide significant cultural resources for a Church in its commitment to charity and justice as they intersect with its religious vision.

But political theology as integral to the Church's mission also entails a self-discovery. The religious symbols, values, and myths have developed within the context of cultural systems, societal structures, and political domination. Critical self-reflection upon this intertwinement is a necessary condition of the Church's retrieval, discovery, and proclamation of its own vision. Since this vision must be constantly reconstructed within the context of the interplay of past and present experience, the Church's present commitments in its social and political mission are important for its own self-reflection. The danger is not that the Church will be too confrontational toward society, but that the Church might lose its own vision because it has become absorbed in its cultural and societal intertwinements; hence, the need for a self-reflective and reconstructive political theology as an essential function of the Church's foundational self-understanding.

Social Ministry and Political Praxis
In addition, the Church's religious identity entails a political ministry because of the parallel development between religious identity, social ministry, and the political structures of society. An adequate theological methodology must take into account two poles: first, the Christian tradition in its development and, second, present structures of experience, thought, and society. Each of these two poles is historical and not a fixed, static point. In regard to the Christian tradition, christology proceeds by reconstructing how the impact of Jesus was successively interpreted by the Church throughout the centuries in order to relate this understanding to the contemporary situation. It is not just

the very first stages or the historical reconstruction of the preaching of Jesus, but the full conciliar development of a wisdom and logos christology that became normative for Christianity. Likewise, the full growth and development of social ministry that went parallel to the christological development, and not just the first or initial endeavors, should be taken as normative for an adequate understanding of social and political ministry. Just as christology does not find explicitly in the preaching of Jesus its total content and criteria—but must move from what is implicit within Jesus' preaching and life-activity to an adequate reception and understanding of Jesus—so too must any understanding of the Church's mission move beyond the initial stages. This methodological principle is often overlooked by those criticizing the Church's political ministry on the basis of the early Church's eschatological expectation. What these criticisms overlook is the need to bring the understanding of social and political mission in line with the development of ecclesiology and christology. The principles of a reception hermeneutic as applied to the foundation of the Church must also be applied to the Church's social and political mission.

A similar point needs to be made about the pole of contemporary experience. For contemporary experience is not simply a combination of present-day factors, but results from historical development and change. The interpretation of present experience, therefore, includes an understanding of the causal and developmental factors leading up to the present, just as an interpretation of the Christian faith involves a reconstruction of the history of its evolution and development. Theological methodology involves the correlation not simply between biblical faith and present experience but between the reconstructions of the history of each. From this perspective, the history of each can be analyzed in regard to the relation between social ministry and political ministry.

From the very beginning the care of the needy and of the poor was central to Christianity.[108] The oblations collected at Eucharistic celebrations were distributed to the poor under the organized supervision of the bishop. Yet the history of Christianity shows that when society became so structured that it took over much of this social activity, the Church's ministry increasingly became a political ministry insofar as the Church became concerned with how the state related to the requirements of social justice. Examples of this interaction can be seen in the fourth century, the Middle Ages, and modern times.

These examples indicate that the Church has understood the

impact of Jesus and the implications of a social ministry to entail a political ministry. The economic crisis of the third century and Diocletian's tax policies led to the impoverishment of broad groups. Constantine, consequently, integrated the Church's care for the poor within the imperial system. This increased episcopal responsibility for the poor and the helpless. But the bishops did not limit their roles to patrons of the poor. They engaged in political criticism; they criticized the effects of the Empire's tax policies, which favored the rich and often led to the disenfranchisement of small farmers. Concrete examples of this criticism in the fourth century are Basil's Epistle 110 and Theodoret's Epistle 23.[109]

A similar intertwinement between social ministry and political organization took place in medieval times.[110] Although at the turn of our century the medieval Catholic practice of almsgiving was criticized as individualistic, arbitrary, and unsystemic, this criticism overlooked, as Catholic scholars have shown, the relationship between the Catholic Church and the cities in regard to social welfare.[111] From the twelfth century onward, the cities passed legislation to provide for the needy and established hospitals for the poor, the sick, and for abandoned children.[112] Church leadership, and even theological faculties, often praised or criticized political leadership when it concerned matters of social justice.[113] Moreover, the social legislation of the modern state was not in contrast to, but a further development of, civic responsibilities in the social area.[114] In this same tradition the Council of Trent urged bishops *ex officio* to supervise the social practices of various cities and provinces. Diocesan and provincial synods were given the task of watching over local economic, civic and political legislation. These synods emphasized the obligation of episcopal surveillance of how the states or cities carried out the care for the needy and unemployed through institutions and legislation.[115]

In the nineteenth century a further interrelationship between social and political ministry took place. Catholic social teachings (e.g., *Rerum novarum*) focused not just on the welfare of those outside the work situation but also on those within it.[116] Reform of economic structures should be based on human dignity and rights. Property ownership should take into account the social function of property. In the last decades the scope was broadened to include the relation between advanced and developing nations, between rich and poor continents. In short, the de facto increase of the interrelation between the social, political, and economic led to a social ministry that increasingly became a political ministry.

In addition to interpreting the paradigmatic convictions and practices of the Christian tradition, one must examine as a relevant background theory the nature of societal evolution and its relation to social welfare. In sociological literature the divisions of social evolution are innumerable. Parsons, Diamond, Eisenstadt, Dobert, Bellah, Habermas, and Luhmann have all sketched in broad outlines various divisions of societal evolution.[117] Although some important objections can be raised against Luhmann's theoretical presuppositions and concrete details, his division of societal evolution into three stages (archaic, high-culture, and modern) is helpful to illustrate important changes in societal evolution and the corresponding changes regarding social help and social virtue.[118] These three stages are not intended to be evaluative in any way. Moreover, although a certain chronological evolution does exist, it is possible for there to be a coexistence of stages, and individuals can be in situations that typify more than one stage.

Archaic societies are characterized by mutual help and *immediate reciprocity*. Persons face common situations and needs. Mutual assistance is necessary in order to survive. Persons help one another against the fluctuations of the environment. What takes place structurally in archaic societies is the institutionalization of reciprocity based upon the possibility that situations might be reversed or that a given task demands two or more persons. Society has not yet become so structured that specified organizations invariably perform specified tasks or take care of specified needs. Instead, mutual help and immediate assistance is religiously sanctioned and characterizes the structure of archaic society.

High culture societies are characterized by a differentiation of society. The division of labor, agriculture, trade, and property leads to new forms of social interaction, political domination, and religious institutionalization. As a result of the division of labor and the more complex organization of society, a new social context for the realization and interpretation of help and social welfare emerges. Help is no longer exclusively based upon immediate reciprocity and its necessity is not due to the reversibility of situations. Instead, help often becomes stabilized in the form of contracts. The division of labor within a differentiated society entails that individuals contract out for specific needs and tasks. Consequently, the more highly structured society becomes, the more contractual agreement rather than mutual help becomes central to the functioning of society. One obtains the assistance of diverse specialized individuals, for example, doctors, teachers, bakers, or construction workers, in a contractual exchange for money; one offers one's own services to others in the same way.

But at the same time that society becomes more highly structured, there emerges not only a division of labor but also a division of wealth, divisions into rich and poor, propertied and nonpropertied, advantaged and disadvantaged, and so forth. With such division neither the reciprocity of mutual help nor the contractual agreement is possible. What remains is liberality (e.g., the Roman religious attitude in antiquity) or charity (the traditional Christian attitude). Those possessing more wealth, property, and advantage have an obligation to assist those in need. The virtue of almsgiving may be seen as the virtue of charity and liberality; and in some cases it was even viewed as the virtue of justice.[119]

In highly structured societies, often called *modern* societies, the complexity of societal structures and interactions has become such to produce a need for a systemic solution to the problems of the needs for assistance and help, especially by the disadvantaged and needy. Society develops highly organized and structured social systems for a systemic solution to the problems of human needs and social hardships. In these situations what was previously a matter of mutual assistance or charity now becomes institutionalized in various social programs; social security, unemployment insurance, health insurance, welfare programs, and the like. What was previously taken care of by individuals or by local groups now becomes integrated within the total organizational pattern of society. Such an institutionalization of social aid has the implication that what is at stake is not merely personal assistance but also social programs. Whether needy persons or groups are helped is the object of a double decision. A decision must be made both about a program and then about whether an individual case is covered by the program. From the perspective of such an interpretation of modern society, one may ask where the Church's social responsibility rests today. As we have noted above, many argue (e.g., Helmut Schelsky, Niklas Luhmann, Wolfhart Pannenberg, and Richard McBrien) that the Church has primarily a substitutional role in such a situation.[120] Its primary role does not involve social concerns and political programs, except when a dysfunctioning takes place. In this view, the Church has a function analogous to that of the Red Cross. Just as the Red Cross steps into particular disaster situations that are exceptional so too does the Church. For example, it sets up soup kitchens for those not covered by government programs, but it is properly and officially not involved in such social programs per se.

This interpretation, however, overlooks the dynamics of contemporary society and of the decision-making process. The situation has changed from that of the need for mutual help in the face of the environment or from the mere division into the more fortunate and the less fortunate. Instead, the situation is characterized by a scarcity of goods and natural resources, by competition on a national and a world market, by an intertwinement of ecological, economic, social, and political decisions.

Economic and political decisions cannot be made without affecting each other. Economic decisions will have their effect not only on social programs but also on the lives of large groups of persons. The need for political parties to gain and to retain political power will mean that political decisions affecting the economy will be made not simply on the basis of "economic rationality" but rather in relation to particular influential interest groups, voting blocks, and power groups.[121] In such a situation, the Churches as religious institutions should have the role not only of sanctioning mutual assistance or of encouraging charity and almsgiving but also of examining critically and of reflecting consistently upon how political decisions affect the demands of justice in relation to human lives and interaction.

The task of the Churches has, therefore, two dimensions in modern differentiated society: (1) the role of critique and advocacy in regard to social justice and social programs; (2) the role of the formation of personal community. Since social welfare is determined primarily through political legislation, the major means of fostering social justice is through the criticism of existing legislation or the advocacy of legislation and programs. However, since modern society achieves its social goals primarily through legislation establishing entitlements, rights, and priorities, and through the distribution of money, social welfare is of an impersonal and anonymous character. Problems of loneliness and individual personal needs cannot be reached by social legislation or the distribution of money. In these cases, the Churches' social ministry takes on the role of the formation of personal contact and communities.

One example can illustrate this point. In the United States a medical-industrial complex of profit-making companies has not only become firmly established but is growing at a spectacular rate.[122] Health care has become an investor-owned profit business. Today profit-making conglomerates own chains of hospitals, nursing homes, kidney dialysis centers, ambulatory surgical centers, diagnostic laboratories, and medical office buildings. In the 1970s these profit-making chains grew faster than the computer industry; and in 1981 nearly 80 percent of all nursing homes were run by profit-making companies. It is estimated that in the near future the health-care industry will rival the defense establishment in revenues and scope. In the case of profit-making medical groups, corporations develop criteria to evaluate doctors: how many tests and procedures were ordered, how many hospital admissions were generated, and the like. In the case of hospitals, admission is dependent upon the financial ability to pay or the appropriate insurance. Obviously, in a situation where health care has become an industrial profit-making complex, questions about the availability of this health care for the poor cannot be resolved by means of mutual assistance or liberality and charity, but only by effective legislation that assures social equity in the availability of health care. At the same time, the interrelationship of the religious and medical dimension involved in health care requires personal contact and involvement by religious communities and groups. The Church's tradition of taking care of the poor and the sick as a religious function demands the double role of political advocacy and personal involvement. A reconstruction, therefore, of the Christian tradition, as well as of the evolution of societal forms of social assistance, points to the necessity of social ministry becoming a political ministry.

My proposal in regard to the political ministry of the Church can be compared with Paul Ramsey's suggestions that the Church primarily has a ministry of criticism and, at the most, should limit itself to middle axioms between theory and praxis.[123] The relation between religion and social-political ministry points to a much more fundamental dimension. It emphasizes that Christianity as a religion provides an interpretation of human reality that intersects with other interpretations. The Church's political ministry is, therefore, much more basic than middle axioms because it is concerned with symbols, vision, and values. Since the religious intersects with the social, political, and ethical, the Church has the obligation to take concrete stances, be they of criticism or of advocacy. Such criticism or advocacy need not be based solely on theological warrants, as Ramsey would claim, but can and should also be based on rational and ethical grounds that are illumined or intersected by the religious vision.

My proposal did not raise the issue of appropriate strategy.[124] What is appropriate for an episcopal conference or a specific organization might not be appropriate for a sermon or a parish. Voluntary groups or ecclesial agencies might have different roles than bishops. Such strategic issues need deliberate and prudent resolution for a Church that is aware of how its religious identity demands a social and political ministry. In the past, there has been the episcopal criticism of the Roman Empire's exploitative tax policies, the local ordinary's concern for adequate social legislation by the cities, and papal concern for the effects of the industrial revolution and the division between rich and poor nations. The present intertwinement between economic, national, and social planning may mean that the Church will be increasingly called upon to take an advocacy stance in behalf of the helpless and voiceless. Increasingly, organizations such as Network and the United States Catholic Conference may assume roles for the sake of goals previously achieved through diaconal organizations. Throughout its history the Church's political ministry arose out of its social ministry for the poor and the oppressed. Its obligation to speak out on social and political issues does not stem from a "better knowledge" of economic problems (e.g., how to have growth without excessive inflation), but from its option for those in misfortune, for its option to exhibit its reception of the meaning and praxis of Jesus in a new historical and societal situation. The Church's religious vision does not produce isolated reasons for such options, but rather its vision intersects with the ethical reasons of justice. Its vision gives ultimacy to justice over political solutions of expediency, interest groups, and power blocks.

The Church's Mission and Foundational Theology

Since traditional fundamental theology discussed the mission of the Church under the rubric of the goal and truth of the Church, the reconstructive interpretation of the Christian tradition and praxis of social mission needs to be related to this rubric. Within a foundational theology seeking to overcome the aporia of the traditional fundamental theology, these two issues remain crucial but have a different locus and distinct interpretation.

Distinction between Function and Goal
Within fundamental theological discussions about the mission of the Church, teleological language is used to express the Church's purpose. References to the Church's function, purpose, goal, end, and mission are often used interchangeably and indiscriminately. It is important, however, to distinguish carefully between two different types of teleological statements: goal and function ascriptions.[125] A *goal* statement refers to some outcome or to some goal toward which certain activities are directed. When woodpeckers peck, their goal is to discover the larvae of insects. *Functional* statements are descriptions of the effects of an activity within an organism. The heart valves have the function of giving direction to blood. These two (goal and

function) are distinct in that it could be said that the function of the eye is to see whereas the goal of a rabbit's flight from a fox is to escape. Flight is a goal rather than a function. Sight is a function of the eye whereby it achieves certain goals.

The distinction between goal and function ascriptions is important for the mission of the Church. Does mission of the Church refer to the goal or to the function of the Church? In traditional fundamental theology it was asserted that all societies have their proper goals but, whereas societies have natural goals, the Church has a distinctive supernatural goal. Therefore, all the Church's activities should be directed to the ultimate goal of the beatific vision of God. Consequently, it was concluded that all activities that are anticipations of this goal are properly religious activities. Contemplation and worship are the most proper activities of the Church because they are most intrinsically related to its goal.

Such an argumentation overlooks the important distinction between goal and function. The mission of the Church relates to the Church's function within the world. This function is, however, determined by the religious identity of the Church. Religious identity consists not in a specific difference but in an overlapping and intersecting of a variety of actors determined, in large part, by religious tradition and history: the intertwinement between belief in Jesus and the interpretative meaning of his significance, on the one hand, and the practice of a social and political ministry, on the other. The religious function of the Church, therefore, takes place when it exhibits this intertwinement in its proclamation, praxis, and ministry. The nature of religion—to offer an interpretation of reality, self, and action—as well as the Christian vision that identifies the saving life-praxis of Jesus with the wisdom, logos, and justice underlying creation is the theological foundation of the Church's religious identity in its social and political mission. The more an action or a ministry can be integrated in the vision and meaning historically articulated by Christianity, the more the ministry is proper to Christian evangelization and constitutive of the Church's mission. Such a ministry and mission belongs to the Church's function as a religious institution.

Foundational Theology: Praxis as Warrant

Traditional fundamental theology sought to demonstrate the truth of Christianity by historical arguments for the facticity of Jesus' resurrection and his de facto foundation of the Church with a supernatural mission. Transcendental fundamental theology sought to demonstrate the existential meaningfulness of Jesus' resurrection and of ecclesial existence. When foundational theology is developed as a reconstructive hermeneutic, then the mission of the Church is central to foundational theology not only as the historical problem of what the Church's mission should be if it is historically rooted in Jesus, not only as the transcendental question of the existential significance of community, but also and especially as the hermeneutical issue of the meaning and truth of the Christian vision.

A well-known and much discussed slogan is: "That may be right in theory but it won't work in practice."[126] This slogan bifurcates theory and practice. Applied to theology it means that the truth of Christianity is a theoretical problem, the practice of Christians and of the Christian Churches is a practical issue. No matter what the de facto practice of the Church in its social and political ministry is, the credibility of Christianity is based upon a historical or existential demonstration.

Nevertheless, it is a characteristic of contemporary understanding of theory that a theory is valid only in relation to its practice. This interrelation can be illustrated with relation to the notion of "reception" (developed in chapter 5) and that of "reflective equilibrium" (to be developed in chapter 11). The notion of reception points out that meaning and truth do not exist as independent identities, but rather in their reception. The importance of reception is not that there is a clear-cut meaning whose reception gives it its truth, but rather that the meaning of a religious vision depends on how it is continually received and transformed into a living belief and praxis.

The notion of reflective equilibrium underscores how various justificatory elements play a role in truth. If beliefs provide the warrants for certain practices in our relation to society, nature, and self, then to affirm the belief is, at the same time, to point out the differences that the beliefs make for the community of believers and how the community relates to society, the world, and to one another. To the extent that a religious vision is offered as a warrant for a particular praxis, then that particular praxis, in its perception as illuminative, right, and true—especially in comparison with alternatives—warrants the religious vision. There is an equilibrium between the warrant of the hermeneutical disclosure of the religious tradition and the warrant of the practice of this tradition. This reflective equilibrium must be balanced against the relevant background theories of societal evolution and political structures.

The notion of praxis as a warrant in reflective equilibrium pertains not only to the justification of truth but also to the discovery of truth. In classical philosophy and theology, it was argued that personal purgation was necessary for the discovery of the truth.[127] Unless one desired the good, one could not know the good. Unless one disciplined oneself to the love of the other and the transcendent, one could not uncover the meaning of the love of the other and the love of the transcendent. In the wake of scientific methodology and technocratic rationality, this interrelation between praxis and truth has become overlooked and neglected. The Church's commitment to truth, justice, and charity is essential to its discovery of the meaning of its religious tradition's vision of truth, justice, and charity. Consequently, the praxis of the Church is not simply a warrant that discloses the truth of its religious tradition, but that praxis is a source of the discovery of such meaning and truth in the Church's religious vision. This is the goal of foundational theology.

NOTES

1. Michael Fahey, "The Mission of the Church: To Divinize or to Humanize?" *Proceedings CTSA* 31 (1976) 56–69.

2. Lothar Rütti, *Zur Theologie der Mission* (Mainz: Matthias Grünewald, 1977); and Thomas Kramm, *Analyse und Bewährung theologische Modelle zur Begründung der Mission* (Aachen: Missio Aktuell, 1979).

3. Roger D. Haight, "Mission: Symbol for Church Today," *TS* 37 (1976) 620–49. See also the response by Robert T. Sears, ibid., pp. 649–51.

4. David Power, *Gifts That Differ* (New York: Pueblo, 1980).

5. See the special issue of the *Jurist* 41 (1981).

6. Dean M. Kelley, *Why Conservative Churches Are Growing* (New York: Harper and Row, 1972; 2nd ed. 1977); Jeffrey K. Hadden, *The Gathering Storm in the Churches* (Garden City, N.Y.: Doubleday, 1969).

7. Charles E. Curran, "Theological Reflections on the Social Mission of the Church," in *The Social Mission of the Church: A Theological Reflection*, ed. Edward J. Ryle (Washington, D.C.: National School of Social Service, Catholic University of America, 1972), pp. 31–54.

8. This point is often overlooked by critics of the Church's political and social mission when they appeal to eschatology.

9. Patrick Granfield, "The Rise and Fall of *Societas Perfecta*," *Concilium* 157 (1982) 3–8.

10. For a survey of options, see Joachim Salaverri, *De ecclesia Christi,* in *Sacrae Theologiae Summa,* vol. 1 (Madrid: BAC, 1958), pp. 822–30.

11. K. Walf, "Die katholische Kirche—eine 'societas perfecta'?" *TQ* 157 (1977) 107–18.

12. Adolf Deneffe, "Geschichte des Wortes 'supernaturalis,' " *ZKTh* 46 (1922) 337–60.

13. See Henri de Lubac, *The Mystery of the Supernatural* (New York: Herder and Herder, 1967) and *Augustinianism and Modern Theology* (New York: Herder and Herder, 1969).

14. Konrad Feiereis, *Die Umprägung der natürlichen Theologie in Religionsphilosophie* (Leipzig: St. Benno, 1965).

15. *Semaines sociales de France* (Versailles, 1936), pp. 461–62; quoted in Walter M. Abbott, ed., *The Documents of Vatican II* (New York: America, 1966), p. 264, n. 192.

16. Pius XII on 9 March 1956: The Church is not given "any mandate or fixed any end of the cultural order" (*AAS* 48 [1956] 212).

17. *Gaudium et spes*, no. 42, in Abbott, *Documents*, p. 241. The text goes on to say: "The Church is willing to assist and promote all these institutions to the extent that such a service depends on her and can be associated with her mission" (p. 242).

18. See Richard S. Wheeler, *Pagans in the Pulpit* (New Rochelle, N.Y.: Arlington, 1974). See also the critique of liberation theology by Roger Vekemans, *Caesar and God: The Priesthood and Politics* (Maryknoll, N.Y.: Orbis, 1972).

19. The classic expression is Jacques Maritain, *Scholasticism and Politics* (New York: Macmillan, 1940). See also his *Christianity and Democracy* (London: Centenary, 1945).

20. For a more positive evaluation of the Lutheran position in contrast to the neo-Lutheran, see Ulrich Duchrow, *Christenheit und Weltverantwortung: Traditionsgeschichte und systematische Struktur der Zweireichelehre* (Stuttgart: Ernst Klett, 1970). For a discussion of the pros and cons of the Lutheran doctrine, see Hans Schwarz, "Luther's Doctrine of the Two Kingdoms: Help or Hindrance for Social Change," *LQ* (1975) 59–75, and the exchange with Karl Hertz, ibid., pp. 76–79 and 257–59.

21. For a survey, see Bernhard Stockle, *"Gratia supponit naturam": Geschichte und Analyse eines theologischen Axioms* (Rome: Herder, 1962).

22. *Theology and the Kingdom of God* (Philadelphia: Westminster, 1969), pp. 90–91, and "Christian Morality and Political Issues," in *Faith and Reality* (Philadelphia: Westminster, 1977), pp. 123–38.

23. "The Church and Social Change: An Ecclesiological Critique," in Thomas M. McFadden, ed., *Theology Confronts a Changing World* (West Mystic, Conn.: Twenty-Third Publications, 1977), pp. 41–62, here p. 52. See his *Catholicism*, vol. 2 (Minneapolis: Winston, 1980), pp. 720–22, for a more constitutive than substitutive role with regard to social justice. For Segundo, see *The Community Called Church* (Maryknoll, N.Y.: Orbis, 1972), p. 96.

24. McBrien, "Church and Social Change," p. 52.

25. "The Church's Commission to Bring Salvation and the Humanization of the World," in *Theological Investigations* 14 (New York: Seabury, 1976), pp. 295–313, here p. 312. Rahner's earlier essay, "The Function of the Church as a Critic of Society" (in *Theological Investigations* 12 [New York: Seabury, 1974], pp. 229–49, asserts: "It can be justifiably said, therefore, that the function of the official authorities of the Church as critics of society has still not found any clear theological *topos* for itself" (p. 243). Influenced by Metz's political theology, Rahner characterizes the Church's task of criticism as "prophetic instruction in social criticism" that must however leave freedom to individual Christians for their own political responsibility (pp. 243–44). In discussing the relation between Church and society, Rahner appears to identify Church with the official Church or the "official authorities" and does not take into account the broader understanding of Church developed elsewhere in his writings.

26. "Theological Reflections on the Problem of Secularization," in *Theological Investigations* 10 (New York: Herder and Herder, 1974), pp. 318–48.

27. On the social and political mission of Catholic Action, see William Bosworth, *Catholicism and Christ in Modern France* (Princeton, N.J.: Princeton Univ. Press, 1962); and Michael Fogarty, *Christian Democracy in Europe* (Notre Dame: Univ. of Notre Dame Press, 1957). A classic theological defense of this position is Yves Congar, *Lay People in the Church* (Westminister, Md.: Newman, 1957).

28. John A. Coleman has articulated the importance of cultural pluralism and ecclesial voluntarism as an appropriate form of American political theology. See his *An American Strategic Theology* (New York: Paulist, 1982). for an appraisal of the principle of voluntarism, see James M. Gustafson, *The Church as Moral Decision Maker* (Philadelphia: Pilgrim, 1970). Although voluntarism is advocated as specifically appropriate to the situation in the Unites States, the Latin American base communities are also well-established examples of such voluntarism in relation to social action.

29. For a criticism of the theology implied in this position, see Elisabeth Schüssler [Fiorenza], *Der vergessene Partner* (Düsseldorf: Patmos, 1964).

30. See Gustavo Gutierrez, *A Theology of Liberation* (Maryknoll, N.Y.: Orbis, 1973). Gutierrez's criticism of the distinction of planes within liberalism is applicable also to the ecclesiologies of Congar and Rahner. Nevertheless, it is Rahner's understanding of

the Church as sacrament that allows him to show the interrelation between salvation history and world history. See Karl Rahner, "History of the World and Salvation-History," in *Theological Investigations* 5 (New York: Seabury, 1966), pp. 97–114.

31. Fahey, "Mission," pp. 56–69. For a similar emphasis upon plurality of tasks, see Jerome P. Theissen, *The Ultimate Church and the Promise of Salvation* (Collegeville, Minn.: St. John's Univ., 1976), pp. 152–82.

32. *Models of the Church* (Garden City, N.Y.: Doubleday, 1976), p. 95.

33. Gutierrez, *A Theology*, pp. 213–85.

34. Dulles, *Models*. See his emphasis on the relation between faith and social mission in "The Meaning of Faith Considered in Relationship to Justice," in *The Faith That Does Justice*, ed. John C. Haughey (Woodstock Studies 2; New York: Paulist, 1977), pp. 1–46.

35. René Coste argues that the Church should have a liberating political impact, but "only on the condition that it remain faithful to its specific mission" ("Foi et société: Liberátion et salut," *Esprit et vie* 85 [1975] 577–88).

36. Coleman (*An American*) weakens the link by relegating social mission to the role of precondition or consequence of evangelization.

37. Peter Wagner argues that the Church's primary function is individual reconciliation and salvation; the concern for social justice is secondary and derivative. See his *Latin American Theology: Radical or Evangelical* (Grand Rapids: Eerdmans, 1970).

38. For the difference between political theology and Latin American liberation theology, see Francis Fiorenza: "Political Theology and Liberation Theology: An Inquiry into Their Fundamental Meaning," in *Liberation, Freedom, and Revolution*, ed. Thomas E. McFadden (New York: Seabury, 1975), pp. 3–29; "Political Theology as Foundational Theology," *Proceedings CTSA* 32 (1977) 142–77; and "Political Theology: An Historical Analysis," *TD* 25 (1977) 317–34.

39. See Johann B. Metz, *Faith in History and Society* (New York: Seabury, 1980) and *The Emergent Church* (New York: Crossroad, 1981). Jürgen Moltmann's *The Church in the Power of the Spirit* (New York: Harper and Row, 1977) emphasizes the Church's messianic role. The option for socialism and the concept of symbiosis modify the earlier emphasis on the critique of political religion that dominated *The Crucified God* (New York: Harper and Row, 1977).

40. For objections to Metz's emphasis on negative critique, see J. Bryan Hehir, "The Idea of a Political Theology," *Worldview* 14 (January 1971) 5–7 and (February 1971) 5–7.

41. For a general survey, see José Miguez Bonino, *Doing Theology in a Revolutionary Situation* (Philadelphia: Fortress, 1975), esp. pp. 132–53; Also Alfred T. Hennelly, *Theologies in Conflict: The Challenge of Juan Luis Segundo* (Maryknoll, N.Y.: Orbis, 1979); and R. Gibellini, ed., *Frontiers of Theology in Latin America* (Maryknoll, N.Y.: Orbis, 1979).

42. Juan L. Segundo, *Masas y minorías* (Buenos Aires: La Aurora, 1973), pp. 67–71.

43. For a survey of criticisms, see Bonaventure Kloppenburg, *Temptations for the Theology of Liberation* (Chicago, Franciscan Herald, 1974); and H. Lepargneur, "Theologie de la libération et théologie tout court," *NRTh* 98 (1976) 109–25. Unfortunately, some criticisms border on caricature; for example, Dennis McCann's *Christian Realism and Liberation Theology* (Maryknoll, N.Y.: Orbis, 1981) reduced liberation theology to an aphophantic vision. See the response by Matthew Lamb, "A Distorted Interpretation of Latin American Liberation Theology," *Horizons* 8 (Fall 1981).

44. Joseph Gremillion's introduction to *The Gospel of Peace and Justice* (Maryknoll, N.Y.: Orbis, 1976), pp. 1–38; also the commentaries on *Gaudium et spes*, especially Charles Moeller, *L'Élaboration du schème iii: dans le monde de ce temps* (Paris: Casterman, 1968); and Yves Congar, "The Role of the Church in the Modern World," in Herbert Vorgrimler, ed., *Commentary on the Documents of Vatican II* (New York: Herder and Herder, 1969), pp. 202–23.

45. *De justitia in mundo* (Vatican, 1971) 5; E.T. in Gremillion *The Gospel*, pp. 513–29, here p. 514.

46. Trans. Walter J. Burghardt, *Origins* 7, no. 20 (3 November 1977), 311. The text states: "it seems more accurate to interpret [*ratio constitutiva*] as meaning an integral part, not an essential part." See the papers of the commission in Karl Lehmann, ed., *Theologie der Befreiung* (Einsiedeln: Johannes, 1977); and the comments by Bonaventure Kloppenburg, *Christian Salvation and Human Progress* (Chicago: Franciscan Herald, 1979), esp. pp. 40–57.

47. *Catholic Mind* 73, no. 1291 (March 1975), 6.

48. Ibid., pp. 50–51. The text argues that the relation between evangelization and social ministry is based upon human rights. Social ministry is "required" and is "central" to the Church's ministry.

49. Ibid., pp. 52–57, here p. 55. The document refers to the "mutual relationship" and "intimate connection between evangelization and liberation." The Gospel contains "profound reasons" and "new incentives for social ministry that should eliminate the unjust social and political structures flowing from sin."

50. *Catholic Mind* 73, no. 1291 (March 1975), 58–64.

51. *Evangelii nuntiandi* (Washington, D.C.: United States Catholic Conference, 1976), no. 31.

52. Ibid., nos. 34 (kingdom of God) and 35 (human nature).

53. Ibid., no. 9, explains that the kernel of evangelization is salvation, and salvation includes liberation from everything that oppresses human beings, especially sins.

54. See *Addresses and Homilies* (Washington, D. C.: USCC, 1979), pp. 22–38, for the Puebla Address; *Redemptor hominis* and *Laborem exercens* (Washington, D.C.: USCC, 1979 and 1981 respectively).

55. Puebla Address 1, 7 and 3, 2.

56. Ibid., 3, 2.

57. "Der Weg der Kirche ist der Mensch: Sozialtheologische Aspekte des Enzyklika 'Redemptor hominis' Papst Johannes Pauls II," *MTZ* 30 (1979) 278–92.

58. See no. 27.

59. See J. Brian Benestad, "The Political Vision of Pope John Paul II: Justice through Faith and Culture," *Communio* 8 (1981) 3–19; Ernst-Wolfgang Böckenförde, "Das neue politische Engagement der Kirche: Zur 'politischen Theologie' Johannes Pauls II," *Stimmen der Zeit* 198 (1980) 219–34; Otfried Höffe, "Die Menschenrechte als Prinzipien eines christlichen Humanismus: Zum sozialethischen Engagement von Johannes Pauls II," *Communio* 10 (1981) 97–106.

60. Paul VI, *Octogesima adveniens* (Washington, D.C.: USCC, 1971), no. 46: "That is why the need is felt to press from economics to politics. It is true that in the term 'politics' many confusions are possible and must be clarified, but each person feels that in the social and economic field, both national and international, the ultimate decision rests with political power." Note that no. 45 affirms that liberation begins with "interior freedom."

61. See Francis Schüssler Fiorenza, "Religion and Society: Legitimation, Rationalization or Cultural Heritage," *Concilium* 125 (1979) 24–32, for the neo-Marxist critique of communism.

62. *Redemptor hominis*, no. 8; Paul VI, "On Evangelization," no. 31.

63. David Hollenbach, "Modern Catholic Teachings concerning Justice," in Haughey, *Faith That Does Justice*, pp. 207–31.

64. For human dignity as a basis for the relation between evangelization and social mission, see Richard McCormick, "Human Rights and the Mission of the Church," *Mission Trends* 4, ed. Gerald H. Anderson and Thomas F. Stransky (New York: Paulist, 1979), pp. 37–50; reprinted from *TS* 37 (1976) 107–19.

65. *Lumen gentium* emphasizes eschatology as the goal to which the People of God moves. *Gaudium et spes* illumines how eschatology provides a focus for the Church's vocation within the world and in tension with it. By locating the Church's ministry within an eschatological purview, it prepares the way for the critical function of eschatology in the post-Vatican II documents.

66. Puebla Address 3, 1.

67. "The Church in Mission: Canonical Implications," *Canon Law Society Proceedings* 37 (1975) 1–11, here p. 6.

68. *Systematic Theology*, vol. 3 (Chicago; Univ. of Chicago Press, 1963) p. 166.

69. Francis Schüssler Fiorenza, "The Response of Barth and Ritschl to Feuerbach," *Studies in Religion* 7 (1978) 149–66, and "The Significance of On the Glaubenslehre," introduction to F. D. E. Schleiermacher, *On the Glaubenslehre* (AAR Texts and Translations 3; Chico, Calif.: Scholars, 1981), pp. 1–32.

70. David Tracy, *Blessed Rage for Order* (New York: Seabury, 1975), p. 93.

71. Stephen Toulmin, *Reason in Ethics* (New York: Cambridge Univ. Press, 1970), pp. 202–21; and Paul Ricoeur, "Biblical Hermeneutics," *Semeia* 4 (1975) 27–148.

72. Langdon Gilkey, *Reaping the Whirlwind* (New York: Seabury, 1976), pp. 210–16 and 236–38. See my critical review essay in *RelSRev* 4 (1978) 237–40.

73. "While aesthetic existence is essentially enjoyment, and ethical existence essentially struggle and victory, religious existence is essentially suffering" (*Concluding Unscientific Postscript* [Princeton, N.J.: Princeton Univ. Press, 1944], p. 256).

74. *Herrlichkeit: Eine theologische Ästhetik*, vol. 1 (Einsiedeln: Johannes, 1961), pp. 42–120. See also *The von Balthasar Reader*, ed. Medard Kehl and Werner Löser (New York: Crossroad, 1982).

75. *Celestial Pantomime: Poetic Structures of Transcendence* (New Haven, Conn.: Yale Univ. Press, 1979).

76. *Philosophical Investigations* (Oxford: Oxford Univ. Press, 1958), nos. 66 and 67.

77. Francis Schüssler Fiorenza, "Religious Beliefs and Praxis: Reflections on Catholic Theological Views of Work," *Concilium* 131 (1980) 81–89, and "Work and Critical Theology," in *A Matter of Dignity: Inquiries into the Humanization of of Work*, ed. William J. Heisler and John Houck (Notre Dame: Univ. of Notre Dame Press, 1977), pp. 23–44.

78. *Summa theologiae* 2–2, 32 a. 1. For a similar pattern of crisscrossing, see his discussion of religion: 2–2, a. 1 and a. 4.

79. *Cartesian Meditations: An Introduction to Phenomenology* (Hague: Nijhoff, 1970), secs. 49–62, pp. 106–50. See the analysis by Paul Ricoeur, *Husserl: An Analysis of His Phenomenology* (Evanston: Northwestern Univ. Press, 1967), pp. 123–30.

80. Niklas Luhmann, *Funktion der Religion* (Frankfurt: Suhrkamp, 1977), pp. 20–27.

81. The suggested approach relies on Wittgenstein's notion of family resemblance and the more analogical and associate use of "appresentation" rather than the more intuitive appropriation of Husserlian phenomenology. For that approach, see Edward Farley's *Ecclesial Man: A Social Phenomenology of Faith and Reality* (Philadelphia: Fortress, 1975).

82. David Little and Sumner B. Twiss, Jr., "Basic Terms in the Study of Religious Ethics," in *Religion and Morality*, ed. Gene Outka and John P. Reeder (Garden City, N.Y.: Doubleday, 1973), pp. 35–37.

83. Melford E. Spiro, "Religion: Problems of Definition and Explanation," in Michael Banton, ed., *Anthropological Approaches to the Study of Religion* (London: Tavistock, 1966), pp. 85–126; and Frederick J. Streng, "Studying Religion: Possibilities and Limitations of Different Definitions," *JAAR* 40 (1972) 219–37.

84. Peter Berger, "Some Second Thoughts on Substantive versus Functional Definitions of Religion," *JSSR* 13 (1974) 125–33; and Wolfhart Pannenberg, *Theology and the Philosophy of Science* (Philadelphia: Westminster, 1976), pp. 297–345.

85. For the complexities as outlined in a field-theory approach, see, for example, J. Milton Yinger, *The Scientific Study of Religion* (London: Macmillan, 1970).

86. Philip E. Hammond, "The Durkheim Integration Thesis Reexamined: A Study of Religious Pluralism and Legal Institutions," in *Changing Perspectives in the Scientific Study of Religion* ed. Allan W. Eister (New York: Basic, 1974), pp. 115–42; and François Houtart, "Les variables qui affectent le role intégrateur de la religion," *Social Compass* 7 (1960) 21–38.

87. Clifford Geertz, *The Interpretation of Culture* (New York: Basic, 1973).

88. Trutz Rendtorff, *Gesellschaft ohne Religion: Theologische Aspekte einer sozialtheoretischen Kontroverse* (Munich: Piper, 1975); and Frithard Scholz, *Freiheit als Indifferenz*. *Alteuropäische Probleme mit der Systemtheorie Niklas Luhmanns* (Frankfurt: Suhrkamp, 1982).

89. *Basic Questions in Theology*, vol. 2 (Philadelphia: Fortress, 1970), pp. 201–33, here p. 230; see also *The Idea of God and Human Freedom* (Philadelphia: Westminster, 1973), pp. 80–98.

90. Karl Rahner, *Foundations of Christian Faith* (New York: Seabury, 1978).

91. Rainer Döbert, *Systemtheorie und die Entwicklung religiöser Deutungssysteme* (Frankfurt: Suhrkamp, 1973).

92. Francis Schüssler Fiorenza, "Joy and Pain as Paradigmatic for Language about God," *Concilium* 5 (1974) 67–80.

93. Francis Schüssler Fiorenza, "Christology after Vatican II: A Shift of Horizons," *Ecumenist* 18 (1980) 81–89. The four trajectories developed by Helmut Koester form the grid of Edward Schillebeeckx's *Jesus: An Experiment in Christology* (New York: Seabury, 1979).

94. See Burton L. Mack, *Logos und Sophia: Untersuchung zur Weisheitstheologie im hellenistischen Judentum* (Göttingen: Vandenhoeck und Ruprecht, 1973); for Q, see Felix Christ, *Jesus Sophia: Die Sophia-Christologie bei den Synoptikern* (Zurich: EVZ, 1972); and Paul Hoffmann, *Studien zur Theologie der Logienquelle* (Münster: Aschendorff, 1972); for the New Testament hymns, see Elisabeth Schüssler Fiorenza, "Wisdom Mythology and the Christological Hymns of the New Testament," in *Aspects of Wisdom in Juadism and Early Christianity*, ed. Robert L. Wilken (Notre Dame: Univ. of Notre Dame Press, 1975), pp. 17–41. For a popular presentation of the relation between wisdom and christology, see Reginald H. Fuller and Pheme Perkins, *Who Is This Christ?* Philadelphia: Fortress, 1983).

95. See Friedo Ricken, "Das Homousios von Nikaia als Krisis des altchristlichen Platonismus," in *Zur Frühgeschichte der Christologie*, ed. Bernhard Welte (Freiburg: Herder, 1970), pp. 74–99; Alois Grillmeier, "Hellenisierung-Judaisierung des Christentums als Deuterprinzipien der Geschichte des kirchlichen Dogmas," in his *Mit Ihm und in Ihm* (Freiburg: Herder, 1975, 2nd ed.), pp. 423–88; for a discussion of the Arian denial of Jesus as *sophos*, see Robert C. Gregg and Dennis E. Groh, *Early Arianism—A View of Salvation* (Philadelphia: Fortress, 1981), pp. 13–19.

96. For ancient wisdom traditions, see Hartmut Gese, *Lehre und Wirklichkeit in der alten Weisheit* (Tübingen: J. C. B. Mohr, 1958). For the element of protest, see James L. Crenshaw, "The Human Dilemma and the Literature of Dissent," in *Tradition and Theology in the Old Testament*, ed. Douglas A. Knight (Philadelphia: Fortress, 1977), pp. 235–58; F. Charles Fensham, "Wisdom, Orphans and the Poor in Ancient Near Eastern Legal and Wisdom Literature," *JNES* 21 (1962) 129–39.

97. H. Ringgren, *Word and Wisdom: Studies in the Hypostatization of Divine Qualities and Functions in the Near East* (Lund: Ohlssons, 1947).

98. James Dunn, *Christology in the Making* (Philadelphia: Westminster, 1980), pp. 162–250, here p. 190.

99. Francis Schüssler Fiorenza, "Critical Social Theory and Christology," *Proceedings CTSA* 30 (1975), 63–110.

100. Criticisms of Ernesto Cardenal's appointment as minister of education in Nicaragua as an improper role for a priest overlook how traditionally the work of Alcuin (a religious and a deacon) has been seen as a symbol of the Church's positive influence on Western civilization.

101. See Walter J. Burghardt, "Towards a Theology of the Health Apostolate," *Hospital Progress* 52, no. 9 (September 1971), 66–71; and Joseph Fichter, *Religion and Pain* (New York: Crossroad, 1981).

102. Karel Dobbelaere, Jan Lauwers, and Mieke Ghesquiere-Walkens, "Sécularisation et humanisation dans les institutions hospitalières chrétiennes," *Social Compass* 20 (1974) 553–68.

103. See Richard K. Fenn, *Toward a Theory of Secularization* (Storrs, Conn.: SSSR, 1978). For America, see Robert N. Bellah, *Beyond Belief* (New York: Harper and Row, 1970) and *The Broken Covenant* (New York: Seabury, 1975); Russell E. Richey and Donald G. Jones, ed., *American Civil Religion* (New York: Harper and Row, 1974). The last volume surveys the debate on the subject.

104. See the critical analysis of John F. Wilson, *Public Religion in American Culture* (Philadelphia: Temple Univ. Press, 1979).

105. For the historical locus of the notion of civil religion, see my "Political Theology as Foundational Theology," *Proceedings CTSA* 32 (1977) 142–77.

106. See for example, Conrad Cherry, ed., *God's New Israel: Religious Interpretations of American Destiny* (Englewood Cliffs, N. J.: Prentice-Hall, 1971); and Sidney E. Mead, *The Nation with the Soul of a Church* (New York: Harper and Row, 1975).

107. See my "Religion und Politik," in Franz Böckle et al., eds., *Christlicher Glaube in moderner Gesellschaft*, vol. 27 (Frieburg: Herder, 1982), pp. 59–101.

108. Still indispensable for its comprehensiveness is Georg Ratzinger, *Geschichte der kirchlichen Armenpflege* (Freiburg: Herder, 1884, 2nd ed.).

109. See Wilhelm Schneemelcher, "Der diakonische Dienst in der alten Kirche," in *Das diakonische Amt der Kirche*, ed. Hubert Krimm (Stuttgart: Evangelische Verlagsanstalt, 1962, 2nd ed.), pp. 61–105; Wolf-Dieter Hauschild, "Christentum und Eigentum," *ZEE* 16 (1972) 34–49; Robert M. Grant, "The Organization of Alms," in his *Early Christianity and Society* (New York: Harper and Row, 1977), pp. 124–45.

110. A survey of the medieval period would obviously have to take into account important differences between various countries and the profound changes that took place from century to century. See Otto Gerhard Oexle, "Armut und Armenfürsorge um 1200," in *Sankt Elisabeth* (Marburg: Jan Thorbecke, 1981), pp. 78–100; M. Mollat, ed., *Études sur l'histoire de la pauvreté*, vol. 1 (Paris: Publications de la Sorbonne, 1974). For the ninth century, see E. Boshof, "Untersuchungen zur Armenfürsorge im fränkische Reiche des 9. Jahrhunderts," *Archive für Kulturgeschichte* 58 (1976) 265–339. For the fifteenth century, see Thomas Fischer, *Stadtische Armut und Armenfürsorge im 15. und 16. Jahrhundert* (Göttinger Beiträge zur Wirtschafts- und Sozialgeschichte 4; Göttingen, 1979).

111. See Gerhard Uhlhorn, *Die christliche Liebestätigkeit* (Stuttgart: Gundert, 1895, 2nd ed.); and the Catholic response by Johann Nepomuk Foerst, *Das Almosen* (Paderborn: Schöningh, 1909).

112. In addition to Ratzinger, Mollat, and Fischer (cited in notes 108 and 110 above), see also Brian Tierney, *Medieval Poor Law* (Berkeley: Univ. of California Press, 1959); and E. Maschke, "Die Unterschichten der mittelalterlichen Städte Deutschlands," in Carl Haase, ed., *Die Stadt des Mittelalters*, vol. 3 (Darmstadt: Wissenschaftliche Buchgesellschaft, 1979), pp. 345–454.

113. Franz Ehrle, "Die Armenordnung von Nürnberg (1522) and von Ypern (1525)," *HJ* 9 (1888) 450–79; and Otto Winckelmann, "Die Armenordnungen von Nürnberg, Kitzingen, Regensburg und Ypern," *ARG* (1912–13) 242–80.

114. See Foerst, *Almosen*, pp. 146–53. For the contrary thesis, see Lotte Koch, *Wandlungen der Wohlfahrtspflege im Zeitalter der Aufklärung* (Erlangen: Univ. Erlangen, 1933).

115. Council of Trent, Sess. 22, *De reform.*, c. 8: "Omnia quae ad cultum Dei aut salutem animarum seu pauperes sustentandos instituta sunt, ipsi [episcopi] ex officio suo juxta canonum sacrorum statuta cognoscant et exequantur non obstantibus quacumque consuetudine etiam immemoriabili, privilegio aut statuto." See Ratzinger, *Geschichte*, pp. 469–72 for the Council of Cologne in 1536.

116. See Gremillion's introduction to *The Gospel of Peace and Justice* (cited in n. 44 above). For the development of Catholic social ethics in the United States, see the comprehensive and erudite treatment of Charles E. Curran, *American Catholic Social Ethics: Twentieth Century Approaches* (Notre Dame, Univ. of Notre Dame Press, 1982).

117. See Talcott Parsons, *Societies: Evolutionary and Comparative Perspectives* (Englewood Cliffs, N.J.: Prentice-Hall, 1966); S. N. Eisenstadt, *The Political Systems of Empires* (New York: Free Press, 1963); Robert Bellah's essay "Religious Evolution," in *Beyond Belief* (New York: Harper and Row, 1970), pp. 20–50; Jürgen Habermas, *Communication and the Evolution of Society* (Boston: Beacon, 1977); Niklas Luhmann, *Funktion der Religion* (Frankfurt: Suhrkamp, 1977); and Döbert, *Systemtheorie* (cited in n. 91 above).

118. See Niklas Luhmann, "Formen des Helfens im Wandel gesellschaftlicher Bedingungen," in Hans-Uwe Otto and Siegfried Schneider, eds., *Gesellschaftliche Perspektiven der Sozialarbeit* (Berlin: Neuwied, 1973), pp. 21–43; and Luhmann's "Die Organisationsmittel des Wohlfahrtsstaates und ihre Grenzen," in Heiner Geissler, ed., *Verwaltete Bürger—Gesellschaft in Fesseln* (Frankfurt: Ullstein, 1978), pp. 112–20.

119. See Joachim Giers, *Gerechtigkeit und Liebe. Die Grundpfeiler gesellschaftlicher Ordnung in der Sozialethik des Kardinals Cajetan* (Düsseldorf: Patmos, 1941). Cajetan interpreted almsgiving not merely as an act of charity but as an act required by justice.

120. See nn. 22, 23, and 118 above.

121. Quite often political theology is criticized (e.g., Lehmann, *Theologie*, pp. 9–44) for its ability to provide "merely" theological solutions to economic and social problems. This criticism overlooks the fact that political rationality should not be reduced to rationality *in se*, since it is often based not on ethical theory, but on voting power and political influences; see Edward C. Banfield, *Political Influence* (New York: Free Press, 1961).

122. Paul Starr, *The Social Transformation of American Medicine* (New York: Basic, 1983).

123. *Who Speaks for the Church?* (Nashville: Abingdon, 1967). For a critique of Ramsey's limitation of the Church to theological warrants, see the perceptive criticisms of Charles E. Curran, *Politics, Medicine and Christian Ethics: A Dialogue with Paul Ramsey* (Philadelphia: Fortress, 1973).

124. For some judicious suggestions, see George G. Higgins, "The Problems in Preaching and Politics: What Place in the Church?" *Origins* 2, no. 13 (21 September 1972), 207, 212–14; Walter J. Burghardt, "Preaching the Just Word," *Liturgy and Social Justice*, ed. Mark Searle (Collegeville: Liturgical Press, 1980), pp. 36–52; and for a more general treatment, Edward Schillebeeckx, "Church, Magisterium and Politics," in *God the Future of Man* (New York: Sheed and Ward, 1968), pp. 141–66.

125. Ernest Nagel, *Teleology Revisted and Other Essays in the Philosophy and History of Science* (New York: Columbia Univ. Press, 1979), pp. 275–316.

126. Immanuel Kant, *On the Old Saw That May Be Right in Theory But It Won't Work in Practice* (Philadelphia: Univ. of Pennsylvania Press, 1974; orig. 1794).

127. St. Augustine, *On Christian Doctrine* (Indianapolis: Bobbs-Merrill, 1981), bks. I and II.

PART IV

FROM FUNDAMENTAL TO FOUNDATIONAL THEOLOGY

Introduction

Our treatment of the specific foundational issues showed that important philosophical and theological differences are at stake within the current debates. These debates, however, center not simply on specific issues of fundamental theology, but on the very enterprise itself. Even the notion of fundamental theology remains ambiguous, with innumerable connotations and denotations. Is fundamental theology an apologetic of the Christian faith? Is it quite clearly distinct from apologetics in that fundamental theology elaborates the meaning at the basis of the Christian faith, whereas apologetics demonstrates the truth of that basis? Is fundamental theology a philosophy of religion or a philosophical theology independent of faith and prior to systematic theology? Or is fundamental theology properly a theological discipline distinct from any rational philosophy of religion? Does it employ historical, philosophical, phenomenological methods that have their validity independently of the context of faith and theology, or does it ultimately depend upon this context for the validity of its arguments?

These diverse questions reflect different views of fundamental theology and are mirrored in the diverse names used to describe it. Apologetics, fundamental theology, foundational theology, formal-fundamental theology, basic science of faith, prolegomena to dogmatics, philosophical theology, and philosophy of religion have all, at one time or other, been used to refer to the enterprise most commonly known today as fundamental theology.[1] Indiscriminately used, they refer to quite distinct philosophical and theological conceptions of the task of fundamental theology.

Not only the task and terminology but the discipline itself is in flux, so much so that it has been observed that a sign should be posted on all fundamental theological seminar rooms: "Temporarily closed due to extensive renovations."[2] But even this sign would be overly optimistic. It would characterize the state of other theological disciplines more than of fundamental theology. Although historical research and theological advances have changed much in the traditional fields of christology, ecclesiology, sacramental theology, and the like, this research has not challenged their very existence as theological disciplines. But this is not the case for fundamental theology. Perhaps, therefore, the sign should read: "Demolition Experts at Work."

Rather than temporarily closing down the seminar room of fundamental theology in order to hammer away at the renovation of existing structures, one should begin by inquiring into what has led to the emergence of fundamental theology as an independent theological discipline prior to systematic theology. To this purpose, it is necessary to search for the conditions and presuppositions of its origins, the stages and impetus of its development, and the structure and organization of its present status. Such a historical analysis would be like an archaeological investigation in that it would uncover the very foundations underlying the existence, structure, and nature of fundamental theology. And this uncovering would in turn point to the way in which fundamental theology needs to be reconstructed and rebuilt—not in its traditional or contemporary forms, but as a reconstructive hermeneutic.

A sketch of the origin and development of fundamental theology as a theological discipline will therefore serve several historical and systematic purposes. It will dispel some widespread myths about the origin and development of fundamental theology. It will show how the reaction to the deism of the Enlightenment and the appropriation of rationalism and Idealism decisively influenced the discipline. The root metaphor of "foundation" and the very division of the discipline stems from this historical context. Its goal, method, and content, can be traced to the same influence.

Chapter 9

The Emergence
of Fundamental Theology

There is a popular consensus that fundamental theology originated in the nineteenth century; it was (and is) primarily a Roman Catholic endeavor; and the move from apologetics to fundamental theology represented a move toward pluralism and diversity within theology. However, despite this general consensus, all three assumptions are false. The point of origin should not be sought in the nineteenth but in the seventeenth and eighteenth centuries. The major forces for its development and structure came not from Roman Catholic authors but from Protestant authors. The move from apologetics to fundamental theology did not necessarily lead to the enrichment of theology but to the attempt to reduce all theology to an archimedean foundation.

To uncover these historical misconceptions about the origin and development of fundamental theology entails a historical search for its roots, the context of its emergence, the forces propelling its development, and the underlying presuppositions. Such a historical survey should not proceed as if it were tracing the history of an idea that like a seed finally arrived at its full fruition, but rather it should proceed as would an archaeologist looking at different levels for distinct cities embodying contrasting cultures. This historical survey will uncover the conception of fundamental theology as a basic theology in relation to positive theology, as an apologetics in reaction to the deism of the Enlightenment, and as a foundation of theology under the influence of fundamental theology. Each of these three constellations merged to form what in the twentieth century came to be taken for granted as fundamental theology.

The Search for Roots: Fundamental Theology and Positive Theology

Fundamental theology as an appellation for a discipline of theology emerged for the first time in association with positive theology. Therefore, the first and preliminary stage of the development of fundamental theology is to be seen in its relation to positive theology. This suggestion might at first appear implausible; after all, a world of difference exists between fundamental theology and positive theology.[3] Moreover, the very notion of positive theology is unclear. Nevertheless, the important beginnings of fundamental theology, or more precisely the seeds for the development of classic fundamental theology, were established in the context of positive theology.

In ordinary usage the term "positive" is obscure. The antonym of positive is negative. Etymologically, the term comes from the past participle *positivus* and refers to what has been laid down, what has been posited.[4] The very historical meaning of the term "positive theology" was ambiguous in the seventeenth century when it became current. Positive theology could refer to any one of the following: scriptural scholarship or exegesis, controversial theology, especially between Catholics and Protestants; it could also refer to positive as the basic smattering of knowledge about the various theological disciplines; or positive as the practical orientation of a body of knowledge to a specific goal, for example, church governance and ministry; and finally, positive as a contrast term to scholastic theology.

A common denominator underlies all these diverse conceptions and multifaceted contexts of positive theology, that is, the study of the sources of revelation. Whereas scholastic theology went beyond the sources of revelation, positive theology took them as its proper object. In the sixteenth century, the positive and the scholastic stood in contrast to each other as two distinct intellectual orientations.[5] The term positive designated the humanists and those theologians desireous of a direct contact with the word of God in the Bible. The positive theologians sought the living expressions of this word in the sources of tradition and recommended the study of languages and of history to discover this word in its original and authentic expression. Scholastic theologians employed an Aristotelian dialectic in use since the Middle Ages.

Positive theology as it developed in the sixteenth and seventeenth centuries was quite distinct from the neoscholastic conception that developed within the nineteenth century.[6] Neoscholasticism understood positive and scholastic theology not as two distinct intellectual orientations, but as two distinct branches of the one and the same theological science. Taking as its staring-point the distinction between *an sit* (whether it is) and *quid sit* (what it is) as employed by Aquinas,[7] neoscholasticism understood positive theology to be that branch of theology which established the basic data of theology, whereas speculative theology was the branch seeking to understand the data, once established.[8]

Positive theology in the sixteenth century thus represents distinct intellectual orientation. It sought to go back to the roots of faith within the sources of faith in order to understand them better. It turned away from speculation upon belief and it turned toward the roots of faith precisely because it viewed scholasticism and Aristotelian dialectics not as a deeper understanding but as a system without a living foundation.[9] In searching for the roots and sources of the Christian faith, positive theology did not search only for the data or for the foundations, but also for the deeper understanding of faith.

This contrast between two distinct intellectual orientations of the sixteenth century points to the meaning of fundamental theology as it emerged in relation to the then current understanding of positive theology. In 1700 Pierre Annat (Petrus Annatus, nephew of the well-known anti-Jesuit and anti-Jansenist, François Annat) published the widely distributed and reprinted *Apparatus ad positivam Theologiam methodicus* in which he related positive and fundamental theology.[10] Contrasting positive and scholastic theology, Annat asserts that positive theology is called by many "fundamental theology,"[11] and rightly so. For as he contends, scholastic theology is much more methodic and much more subtle in its use of syllogistic arguments, whereas positive theology seeks to go back to the basic propositions and fundamental articles of faith. Scholastic theology needs to be solidly grounded as theology. Therefore, it must be based upon the basic truths of faith found in the tradition. Since the study of these truths is the task of positive theology, it is a fundamental theology.

Annat explicitly uses the metaphor of foundation to explain this task of fundamental theology.[12] Just as a house cannot be built without a foundation or without foundational walls, so too, he argues, scholastic theology cannot stand without a positive or fundamental theology. If scholastic theology is to be solidly grounded, it must be based on a fundamental theology that searches out the foundations and the sources of Christian faith. It is God's word in these sources that provides the basic foundation upon which the truths of theology are built. It is not the propositions themselves or the written and verbal traditions themselves that are properly the foundation, but the word of God present in them. Annat's use of the metaphor of foundation displays how the basic propositions of faith are presupposed and believed. These derive from the tradition of the Church that has specified their meaning. Fundamental theology does not prove so much as point to what has been believed in this tradition.

Annat's conception of positive theology as a fundamental theology can be better understood if it is profiled against the two classic models of positive theology: Melchior Cano's *De locis theologicis* (1563)[13] and Denis Petau's *Theologicorum dogmatum* (1644).[14] Cano's monograph focused on the ten sources of theology: seven proper sources: Scripture and tradition as constitutive of revelation and the Catholic Church, councils, papacy, fathers, and scholastic theologians as interpretative of religion; three important sources: human reason, philosophy, and human history were extraneous sources; they provided a valid basis for theological argument, but were not constitutive. Cano's concern was with the degree of authority of these sources.

Denis Petau provides a contrasting example, for his volumes of positive theology collect the positive sources not so much according to the type of source and authority as to the fundamental articles of faith or the basic doctrines of Christian faith. Petau also develops his conception of positive theology with relation to the metaphor of a foundation and the image of a building. He refers to the "fundamental articles" and the "fundamental truths" that characterize those central beliefs which are the foundation for the rest of Christian doctrine.[15] Just as a building would collapse without its foundation, so too would the Church collapse if these foundational truths were denied. These fundamental doctrines are: monarchy, trinity, incarnation, infallibility, the Church's possession of the power of the keys. It is not the existence of supernatural revelation so much as these central truths that constitute the object of positive theology.[16] Except for the last two doctrines, these basic teachings will not be at the center of fundamental theology as it will be later developed.

The *structure* and outline of Annat's *Apparatus* is closer to Cano than to Petau. The volume is divided into seven sections. After an explanation of the differences between positive and scholastic theology and an analysis of the various qualifications of the theological affirmation, Annat discusses sacred Scripture, its authority and its rules of interpretation; sacred tradition, especially the apostolic tradition, the fathers of the Church from Clement of Rome to Thomas and Bonaventure; the councils of the Church; and finally, the heresies in the Church, especially in the early Church. The sections on the Fathers and councils are three times more extensive than the other sections. Each section discusses not only content but also methodological and historical issues, especially in regard to the foundation of faith and the sources of the word of God. Annat's six sources correlate with the seven proper sources that Melchior Cano had enumerated. Philosophy, history, and human reason are not included with Annat's division—a significant fact because in the eighteenth and nineteenth century fundamental theology will proffer an almost exclusively historical and philosophical demonstration.

Yet Annat's *conception* is closer to Petau's on several accounts. In Annat's discussion of positive theology, scholastic and positive theology are sharply contrasted. He criticizes scholastic speculation and seeks to go beyond it by means of positive theology.[17] His work is removed from the scholastic conceptuality pervading Cano's. Moreover, in contrast to Cano he does not seek the foundation in the formal authority of the individual sources but in the revelation of God that is transmitted through the sources. His use of the metaphor of foundation and the imagery of a building is close to Petau. Annat's positive theology as a fundamental theology, therefore, stands at the crossroads between Cano and Petau.

Standing at the crossroads between the positive theology of the sixteenth century and the fundamental theology of the eighteenth and nineteenth centuries, Annat has the distinction of being the first to have used the term fundamental theology. He thought of fundamental theology as a positive theology that sought the foundation of the basic Christian truths in the sources of Christian faith. His conception was still far removed from the conception of fundamental theology as a historical and a rational demonstration of the truth of faith. Nevertheless, his conception remains the first, even if preliminary, step toward a new discipline. Some of its features will remain; others will be lost in the development of the discipline.

Noteworthy are the following features of his conception. (1) Fundamental theology is retrospective rather than prospective. It does not seek to build a foundation for the faith so much as to search for the foundations already existing. Fundamental theology as a positive theology is much more of an archaeological than a constructive activity. (2) Fundamental theology is a theological rather than a philosophical enterprise. It searches for the foundations of faith not independently of faith, but by investigating the historical foundations of faith that disclose God's revelation. (3) Fundamental theology is not focused on the authority of revelation as a singular point of foundation, but on a set of basic beliefs that express Christian faith. These characteristics are retrospective rather than prospective, theological rather than philosophical, basic doctrines of identity rather than a formal foundational element. On each of these points the later development of fundamental theology will differ.

The Search for Proofs:
Fundamental Theology and Apologetics

The return to the roots and sources of the Christian faith in the humanism of the renaissance and in the controversial confessional debates provided the context for the first stage of the development of fundamental theology. The second stage was provided by deism and rationalism with its critique of positive religion and of institutional Christianity. This critique was not primarily directed against a specific belief of Christianity or a specific doctrine of the individual Christian Churches. Instead, it was directed against the claim of the Christian religion to be based upon supernatural divine intervention. The critique did not emerge in a vacuum but as a reaction to the confessional debates and the ensuing religious wars. In contrast to the diverse confessional claims based upon supernatural revelation, rationalism proposed a natural and rational religion.

One of the first theologians to undertake the defense of Christianity as a true religion based on divine revelation was Phillip de Plessis-Mornay, a Protestant theologian. His *De la vérité de la religion chrétienne*, published in 1579,[18] sought to provide a philosophical defense of the fact of Christian revelation. He was followed by Pierre Charron, a Roman Catholic and a friend of Michel de Montaigne. His apologetic, *Les trois vérités*, attempted to demonstrate the existence of God, the truth of Christianity and of the Roman Catholic Church.[19]

The next significant publication for the development of fundamental theology was Hugo Grotius's *De veritate religionis*,[20] published in 1622, for it sought to differentiate apologetics from dogmatics and focused the apologetical task on the defense of the truth of Christian religion. In his apologetic, Grotius refused to present demonstrations of the truth of individual Christian doctrines, but sought to demonstrate that Jesus Christ was the divine legate sent by God to establish the true religion. This procedure was criticized by his contemporaries. In a letter to his brother, Grotius responded to these criticisms by arguing that the defense of the individual teachings of Christianity is not the proper task of apologetics but of dogmatics.[21] Apologetics has as its fundamental task the demonstration of the divine origin of

Christianity, through the demonstration of Jesus as a divine legate. If this truth is demonstrated, then the truth of the individual Christian dogmas follows from that demonstration.

In 1684 Jacques Abbadie's *Traité de la vérité de la religion chrétienne* developed Grotius's project;[22] what Grotius wrote in outline form, Abbadie rhetorically unfolds. His book had an enormous influence in the eighteenth century and overshadowed by far Pascal's *Pensées*.[23] Abbadie introduces a section in which he argues for the necessity of demonstrating the truth and necessity of religion as revealed in contrast to the deist conception of natural religion. His argument seeks to demonstrate the necessity of a revelation that is added to that of nature and to establish that Christianity offers us this revelation.

At approximately the same time, the Catholic bishop, Pierre Daniel Huet, wrote an apologetic, *Demonstratio evangelica*, in which the term and metaphor of foundation but not that of fundamental theology is used.[24] In the preface to the later editions, he underscores his search for a proof and a demonstration that is, at the same time, the foundation (*fundamentum*) of all theology. Although he sought a foundation against rationalism, his argument shared many of the rationalistic presuppositions of the seventeenth century, especially the conviction expressed by Descartes in his *Discourse on Method* that geometry was the paradigm of scientific method.[25] Just as Spinoza's ethic sought a geometric demonstration, just as Galileo divided physics into an a priori, axiomatic, proto-physics and into an a posteriori experimental physics,[26] so too did Huet develop a geometric method of demonstration for theology with the use of definitions and axioms. These axioms seek to prove the authenticity and historical trustworthiness of the biblical sources, the validity of the messianic prophecies, the messiahship of Jesus, and the truth of the Christian religion. With what will become the threefold demonstration in classical fundamental theology (religious, Christian, and Catholic), Huet's work deals only with the Christian demonstration.

At the beginning of the next century, Vitus Pichler divided his *Theologia polemica* (1713) into a more general section, a controversial fundamental theology, and a more particular one.[27] The first section entitled "general and fundamental controversies" argued for the existence of a religion of revelation. Revelation is treated before the Holy Scriptures and the Church as a general presupposition of controversial theology. Pichler remains within the framework of rationalism when he argues against deism that the principles of natural reason suffice to demonstrate the necessity of revelation and the unicity of the Christian belief.[28]

The antideist apologetic led increasingly to the defense of supernatural revelation and of the legitimacy of the Christian religion. This defense in turn led to the formation of the classic structure and division of fundamental theology. Three influential eighteenth-century theologians were decisive in this theological development: Houtteville, Hooke, and Gazzaniga. The first, Abbé Houtteville, argued in *La religion chrétienne prouvée par les faits*[29] (published in 1722 and reprinted throughout the century) that the true task of the apologist is to meet the opponents on their own grounds. He took care to ascertain what were the facts according to the rules of historical investigation. Thus, the miracles in the Scriptures were described by eyewitnesses and contemporaries; their honesty was beyond question and the testimony of their subsequent lives was incontestable. These facts had to be admitted whether they contradicted nature or not. Such a contradiction was due to the limitation of human reason and would disappear in the light of divine reason. Houtteville's emphasis upon historical demonstration, miracles, and the limitations of human reason would be given further justification by Gazzaniga.

The second influential figure was Luke-Joseph Hooke, a professor of Irish extraction at the Sorbonne. His *Religionis naturalis et revelatae*, published in 1754, was divided into three sections: natural religion, revealed religion, and the Church of Christ and the principle of the Catholic faith.[30] This tripartite division, that went back to Grotius and Charron, in Hooke's treatise became the prototype of all fundamental theological handbooks. Its outline and structure can be considered the classic structure of fundamental theology. Hooke combined two distinct areas into one apologetical work. (The controversial apologetic treatise of the sixteenth century focused on the truth of the Catholic Church, the seventeenth-century and early eighteenth-century treatise emphasized divine supernatural revelation against deism.) Hooke combined the defense of revealed religion and the defense of the Catholic Church into one treatise. His defense of revealed religion first argued for the possibility, utility, and necessity of revelation. Then it analyzed miracles and prophecies as the characteristics of divine revelation. These characteristics would demonstrate the divine nature and origin of the Christian religion and this culminated in a defense of the Catholic Church. So influential was Hooke's volume that within fifteen years, it was adopted by two standard textbooks for seminaries. Louis Bailly's *Tractatus de vera religione*[31] and Ignatius Neubauer's *Tractatus de religione* (both published in 1771)[32] follow his scheme. The textbooks of the nineteenth century (Liebermann and Peronne) are strongly influenced by the treatise and its structure.[33] And at the beginning of the twentieth century, he became acknowledged as a founding father of modern apologetics because of the organization of his treatise.[34]

The third author, Petrus Maria Gazzaniga, professor at the University of Vienna, sought to demonstrate that the defense of religion exclusively on philosophical principles would lead only to the abandonment of revelation.[35] His *Praelectiones theologicae* argued that the critique of revelation undermines religion itself.[36] Against the rationalism of deism, he argues that divine revelation is necessary even for the knowledge of the natural law because of the sinful state and weakness of human nature. Consequently, revelation is necessary even for the recognition of the truths of natural religion—a position contrary to that of Huet. In addition, Gazzaniga proposes that since religion deals with mysteries, it cannot produce any direct or intrinsic evidence as geometric teaching does. Instead, the only evidence is indirect through prophecies and miracles. The historical demonstration became in his treatise a demonstration of the authority of indirect evidence for the truth of revelation. Hence, it was not the intrinsic meaning of Jesus' resurrection or of the Church but the extrinsic authority and evidence that counted.[37]

The Search for Foundations:
Fundamental Theology and the Foundation of Theology

A transformation took place in the nineteenth century that is equally as significant as the transformation in the eighteenth century. The transformation from fundamental theology as a theology of basic doctrines—that is inspired by the humanist return to the sources and motivated by the confessional theological controversies—to the development of an antideist apologetic is now complemented by the influence of German Idealism with its development of a fundamental philosophy. In the eighteenth and nineteenth centuries, the disciplines of the philosophy of religion and of fundamental philosophy emerged. These new philosophical disciplines had a decisive impact upon the understanding of fundamental theology.

Influenced by Christian Wolff's philosophy, L. Barbieri and F. T. Canzius introduced the term "fundamental philosophy" in 1734 to express a basic philosophical science.[38] In 1803 the conception of a fundamental philosophy was fully developed by W. T. Krug's *Fundamentalphilosophie oder Urwissenschaftliche Grundlehre*. Influenced by

Kant, Reinhold, and Fichte, Krug argued that fundamental philosophy constitutes the first section of philosophy and should deal with the possibility of philosophy itself, its method and principles. Fundamental philosophy thus contrasts with ontology, metaphysics, aesthetics, ethics, and so forth. Whereas these are derivative branches of philosophy, fundamental philosophy is basic since it explores the very principles of philosophical knowledge. It establishes those principles that are valid for all areas and branches of philosophy. By establishing the validity of these principles, fundamental philosophy provides the foundation of all philosophy.

What led to fundamental philosophy's role as the basic philosophical discipline, prior even to ontology and metaphysics, was the transcendental turn toward the subject brought about by Descartes and Kant within modern philosophy.[39] Insofar as fundamental philosophy analyzed the cognitional operations and structures of the human mind underlying all areas of human intellectual activity, fundamental philosophy became a basic and all-encompassing discipline. In analyzing the a priori structures of human intellection, it studied what was at the basis not just of philosophy but of every science and human endeavor. In this sense, fundamental philosophy became commonly designated in the nineteenth century as the foundational philosophical discipline. Its basic conception was made widespread through the publications of G. W. Gerlach (1825), J. L. Tafel (vol. 1, 1848), F. C. Biedermann (1857), and H. M. Carybeaus (1861).[40]

The emphasis upon a fundamental philosophy indicated a basic shift in the understanding and function of philosophy. Previously, metaphysics had been considered the apex of philosophy, because it was concerned with the most universal and the most spiritual. Now epistemology became the most basic of the philosophical disciplines; yet it became such not as the "highest" or "most spiritual" but rather as the "underlying" or "foundational" discipline. The shift to epistemology, moreover, entailed a new starting-point for philosophy. Its proper area of inquiry was prior to the subject matter of traditional philosophy, for epistemology began with the human subject. Moreover, epistemology sought by its analysis of human subjectivity to provide certainty and certitude for philosophical knowledge. Its transcendental analysis would engender a degree of certitude previously unattainable in philosophy—at least so it was claimed.[41]

This turn toward the human subject and the priority given to epistemology as the basic philosophical science led to a reconception of the theological task of grounding theology and legitimating the

Christian faith. The objectivism of previous apologetical endeavors was no longer scientifically acceptable and philosophically justifiable. As a result the discipline of fundamental theology developed in dependence upon fundamental philosophy and in dependence upon its methodological constraints. The transcendental turn within theology came to the fore in the work of Hermes, Günther, Drey, and others.[42] It was especially Güntherians—the most influential direction of theology within German speaking countries until Günther's censure—that produced works on fundamental theology as a basic theological science.

Johann Sebastian Drey's development of an independent apologetic (published only in the middle of the nineteenth century) was the halfway point between the previous approaches of the eighteenth century and the transcendental fundamental theology developed in the nineteenth century. Distinguishing between apologies and apologetics, he sought to develop apologetics as an independent discipline prior to theology. It would defend not just particular beliefs of Christianity, but provide the foundation of all of Christianity through its defense of a philosophy of revelation. Although he had originally been influenced by Schleiermacher's conception of philosophical theology and apologetics and had limited the role of apologetics to the elaboration of the essence of Christianity, Drey follows the outline developed in the eighteenth century by Luke-Joseph Hooke and Petrus Maria Gazzaniga.[43] The threefold division, revelation, Christian revelation with its culmination in the resurrection of Jesus, and Catholic revelation or the foundation of the Church, was the basic framework. Nevertheless, the influence of Lessing, Schleiermacher, and Schelling led him to play down and even to criticize the previous reliance on external criteria. Instead, he sought to show the correlation between the objective ideas of history and the human spirit.

In 1859 Johann Nepomuk Ehrlich, a student of Gunther and a professor at the University of Prague, published the first volume of a *Fundamental-Theologie* which sought to give the theoretical foundation for a new and distinctive theological discipline.[44] In his opinion, the development of apologetics into an independent discipline by Johann Sebastian von Drey was a significant achievement, but it did not go far enough. It was not sufficient to defend the Christian faith against the critical skepticism of the day. What was needed was a new synthesis that would combine into one discipline two distinct foundational tasks. In the face of the increasing attacks of the secular sciences upon the scientific character of theology, a need existed to ground and to justify theology as a scholarly and scientific discipline.

Fundamental theology had the task of grounding the scientific character of theology by providing the transition from scholarly disciplines to the disciplines within theology. In addition to this task coming from the outside, there was the need to establish the inner foundation of theology, to secure the scientific unity of theology as a discipline, and to ground the unity of the various theological disciplines *precisely as unified* in the theological task.[45]

Ehrlich's proposal was distinctive and original. Its originality, however, was not so much in its organization and content, patterned on the eighteenth-century apologetics, as in its methodological goal to justify theology as a science and to ground its unity. In line with the turn to the human subject that characterized fundamental philosophy, his fundamental theology took as its starting-point religion as a moment of human self-consciousness. The necessity of revelation and its historical realization was developed from this starting-point.

The parallel between Ehrlich's conception of fundamental theology and the discipline of fundamental philosophy is noteworthy, for it concerns goal, purpose, and method. Just as fundamental philosophy sought to demonstrate the truth of philosophy by demonstrating the validity of its basic principles, so too did fundamental theology seek the truth of the principles underlying theology as a discipline. Just as fundamental philosophy strove by this demonstration to establish the scientific nature of philosophy as a discipline, so too did fundamental theology seek to establish theology as a scientific discipline that could exist with dignity alongside of secular disciplines. Both sought to establish the foundations of their respective disciplines with reference to their truth character and their status as scientific disciplines. Both sought to reach this double foundational goal by a common methodological starting-point. Just as fundamental philosophy took the subjectivity of the knower as the ground of all philosophical knowledge, so too did fundamental theology start with human subjectivity in order to ground not only religion and revelation but also theology. Through this endeavor, Johann Ehrlich, the first professor holding a university chair for fundamental theology, ably represented the high-point of the theological reception of Idealism.

Ehrlich's fundamental theology represented an exemplary development of Güntherian theology.[46] But although Günther's theology was the most widespread and his students were the most influential in Germany (one even replaced Drey at Tübingen), a reaction soon set in against this theological openness to modern philosophy, its principles, goals, and methodology. Günther was censured, as were other theologians. The attempts to construct a fundamental theology with the goal of overcoming the dichotomy between the objectivity of faith and the subjectivity of the human person came to a halt with the emergence of neoscholasticism.

The neoscholastic revival sought to counter the influence of modern philosophy by the principles of Thomistic philosophy, which were to be the remedy against the aberrations of rationalism and Idealism.[47] In reality, however, the neoscholastic fundamental theology was much more indebted to eighteenth century rationalism than it realized. The world view of nature as a closed system with its own telos was implicitly embraced by the neoscholastic emphasis on the radical distinction between nature and supernature—a view that sharply contrasted with Thomas's own. Moreover, it had the effect that revelation and the signs of revelation were increasingly seen as being distinct from nature. Revelation as a supernatural event was separate from and beyond human rationality.[48] Consequently, Gazzaniga's distinction between internal and external criteria of revelation became central to the neoscholastic fundamental theology that sought to demonstrate the authority of the revealer and of the magisterium rather than the intelligibility and intrinsic meaning of Christian faith.[49]

Neoscholastic fundamental theology dominated twentieth-century Roman Catholic theology until Vatican II.[50] The influence of the Roman reaction to modernism denigrated significant new approaches, particularly the work of Maurice Blondel and even of Pierre Rousselot.[51] At the same time, Protestant neo-orthodoxy rejected any apologetical natural theology.[52] It was not until the 1950s and Vatican II that the situation changed drastically. Transcendental theology emerged within Roman Catholicism under the banner of a genuine retrieval of Aquinas and a serious confrontation with the philosophical problems raised by Kantianism and the historical-critical questions raised in the nineteenth and twentieth centuries.[53] Likewise, a renewed interest in fundamental theology took place in Protestant theology.

The historical and transcendental approaches to fundamental theology have dominated the contemporary situation. Both have been challenged in the last decade by political and liberation theology and by hermeneutical theology.[54] Political theology argues that previous approaches to fundamental theology overlook the societal situation of the human subject, give insufficient attention to ideology and the need for ideology-criticism, and fail to recognize that the theoretical foundation of faith, as well as of theology, involve problems of social and political praxis. Political theology, however, has been stronger in its critique than in its constructive proposals. Many of the traditional topics of fundamental theology, for example, the resurrection of Jesus and the foundation of the Church, have not been discussed with relationship to the problems of ideology-criticism or of the societal conditioning of the human subject. Instead, political theology has tended to concentrate on the mission of the Church and to interpret other issues primarily within that context.[55]

Hermeneutical theology as well as narrative theology has criticized the interpretation of human experience within historical and transcendental theology. The emphasis upon facticity or upon unthematized or implicit experience fails, it is suggested, to give due account to the interpretative dimension of history and experience. Much of hermeneutical theology has relegated hermeneutical retrieval to systematic theology rather than to fundamental theology.[56] It has thereby overlooked the very points that political and liberation theology have brought to the fore, namely, the social conditioning of knowledge, the need of ideology-criticism, and the relevance of praxis to the formation of theory. Hermeneutical theology has, however, underscored the necessity of the retrieval of a tradition in the very act of criticizing the tradition. The theological need, therefore, in this situation calls for a sensitivity to both the political and hermeneutical contributions to fundamental theology, and especially to the historical and transcendental versions. But first we must examine the nature and characteristics of fundamental theology and the presuppositions of its major directions.

Chapter 10

Fundamental Theology: Characteristics and Presuppositions

The historical survey has traced three distinct stages with diverse conceptions of fundamental theology: the retrieval of the basic teachings of Christianity, the apologetical defense of Christianity as a historical revelation, and the transcendental foundation not only of Christian revelation but also of Christian theology. Although each stage represents a significant transformation, each stage has significantly contributed to what has now in the twentieth century become established and well known as fundamental theology.[57] The problems, ambiguities, and difficulties that fundamental theology faces as an independent theological discipline have, in no small measure, been determined by its historical genesis.

Against the background of this historical development, this chapter sketches those common characteristics of fundamental theology that have resulted from the various influences upon this development.[58] Then it will examine the claim of fundamental theology to be an independent and distinct theological discipline. Finally, it will examine how the disciplinary independence of fundamental theology is grounded within the historical and transcendental conceptions of fundamental theology, each having its own conception of truth and criteria of truth.[59] The inadequacies of these conceptions, moreover, will point to the need for a conception of fundamental theology as a hermeneutical foundational theology.

General Characteristics

The historical evolution that has led to fundamental theology as it is now known has contributed not only diverse elements but even contradictory orientations.[60] The apologetical defense of the truth of Christian faith and the attempt to establish the scientific foundation of theology as an academic discipline are quite distinct endeavors and yet both of them have been combined into one discipline. Consequently, the discipline of fundamental theology has not only common characteristics but also distinct elements that stand over and against these common characteristics.[61]

One common characteristic of fundamental theology in its classic form is the universality or comprehensiveness of its theological goal.[62] Irrespective of whether the apologetic or theological goal predominated, fundamental theology sought to provide a foundation for all of Christian faith or theology. The distinction that Drey made between apologies for the diverse truths of Christianity and the apologetic defense of the foundation of Christianity in itself remains a constant for all forms of fundamental theology.[63] The demonstration of truth that is sought by fundamental theology is not a particular but a general demonstration. Similarly with the foundation of theology, the fundamental theological focus has not been upon the foundation of any particular theological doctrine or discipline, but rather has been upon the grounding of all of theology.

Another common characteristic was the presupposition that certain truths were more basic or "fundamental" than others.[64] At first, a whole range of central doctrines was considered basic. However, as the discipline developed the foundational truths became limited to the fact of divine revelation, the resurrection of Jesus as a confirmation of his divine mission, and the foundation of the magisterium of the Catholic Church in the Petrine promises to safeguard this revelation. These were the basic beliefs upon which all other beliefs could be grounded, for they involved the fact of Christian revelation, its truth, and its transmission. The apologetical task of fundamental theology, therefore, culminated in the demonstration of the magisterium, whereas the theological task elaborated those sources (Scripture, tradition, magisterium) that contained and preserved revelation and therefore formed the basis of theology.

The endeavor to be scientific is, however, the characteristic qualifying the discipline.[65] Even though it was understood quite differently, its nature as a scientific discipline was central to its self-understanding. In the seventeenth century, the influence of humanism and historical studies pervaded fundamental theology. In the eighteenth century, it sought through a positivistic historical demonstration to ground its claims scientifically. In the nineteenth century, it was the scientific ideal of transcendentalism and Idealism; and in the twentieth century, Rahner's transcendental-existential fundamental theology sought to take into account Heidegger's critique of objectivizing scientific rationality for the sake of a more foundational rationality. Taking a different direction, Bernard Lonergan sought to show the isomorphism between contemporary scientific methodology and theological methodology at the level of cognitional structures. In all these conceptions of fundamental theology the common characteristic was not just to provide a foundation for faith and theology but a "scientific" foundation.

Another characteristic of fundamental theology is the general structure that emerged at the end of the eighteenth century, namely, the demonstration of the possibility of revelation, the facticity of Christian revelation, and the truth of the Catholic Church. Nevertheless, two basic forms of fundamental theology have developed.[66] They have come to be known as the "German" and the "Roman," though the labels are somewhat arbitrary, and even misnomers, because many Germans, for example, Drey, followed the Roman form. The Roman differs from the German in two respects. First, since the demonstration of the truth of religion can be discussed in philosophy of religion, it is often omitted from fundamental theology and relegated to philosophy of religion. Instead, a philosophy of revelation takes its place.

Second, whereas the German form has the threefold demonstration—revelation, the Christian fact, and the Catholic Church—the Roman includes the theological principles, that is, the sources and principles of dogmatics after a treatise on faith. The German form excludes these two and includes them within dogmatics rather than fundamental theology. In this respect, the Roman form is much more comprehensive than the German in that it includes within fundamental theology what the latter relegates to dogmatics. This division has led to some severe criticism by Ambroise Gardeil who argued that the inclusion of these sections in fundamental theology went contrary to the very apologetical defense of Christianity based upon human experience and human reason.[67] It confused the distinction between the truth of Christian theology and that of Christian faith. It points, therefore, to one of the main ambiguities of fundamental theology that needs to be uncovered and analyzed.

A final significant characteristic of all fundamental theology is its concentration on the Christian religion, especially, its origin and foundation.[68] Fundamental theology was distinct from the philosophy of religion and from any philosophical apology because it sought to demonstrate the truth of a particular revelation and its presence in a specific religious community. In addition, the concentration upon revelation distinguished fundamental theology from the scholastic endeavor of demonstrating the preambles of faith, for example, the existence of God, the immortality of the soul, and the like. Whereas scholastic theology had argued that the preambles of faith could be demonstrated by reason independent of faith, the argument in fundamental theology noted that these truths had not been challenged by deism; deism challenged the fact of a supernatural revelation. Therefore, this revelation as the foundation of the Christian religion and Church was in need of demonstration.[69]

This characteristic influences the nature of the theological task. If the apologetical task focuses on the existence of God as a preamble of faith and the theological task is to interpret reality and faith in relation to God, then a certain continuum exists between the apologetical and the theological task. If, however, the fundamental theological task is considered to be the rational and historical demonstration of the external signs of the credibility of a supernatural and gratuitous revelation, and the theological task is primarily the exposition of the teachings of the magisterium to which this revelation has been entrusted, then a strong discontinuity exists between foundational theology as a natural theology and systematic theology as a natural theology. Through this characteristic, however, traditional fundamental theology sought to demonstrate the unity of theology and to combine two tasks into one. By concentrating on the Christian revelation, religion, and community, it could combine into one both the demonstration of the truth of the Christian religion and the establishment of the basis of Christian theology. This double task tended to reduce the foundation of faith and the foundation of theology to one task. Moreover, since the relation between fundamental and systematic theology was distinct, it enabled systematic theology, once its foundation was established, to operate independent of the foundational task.[70]

The Independence of Fundamental Theology from Systematic Theology

The general characteristics of fundamental theology indicate the extent to which it has developed into a distinct and independent theological discipline prior to systematic theology.[71] Fundamental theology had the distinct twofold goal of defending the Christian faith in general and of providing the foundation of Christian theology. Its thematic and content focused on Christian revelation as demonstrated by the resurrection of Jesus and on the foundation of a Christian Church with a supernatural mission. The development of fundamental theology as an independent discipline was the result of a long historical process. The emergence of separate treatises on religion and revelation in the eighteenth century, the development of apologetics as an independent discipline in the eighteenth and nineteenth centuries, and the transcendental foundations of theology in the nineteenth centuries—all provided the stimuli for the development of fundamental theology as an independent discipline.

The independence of fundamental theology from systematic theology, however, is not simply an issue of the division of labor within theology, but touches on the nature of fundamental theology. Therefore, the consensus about this independence of fundamental theology needs to be carefully examined for it concerns the very nature of the field. Stephen Toulmin's distinction between "fields of arguments" and "fields of study" needs to be applied to the relation between fundamental theology and systematic theology.[72] A field of study is the subject matter or the area of study; fields of argument refer to the logical status of those propositions constituting the data and the arguments within a field. When the independence of fundamental theology has been maintained, what has been claimed is that fundamental theology differs from systematic theology, not just as a field of study but as a field of argument. Much of the same field of study, Christ, the Church, has been analyzed both in fundamental and in systematic theology. The same subject matter was studied with a distinct methodology because the fields of argument in fundamental and in systematic theology differed.

The distinction between fundamental and systematic theology does not, in this conception, rest upon a division of labor as does the sectioning within systematic theology among christology, ecclesiology, and sacramental theology. In the latter instances, the methodology, warrants, data, and goals are in principle the same. The field of study has been divided up merely for the sake of specialization in research and teaching. The distinction between systematic and fundamental theology is much more basic. Even in treating the same subject matter the claim is advanced that the logical status of the propositions differs in principle depending upon whether it is analyzed within fundamental or systematic theology. The specific issues of this volume, the resurrection of Jesus, the foundation of the Church, and its mission, were generally treated in fundamental theology. They could, however, also be treated in systematic theology as long as different fields of argument were used and different goals were pursued.[73]

At stake, therefore, in any discussion of the relation between fundamental and systematic theology is not simply the place of fundamental theology within the organization of the theological disciplines, but rather the very status of fundamental theology itself. Since fundamental theology traditionally sought to establish not only the truth of the Christian faith (an apologetical task) but also the truth of Christian theology (a disciplinary task), its independence from systematic theology has been quite differently conceived. Understood as the retrieval of the basic truths of Christian faith, fundamental theology sought through a positive historical theology to uncover the presence of these truths in the primary sources of Christian faith. Understood as the apologetical defense against deism, fundamental theology sought through historical demonstration to show the factual basis for the Christian claim of a supernatural revelation. Understood as the transcendental justification of both theology and faith, it sought to demonstrate the correlation between Christian faith and human subjectivity.[74]

The independence and distinction of fundamental theology, therefore, rests on two claims: a distinct method and distinct criteria of truth.[75] The historical survey of fundamental theology indicated that what had originated as two distinct stages within the history of theology resulted in two distinct approaches to fundamental theology: the historical and the transcendental. The historical approach to fundamental theology tends to presuppose a correspondence theory of truth and seeks through historical argumentation to demonstrate a correspondence between belief statements and historical facts that support them either directly or indirectly. The transcendental approach operates with a coherence and disclosure theory of truth. It seeks to show the correlation between present human experience and belief statements. Perhaps this distinction can be expressed through what contemporary philosophy calls the difference between a historical genetic justification and a current-time-slice justification.[76] The historical genetic makes the justificational status of a belief dependent upon its previous history and warrants, whereas the current-time-slice approach correlates the belief primarily with what is true of the believer at the time of belief. Such an ideal-type division is obviously inadequate to cover all the concrete differences, but it does provide a helpful way of viewing two basic approaches of fundamental theology, and thereby of analyzing the presuppositions of their methods and criteria of truth.

Traditional Fundamental Theology: Truth as Historical Correspondence

The classic Roman form of fundamental theology divided the discipline into the apologetical defense of the supernatural nature of the Christian fact and the theological and historical demarcation of the positive sources and norms of Christian belief. In the Aristotelian conception of science with its distinction between formal and material elements, fundamental theology has as its formal object the credibility of the Christian religion as this credibility was demonstrated by human reason alone without any appeal to faith.[77] In such a conception fundamental theology had an intermediary role between philosophy or historiography, on the one side, and systematic theology on the other. Fundamental theology studies the origins of the Christian religion with common human rationality and with the normal means of historiography. From that perspective, fundamental theology appears basically as a historical analysis of the data at the basis of the Christian fact: the resurrection of Jesus, the foundation and the purpose of the Church. Yet it had the same content as theology: God's revelation. Thus, where fundamental theology sought to demonstrate the credibility of the faith, systematic theology took that faith as its standpoint and sought understanding.

Since fundamental theology was defined within this conception primarily in terms of the credibility of the Christian religion, it defined credibility in such a way that it could be accessible to all; and it defined the Christian religion in terms of its accessibility: what are the facts at the basis of the Christian religion.[78] Its approach to the problem of credibility was, however, primarily in terms of what it called external signs of credibility.[79]

Two sorts of criteria were distinguished within this conception of fundamental theology: internal and external. The internal criteria referred to the sublimity, goodness, and truthfulness of a belief, whereas the external criteria referred primarily to the miracles and prophecies corroborating it. The external criteria of credibility, however, outweighed the internal criteria. Since any evaluation of the meaningfulness, goodness, and sublimity of a belief depends upon subjective dispositions and personal judgments, the internal criteria were viewed as arguments ad hominem that could only have an auxiliary and supportive role. It was the historical demonstration of the external signs, especially prophecies and miracles—of which the resurrection of Jesus was the culmination—that constituted the argument for the credibility of the Christian fact. It was argued that these external signs were the most probable means of showing the credibility of the Christian religion because they were capable of a historical demonstration that would be publicly accessible. Moreover, since the Christian religion is primarily a historical reality, it "as such should be proved mainly on historical grounds."[80]

The link between demonstration of credibility and historical argumentation was developed in such a way that traditional fundamental theology combined two distinct tasks: the apologetical foundation of faith and the theological establishment of the foundation of theology. Such a combination took place by means of the conception of an authoritative mediation of revelation. The historical demonstration of the credibility of Jesus' resurrection served to establish his authority as God's legate and agent of revelation, just as his establishment of a hierarchically ordered Church with a supernatural mission guaranteed the sources and transmission of that revelation. The apologetical task of demonstrating the truth of the Christian belief in Jesus' resurrection and in the divine foundation and purpose of the Church established the basis and foundation of theology at the same time. Since this apologetical task was primarily historical and employed external criteria, the relation of faith, as well as theology, to its object and content was primarily extrinsic rather than intrinsic.

Underlying the historical argument was a definition of truth as correspondence that provided the main presupposition of the criteria of the traditional fundamental theology. In a correspondence theory of truth, to claim that an assertion is true is to claim "that what is said has actually said things as they actually are; it has stated a fact."[81] When what is stated corresponds to the facts, then the statement is true. This definition, originating with Aristotle, has come down to us through Isaac ben Israeli and Thomas Aquinas. According to Aristotle's *De interpretatione* (1, 16a 6), the soul's experience, its representations, are the likeness of things. This assertion became formulated later as an explicit definition of truth. Aquinas refers to Avicenna's definition of truth that comes from Isaac ben Israeli's *Book of Definitions: "Veritas est adequatio (convenientia, correspondentia) intellectus et rei."* "Truth is the adequation, (the coming together or correspondence) of understanding and reality." The *Summa Contra Gentiles* I expresses this definition so: "truth of understanding is the suitability of understanding and reality according to which the understanding says what is and what is not."[82]

The effect of such a conception of truth upon fundamental theology is to make the truth of religious claims dependent upon whether or not they correspond to reality. Religious claims are consequently interpreted primarily as propositional statements or factual affirmations. Hence, the major issues of traditional fundamental theology were posed in terms of factual propositions. The resurrection of Jesus implied primarily a factual claim about an empty tomb. The foundation of a Church with a supernatural mission expressed a factual claim about specific historical intentions and actions on the part of Jesus in relation to the Church. The resurrection of Jesus, the foundation of the Church, and the mission of the Church entailed religious claims, but these religious claims were true to the extent that a correspondence existed between them and historical facts. This line of argument inaugurated with Abbé Houtteville in *La religion chrétienne prouée par les faits* is continued in the neoscholastic distinction between *an sit* and *quid sit*, with its relegation of the former issue to fundamental theology and the latter to systematic theology. Fundamental theology demonstrates the truth as the existence of the object of belief, whereas systematic theology explicates the meaning of belief once its existence has been demonstrated.

The correspondence theory of truth represents a common and widespread notion. Nevertheless, it is inadequate to the foundational theological task. Philosophically, the correspondence theory of truth is valid only to the extent that it fits with one feature of truth claims, namely, the propositional content of sentences.[83] When sentences describe a state of affairs, then the truth of correspondence makes sense because a correspondence is entailed in the very nature of the description. Correspondence is the criterion of truth in descriptive propositional sentences because such descriptive sentences are constituted by such correspondence.

But it is questionable whether the correspondence theory of truth can be generalized to a universal theory of truth. Its inadequacy comes to the fore in its inability to express what is not descriptive or propositional. The correspondence theory of truth cannot deal with the normative, expressive, and existential dimensions. Moreover, a correspondence theory of truth overlooks that a correspondence between an assertion and a state of affairs is not a correspondence between two simple entities, but entails interpretations of both factual and the assertional.[84] The question of facticity cannot be separated from that of meaning and resolved prior to the meaning question. If, for example, one were to ask whether Antigone's actions express an authentic mode of human behavior, the answer could not be given and then evaluated in terms of a correspondence theory of truth because the very meaning of the assertion and of the state of affairs is not a simple observable fact. It is for these reasons that Heidegger's notion of truth as an unconcealment or an unveiling uncovers a dimension much more basic than correspondence.[85] Likewise, Habermas's division of validity claims into the propositional, normative, and expressive points to the limitations of a correspondence theory of truth that cannot be generalized to cover all validity claims.[86]

For these reasons, the correspondence theory of truth has limited value for fundamental theology, which is not to deny that it has any validity. In arguing against the appropriation of Heidegger's conception of truth by Rudolf Bultmann and Gerhard Ebeling, Wolfhart Pannenberg has noted that religious truth is more than disclosure and communication; it is a communication and disclosure about something.[87] A statement is true only if there is something in the world in virtue of which it is true. Pannenberg's critique and his affirmation of realism points to the dimension of truth as correspondence that has been presupposed in traditional fundamental theology and its historical demonstration.

Nevertheless, his critique fails to take into account that religious truth is more than facticity, and this "more" constitutes the religious dimension.[88] For example, Christians claim as true that Jesus has redeemed us through his death on the cross. It is certainly valid to argue against any existential interpretation of this truth that the statement presupposes a factual death on the cross. But such an argument, albeit valid, is much too facile. The belief that Jesus' death is redemptive is not simply a propositional statement about a fact, but brings to the fore the existential, normative, and expressive dimensions of Jesus' crucifixion. These dimensions cannot be reduced to the merely factual. The same problem affects those three issues of fundamental theology: the resurrection of Jesus, the foundation of the Church, and the mission of the Church—all make a more than factual claim. Resurrection is not just resuscitation; foundation of the Church is more than the gathering of disciples; and mission is much more than the sending out of disciples. In each instance the meaning of what is claimed is as crucial to its "truthfulness" as the factual dimension. A fundamental theology that presupposes exclusively a realism and a correspondence theory of truth will overlook the religious and interpretative dimension at the foundation of faith.

The emphasis within traditional fundamental theology upon the credibility of faith and the historical demonstration of the signs of credibility necessarily led to a reductionistic conception of fundamental theology. Such a reduction was seen as early as the turn of the century by Ambroise Gardeil, who argued for the distinction between apologetics and fundamental theology.[89] Whereas apologetics sought to demonstrate the rational and historical credibility of faith, fundamental theology sought to elaborate the foundation of theology itself as a theological discipline. The former went from the external to the internal, whereas the latter sought to elaborate from within the foundation of theology itself. The conflation between fundamental theology and apologetics reduced fundamental theology to a rational defense of the faith. However, fundamental theology based on faith, should proceed from faith, for its proper object is not the credibility of faith but the proper sources, authorities, and ground of faith. This distinction between fundamental and apologetic theology has been reformulated by Bernard Lonergan in his development of the eightfold functional specialties.[90] Lonergan distinguishes between the functional specialties of interpretation, history, and dialectics and those of foundations, doctrines, and systematics. Whereas the former (culminating in dialectics) show the diverse horizons of contrasting positions, the latter explicate the conversion experience as the foundation of theology that is further thematized in doctrinal and systematic theology. Since Lonergan's foundational theology is based upon conversion, it has been criticized as fideistic by Langdon Gilkey and David Tracy because it has removed foundational theology from the public defense of the Christian faith.[91]

This debate points to the basic problem of the very conception of traditional fundamental theology. It does too little and goes too far: too little, because insofar as fundamental theology was considered primarily the apologetical defense of the credibility of the Christian religion and was thereby thought to provide the foundation for theology, it only demonstrated—at best—historical credibility that was extrinsic to belief. It went too far insofar as it assumed an abstract conception of historical demonstration and human rationality, whereby it hoped through historical arguments to demonstrate rationally and in a publicly accessible manner the truth of the Christian faith. In this respect, Lonergan's insight into the role of conversion as the foundation of theology takes into account the weakness of the abstract demonstration of credibility—but then it also opens itself to the problem of fideism. This dilemma between abstract rational demonstration and public demonstration is a problem that transcendental fundamental theology sought to wrestle with much more successfully than did traditional fundamental theology. But its method of correlation and its conception of truth undercut the very aspects that the traditional fundamental theology emphasized.

Transcendental Fundamental Theology: Truth as Existential Correlation

The turn toward the human subject in modern philosophy not only has historically influenced fundamental theology but also has exercised an influence even today. In the wake of Schleiermacher, a whole school of theology, "the mediation theologians"[92] sought to mediate between Christian faith and modern consciousness. Johann Sebastian von Drey and Johann Ehrlich had profound influence upon the development of fundamental theology in that they made the correlation between human subjectivity and the content of Christian belief the explicit goal of apologetics and fundamental theology. At the beginning of the twentieth century, Maurice Blondel's "apologetics of immanence" sought a similar correlation. In recent years, such a correlation was the explicit goal of Paul Tillich's apologetical method in his systematic theology and of Karl Rahner's transcendental method in his fundamental theology. Currently, the method of correlation has been proposed as an ecumenical theological method suitable for Catholic and Protestant theologians alike. Peter Hodgson, Schubert Ogden, David Tracy, Edward Schillebeeckx, Langdon Gilkey, and Hans Küng have all favored the method of correlation for fundamental theology.[93]

The advocacy of correlation as a basic method has affected not only how the task of fundamental theology is understood but also how fundamental theology is related to systematic theology. The method of correlation has, moreover, presupposed a coherence theory of truth, and disclosure and coherence as major criteria of truth. Although the method of correlation has received a phenomenological, existential, and a transcendental interpretation, it has basically entailed two distinct steps.

The first step is the transcendental, existential, or phenomenological analysis of the religious dimension of human experience. The second is the attempt to correlate this experience with the content of the Christian faith, or more specifically, with Christian revelation. The method does not simply correlate human experiences and divine revelation, but correlates human experience as transcendentally and phenomenologically analyzed so as to uncover its religious dimension, while the content of Christian faith is interpreted to show its disclosive meaning and its coherence with this religious dimension of human experience.

These two steps are the common characteristic of the fundamental theological method of correlation, which, in fact, has become the dominant method within contemporary theology. Nevertheless, significant differences exist because of diverse interpretations of either human experience or the Christian revelation. In addition, the method of transcendental correlation has been formulated with distinct categories, since the correlation has been understood as the relation of possibility and actuality; implicit and explicit; situation and message. The notion of truth presupposed and the validity of each approach needs to be analyzed with a view to determining its adequacy.

Possibility and Actuality

A phenomenological method is used by Peter Hodgson to distinguish fundamental (which he calls foundational to avoid connotations of a natural theology) from symbolic and systematic theology.[94] This foundational theology develops a phenomenological analysis of the basic structures of human existence and strives to uncover those structures for which revelation is a real possibility. It thereby provides the foundation for the experience of revelation and religious language.

Through a phenomenological description, foundational theology uncovers the universal existentials of human existence. These existentials, descriptions of human existence within the world, are essential freedom, fallibility, and redeemability. These are explicated through divisions of foundational theology: the essential structures of human freedom through eidetics; those of human fallibility through empirics; and those of redeemability or openness through poetics. These foundational theological descriptions are then correlated through a symbolic theology with systematic theology. Symbolic theology explicates those religious symbols that are correlated with these structures: revelation, bondage, and liberation. Systematic theology then formulates and translates these symbols into concepts. The symbol of revelation is thematized as authority, bondage as sin, and liberation as creation, redemption, and sanctification. The phenomenological description of human existential structures in foundational theology finds, thereby, its correlation in the doctrines of systematic theology.

The truth of systematic theology is based in this conception not so much on historical demonstration and the interpretative experience of a religious tradition as it is on the correlation between anthropological structures and the doctrines of systematic theology. Foundational theology elaborates the possibility that stands in correlation to the actual symbols of symbolic theology and the actual doctrines of systematic theology. The historical concreteness of a religious tradition, with the concrete meaning disclosed in its expressions of language and praxis, is basically only the concrete actualities of more general existential structures. This division within foundational theology is similar to Ricoeur's division of anthropology into essential structures, fallible and redeemable structures, as well as to Schleiermacher's systematic theological division into experience of dependency, sin and redemption.[95] Nevertheless, where Schleiermacher correlated actual experience to actual doctrines, this foundational theology moves from possibility to actuality.

Implicit and Explicit

The formal fundamental theology developed by Karl Rahner uses a phenomenological and transcendental method not to move from possibility to actuality but from the implicit to the explicit, from an experience of grace to its explicit symbolic thematization. A difference in goal and method exists for Rahner between fundamental theology and systematic theology. Whereas fundamental theology presupposes nothing of Christianity and has the task of providing all Christian truths, systematic theology presupposes the community's faith and has the task of showing that a statement is legitimate in that it is held in the faith convictions of the community and exists in conformity with Scripture and tradition.[96]

This difference of presupposition and goal determines the methodological differences, especially the criteria of truth employed. Formal fundamental theology elaborates the correlation between the transcendental and existential structures of human existence and the content of faith. For systematic theology, the criterion for the truth of a doctrine is the authority of Scripture and tradition, as well as that of the Church's teaching office. Since, however, fundamental theology does not presuppose faith but must demonstrate it, its existential and transcendental correlation provides the criteria of truth. Nevertheless, because the method of correlation is not that of possibility to actuality, a formal fundamental theology actually lessens the traditional gap between systematic and fundamental theology. It does not extrinsically justify faith on the basis of a demonstration of the Church's authority, but on the basis of a correlation between the content of faith and the transcendental analysis of human existence. Fundamental theology, therefore, presupposes the content of systematic theology in its elaboration of the transcendental and existential correlation between revelation and experience. This presupposition takes place because the basic move of correlation is from the implicit to the explicit. In fact, it is more accurate to state that a twofold movement of making explicit takes place and this double explication is the center of Rahner's method of correlation.[97]

The step of making explicit is characterized by Rahner himself as "mystagogical" or "maieutic" function. The Eastern Fathers, for example, Cyril of Jerusalem's *Mystagogical Catecheses* and Maximus the Confessor's *Mystagogy,* use the term "mystagogy" to refer to the deeper introduction of Christians into the rites of sacramental initiation. For Rahner, a transcendental mystagogy has primarily a "maieutic function"; it does not make known new experiences as it makes explicit what is implicit; it brings to consciousness the religious dimension present within experience; it explicates the openness to the absolute present in human life. Psychological and metaphysical categories are also used to describe this mystagogical step of formal fundamental theology. It is called a "logotherapy" insofar as it involves an awakening, a bringing to consciousness, and an activating of what is already experienced in a prethematic fashion. Likewise, Martin Heidegger's concept of "pre-understanding" or "pre-grasp" is theologically adapted and modified to explain this mystagogical function. According to Heidegger, human existence in the world already stands in the presence of being and this pre-apprehension of being constitutes a human existential that makes possible human understanding. For Rahner, humanity exists in the presence of divine grace and it is this pre-apprehension of the transcendent resulting from the divine presence and call that becomes thematized as the knowledge of the transcendent. Fundamental theology's mystagogic function is to explicate and to thematize this pre-apprehension.

A second step of explication takes place with reference to the content of Christian belief. The focus is not upon Christian origins or the diverse New Testament writings, but rather on the Chalcedonian dogma as the central mystery of Christianity that proclaims the union between the divine and human in Christ. This christological affirmation is taken not only as the key belief expressing the "essence" of Christianity but also as a central belief expressing the mystery of human nature and its experience of the longing for union with the absolute.

Formal fundamental theology, therefore, correlates a specific transcendental analysis of human existence with a specific transcendental interpretation of Christian belief. The christological dogma of the union between the divine and the human is an explicit formulation of the deepest human desires that are given through the divine presence to the human spirit and uncovered in the mystagogical analysis. This correlation is then seen as a confirmation of the truth of Christian beliefs. Formal fundamental theology, therefore, brings this correlation to the forefront of its argumentation and places historical questions into the background.

Against the criticisms of naturalism, formal fundamental theology so appropriates Heidegger's notion of existential that human beings differ from nonhuman reality insofar as they have a historical existence. The existentials, human structures, resulting from the historicity of human existence, include a supernatural existential. Since human beings were created with a historical and gratuitously given goal of union with the divine, this goal and givenness constitute historical human nature. Therefore, the orientation toward the absolute that is uncovered in the mystagogical analysis of human existence and in the interpretation of Christian beliefs results from the divine presence both in human experience and in its symbolic expression in the symbols of faith. This use of correlation does not move from possibility to actuality, but from an implicit actuality that is made explicit through mystagogy and then correlated with the explicit creedal formulas of the Christian faith.

The argument from a formal fundamental theological correlation can be contrasted with the historical demonstration of fundamental theology.[98] Although this historical demonstration is not excluded—and *Spirit in the World* emphasizes the role of judgment and correspondence—formal fundamental theology operates with the criteria of a disclosure and a coherence model of truth. Formal fundamental theological treatment of the resurrection deemphasizes the historical demonstration in favor of an indirect method disclosing the resurrection as the historical manifestation and disclosure that coheres and correlates with the human affirmation of freedom and of permanence. Likewise, the foundation of the Church is approached not so much by historical arguments as by the indirect method; for example, that salvation must be communitarian if it is to be correlative with the social nature of human beings and if it is to be publicly and permanently manifest within the human world.

The criterion of truth is sought in the demonstration that Christian beliefs are explicit symbols that disclose and manifest the most profound dimension of human experience. This formal fundamental theology presupposes Heidegger's conception that unconcealment and disclosure are more fundamental and basic to truth than correspondence.[99] The method of correlation between human experience and Christian belief affirms a basic coherence between the two because of a more original disclosure of the meaning and truth of each.

The coherence and harmony between human experience and Christian faith is therefore achieved by a very specific interpretation of human experience and of Christian faith. Not only is the dogma of Chalcedon chosen as the Christian belief par excellence, but this dogma is given an anthropological interpretation. This double explication of human experience and of Christian belief is, however, extended to other religious traditions, cultures, and experiences. Both the religious experience as well as the religious tendencies underlying other religious traditions are interpreted as latent, implicit, or anonymous dimensions of what has become explicit and thematized within Christian belief.

Unfortunately, this method of correlation has several methodological deficiencies. Transcendental arguments primarily tend to be circular and to overlook the historical and hermeneutical dimension of human experience. They overlook the extent to which human experience and its theological interpretation is situated within the cultural tradition of Christianity and Western civilization. Both the experience and its interpretation have been predetermined by Christian beliefs. The human longing for the unconditional, for personal permanence, for union with the divine and the absolute results in some measure from the cultural influences and historical determination that Christian beliefs have had within Western civilization upon images of the self. Such transcendental correlations have a circular character. Like using a diagram to illustrate a geometric theorem, the diagram might be illustrative but it should not be construed as evidence for the theorem.

A final weakness of this transcendental fundamental theology lies in its inability to distinguish adequately between the foundation of faith and the foundation of theology. The transcendental method of correlation uncovers the a priori foundations of human experience, but not the presuppositions of theology as a research praxis and as an intellectual discipline. Grounding Christian faith is not necessarily identical with grounding Christian theology. If traditional fundamental theology grounded theology in external criteria and extrinsic authority, transcendental fundamental theology grounds theology in the intrinsic correlation between experience as religiously interpreted and faith. Nevertheless, theological statements represent not only the faith of an individual or a community but also constitute a disciplinary matrix with a plurality of justificatory elements. Theological reflection involves more than correlation because it entails a reflective equilibrium among several sources, each with different criteria.

Situation and Message

The categories of possibility-actuality or implicit-explicit are replaced by those of situation and message in David Tracy's development of the method of correlation. His own proposals are made against the background of the inadequacies of Paul Tillich's question-answer and Bernard Lonergan's correlation of Christian doctrine with thematizations of religious conversion.[100] Tillich's correlation between question and answer overlooks that the present situation contains answers as well as questions, just as the message is itself a response to certain questions. The situation (both questions and answers) must be correlated with the message also (both questions and answers). Bernard Lonergan's foundational theology starts out from the religiously converted subject. His method of correlation does not adequately take into account the pluralism, secularity, and common human experience of the situation.

For Tracy, the two poles, situation and message, are correlated with each other. A phenomenological analysis of everyday and of scientific situations discloses their religious dimension. This religious dimension is uncovered in the limit-situations of everyday experience or in the limit-questions to science, art, and morality, where the religious possibilities of existence emerge. The other pole, at first described as the Christian fact, is later described with reference to the religious classic. It is the religious classic that discloses the limit-to experience. It represents "the religious intensification of the common experience" and discloses "an event of manifestation by the whole of a limit-of, ground-to, horizon-to experience—in sum, an authoritative-because-classic expression of the whole that promises a wholeness to life."[101]

Tracy's conception of the fundamental theological correlation is consequently very close to the previous positions. The categories of possibility-actuality and implicit-explicit are replaced with the categories of "intensification" and "manifestation." The truth of the religious tradition consists in its ability to disclose what coheres with the religious dimension of human experience. This disclosure-coherence model of truth underlies all these diverse conceptions of correlation irrespective of whether the disclosure is seen as actualization, explication, or intensification and manifestation. Such a model tends to view the Christian tradition primarily as a specification of what is universally experienced as religious. The historical particularity of the tradition as well as the force of its conflict with experience tends to be minimized in such a model.

In *The Analogical Imagination*, this model of correlation between message and situation is made much more precise through the distinction of social publics: the academy, Church, and society.[102] These distinct publics represent distinct communities with their own criteria and paradigms of truth and they form the basis for the distinction of theology into fundamental, systematic, and practical. With this nuance, Tracy brings to the fore what Rahner has overlooked. Foundational theology is concerned not only with the foundation of faith, but with the foundation of theology as a discipline. The three publics become focal points for a distinction of disciplines.

Yet a problem exists within this analysis, the three publics do not represent distinct communities and therefore are, at best, logically but not really distinct publics. In the history of science, the switch from Ptolemaic to Copernican, from Newtonian to quantum physics consisted of radical innovations in which one scientific community replaced another scientific community, each with its own paradigms and incommensurable theories. The transferral of socially and historically distinct communities of scientists to the three publics of theology breaks down because individuals may very well be members of more than one community—or of all three.

Nevertheless, the point is well made that fundamental theology, in its correlation between message and situation, addressed primarily the issue of the adequacy to common human experience in terms of the approach and methods of some academic discipline or of the philosophical dimension of that discipline. The arguments of that discipline are used to explicate and to adjudicate the truth claims of the religious tradition. In this affirmation, the weaknesses of the correlation model are evident. On the one hand what is correlated is precisely what transcends or is a limit to experience and scientific endeavor. On the other hand it is the mode of argument of these disciplines that adjudicates the truth claims. The danger then arises that the nontheological disciplines may be given too much weight in deciding and adjudicating the truth of religious claims and that they might become the foundational fulcrum of theology.

Moreover, all three versions of the method of correlation with its disclosure-coherence model of truth have to ask what value is a coherence between a tradition and an experience when the experience stands within the religious and cultural tradition affecting that very experience. How does it avoid that circularity of argument which is common to all transcendental arguments?[103] If it should seek to avoid circularity by locating a foundation of religious truth outside of the religious tradition, then it undergoes the risk of making the nonreligious the criterion of evaluating the religious and the nontheological the theological. These problems need to be addressed by analyzing the foundational fallacy, the hermeneutical dimension of both tradition and experience, and the distinctive elements constituting the foundational theological task.

Chapter 11

Foundational Theology as a Reconstructive Hermeneutics

The Foundational Fallacy: The Pyramid or the Raft

Foundationalism, a common and technical term within contemporary philosophy, refers to the conviction that knowledge as a true and justified belief is based on foundations.[104] Humans have beliefs and opinions that they need to justify if these beliefs and opinions are to become knowledge. A foundation, however, is neither justified by other beliefs nor based upon other beliefs, but rather provides the support for all other beliefs, itself needing no such support. Foundationalism presupposes certain basic truths that can be described either as self-justified (that is, not as justified through something else) or as irrefutable. All other truths are either justified by these basic foundational truths or are foundational in that they are self-justified, irrefutable and justify others.

Foundationalism can be either "hard" or "soft," either empiricist or rationalist. A soft foundationalism maintains that all noetic structures have a foundation, that is, a set of propositions according to which all others are believed. A hard foundationalism adds to soft foundationalism a set of criteria that defines the allowable basic propositions that can be ascertained as foundational. These criteria are self-evidence, incorrigibility, and evidence to the senses. In the distinction between an empiricist or a rationalist foundationalism,[105] the empiricist maintains that basic beliefs are justified by empirical statements and thereby become knowledge. The rationalist believes that the basic beliefs are justified by a transcendental deduction or through a conceptual analysis that shows their clarity and intelligibility. Whereas the empiricist relies heavily on the criterion of evidence to the senses, and the rationalist on the criterion of self-evidence, both view their foundations as incorrigible. Both see justification as a guarantor of truth, irrespective of whether the justification consists of the self-justification of basic beliefs (direct and immediate justification) or the derivative justification through these basic beliefs (mediate justification).

Both traditional and transcendental versions of fundamental theology display parallels to these diverse types of philosophical foundationalism. The historical demonstration of the credibility of Christian revelation through the "fact" of Jesus' resurrection and the "fact" of the Church's foundation with a supernatural mission provided the foundation for a whole system of Christian beliefs. The formal transcendental fundamental theology correlated the basic truths of Christian revelation with human subjectivity. Revelation, resurrection, and Church received their justification not so much on the basis of historical empirical data (although such arguments were also used) but primarily as existential truths that illumined the condition in the presence of God's grace. The transcendental as well as the historical types sought a foundation in either historical facticity or human subjectivity that would provide the foundation for all the truths of Christianity.

Severe criticisms have been raised against foundationalism and the metaphor of foundation.[106] The most influential criticisms are the Duhem-Quine thesis and Sellars's critique of the "Myth of the Given." Developing the theoretical position of Pierre Duhem, W. V. Quine has shown that statements about the external world face the court of sense experience not individually nor singularly but only together and as a corporate body.[107] Against the conventional wisdom that the truth status of observation statements is independent of the truth status of interpretative systems, the Duhem-Quine thesis argues that observational reports do not have their status in isolation from the theoretical context in which they occur. An individual statement must be judged and interpreted within its total context.

Foundationalism and its metaphor of foundation have been given the label of the "Myth of the Given" by Wilfrid Sellars,[108] not because empirical knowledge has no foundation, but because the metaphor is misleading for its static character. Not only is a logical dimension present in basing observational statements upon observational reports, but a logical dimension is also present in the observational reports themselves. Even a simple observational statement, "this is green," entails not only the symptom or sign of a green object, but this must also be recognized by those perceiving it as such. Simple observational statements and judgments about true facts cannot be made without a broad knowledge of all the relevant elements. In his critique of foundationalism, Sellars concludes, "one seems forced to choose between the picture of an elephant which rests on a tortoise (What supports the tortoise?) and a picture of a great Hegelian serpent of knowledge with its tail in its mouth (Where does it begin?)."[109] One escapes from this impasse by acknowledging that a discipline is rational not because it has a foundation, but because it is a self-correcting enterprise that examines all claims, all relevant background theories—even though not all at once.

The philosophical critique of foundationalism is valid because the demands of foundationalism are impossible to meet. Foundationalism requires a clearly recognizable condition by which a particular belief is conclusively justified. Such a requirement is impossible because the relation between conditions and beliefs (justified beliefs) is very complex. Even in the case of sensory experience, the same sensory stimulation can lead to different experiences because of differences in past experiences and present beliefs. Consequently, "no belief is conclusively justified. Each belief is tied loosely to a range of conditions in which relative to other beliefs, it is justified in varying degrees."[110]

The inability of foundationalism to specify a clearly recognizable condition according to which a particular belief is independently and conclusively justified is also shown by the notion of "structures of justification." Contemporary philosophy refers to "noetic" structure or "doxastic system,"[111] and sociology of knowledge in a different context refers to "plausibility structures."[112] Such terms express the hermeneutical circle involving beliefs, justifications, and knowledge. Whenever persons justify their beliefs, they appeal to other beliefs. One cannot break out of the circle. Even the direct appeal to an immediate observational experience is caught within the circle. What one believes when one experiences a particular sensory stimulation depends upon antecedent convictions and beliefs. An observational experience may appear to be immediately self-evident and independent of prior beliefs or convictions. Nevertheless, it depends upon the prior conviction that one can trust one's senses, one is not dreaming, one knows what the object is. Experiences are interpreted and judged insofar as they cohere with a cluster of justifying beliefs and convictions. This justificatory system ("structures of justification") articulates what a person experiences, and beliefs must cohere with it in order to be justified. It does not refer so much to the content of what is believed as to what counts as relevant to justification.[113]

What counts as justification or what are the relevant structures of justification can be diverse, simple or complex, adequate or inadequate. If one wants to know what constitutes the ingredients of apple pie, one looks it up in a cook book. In this case, it is a justifiable approach to knowledge. If someone proclaims that Beethoven's Ninth Symphony is the best of all symphonies because the roll of the drums in the first movement is quite thrilling, then such a structure of justification appears inadequate. The justification of beliefs is rather complex and cannot be reduced to a simple or singular foundation. What counts as rational and justifying in regard to the claims of truth would be quite different according to the structures of justification of the individual, community, or culture.

In his classic essay of 1932, "Protocol Sentences," Otto Neurath used the metaphor of a ship in arguing against the positivism of Rudolf Carnap.[114] There are no secure, clean and definitive protocol sentences that can be made the starting-point of a science. Philosophers are on a ship on the open sea. They have to constantly rebuild the ship without having the opportunity to arrive in a port and to put the ship in dry dock. Instead amidst the waves of the sea, they have to take apart the ship and rebuild it out of its own planks. Recent discussions on foundationalism have picked up Neurath's image, but changed the ship into a raft.[115] Against the metaphor of knowledge as a pyramid in which one stone is laid upon another stone, the present situation is described as that of a raft upon the sea.

The critique of foundationalism poses a historical and systematic challenge to fundamental theology. Historically, the critique moves against the very direction of the discipline's development. The first stage of fundamental theology sought a foundation in those basic beliefs uncovered by positive theology. The second stage sought a foundation in the facts demonstrated by historical arguments. The third stage explicated a foundation in human subjectivity. The tendency of this development was to intensify the foundationalism of the discipline and to secure even more firm foundations for both faith and theology. In its final stage of development, fundamental theology had as its task to seek a single foundation for theology as well as for faith.

The critique also raises some important systematic challenges. It asks whether fundamental theology can uncover historical or empirical, transcendental or existential foundations independent from cultural traditions and interpreted experiences, or whether fundamental theology is forced to start out amid diverse religious, cultural, and social traditions as they intersect with diverse contemporary interpretations of human experience. It thereby challenges the traditional assumption of fundamental theology that the credibility of a religious tradition can be established by ascertaining the events, facts, proclamations, and miraculous occurrences at the basis of the tradition. It challenges whether the central beliefs of a religious tradition can be grounded as expressions of the diverse structures of the human experience of the transcendent. No external standard, be it history or human experience, exists independent of cultural tradition and social interpretation that can provide an independent foundation of either faith or theology. The rejection of the independence of such evidential standards does not imply that there are no standards but that historical and transcendental standards are only available within a cultural and interpretative framework.[116]

The critique of foundationalism questions whether fundamental theology can provide Christian faith and theology with an independent criterion and foundation. Therefore, it challenges the independence of fundamental theology from systematic theology in that it questions whether the former has its own distinct criteria of truth and its own fields of argumentation. Since the critique of foundationalism points to the cultural, social, and hermeneutical dimensions of "all foundations," it challenges attempts to limit hermeneutical retrieval of meaning to systematic theology and to the public of the Church in a way that would relegate the historical and transcendental analysis primarily to fundamental theology.[117] The implications of the critique of foundationalism become evident in the following sections that develop foundational theology as a reconstructive hermeneutic, for these sections seek to take seriously the critique of foundationalism. To this purpose, I shall argue that the task of retrieving the meaning of a religious tradition not only raises issues of interpretation but also those of truth. Likewise, I shall argue that experience, be it transcendental or religious, is itself hermeneutical and dependent upon determinative religious and cultural traditions. Foundational theology, therefore, requires a method seeking a reflective equilibrium between the reconstruction of meaning, retroductive warrants, and background theories.

Interpretation of Meaning and Truth Claims

The philosophical critique of foundationalism has uncovered the degree to which meaning and truth are not simply evidential objective qualities. In this respect, this critique stands within a tradition of philosophy increasingly aware that meaning is context dependent. In linguistic philosophy, Wittgenstein has shown how the meaning of words is intertwined with their use within life. The phrase "language game" expresses the interrelation between meaning and forms of life.[118] The development of hermeneutical theory from the nineteenth century to the present has shown how illusory are those abstract, universal, and a priori structures of rationality claimed by a Kantian transcendental philosophy.[119] The role of pre-understanding (Heidegger), the significance of tradition (Gadamer), and the creativity of language itself (Ricoeur) show the inadequacy of transcendental philosophy not only for interpretation and understanding but also for criteria of application, evaluation, and judgment.[120] The work of Thomas Kuhn, Paul Feyerabend, and to a lesser degree Stephen Toulmin show how the paradigms employed by the communities of scientists determine not only the meaning but also the criteria of truth for various scientific theories.[121]

The theological appropriation of these philosophical analyses of human understanding and rationality has been one-sided. The appropriation has been directed against fundamental theology and not just foundationalism. The appeal to language games and to the interrelation between religious beliefs and religious forms of life has been used to argue that faith cannot in principle be justified to those outside the language game, to those outside of the faith.[122] The notion of paradigms had been used to show how faith may be grounded, but how such a grounding takes place primarily within the context of a particular faith community with its own specific paradigms and criteria.[123] The hermeneutical significance of the tradition has been used, with an appeal to Gadamer, to ground a dogmatic appeal to the classic rather than to see the limitations of classics with their expressions of particular interests, cultures, and subjects.

Hermeneutics refers to the process of interpretation. Within theology hermeneutics refers to the interpretation of the meaning of a religious belief, praxis, or tradition. Since meaning and truth are distinct, it has often been assumed that hermeneutics deals with meaning and not truth. Foundational theology, therefore, cannot be a hermeneutical discipline because its primary object is not the meaning, but the truth of religious claims. Although widespread, such a view is false. Meaning and truth are indeed distinct, but it is not possible to separate the interpretation of a tradition's meaning and identity from that of its truth. To interpret the meaning of a religious claim entails examining its truth. Such a contention has important ramifications for the nature and method of foundational theology. These can be shown by demarcating the distinctive hermeneutical problem of theology, the interrelation between meaning and truth, and the significance of symbolic interaction for understanding a religious tradition.

The "Double Hermeneutic" of Theology

Theology has a distinctive hermeneutical problem for, as opposed to the natural sciences, it is constituted by a "double hermeneutic." The hermeneutical dimension within the natural sciences exists because the data upon which scientific theories are based and tested cannot be described independently of the respective linguistic framework of the theory itself. The paradigms operative within the theoretical framework often affect both the data and the criteria for its verification. Since scientific theories are dependent upon those frameworks and paradigms used by concrete scientific communities, they cannot be simply falsified or verified. This problem has been well formulated by Mary Hesse's description of the present consensus: "it has been sufficiently demonstrated that data are not detachable from theory, and that their expression is permeated by theoretical categories; that the language of the theoretical science is irreducibly metaphorical and unformalizable, and that the logic of science is circular: interpretation, reinterpretation, and self-correction of data in terms of theory, and theory in terms of data."[124]

In contrast, theology faces another hermeneutical dimension and is constituted by a double hermeneutic. In addition to the hermeneutical problem that all scientific theories presuppose distinct paradigms, theoretical frameworks, meaning schemes, and the like, the further problem is that theology deals with a preinterpreted world. Meaning is part and parcel of the very object of theological study. Theology is, therefore, hermeneutical not just because theological theories are dependent upon the specific paradigms, models, and frameworks (as in the case of the natural sciences) but also because understanding and meaning are operative in the very object of theological study. The object of theological study is not simply observational data, but symbolically structured data that is meaning-laden and interpretation-constitutive.

This difference between theology and the natural sciences has enormous implications. The natural sciences are hermeneutical in that their observational propositions are dependent upon the theoretical frameworks chosen. Theology is hermeneutical in addition because what it studies consists of structured meaning.[125] Since interpretation and meaning form the very object of theology, and not just the means of approach to the object, it becomes necessary that the theologian as an "observer" must participate in the very process of understanding in order to grasp the constitutive meaning of the object of study.

An example easily illustrates this abstract claim. A theologian attempting to understand and to interpret a liturgy differs from a natural scientist attempting to understand atoms. The models and paradigms both have chosen will determine how they understand their objects. However, a liturgy and liturgical action differs from the movement of atomic particles in that a liturgical action is meaning laden. The participants in a liturgy are through their words and actions expressing meaning. The theologian as an "observer" and an interpreter can understand and interpret this meaning only if she somehow participates in the meaning of what liturgy involves. Without such participation the theologian would not have access to the meaning that is symbolically structured in the actions of those performing the liturgy.

Meaning and Truth Conditions

The double hermeneutic of theology, however, raises the further and highly controverted question: what is entailed in grasping meaning? Although linguistic philosophy and hermeneutical theory have provided diverse answers, a certain convergence appears to emerge between the two.[126] Nevertheless, we shall look first at the development within linguistic philosophy, and then at hermeneutical theory.

A consensus exists within linguistic philosophy that in order to understand the meaning of utterances, it is necessary to know the truth conditions of an utterance. From the early Wittgenstein ("to understand a proposition means to know what is the case if it is true") to contemporary American philosophers, such as Donald Davidson ("to give truth conditions is a way of giving meaning the meaning of a sentence") and W. V. Quine (one "understands a sentence" insofar as one "knows its truth conditions"), the correlation between knowledge of meaning and knowledge of truth conditions is affirmed.[127]

Nevertheless, as Strawson has noted, "it is indeed a generally harmless and salutary thing to say that to know the meaning of a sentence is to know under what conditions one who utters it says something true . . . the dictum represents, not the end, but the beginning of our task. It simply narrows, and relocates, our problem, forcing us to inquire what is contained in the little phrase . . . says something true."[128] Indeed, the controversies have no end, for some understand truth conditions in terms of a causal theory of reference; others take them as conditions of assertibility.[129] Formal semanticists suggest that the notion of truth conditions can be explicated without reference to communication, whereas communication theorists convincingly argue that truth conditions are understood only in connection with speech-acts and communication.[130]

In affirming truth conditions as determinative of meaning, "the argument is that we determine the sense of a sentence by laying the conditions under which it is true, so that we could not first discuss the sense of a sentence and then apply some criterion to decide in what circumstances it was true."[131] Take the example of a game. One does not know the meaning of a game independently of knowing the criterion for winning it. When one learns a game, one learns what it takes to win the game. Likewise, one does not learn the meaning of a sentence and only afterwards learn its truth conditions. But in learning its truth conditions, one learns its meaning. An analogous example is the utterance of a command. The meaning of a command is known only if one knows what constitutes obedience or disobedience to a command. If one does not know these conditions, then one does not know what the command is about. Likewise, unless one knows what are the truth conditions of a statement, then one does not know the meaning of the statement.

The meaning of a sentence is, however, not simply explained by correlations between sentences and possible states of affairs, but rather has to include how one seeks to communicate. In order to communicate individuals must not only produce grammatically correct sentences, they must also perform successful speech-acts. Communication involves not only propositional content, but the force of performative actions. A hermeneutical theory that abstracts from the performative aspects of communication fails to grasp precisely what makes an act of communication successful or how a speech-act successfully communicates.[132] This performative aspect of communication has been developed by the later Wittgenstein, Strawson, and Searle.[133] More recently, Habermas has extended their analyses by moving from the specific context of speech-acts to the more general presuppositions of all speech-acts and by elucidating the interrelation between speech-act theory and hermeneutical theory.

An analysis of those features present in every successful communication shows that a speech-act is twofold.[134] It contains a propositional component with referential and predicative expressions and an illocutionary element that specifies the engagement with which the speaker communicates. Successful acts of communication comprise, therefore, two levels. Persons do not just speak about something, but they interact with others. A successful communication therefore takes place not only on the level of objects but also on the level of intersubjectivity. This intersubjective relation is established because in every act of communication a speaker explicitly or implicitly raises certain validity claims and these validity claims are reciprocally acknowledged, sometimes explicitly, often implicitly.

Four validity claims can be distinguished in every act of communication.[135] The speaker implicitly claims intelligibility for the utterance. In addition, an utterance situates a sentence in relation to external reality, social reality, and internal reality. The propositional content of the utterance relates to external reality, to the world of objects and events about which one can make true or false claims. An utterance is performatively related to the normative reality of society, to the social life-world with its norms and values. This involves the validity claim of correctness or rightness. An utterance is related to the speaker's own internal world, the world of intentional experiences that come to expression. This expressive dimension raises the claims of truthfulness or sincerity. In short, utterances imply claims of intelligibility, truth, rightness, and truthfulness.

Symbolic Interaction and Hermeneutics

The significance of diverse validity claims within communication needs to be placed within the conception of symbolic interaction. Language is a symbolic structuring of the experienced world, as Durkheim, Mead, Blumer, and Goffman document.[136] Everyone learning a language is initiated into the symbolic structures of a language and into the intersubjective social world. Its norms and rules become internalized through the learning of the language and its specific symbolic structuring of the experienced world.

Interpreters, therefore, retrieve the meaning of past texts insofar as they learn to differentiate between the life-world of the author and their own life-world. The text to be interpreted must be located within the life-world of the past in order that its diverse truth claims with their reference to distinct reality domains be acknowledged. The division into distinct validity claims (intelligibility, truth, rightness, and truthfulness) and distinct reality domains (language, external, social, and internal reality) has significant implications for hermeneutics. Interpretations of meaning must attempt to reconstruct how the statements stand in relation to distinct validity claims and reality domains. The knowledge of the life-world that has become symbolically structured in the language of the text is also a requirement in that precisely what is affirmed in the text can be acknowledged insofar as the claims are either accepted or rejected.

The relation between acknowledging validity claims and understanding the meaning of a statement not only requires that the interpreters participate in the process itself but also makes possible that the interpreters can criticize the text and its claims. The interpreter knows the meaning of a text insofar as he or she knows the claims of the text and to which domains the test is referring. To stand in relation to these object domains makes understanding possible, as well as criticism.

This hermeneutical proposal goes counter to two tendencies within some schools of hermeneutical thought. Paul Ricoeur has pointed to Saussure's distinction between parole and language, between the spoken dialogue and the written text in order to emphasize the importance of the text's meaning apart from the author's original intention and the reader's original reception.[137] Nevertheless, this emphasis overlooks the fact that what takes place in language is communication, a communication based upon performative aspects of language and upon the validity claims raised in communication. This cannot be bypassed without falling into textual idealism that overlooks the degree to which language is structured symbolic interaction.

The analysis of the interrelation between validity claims and interpretation also goes contrary to the emphasis upon the classic, as developed in Gadamer's hermeneutics; for such a hermeneutics presupposes that what is to be interpreted is normative.[138] Therefore, it argues that one must learn from a text and can understand a text only insofar as one can apply the text to one's present situation. The truth claim and meaning of a text become understood in the act of accepting and applying the text. Such a hermeneutic overlooks the fact that the author of a text, even a classic, could also have learned from us. An adequate hermeneutic would therefore require that the interpretation of text come to terms with its validity claims.[139] Such a requirement does not mean that in order to understand a text one must immediately know whether what the text has asserted is in fact true, right, or truthful, but that one is capable of recognizing what its truth conditions are. This requirement presupposes, therefore, that the interpretation of a text includes a knowledge of what a text is about and includes a knowledge of the text as an expression of a particular socialized view about the subject matter of the text.

The interrelation between interpretation and truth conditions has implications for foundational theology. Moreover, it represents an important shift in hermeneutical orientation. In the earlier part of the twentieth century, a priority of meaning over truth was claimed by analytical philosophy and hermeneutical theory; today, the significance of truth conditions for the interpretation of meaning has come to the fore within linguistic and hermeneutical theories critical of the previous consensus.[140] The implication for fundamental theology touches on its ability to retrieve and to interpret its own religious tradition. Since any interpretation of the tradition entails the ability to perceive the truth conditions of what is claimed by the tradition, the crucial question becomes how does one know the truth conditions, or how does one evaluate what is asserted by the tradition. Some would appeal to contemporary experience or to criteria of a transcendental analysis of contemporary experience, but such an appeal overlooks the fact that experience itself is hermeneutical.

Experience as Hermeneutical

Experience is a complex and often misused concept. Contrary to popular understanding, experience is primarily an act of interpretation. Experience is not an immediate act of consciousness or some feeling underlying human thoughts and concepts. Instead, experience takes place within the context of memory, the memory of previous examples and similar cases. Moreover, experience is embedded within a cultural tradition and a network of social interaction and mutual interpretation. Memory, tradition, and interpretation are as much a part of experience and as determinative of experience as are the acts of consciousness, sensation, or feeling.

This view goes beyond the common understanding of experience. The term "experience" normally has two uses with diverse connotations. In one sense experience refers to the immediate, personal, and evidential. It is immediate. Persons claim that they have experienced something. They mean that they have not simply heard or learned of it from others. Nor have they indirectly deduced it by some sort of logical inference. Instead, they have a direct and immediate knowledge. Therefore, experience also refers to the personal. To have an experience is to have a personal and direct involvement with something. No one can experience something vicariously. In this immediate and personal sense experience is contrasted with the remote, the conceptual, and the abstract. Experience also refers to the evidential. Because experience is immediate and personal, it often refers to the direct knowledge of something. Experience is what provides the material for thought, supplies the warrants for conclusions, and is the material evidence is made of. All these connotations are included in one strain of the use of the term "experience."

Yet experience is often used with another connotation and meaning, when, for example, one refers to an experienced doctor or experienced teacher. To be experienced results from having gone through a series of experiences and having learned from them. The result of the succession of experiences is to make someone learned and prudent in judgments. This understanding of experience is related to the other. An experienced doctor is not simply one who knows all that is in medical books about health and medicine, but has personal knowledge of individual cases. The result of remembering and connecting individual cases makes a person experienced. The result of acquiring the ability to unite the theoretical and practical based upon a knowledge of exemplary cases makes one experienced.

Memory and Practical Judgment

It is in this latter sense that Aristotle develops the conception of experience within his *Metaphysics* (980b–981a): "From memory, persons can get experience, for by often remembering the same thing they acquire the power of unified experience. Experience, though it seems quite like scientific knowledge and art, is really what produces them."[141] He argues that experience gives one the skill to know which similarities are important and form a whole. Using the example of medicine, he argues that medical skill comes when, through memory, one has the experience of what is appropriate. This type of experience is not inferior but superior to the merely theoretical. Experienced persons succeed better than those with theoretical knowledge because one does not heal "humanity" but a particular person. "If, then, someone lacking experience, but knowing the general principles of the art, sizes up a situation as a whole, he will often because he is ignorant of the individual within that whole, miss the mark and fail to cure; for it is the individual that must be cured."[142]

Experience gives knowledge of the particular existing in the interrelation between the particular and the universal. Someone lacking experience but knowing abstract principles may misjudge the particular. A judgment that is "considered" is reached when individual cases are remembered so that one can distinguish the general and the particular and can make prudent and considered judgments as to what is applicable. Two elements are present in this conception of experience: the definitional and assertional. Through the memory of the individual and particular cases one gains not only a definitional knowledge of the general but also an assertional knowledge of how the general is applicable to the particular. Experience is therefore not merely a perception of something immediate, but rather an interpretation dependent upon knowledge and memory.

The Aristotelian conception of experience has been pushed into the background within modern philosophy.[143] Although John Locke offers a description of experience that entails going beyond isolated data, his distinction between perception and judgment has led to an empiricist conception of experience. Even though he concedes that sensations are often influenced by judgments, Locke's philosophical emphasis is to separate perception and judgment. Judgment follows perception and is based upon the material that perception provides.[144] In his analysis of judgment, Kant argues even more strongly than Aristotle that "examples are the go-cart of judgment."[145] Judgment involves a talent that can be practiced and learned from examples. It cannot be taught on the basis of universals, because judgments in new situations demand the crisscrossing of the universal and concrete in new ways. Nevertheless, Kant strove to develop a transcendental philosophy which, like mathematics, would have an a priori basis. In short, both the empiricism stemming from Locke and the transcendentalism stemming from Kant played down the role of considered judgments in regard to examples as a basis for understanding experience.

From a methodological viewpoint, experience should not be seen simply as a category of theoretical reason, but rather as one of practical reason.[146] The appeal to experience is then not made as an appeal to a self-evident or to an immediately and directly evident foundational principle, but rather to a prudential and reflective judgment. The appeal to experience is, therefore, of itself not foundational; nor can it be. Only in consideration with other factors does it play a significant role in the theoretical and theological task of foundational theology.

Historical Tradition and Experience

The inadequacy of the Cartesian starting-point and the Kantian transcendental analysis of the human subject has been demonstrated by a philosophical analysis of "pre-understanding" and "effective history." These notions not only point out the historical conditioning of human subjectivity, but they also elevate this historical conditioning

into a hermeneutical principle. The circular nature of human understanding is well illustrated by Heidegger's notion of pre-understanding.[147] Human beings exist in the world. As such, they have a relation
to the world and to the world of meaning. They come to understand a
text or an event insofar as they already pro-ject a pre-understanding.
This projective pre-understanding may be revised as a result of the
encounter with a text or an event, and what may emerge is a further
understanding. Nevertheless, without this pre-understanding, further understanding is not possible. Moreover, the pre-understanding
influences how understanding will take place.

This Heideggerian insight has been expanded by Gadamer to
show that the Enlightenment belief in the freedom of human subjectivity from all prejudice is illusory.[148] Persons stand within the history
of a tradition of ideas and values. The classics of a culture, for example, have a momentous importance because they do not represent
ahistorical ideals, but rather because they bring to the fore a "notable
mode of being historical" that has a determinative influence upon a
culture and a tradition. As such, a classic in being handed down,
preserved, and taken as normative has an effective history. It pre-
cedes historical reflection and it continues to have an effect upon
historical reflection. As exemplary disclosures of human self-understanding, classics have not only value for the past but affect contemporary understanding and experience. A person within Western civilization stands within a culture, civilization, and tradition that has
been conditioned by the classics of its tradition. That person's mode
of subjectivity has been so conditioned by these classics that when he
or she experiences as a very immediate and personal experience often
expresses the very values of the classics in their effective history.

To take the conditioning of human experience by historical tradition as a hermeneutical principle is to challenge the notion of a transcendental experience or of a transcendental analysis of the religious
dimension of experience. Within contemporary fundamental theology, an appeal is made to human experience and to the disclosure
within human experience of a common faith, a common trust in reality, and an underlying religious dimension.[149] This appeal overlooks
the extent to which human experience takes place within a cultural
tradition that provides concepts and paradigms according to which
that experience is interpreted. There are no experiences of the religious dimension of reality that can escape the influence of the historical tradition in shaping religious experience.

Even the fundamental experience of contingency illustrates this
hermeneutical dimension of experience. Human experience of contin-

gency is universal. Everyone experiences the limitations of birth and death. Even acts of human freedom depend upon a certain receptivity and givenness of ability. No experience of freedom is such that one can determine and effect one's own being in existence. But what is experienced when finitude and limitation are experienced? Such experiences are susceptible to two radically different interpretations. One can experience contingency as the radical dependence upon the system of nature as the absolute within the universe of meaning. Or one can experience contingency as the radical dependence upon God as the ground of all nature. The one experience is religious; the other is not. Thus, persons experience their contingency in relation to their notions of ultimacy according to the paradigms of the tradition affecting their own consciousness.

When persons claim to have had an experience of God, this experience is not a pure experience, but is an experience mediated through the paradigms of cultural religious history as to what is the meaning of God and what counts as an experience of that meaning. It has often been pointed out that even the classic five ways of Aquinas do not end inferentially with God, but with the acknowledgment that what has been arrived at is in the language of the tradition commonly called God. The point of referring to the role of cultural tradition in determining experience is not that one cannot argue for the superiority of a religious interpretation of the experience of contingency over a nonreligious interpretation; but rather the point is that such an argument does not make an appeal to experience as an evidential criterion independent of the interpretations of tradition and culture. Likewise, the appeal to a common faith in the trustworthiness of reality is an appeal less to a substratum of all particular religious faiths, than an appeal to one rather specific interpretation of faith and of reality. Its evidential quality does not stand more secure over against more determinate religious interpretations.

This conclusion, that experience is based upon memory, practical judgment, and cultural tradition, implies that fundamental theology cannot appeal to a transcendental experience as primal experience, prior to the encounter with the religious tradition. Such an experience stands within the effective history of that tradition. Therefore, fundamental theology is faced with the problem that, on the one hand, the tradition can only be known and interpreted insofar as one acknowledges its truth claims, to be accepted or to be rejected and that, on the other, contemporary experience is not an independent source or criterion that is totally free from the tradition itself. The way through the impasse is to develop a reconstructive hermeneutic that implies a method of justification commonly called a wide reflective equilibrium.

Hermeneutical Reconstruction and Reflective Equilibrium

The basic problem is: how does foundational theology take into account the criticisms of foundationalism without surrendering its foundational task of disclosing the meaning and truth of its religious tradition? The relation between meaning and truth requires that the meaning of a tradition cannot be recovered without at the same time raising the truth claims constitutive of that tradition. The hermeneutical dimension of experience shows that experience cannot be simply appealed to as an evidential proof because it is embedded within a tradition of meaning and truth. Fundamental theologies have tended to give a priority to one or the other without taking fully into account their intertwinement. The way out of the impasse is a conception of foundational theology as a reconstructive hermeneutic employing what has come to be known as the method of wide reflective equilibrium. These technical terms of "reconstruction" and "wide reflective equilibrium" need to be elucidated.

The term "reconstruction" has within contemporary philosophy, especially moral philosophy and linguistic philosophy, a rather specific meaning.[150] When it is used to describe a method of moral philosophy, a distinction is often made between a virtual and a real reconstruction.[151] A virtual reconstruction takes as its starting-point concrete moral judgments. It seeks to organize these diverse judgments into overarching principles. A virtual reconstruction strives for a useful systematization of diverse moral beliefs, but does not seek to give them independent justification. A real reconstruction, however, seeks to uncover the principles present in moral judgments for the sake of giving insight into the reasons for presystematic moral beliefs. Moving first from the particular to the general, it moves back from the general to the particular. The general principles are then brought to bear on the particular and vice versa. Its circular method of mutual critique, justification, and adjustment has led to a further refinement of the tool of reconstruction.

The notion of reconstruction can be further specified through the distinction between narrow and wide reflective equilibrium.[152] A narrow equilibrium consists of a twofold procedure of mutual correction and justification, as, for example, in moral philosophy between considered moral judgments and moral principles or in linguistics between linguistic practice and grammatical rules. On the one hand are the concrete moral judgments or the concrete linguistic practices; from these universal moral principles or grammatical rules are reconstructed. The reconstructed rules then serve, on the other hand, as guidelines by which the concrete practice is criticized. In narrow equilibrium the reconstruction of general rules from concrete practice allows the rules to criticize the practice or the practice to lead to a revision of the rules. The equilibrium is reflective because it is not static but is a constantly revising movement. Through a back and forth movement the method of reflective equilibrium seeks to bring into equilibrium the principles reconstructed from practice with the practice itself.

In view of the spiral character implied in a reconstructive method, ethical theorists have suggested that wide reflective equilibrium more adequately encompasses the diverse elements of practical reasoning.[153] In addition to the considered judgments or the practice and the principles, the relevant background theories are also brought into consideration. The advantage of wide reflective equilibrium consists in the ability of the background theories to provide independent constraints that prevent the principles from being mere generalizations of the considered judgments or practice, even though they themselves are also under constraint from the judgments and principles. The method of wide reflective equilibrium is employed by Rawls's *Theory of Justice* and seeks to take into account concrete considered moral judgments about justice, principles of justice reconstructed from them, and the relevant background theories (for example, nature of person, society, role of morality in society, etc.).[154]

The methodological significance and purpose of developing a reconstructive method that employs reflective equilibrium lies in its ability to avoid the dangers of foundationalism.[155] Such a method does not accept a tradition of judgments or practice or some general principles or some items of experience or some background theories as foundational. Instead, the method presupposes a diversity of judgments, principles, and theories, each entailing different kinds of justification that come together to support or to criticize, to reinforce or to revise. Reflective equilibrium entails, as one author has phrased it, "the systematic rechanneling of initial commitments in such a way that each act is judged in terms of all others. We do not start from scratch, but always with initial commitments of some degree."[156] It acknowledges that one starts with initial commitments, be these considered moral judgments, linguistic practice, or such, but that these are then related to principles and theories in such a way that the latter are in part independent of the commitments so that they can modify them and yet are also dependent upon them in such a way that they are susceptible to revision.

This method in ethics and practical reasoning seeks to overcome the weaknesses of an intuitive or utilitarian foundation for moral reasoning. Nevertheless, its use has not been without controversy. Some criticize the method as engendering too weak a form of justification; others consider the reliance on initial considered judgments or initial practice to be too strongly dependent on current societal values.[157] Both criticisms mistake a narrow for a wide reflective equilibrium. The point is the interaction between initial judgments or practice, principles, and background theory. Each not only provides a support to the other two elements but also may challenge and correct them. There is not one single element of foundation; rather, the foundation consists in the constant interchange among the diverse sources and principles.

Reflective equilibrium has been appropriated as a method in recent linguistic theory, ethical theory, and philosophy. It has even been suggested as an appropriate method within the philosophy of science. Yet it has not been appropriated as a method for foundational theology. In part, the reasons for this neglect are the pervasive dominance of foundationalism within foundational theology and the identification of the foundation of faith and the foundation of theology.

In contrast, however, to either historical or transcendental fundamental theologies, reflective equilibrium makes possible a theological method that takes into account diverse elements as foundational without reducing the one to the other. The danger of the method of correlation, understood as the correlation between revelation and the cognitional and normative claims of the modern world, consists in the risk of positing one of the two elements as foundational.[158] Either the Christian revelation would be reduced to the criterion of the modern world or the biblical form of revelation would be the criterion of contemporary experience. The analysis of tradition and experience has challenged whether tradition and experience can be separated into two distinct poles that are then correlated. Such a separation not only neglects the intertwinement between interpretation and experience but also allows that one of the poles be taken as foundational.

It therefore seems that the method of wide reflective equilibrium brings to the fore the diversity of criteria that a foundational theology should take into account without falling into foundationalism and without reducing the foundation of theology to that of faith. The question remains what would be the elements and criteria if reflective equilibrium were employed as a method for foundational theology. The following three are in my opinion constitutive of foundational theology: the hermeneutical reconstruction of the Christian tradition; the retroductive warrants for the tradition; and the relevant background theories.

Hermeneutical Reconstruction

The task of hermeneutical reconstruction presupposes the existence of Christian beliefs, convictions, and practices in need of interpretation. A plurality of diverse beliefs, claims, convictions, and practices exists as a religious tradition. In view of this plurality and diversity, a religious tradition does not exist as a self-evident identity, but rather needs to be interpreted so that its identity can be discerned.[159] Some beliefs and practices are more significant than others; some stand in contradiction to others; some are laudable; others are not. The first task of foundational theology would therefore be to offer an interpretation of Christian identity: what it means to be a Christian; in what does the Christian vision consist; and what is Christian praxis.

This task is not an easy task, for although Christianity and Christian traditions are historically and empirically given, Christian identity is not.[160] It is given only as the result of an interpretative reconstruction of the tradition in its past and present forms of existence. Any reconstruction, however, involves the critical discrimination as to what is primary and what is secondary, what is essential and what is accidental, what is authentic and what is distortion. A reconstruction is more than descriptive.[161] A descriptive account would trace the divagations as well as constants of belief and practice throughout the history of Christianity until the present. A hermeneutical reconstruction, however, seeks to ascertain the meaning and identity of Christianity. Such a reconstruction will necessarily produce a *Gestalt* in which certain lines come to the fore as constitutive, whereas others do not. The reconstruction takes as its basis the considered judgments of Christians, both present and past, as to what constitutes the Christian vision in its beliefs and practices and seeks to uncover an identity in the midst of diversity.

The first element of reconstruction is similar to what we have earlier called a narrow equilibrium. It seeks out of the diversity of traditions and judgments throughout the history of Christianity and throughout present Christianity to reconstruct what is Christian identity or what is the identity of a particular belief. Such interpretative reconstructions involve a crisscrossing and a going back and forth from the considered judgments about identity to the reconstructed identity, and then reciprocally from the reconstructed identity to the considered judgments. Such discriminations—albeit quite often implicit—have often been made throughout the history of Christianity. It is the task of foundational theology to make them explicit through hermeneutical reconstruction.

Taking the hermeneutical reconstruction of the tradition as the first element of foundational theology presupposes that the starting-point of foundational theology is neither historical facticity nor transcendental a priori. It presupposes that the starting-point is the givenness of the religious dimension of human life, a dimension not given—I repeat—as a bare fact or as an anthropological a priori, but given as a tradition of interpreted meaning and practice that in turn needs to be further interpreted. Ever since Dilthey, it has been an insight of hermeneutical theory that one gains knowledge of human existence primarily through the cultural expression of human existence, through language and praxis.[162] The starting-point of foundational theology is, therefore, not a transcendental a priori or a phenomenological analysis of abstract structures of possibility, but rather the historical manifestation of the religious dimension of life as it is exhibited in a particular religious tradition. It is then the task of hermeneutical reconstruction to bring to the fore the identity of the tradition in its meaningfulness and truth claims.

An interpretative reconstruction of a religious tradition necessarily goes back to the originating interpretations of a religious tradition, but it does not stop there. Nor does it necessarily make them exclusively normative as in some contemporary fundamental theologies where the appropriateness to the earliest witnesses is the criterion.[163] Instead, it presupposes that the originating interpretations have a reception-history, produce consequences and effects, lead to modifications, reinterpretations, shifts in argumentation, and new paradigms. Any reconstructive analysis would have to trace some of these shifts and changes, show the role of reception, and indicate differences of paradigms.

Since a hermeneutical reconstruction can be accused, as all hermeneutics of retrieval have been, of justifying the existent or of legitimating the development, it is necessary to consider how a hermeneutical reconstruction is critical and how it avoids the dangers of false legitimation.[164] A hermeneutical reconstruction is critical in that it has the task of bringing to the fore the identity of the tradition as it exists in the paradigmatic ideals, both in theory and practice, of the tradition. These paradigms provide criteria for evaluating certain developments as legitimate and others as deformations.

An interpretation of Christian history and praxis can show that certain patterns of behavior are more consistent and coherent with what Christianity considers a paradigmatic statement of Christian identity and praxis. Such judgments are in many cases not very complex. Historical examples of anti-Semitism, inquisitional torture, colonial exploitation, and the like are easily identifiable as inconsistent with what, in the considered judgment of Christians, is ideal and paradigmatic for Christian existence, for example, the Sermon on the Mount. In other cases the discriminating judgment is not so simple. Some Christians might argue that social welfare legislation and the reform of political structures represent the drawing out of the implications of the Sermon on the Mount. Others might argue that personal almsgiving expresses the meaning and truth of the Sermon on the Mount; therefore, personal charity rather than social reform represents what is paradigmatically Christian. In such instances, it does not suffice to refer to the disclosure power of the Sermon on the Mount or to the coherence of a practice with its ideals. Instead, one must appeal to additional criteria. These may be background theories about societal evolution and the forms of mutual assistance. These may be retroductive warrants in regard to the practice of the Sermon in a particular historical situation.

The methodological point is that the hermeneutical reconstruction of Christian identity and its ideals has a critical function, but it does not suffice as a methodological principle. In addition to the disclosive power of the Christian vision, foundational theology must take into account relevant background theories and retroductive warrants. The foundational theological task is only achieved when all these elements are brought into reflective equilibrium. Only then can theology demonstrate which concrete paradigms of behavior and belief represent legitimate developments and new paradigms of Christian identity.

Retroductive Warrants

"Retroductive" is a philosophical term that refers to an argument which is neither deductive nor inductive.[165] Where a deductive argument moves from axioms to theorems, an inductive argument generalizes particular cases. A retroductive warrant, a much weaker confirmation than the above two, argues from the variety and diversity of inferences that can be drawn from a hypothesis. The argument is not accepted because of logical cogency as in deduction or because of the generalizations of data as in induction. Instead, the argument is accepted because the hypothesis generates illuminative inferences. Retroductive is explained by Charles Peirce with the example of making inferences from a person's traits, knowledge, carriage, ability, and the like to that person's character or profession.[166] Such warrants are weaker than inductive and deductive ones, but they are important criteria for decisions.

The adequacy of warrants for theories has become an acute question today because it has become generally acknowledged that not only theories themselves but also the warrants for theories are dependent upon diverse paradigms. Accordingly, the context of the discovery of a theory and the context of its justification cannot be separated too sharply. The justification and confirmation of a theory proceeds retroductively from a theory's fertility, that is, from its explanatory and pragmatic success. A theory is confirmed to the degree that it is more successful than others in explaining more data, more problems, and more conundrums. It has a present ability to illumine and it has a potential for further developments. Moreover, a theory is more warranted to the degree that it can guide praxis. This ability to guide praxis generates consensus, leads to further developments, and is a warrant that corroborates the theory.

Explanation and proof are often considered as distinct. However, "in retroduction, the two are indissoluable. The hypothesis is confirmed or justified precisely to the extent that it is shown to have explanatory power."[167] This explanatory power, proven and potential, moreover, is based upon the interrelation between theory and praxis. Since ideas guide practice and structure forms of life, their success becomes a warrant for their validity.[168]

Foundational theology, therefore, has the task not only of hermeneutically reconstructing the religious beliefs and claims of its tradition but also of inquiring into the retroductive warrants for their validity. It does not suffice to point to the coherence between a religious belief and contemporary experience as a warrant because religious beliefs often conflict with experience. The illuminative power of a religious belief often consists not so much in its coherence with experience as in its transformative character to challenge such experience. Likewise, the conflict between experience and religious belief often challenges the religious belief itself. Moreover, beliefs are not only illuminative but also dispositional in that they entail a praxis.[169] This praxis is a critical criterion that either provides a warrant for religious belief and challenges the particular contemporary experience or it challenges the religious belief itself.

Foundational theology faces the problem of the hermeneutical circle when it appeals to retroductive warrants. The illuminative power and the transformative praxis of religious beliefs does indeed provide retroductive warrants that corroborate such beliefs. Yet it is never unambiguously clear as to what constitutes the illuminative and transformative. The religious tradition itself influences judgments and provides criteria according to which beliefs are judged as illuminative or transformative. Nonreligious traditions and attitudes likewise provide such criteria and judgments.

Nevertheless, religious beliefs are subject to retroductive warrants in a manner analogous to other theories, insofar as a belief's ability to illumine experience and to guide praxis has in fact some independence from the belief's traditional coherence. Religious as well as cultural traditions often lose their creative potential and fail to meet new challenges. The ability of a religious heritage to be linked with present experience and praxis, even in critical confrontation, is not given as a constant or as an a priori factor, but only as retroductive warrant. Discrepancies emerge, cognitive dissonances develop, moral inconsistencies become apparent, so that a gap between a tradition and its praxis become manifest. Since the hermeneutical retrieval of a tradition entails the retrieval of meaning and truth conditions, the ability of a hermeneutical retrieval to illumine and to guide praxis provides a warrant for the tradition.

Therefore, although foundational theology is caught within the hermeneutical circle, and although it must concede that every foundational criterion is in part determined by cultural and religious traditions, it can appeal to retroductive warrants as having a limited but significant independence. Religious beliefs illumine experience and affect praxis so that it becomes possible to look at the points of successful intersection between the beliefs and present experience and praxis in order to make retroductive inferences. Currently, the issue of retroductive warrants has become central to the discussions about liberation theology and the conflicting roles of hermeneutical retrieval and ideology-criticism.[170] On the one hand religious and cultural traditions, even their highest ideals, are often ideologically distorted and in need of critique. Yet on the other the question emerges as to the source of the standards and criteria for the critique of the tradition. From experience? But experience is itself often distorted and determined by tradition. From tradition? But the tradition is what is in need of critique.

This dilemma can be dealt with in two ways. Liberation theology generally argues that the oppressed have a hermeneutical privilege so that the experience of the oppressed is the starting-point of theological reflection and critique.[171] This advocacy of the hermeneutical privilege of the oppressed represents a theological appropriation of Marxist class analysis and its attribution of truth to the insights and praxis of a particular class, for example, the proletariat's experience enables it to criticize the ideology of the ruling classes. But this solution does not take sufficiently into account the criticisms of Marxist class analysis that have been developed even by neo-Marxists (from Bloch to Habermas). In addition, the experience of oppression is not only an immediate experience but also results from the conflict between cultural values and present experience. This conflict intensifies the experience of oppression so that without this conflict specific situations might not be experienced as oppressive or alienating. Consequently, a more moderate and modified approach would acknowledge that by opting for the oppressed one gains an insight into ideological distortions of the dominant culture. But it would at the same time appeal to the tradition to uncover those values in conflict with contemporary ideologies, and it would recognize that truth cannot be localized within one class, but must be seen in relation to a plurality of subjects and traditions.

The other approach to the dilemma of hermeneutical circularity is to appeal to the possibility of the universalization of a consensus through public discourse. Within the Enlightenment tradition and its emphasis upon public discourse, Jürgen Habermas has underscored the significance of ideal situations of communication, free of domination and open to individual needs, as conditions for arriving at the truth.[172] This approach points to the "counterfactual" ideal of open discourse, but overlooks the necessity of retrieving the traditions and examining the values present in those traditions that might challenge implicit distortions of the public realm.

The inadequacies of both of these approaches underscore the significance of reflective equilibrium. There does not exist a fulcrum independent of a society's cultural tradition and experience that can provide a firm foundation, as our critique of foundationalism has already noted. The appeal to contemporary experience as a source of criticism of ideologies overlooks that only through a process of mutual adjustment and reflective equilibrium can one approach the truth. The starting-point of foundational theology is therefore the hermeneutical reconstruction of the tradition that raises to the forefront the meaning and truth claims of the tradition. This hermeneutical reconstruction seeks to show that what it elaborates as the concrete ideals and paradigmatic praxis of the tradition can serve to confront contemporary experience and to guide praxis. Its ability to do so provides a retroductive warrant for its veracity. Nevertheless, such an inference is similar to practical and prudential judgments[173] insofar as it is not based on the manifest evidence of one criterion or foundation, but rather on a multiplicity of diverse factors that must be continually reevaluated and reinterpreted. In addition to the reconstruction of the tradition and the retroductive warrants from present experience and praxis, background theories also come into play as the third element of the reflective equilibrium.

Background Theories

"Background theories" within foundational theology can be compared to the use in contemporary philosophy of "auxiliary statements or hypotheses" for the application and assessment of theories.[174] The expression "auxiliary hypotheses" was originally used by Henri Poincaré, the French mathematician and physicist, to describe how the application of geometry to experience necessarily involves hypotheses about physical phenomena.[175] When physical geometry is not in agreement with observation, then an agreement is attained either by different axioms or by modifying the relevant auxiliary hypotheses. The notion of background theory has been expanded within contemporary philosophy of science to explain the development and application of theories. The auxiliary hypothesis mediates between a theory and an experimental situation since it concerns procedures applying the theory to the phenomena. When a coherence between theory and phenomena is not attained, it often results either in a revision of the theory or in a revision of the auxiliary hypothesis.

For example, an astronomer makes photographic observations of stars through a telescope.[176] The results are interpreted evidence because the astronomer has recourse to background theories, for example, theories about photographic processes, the nature of telescopes and their receptive abilities, the correlations between degrees of exposure and the distance to the stars or the size of the stars. If the resulting interpreted evidence conflicts with astrophysical theories, then either the theories are revised or the background theories are revised. Another example: the application of ethical theories involves not only considered moral judgments and moral principles but also relevant background notions about human nature or human society.

Conflicts can lead to a revision of moral principles or judgments or to a revision of the relevant background theories.[177]

The specific issues of foundational theology, which we have previously analyzed, entail several relevant background theories, only some of which were analyzed in detail. Jesus' resurrection was related to the nature of historical testimony, to the interrelation between literary form and content, and to narrative history and identity; the foundation of the Church was related to theories on the relation between intentionality and action, and the nature of reception; the mission of the Church was related to theories about the relation between societal evolution and social forms of welfare assistance.

Such background theories indicate that the relation between religious faith and contemporary experience entails not simply coherence with experience or correspondence to data, but instead involves the analysis of background theories by which data and experience are interpreted and interrelated with creedal statements. Background theories have therefore an important function in relation to religious beliefs. They often provide either constraints or indirect supports to the religious tradition. Of themselves, they do not validate the religious tradition. Nevertheless, when a conflict between a religious belief and contemporary experience takes place not only may the religious belief or the contemporary experience be challenged and modified but so also may be the background theory.

The task of foundational theology is therefore to seek a reflective equilibrium among several elements: the hermeneutical reconstruction of the religious tradition that seeks to display the identity, intelligibility, and truth of the tradition, especially in its disclosure of the ideal potential of the tradition; the retroductive warrants that intersect and flow from the cognitive, normative, and expressive claims of the tradition; and the background theories by which the tradition is related to the phenomena of history and experience.

NOTES

1. See the diverse conceptions reflected in the various essays collected by René Latourelle and Gerald O'Collins, *Problems and Perspectives of Fundamental Theology* (New Jersey: Paulist, 1982).

2. Ferdinand Hahn, "Exegese und Fundamentaltheologie," *ThQ* 155 (1975) 262–80.

3. Tharcisse Tshibangu, *Théologie positive et théologie spéculative* (Louvain: Publications Université de Louvain, 1965), pp. 140–301.

4. *Oxford Dictionary of English Etymology*, ed. C. T. Onions (New York: Oxford Univ. Press, 1966), p. 699. In Latin antiquity, positive referred to the first degree of an

adjective in contrast to the comparative and superlative forms. Abelard testifies to the distinction in use among twelfth-century canonists between natural and positive law. In the sense that positive expresses the antithesis of nature and law, it seems to indicate the distinction between human and divine law. See Stephen Kuttner, "Sur les origines du terme 'Droit positif,'" in *Revue historique de droit français et étranger* 15 (1936) 728–39.

5. See Robert Guelluy, "L'évolution des méthods théologiques a Louvain d'E-rasme a Jansenius," *RHE* 37 (1941) 31–144, esp. pp. 117–44.

6. Tshibangu, *Théologie positive,* pp. 246–50.

7. *Quodlibet* IV.

8. A. Stolz, "Positive und spekulative Theologie," *Divus Thomas* (Freibourg) 12 (1934) 327–43.

9. L. Willaert, *La Restauration catholique* (Fliche et Martin 18; Paris: Beauchesne, 1960), pp. 246ff.

10. Full title is *Apparatus ad positivam Theologiam methodicus, in quo jam reviso, multumque ditato, clara, brevis et expedita delineatur idea positivae et scholasticae Theologiae, Scriptura sacrae,* 2 vols. (Paris, 1770, 1705; from 9th ed. [Venice: Typographia Balleo-niana, 1766]; first Venice edition was in 1717). For a discussion of Pierre Annat, see Heinrich Stirnimann " 'Fundamentaltheologie' im frühen 18. Jahrhundert?" *FZPhTh* 24 (1977) 460–76. See also Michael Hofmann, *Theologie, Dogma und Dogmenentwicklung im theologischen Werk Denis Petaus* (Bern: Herbert Lang, 1976), pp. 468–70.

11. "Unde positiva [theologia] fundamentalis Theologia a nonnullis vulgo voca-tur, et merito" (*Apparatus,* vol. 1, art. 2, p. 2).

12. Ibid., p. 5; see also p. 2.

13. Published in 1563. Pages 1–415 of *De locis* were republished in the eighteenth century under the title *Melchioris Cani opera* (Padua: Edition Sherry, 1742).

14. Petau's *Theologicorum dogmatum* (Paris, 1644) was reprinted in 1700 under the title *Opus de theologicis dogmatibus* (Amsterdam). The latest complete edition was in 8 volumes by J. B. Thomas (Bar-le-Duc, 1864–70). In the Roman School, C. Passaglia and C. Schrader edited and published vol. 1 (Rome, 1857).

15. Petau, *De la pénitence publique et de la prépraparation a la communion* (Paris, 1644; 3rd ed. 1645), II, VII, 2.

16. In connection with his explication of the concept of the substance of dogma, Petau develops the idea of the hierarchy of truth; see Hofmann, *Theologie, Dogma,* pp. 141–58.

17. For a discussion of Cano's theological methodology and his emphasis upon authority, see Elmar Klinger, *Ekklesiologie der Neuzeit. Grundlegung bei Melchior Cano und Entwicklung bis zum Zweiten Vatikanischen Konzil* (Freiburg: Herder, 1976).

18. Anvers, 1579/80.

19. Bordeaux, 1594. Charron's three truths represent: the existence of God against the atheists, the truth of Christianity against Muslims and Jews, and of the Roman Catholic Church against the Huguenots.

20. See the French translation in Migne, vol. 2 (Paris, 1843), cols. 993–1122.

21. *Grotti epistolae quotquot reperiri potuerunt* (Amsterdam, 1687), p. 760; quoted in Aug. Langhorst, "Zur Entwicklungsgeschichte der Apologetik: VI. Das Zeitalter des Deismus," *Stimmen aus Maria Laach* 20 (1881–) 412–31.

22. Published anonymously (Rotterdam, 1684), pp. 152–230.

23. See Henri Bouillard, "De l'apologétique a la théologie fondamentale," *Dieu connu en Jésus Christ. Les Quatres Fleuves,* vol. 1 (Paris: Ed. du Seuil, 1973), pp. 57–70, here p. 60. See also Albert Monod, *De Pascal a Chateaubriand. Les défenseurs du christianisme de 1670–1802* (Paris: Felix Alcan, 1916), for the influence of Pascal.

24. For an analysis of the significance of Pierre Daniel Huet, see Franz-Josef Niemann, "Fundamentaltheologie im 17. Jahrhundert," *ZKTh* 103 (1981) 178–85.

25. René Descartes, *Discourse on Method* (Indianapolis: Bobbs-Merrill, 1950; originally published 1637).

26. Jürgen Mittelstrasse, *Neuzeit und Aufklärung. Studien zur Entstehung der neuzeitlichen Wissenschaft und Philosophie* (Berlin: de Gruyter, 1970), pp. 167–243.

27. *Cursus Theologiae polemicae universae* (Augsburg, 1713; 6th ed. 1719), p. 14.

28. Peter Eicher, *Offenbarung. Prinzip neuzeitlicher Theologie* (Munich: Kösel, 1977), pp. 89–91.

29. Subtitled *Précédée d'un discours historique et critique sur la méthode des principaux auteurs, qui ont écrit pour et contre le christianisme depuis son origine* (Paris, 1742).

30. Paris, 1754; 2nd augmented ed., 1774.

31. Dijon, 1771.

32. See n. 4 in Part I above.

33. The antideist polemic was central to Giovanni Perrone, *Praelectiones theologicae* (Rome, 1835). Vol. 1 was entitled: *De vera religione*. See the important analysis by Peter Walter, *Die Frage der Glaubensbegründung aus innerer Erfahrung auf dem 1. Vatikanum. Die Stellungnahme des Konzils vor dem Hintergrund der zeitgenössischen römischen Theologie* (Mainz: Matthias Grünewald, 1980), pp. 19–45. Bruno Franz Leopold Liebermann, *Institutiones theologicae* (Mainz, 1819).

34. See L. Maisonneuve, "L'Apologétique," *Dictionnaire apologétique de la foi catholique* (Paris: Letouzey, 1912), cols. 1511f. Ambroise A. Gardeil, *La crédibilité et l'apologétique* (Paris: Gabalda, 1928; 1st ed. 1912), pp. 206–7.

35. See Konrad Feiereis, *Die Umprägung der natürlichen Theologie in Religionsphilosophie* (Leipzig: St. Benno, 1965), pp. 205–12.

36. Vienna, 1766.

37. Gazzaniga's notion of extrinsic evidence has influenced the manual tradition as well as Vatican I; see Eicher, *Offenbarung,* pp. 98–150.

38. See C. G. Gethmann, "Fundamentalphilosophie," in *Historisches Wörterbuch der Philosophie,* vol. 2, cols. 1134–35, for the historical material. Gethmann develops his own suggestions in "Logische Propädeutik als Fundamentalphilosophie?" *Kant Studien* 60 (1969) 352–68.

39. See Richard Rorty, *Philosophy and the Mirror of Nature* (Princeton, N.J.: Princeton Univ. Press., 1979), pp. 131–64. But note the critical comments by Ian Hacking, "Is The End in Sight for Epistemology," *JP* 77 (1980) 579–88; and Jaegwon Kim, "Rorty on the Possibility of Philosophy," ibid., pp. 588–97; and Robert Schwartz's extended review, *JP* 80 (1983) 51–67.

40. Gethmann, "Fundamentalphilosophie," cols. 1134–35.

41. See Richard Rorty's criticism of the transcendental method, "Verificationsim and Transcendental Arguments," *Nous* 5 (1971) 3–13, and "Transcendental Arguments, Self-Reference, and Pragmatism," in Peter Bieri, ed., *Transcendental Arguments and Science* (Dordrecht: Reidel, 1979), pp. 77–104; and the response by Dieter Henrich, ibid., pp. 113–20.

42. The unsurpassed history of the period is still Karl Werner's *Geschichte der katholischen Theologie* (Hildesheim: Olms, 1966; reprint of 1866 ed.), pp. 342–642. As a student of Günther, his history represents a sympathetic perspective to the innovative developments by German theologians of a transcendental approach.

43. Johann Sebastian von Drey, *Apologetik,* 3 vols. (Frankfurt: Minerva, 1967; reprint of 1838–1847 ed.), esp. 1:24–78.

44. The complete title is *Leitfaden für Vorlesungen über die allgemeine Einleitung in die theologische Wissenschaft und die Theorie der Religion und Offenbarung als I. Teil der Fundamental-Theologie* (Prague, 1859), *Leitfaden für Vorlesungen über die Offenbarung Gottes als Tatsache der Geschichte. II. Teil der Fundamental-Theologie: Die Offenbarung Gottes in der Zeit vor Christus* (Prague 1860), and *Die Offenbarung Gottes in Jesus Christus und seiner Kirche* (Prague, 1862).

45. See Clemens Engling, *Die Bedeutung der Theologie für philosophische Theoriebildung und gesellschaftliche Praxis* (Göttingen: Vandenhoeck und Ruprecht, 1977), pp. 74–130.

46. Ibid., pp. 131–60.

47. See the historical survey by Franz Schnabel, *Deutsche Geschichte im neunzehnten Jahrhundert. Die katholische Kirche in Deutschland,* vol. 7 (Freiburg: Herder, 1965), pp. 101–27 and 305–36.

48. See Johann Baptist Metz on the cognitive and cultural isolation of the neoscholastic apologetic, in *Faith in History and Society: Toward a Practical Fundamental Theology* (New York: Crossroad, 1980), pp. 16–22.

49. For Vatican I and its background, see Hermann J. Pottmeyer, *Der Glaube vor dem Anspruch der Wissenschaft. Die Konstitution über den katholischen Glauben "Dei Filius" des 1. Vatikanischen Konzils* (Freiburg: Herder, 1968).

50. The best survey on the Catholic fundamental theology, especially of the non-neoscholastic approaches is Johannes Flury, *Um die Redlichkeit des Glaubens. Studien zur deutschen katholischen Fundamentaltheologie* (Fribourg: Universitätsverlag, 1979).

51. See Norbert Trippen, *Theologie und Lehramt im Konflikt. Die kirchlichen Massnahmen gegen den Modernisms im Jahre 1907 und ihre Ausirkungen in Deutschland* (Freiburg: Herder, 1977). For Rousselot, see Erhard Kunz, *Glaube, Gnade und Geschichte. Die Glaubenstheologie des P. Rousselot* (Frankfurt: Knecht, 1969).

52. The reaction to neo-orthodoxy has led to the revival of an interest in fundamental theology by several prominent German Lutheran theologians; see Gerhard Ebeling, "Erwägungen zu einer evangelischen Fundamentaltheologie," *ZThK* 67 (1970) 479–524; Horst Beintker, "Verstehen und Glauben. Grundlinien einer evangelischen Fundamentaltheologie," *KD* 22 (1976) 22–40; Wilfried Joest, *Fundamentaltheologie. Theologische Grundlagen- und Methodenprobleme* (Stuttgart: W. Kohlhammer, 1974). For the Catholic response to this tendency, see Heinrich Stirnimann, "Evangelische Fundamentaltheologie," *FZPhTh* 22 (1975) 375–83; Max Seckler, "Evangelische Fundamentaltheologie. Erwägungen zu einem Novum aus katholischer Sicht," *ThQ* 155 (1975) 281–99; and Peter Knauer, *Verantwortung des Glaubens. Ein Gespräch mit Gerhard Ebeling aus katholischer Sicht* (Frankfurt: Knecht, 1969).

53. Heinrich Fries, "Zum heutigen Stand der Fundamentaltheologie," *TThZ* 84 (1975) 351–63.

54. See my surveys of political and liberation theology in "Political Theology as a Foundational Theology," *Proceedings CTSA* 32 (1977) 142–77; "Political Theology: An Historical Analysis," *TD* 25 (1977) 317–34; and "Religion und Politik," in F. Franz Böckle et al., eds., *Christlicher Glaube in moderner Gesellschaft*, vol. 27 (Freiburg: Herder, 1982), pp. 59–101.

55. Two exceptions are the important methodological works of Matthew Lamb, *Solidarity with Victims: Toward a Theology of Social Transformation* (New York: Crossroad, 1982); and Helmut Peukert, *Wissenschaftstheorie–Handlungstheorie–Fundamental Theologie* (Frankfurt: Suhrkamp, 1978). Within liberation theology, significant fundamental theological considerations are raised by Juan L. Segundo, *The Liberation of Theology* (Maryknoll, N.Y.: Orbis, 1976). See also Alfred T. Hennelly, *Theologies in Conflict: The Challenge of Juan Luis Segundo* (Maryknoll, N.Y.: Orbis, 1979); and Brian Maher and Dale Richardson, eds., *The Challenge of Liberation Theology* (Maryknoll, N.Y.: Orbis, 1981).

56. David Tracy emphasizes the role of transcendental analysis in deciding questions of truth within fundamental theology, whereas hermeneutical retrieval is the primary task of systematic theology. See *Blessed Rage for Order* (New York: Seabury, 1975), pp. 52–56, and *The Analogical Imagination* (New York: Crossroad, 1981), pp. 64–69. For attempts at a fundamental theology as hermeneutical theology, see Peter Knauer, *Der Glaube kommt vom Hören. Ökumenische Fundamentaltheologie* (Graz: Styria, 1978); and Eugen Biser, *Glaubensverständnis. Grundriss einer hermeneutischen Fundamentaltheologie* (Freiburg: Herder, 1975).

57. For surveys of twentieth-century fundamental theology, see Josef Schmitz, "Die Fundamentaltheologie im 20. Jahrhundert," in Herbert Vorgrimler and Robert van der Gucht, eds., *Bilanz der Theologie im 20. Jahrhundert*, vol. 2 (Freiburg: Herder, 1969), pp. 197–245; Henri Bouillard, "La tâche actuelle de la théologie fondamentale," in Charles Kannengeisser, ed., *Le point théologique. Rechecheres actuelles*, vol. 2 (Paris: Beauchesne, 1972), pp. 7–49; Heinrich Stirnimann, "Erwägungen zur Fundamentaltheologie. Problematik, Grundfragen, Konzept," *FZPhTh* 24 (1977) 291–365; and Claude Geffré, "Recent Developments in Fundamental Theology," in his *A New Age in Theology* (New York: Paulist, 1974), pp. 11–30.

58. See the different proposals and suggestions by Adolf Kolping, "Fundamentaltheologie im heutigen Hochschulunterricht, Situation und Vorschläge," *ThGl* 54 (1964) 115–26, and "Zehn Jahre einer neuen Fundamentaltheologie. Gundsätzliche Erwägungen zur Anlage eines fundamentaltheologischen Lehrbuches," *MThZ* 15 (1964) 62–69. For chronicles of the last twenty years of research, see Jean-Pierre Torrell, "Chronique de théologie fondamentale," *Rev Thom* 64 (1964) 97–127; 66 (1966) 63–107, 239–76; 67 (1967) 439–65; 69 (1969) 61–92; 71 (1971) 61–98; 75 (1975) 599–624; 76 (1976) 97–125; 78 (1978) 430–63; 79 (1979) 273–314; 81 (1981) 447–76; and 82 (1982) 357–91.

59. For a different division of directions within contemporary fundamental theology, see G. Ruggieri, "Teologia fondamentale," in *Nuovo Dizionario di Teologia* (Rome, 1979), pp. 1754–67; also Harald Wagner, *Einführung in die Fundamentaltheologie* (Darmstadt: Wissenschaftliche Buchgesellschaft, 1981), p. 49, who distinguishes the neoscholastic, immanence, political, and correlation models of fundamental theology.

60. The distinction between a foundation of faith and a foundation of theology is generally overlooked within classical fundamental theology. One exception is Gardeil, *La crédibilité*, pp. 243–60. See also the perceptive interpretation of the significance of Gardeil's conception of apologetics and fundamental theology by Rudolf Michael Schmitz, " 'Apologetische Theologie—Ein Aktueller Begriff?' Eine Untersuchung zur Fundamentaltheologie bei P. Ambroise Gardeil OP," *Divinitas* 25 (1980) 218–309.

61. See Wagner, *Einführung*, pp. 17–27, for a description of the structure of classic fundamental theology.

62. Maisonneuve refers to a "general apologetics" ("L'Apologétique"; see n. 34 above).

63. *Apologetik*, 1:17–19.

64. See the historical survey in chapter 9. The basic truths were much more doctrinal in content in the earlier stages of fundamental theology. Later the "formal authority" of certain beliefs becomes the foundational truth.

65. Gardeil considers comprehensiveness and scientific character as the two basic characteristics (*La crédibilité*, pp. 206–9).

66. Flury, *Um die Redlichkeit*, pp. 58–60. Adolf Kolping suggests that the division was based on the differences of various school traditions (*Fundamentaltheologie*, vol. 1 [Münster: Regensberg, 1968], p. 71).

67. *La crédibilité*, pp. 249–51.

68. This characteristic stems from the development of fundamental theology out of a philosophy of religion.

69. Bouillard, in "De l'apologétique" and "La tache actuelle," argues that today the situation has changed because not only revelation but the very existence of God has been questioned. Therefore, he suggests that fundamental theology go back to the question of God. The significance of the God question for fundamental theology had been underscored previously by Hermann Schell and Adolf Kolping even though their fundamental theologies followed the tripartite division with its emphasis upon Christian revelation. See Hermann Schell, *Religion und Offenbarung* (Paderborn, 1901; reprint Frankfurt: Minerva, 1967). Adolf Kolping's *Fundamentaltheologie* emphasized the distinctiveness of the Christian conception of God.

70. The independence of fundamental theology from systematic theology, with the concomitant extrinsic rather than intrinsic relation between the two, has led to the major criticisms of traditional fundamental theology in Rahner's formal fundamental theology. Ebeling makes the successful attempt to overcome such extrinsicism insofar as he places fundamental theology not at the beginning of the theological encyclopia (outline of studies) but rather at the end. See Gerhard Ebeling, *The Study of Theology* (Philadelphia: Fortress, 1978), pp. 153–65.

71. See Franz Hettinger, *Lehrbuch der Fundamentaltheologie oder Apologetic* (Freiburg: Herder, 1913), pp. 1–18; and Gerhard Van Noort, *The True Religion* (Westminster, Md., Newman, 1957), pp. xvii–lviii, for two traditional methodological divisions between fundamental theology, on the one side, and systematic theology, on the other.

72. Stephen Toulmin, *The Uses of Argument* (Cambridge: Cambridge Univ. Press,

1958), pp. 11–43. For further precisions, see his *Human Understanding* (Princeton, N.J.: Princeton Univ. Press, 1972), pp. 145–99 and 364–477; and the distinction between "interfield" and "intrafield" in Stephen Toulmin, Richard Rieke, and Allan Janik, *An Introduction to Reasoning* (New York: Macmillan, 1979), pp. 195–327.

73. See Gardeil's lament that in fact this difference was often overlooked (*La crédibilité*, pp. 214–44).

74. See the historical survey in the preceding chapter.

75. The use of social factors to differentiate fundamental and systematic theology entails in the last resort differences of method and of criteria of truth.

76. See Alvin I. Goldman, "What Is a Justified Belief?" in George S. Pappas, ed., *Justification and Knowledge* (Dordrecht: Reidel, 1979), pp. 1–23, esp. 14–18.

77. Albert Lang, *Fundamentaltheologie* (Munich: Max Hueber, 1962), pp. 8–41; Van Noort, *The True Religion*, pp. xviii–xxviii; Michaele Nicolau and Joachim Salaverri, *Theologia Fundamentalis*, vol. 1 of *Sacrae Theologiae Summa* (Madrid: BAC, 1958), p. 15–50.

78. David Tracy's appeal to the "Christian fact" in his conception of fundamental theology seeks to preserve and to retrieve the public intent of classical fundamental theology; see his "The Task of Fundamental Theology," *JR* 54 (1974) 13–34, esp. thesis 4, and its modification in *Blessed Rage*, p. 49; also William M. Shea, "The Stance and Task of the Foundational Theologian: Critical or Dogmatic?" *HeyJ* 17 (1976) 273–92.

79. See the development of the notion of credibility by Gardeil's student, Reginald Garrigou-Lagrange, *De revelatione* (Rome: F. Ferrari, 1950), 1:401–519 and 2:1–124.

80. Van Noort, *The True Religion*, p. 63.

81. Alan White, *Truth* (Garden City, N.Y.: Doubleday, 1970), p. 128, see also pp. 3–40.

82. *On the Truth of the Catholic Faith* (Garden City, N.Y.: Doubleday, 1955), I, 59. The translator and editor Anton Pegis suggests that the usual attribution of this definition to Isaac ben Israeli is incorrect. It should be attributed to William of Auvergne.

83. See George Pitcher, "Introduction," in the collection *Truth* (Englewood Cliffs, N.J.: Prentice-Hall, 1964), pp. 1–15, for a critique of the correspondence theory of truth. See also L. Bruno Puntel, *Wahrheitstheorien in der neueren Philosophie* (Darmstadt: Wissenschaftliche Buchgesellschaft, 1978), pp. 26–40.

84. See Donald Davidson, "True to the Facts," *JP* 66 (1969) 748–64; and Michael Dummett, *Truth and Other Enigmas* (Cambridge: Harvard Univ. Press, 1978), pp. 1–25.

85. *Being and Time* (New York: Harper and Row, 1962), sec. 44, and *The Basic Problems of Phenomenology* (Bloomington, Indiana Univ Press. 1982), no. 18.

86. "Wahrheitstheorien," in *Wirklichkeit und Reflexion. W. Schulz zum 60. Geburtstag*, ed. Hans Fahrenbach (Pfullingen: Neske, 1973), pp. 211–65.

87. Wolfhart Pannenberg, *Theology and the Philosophy of Science* (Philadelphia: Westminster, 1976), pp. 156–224.

88. See Julian N. Hartt, *Theological Method and Imagination* (New York: Seabury, 1977), pp. 45–83.

89. *La crédibilité*, pp. 343–360.

90. Bernard Lonergan, *Method in Theology* (New York: Herder, 1972), pp. 235–94.

91. David Tracy, "Lonergan's Foundational Theology: an Interpretation and a Critique," and Langdon Gilkey, "Empirical Science and Theological Knowing," in Philip McShane, *Foundations of Theology* (London: Gill and Macmillan, 1971), pp. 76–101 and 197–22. See Lonergan's response, pp. 223–34, for his emphasis on the critical nature of dialectics. In *Method*, p. 130, he notes: "By dialectic, then, is understood a generalized apologetic."

92. Ragner Holte, *Die Vermittlungstheologie* (Uppsala: Almqvist & Wiksell, 1965).

93. See the essays by Küng, Tracy, Dulles, and Schillebeeckx, in Leonard Swidler, ed., *Consensus in Theology? A Dialogue with Hans Küng and Edward Schillebeeckx* (Philadelphia: Westminster, 1980); Schubert M. Ogden, "The Task of Philosophical Theology," in *The Future of Philosophical Theology* (Philadelphia: Westminster, 1971), pp. 55–84, and "What Is Theology," *JR* 52 (1972) 22–40; Langdon Gilkey, *Reaping the Whirlwind: A*

Christian Interpretation of History (New York: Seabury, 1976), pp. 117–33; and for a comprehensive analysis of Tillich, see John P. Clayton, *The Concept of Correlation* (New York: de Gruyter, 1980).

94. *New Birth of Freedom* (Philadelphia: Fortress, 1976), pp. 114–21.

95. Among the many writings of Paul Ricoeur, see the two introductions to *Freedom and Nature: The Voluntary and the Involuntary* (Evanston, Ill.: Northwestern Univ. Press, 1966), pp. xi–xxxviii (translator's introduction by Erazim V. Kohak) and pp. 3–34 (by Ricoeur). See also John W. Van Den Hengel, *The Home of Meaning: The Hermeneutics of the Subject of Paul Ricoeur* (Washington, D.C.: Univ. Press of America, 1982). For the outline of Schleiermacher, see my introduction to his *On the Glaubenslehre* (Chico, Calif.: Scholars, 1981), pp. 1–32.

96. Karl Rahner offers concise descriptions of his method in "Formal and Fundamental Theology" and "Transcendental Theology," in *Encyclopedia of Theology*, ed. Karl Rahner (New York: Seabury, 1975), pp. 524–35 and 1748–51. See also his *Foundations of Christian Faith* (New York: Seabury, 1978), pp. 1–23.

97. For critical analyses of Rahner's method of correlation, see Elmar Mitterstieler, *Christlicher Glaube als Bestätigung des Menschen* (Frankfurt: Knecht, 1975); and Karl Neumann, *Der Praxisbezug der Theologie bei Karl Rahner* (Freiburg: Herder, 1979).

98. Rahner's distinction between a first and second level of reflection also expresses the de-emphasis upon historical and scientific rationality in his formal fundamental theology. Under the influence of Heidegger's critique of scientific rationality, Rahner's conception of fundamental theology contrasts with traditional fundamental theology precisely in regard to the "scientific" nature of its method.

99. See the references in n. 85 above. The centrality of Heidegger's notion of truth in his divergence from Husserl has been examined by Ernst Tugendhat, *Der Wahrheitsbegriff bei Husserl and Heidegger* (Berlin: de Gruyter, 1967).

100. *Blessed Rage for Order*, pp. 3–87,

101. *Analogical Imagination*, p. 172

102. Ibid, pp. 3–46.

103. Rorty, "Transcendental Arguments," pp. 77–104 (cited in n. 41 above).

104. The literature on foundationalism is enormous. Especially helpful are: William P. Alston, "Two Types of Foundationalism," *JP* 73 (1976) 165–85; Ernest Sosa, "The Foundations of Foundationalism," *Nous* 14 (1980) 547–64; id., "The Raft and the Pyramid: Coherence versus Foundations in the Theory of Knowledge," *Midwest Studies in Philosophy* 5 (1980) 3–25; and the two collected volumes of essays, George Pappas and Marshall Swain, eds., *Essays on Knowledge and Justification* (Ithaca: Cornell, 1978), and George Pappas, ed., *Justification and Knowledge: New Studies in Epistemology* (Dordrecht: D. Reidel, 1979).

105. See the two essays by Sosa listed in the previous note.

106. See the recent and influential book by Richard Rorty, *Philosophy and the Mirror of Nature* (Princeton, N.J.: Princeton Univ. Press, 1979).

107. Pierre Duhem, *The Aim and Structure of Physical Theory* (New York: Athenaeum, 1962). Among the many works of Willard van Omran Quine, see *From a Logical Point of View* (Cambridge: Harvard Univ. Press, 1953) and *Word and Object* (Cambridge: MIT Press, 1960). See also George D. Romanos, *Quine and Analytic Philosophy* (Cambridge: MIT Press, 1983), esp. 77–106.

108. The by now almost classic essay criticizing the "Myth of the Given" is Sellars's "Empricism and the Philosophy of the Mind," in his *Science, Perception, and Reality* (New York: Humanities, 1963), pp. 127–96.

109. Ibid., p. 170.

110. Michael Devitt, "Dummett's Anti-realism," *JP* 80 (1983) 73–99, here p. 93.

111. See Keith Lehrer, *Knowledge* (Oxford: Clarendon, 1974), p. 214. For a defense of foundationalism, see Roderick M. Chisholm, *The Foundations of Knowing* (Minneapolis: Univ. of Minnesota Press, 1982), esp. 3–85.

112. See Peter L. Berger and Thomas Luckmann, *The Social Construction of Reality*

(Garden City, N.Y.: Doubleday, 1966), pp. 92–189; and Peter L. Berger, *The Sacred Canopy* (Garden City, N.Y.: Doubleday, 1967).

113. For a survey on current theories of justification, see Robert K. Shope, *The Analysis of Knowing: A Decade of Research* (Princeton, N.J. Princeton Univ. Press, 1983).

114. "Protokollsätze," *Erkenntnis* 3 (1932/33) 204–14.

115. Sosa, "Raft and the Pyramid," pp. 3–25. For a fascinating study of the metaphor of ship and raft, see Hans Blumenberg, *Schiffbruch mit Zuschauer. Paradigma einer Daseinsmetapher* (Frankfurt: Suhrkamp, 1979), pp. 70–75.

116. See Richard Rorty, *Consequences of Pragmatism* (Minneapolis: Univ. of Minnesota Press, 1982), pp. xii–xlvii.

117. David Tracy, *Analogical Imagination*, pp. 47–153.

118. *Philosophical Investigations* (New York: Macmillan, 1958).

119. See Wilhelm Dilthey, *Der Aufbau der geschichtlichen Welt in den Geisteswissenschaften* (GS VII; Göttingen: Vandenhoeck und Ruprecht, 1965).

120. This point is at the center of the debate between the hermeneutical standpoint (Gadamer) and the critique of ideology (Habermas). See the instructive survey but from the hermeneutical standpoint by Paul Riceour, "Hermeneutics and the Critique of Ideology," in his *Hermeneutics and the Human Sciences*, ed. John B. Thompson (New York: Cambridge Univ. Press, 1981), pp. 63–100.

121. Thomas Kuhn, *The Structure of Scientific Revolutions* (Cambridge: Harvard Univ. Press, 1957) and *The Essential Tension* (Chicago: Univ. of Chicago Press, 1977); Paul Feyerabend, *Against Method* (London: NLB, 1975) and *Science in a Free Society* (London: NLB, 1978); Stephen Toulmin, *Human Understanding* (Princeton N.J.: Princeton Univ. Press, 1972).

122. See Norman Malcolm, "The Groundlessness of Belief," in Stuart Brown, ed., *Reason and Religion* (Ithaca, N.Y.: Cornell Univ. Press 1977); and Roger Trigg, *Reason and Commitment* (New York: Cambridge Univ. Press 1973).

123. Gary Gutting, *Religious Belief and Religious Skepticism* (Notre Dame: Univ. of Notre Dame Press, 1982), pp. 114–40.

124. Mary Hesse, "In Defence of Objectivity," in *Proceedings of the Aristotelian Society* (1973), p. 9. See also her "Science and Objectivity," in John B. Thompson and David Held, eds., *Habermas: Critical Debates* (Cambridge: MIT Press, 1982), pp. 98–115.

125. The significance of the double hermeneutic applies to theology not in isolation but as a human science. Its value for understanding social action has been demonstrated by Jürgen Habermas, *Theorie des kommunikativen Handelns*, 2 vols. (Frankfurt: Suhrkamp, 1981).

126. The emphasis upon speech acts, competence, and the pragmatics of language within linguistic theory runs counter to the emphasis within hermeneutic theory of the ideal autonomy of the text. In Jürgen Habermas's development of a theory of communicative action, the insights of linguistics, hermeneutical theory, and Marxist philosophy are combined in a more general synthesis.

127. Ludwig Wittgenstein, *Tractatus*, 4.024; Donald Davidson, "Truth and Meaning," in *Philosophical Logic*, ed. J. W. Davis (Holland: Dordrecht, 1969), p. 7; W. V. Quine, "Mind and Verbal Dispositions," in Samuel Guttenplan, ed. *Mind and Language* (Oxford: Clarendon, 1975), p. 88.

128. Peter F. Strawson, "Meaning and Truth," in Ted Honderich and Myles Burnyeat, eds., *Philosophy As It Is* (New York: Penguin, 1979), p. 538.

129. For the notion of truth conditions as conditions of assertibility, see the important work of Michael Dummett: *Truth and Other Enigmas* (Cambridge: Harvard Univ. Press, 1978); "What Is a Theory of Meaning?" in Guttenplan, *Mind and Language*, pp. 97–138; and "What Is a Theory of Meaning? (II)," in Gareth Evans and John McDowell, eds., *Truth and Meaning: Essays in Semantics* (Oxford: Clarendon, 1976), pp. 67–137.

130. Strawson, "Meaning and Truth, pp. 519–40.

131. Dummett, *Truth*, p. 7; see the postscript (pp. 19–21) where it is noted that the notion of truth is much more complex than winning a game, for it includes the linguistic activity of making assertions.

132. See Jürgen Habermas, "What Is Universal Pragmatics," in his *Communication and the Evolution of Society* (Boston: Beacon, 1979, pp. 1–68.

133. See the representative selections and the bibliography in John R. Searle, ed., *The Philosophy of Language* (London: Oxford Univ. Press, 1971), as well as his own work: *Speech Acts, Expression and Meaning,* and *Intentionality* (New York: Cambridge Univ. Press, 1969, 1979, and 1983 respectively).

134. For a critical analysis of this division, see John B. Thompson, "Universal Pragmatics," in Thompson and Held, *Habermas,* pp. 116–33.

135. See Habermas, "Wahrheitstheorien" (cited in n. 86 above).

136. See Habermas's development of the notion of life-world and his discussion of Durkheim and Mead in *Theorie,* 2:7–294.

137. For a summary statement, see Paul Ricoeur, *Interpretation Theory* (Fort Worth: Texas Christian Univ. Press, 1976).

138. Hans-Georg Gadamer, *Truth and Method* (New York: Seabury, 1975), pp. 253–58.

139. See Habermas's critique of Gadamer in its most recent formulation, in *Theorie,* 1:188–96.

140. See L. Bruno Puntel, *Wahrheitstheorien in der neueren Philosophie* (cited in n. 83 above); and Mark de Bretton Platts, *Ways of Meaning* (Boston: Routledge and Kegan Paul, 1979).

141. Trans. Richard Hope (Ann Arbor: Univ. of Michigan Press, 1960), 980b.

142. Ibid., 981a.

143. For the comparison between Locke and Aristotle as well as the history of the reception of Aristotle in modern philosophy, see Friedrich Kambartel, *Erfahrung und Struktur. Bausteine zu einer Kritik des Empirismus und Formalismus* (Frankfurt: Suhrkamp, 1968), pp. 50–86.

144. John Locke, *An Essay Concerning Human Understanding* (Oxford: Clarendon, 1975; critical edition of 1689 text), bk. 2, chap. 1 on ideas and chap. 9 on perception.

145. Immanuel Kant, *Critique of Pure Reason,* B172–B174.

146. See Kambartel, *Erfahrung,* pp. 199–221 and 249–52; and Stanley Cavell, *The Claim of Reason* (Oxford: Oxford Univ. Press, 1979), pp. 3–125, on the relation between criteria and judgment. A classic collection of essays on the renewal of practical reasoning is Manfred Riedel's *Rehabilitierung der praktischen Philosophie* (Freiburg: Herder, 1974).

147. Martin Heidegger, *Being and Time,* secs. 42–44, and *The Basic Problems of Phenomenology,* secs. 15 and 18. See Karl Rahner's modification of Heidegger in *Spirit in the World* (New York: Herder and Herder, 1968).

148. Gadamer, *Truth and Method,* pp. 235–344.

149. See Schubert M. Ogden, "The Task of Philosophical Theology" (cited in n. 93 above); also Tracy, *Blessed Rage,* pp. 43–63.

150. For the distinction between critical and reconstructive, see Fiorenza, "Political Theology as Foundational Theology," pp. 174–77, where its use in political theology is illustrated. John Passmore ("Rational Reconstruction," in Paul Edwards, ed., *The Encyclopedia of Philosophie,* vol. 6 [New York: Macmillan, 1967], pp. 224–25) describes a reconstructive approach as a middle ground between a merely descriptive and a merely normative or prescriptive approach. For a discussion and analysis of Habermas's use of reconstruction as the characterization of his later method, see Thomas McCarthy, *The Critical Theory of Jürgen Habermas* (Cambridge: MIT Press, 1978), pp. 276–79 and 355–56.

151. See Robert Paul Wolff, *The Autonomy of Reason: A Commentary on Kant's Groundwork of the Metaphysics of Morals* (New York: Harper and Row, 1973), pp. 52–55.

152. See the essays of Norman Daniels: "Wide Reflective Equilibrium and Theory of Acceptance in Ethics," *JP* 76 (1979) 256–82; "Reflective Equilibrium and Archimedean Points," *Canadian Journal of Philosophy* 10 (March 1980) 83–103; and "Moral Theory and the Plasticity of Persons," *Monist* 62 (1979) 265–87. See also Peter Singer, "Sidgwick and Reflective Equilibrium," *Monist* 58 (1974) 490–517; Kai Nielson, "Our Considered Judgments," *Ratio* 19 (1979), and "Grounding Rights and a Method of

Reflective Equilibrium," *Inquiry* 25 (1982); and Joseph Raz, "The Claims of Reflective Equilibrium," *Inquiry* 25 (1982).

153. Norman Daniels argues that wide reflective equilibrium overcomes the objections against narrow equilibrium. In addition to the references in the previous note, see his "On Some Methods of Ethics and Linguistics," *Philosophical Studies* 37 (1980) 21–36.

154. See John Rawls, *A Theory of Justice* (Harvard: Cambridge Univ. Press, 1971), pp. 46–53. The advocacy of a wide in distinction to a narrow equilibrium comes to the fore in Rawls's later essays: "The Independence of Moral Theory," *Proceedings and Addresses of the American Philosophical Association* 48 (1974/75) 5–22, and "Kantian Constructivism in Moral Theory: Rational and Full Autonomy," *JP* 77 (1980) 515–72.

155. See the excellent comparison between Rawls's methodology and scientific method by Cornelius F. Delaney, "Rawls on Method," *Canadian Journal of Philosophy* 3 (1977) 153–161. He argues that Rawls's methodological position has increasingly become aware of the philosophical critique of foundationalism and has taken over the methodological work of Nelson Goodman, W. V. Quine, and Morton White. Cf. *A Theory of Justice* with Rawls's earlier "Outline of a Decision Procedure for Ethics," *PhRev* 60 (1951) 177–97. For a defense of the method against charges of intuitionism, see Ronald Dworkin's analysis of reflective equilibrium in "The Original Position" and "Non-Neutral Principles," in Norman Daniels, ed., *Reading Rawls* (New York: Basic, 1974), pp. 16–52 and 124–140.

156. Israel Scheffler, "On Justification and Commitment," *JP* 51 (1954) 180–91, here p. 189. See also Nelson Goodman, "Sense and Certainty," *PhRev* 61 (1952) 160–67, and his *Fact, Fiction, and Forecast* (Indianapolis, Bobbs-Merrill, 1973, 3rd ed.), pp. 59–83.

157. M. B. E. Smith, "Rawls and Intuitionism," *Canadian Journal of Philosophy* 3 (1977) 163–78. See Jürgen Habermas's critique of the method in Willi Oelmüller, ed., *Transzendentalphilosophische Normenbegründungen* (Paderborn: Schöningh, 1978), pp. 123–59; also Fred R. Dallmayr, "Toward a Critical Reconstruction of Ethics and Politics," *Journal of Politics* 36 (1974) 926–57; and Steven Lukes, "Relativism: Cognitive and Moral," *Aristotelian Society Suppl.* 68 (1974) 165–89, esp. pp. 182ff.

158. The method of correlation also presupposes an interchangeability between concepts and content. See the critique of Tillich by John P. Clayton, "Was ist falsch in der Korrelationstheologie," *Neue Zeitschrift für systematischen Theologie* 16 (1974) 93–111.

159. Still posing a challenge to systematic theology are the historical problems raised by Walter Bauer's *Orthodoxy and Heresy in Earliest Christianity* (Philadelphia: Fortress, 1971).

160. See Ernst Troeltsch, "What Does 'Essense of Christianity' Mean?" in *Ernst Troeltsch: Writings on Theology and Religion*, ed. Robert Morgan and Michael Pye (Atlanta: John Knox, 1977), pp. 124–81.

161. Fred R. Dallmayr, "Toward a Critical Reconstruction of Ethics and Politics," *Journal of Politics* 36 (1974) 926–57.

162. Wilhelm Dilthey, *Der Aufbau der geschichtlichen Welt in den Geisteswissenschaften* (GS VII; Göttingen: Vandenhoeck und Ruprecht, 1927, 2nd ed. 1958).

163. Cf. Schubert M. Ogden, *The Point of Christology* (New York: Harper, 1982).

164. See also Stephen Toulmin, "The Construal of Reality: Criticism in Modern and Postmodern Science," in *The Politics of Interpretation*, ed. W. J. T. Mitchell (Chicago: Univ. of Chicago Press, 1983), pp. 99–117.

165. Ernan McMullin: "Structural Explanation," *American Philosophical Quarterly* 15 (1978) 139–147, esp. part 4, "Realism and Retroduction"; "The Fertility of Theory and the Unit for Appraisal in Science," in R. S. Cohen, ed., *Essays in Memory of Imre Lakatos* (Boston: Reidel, 1976), pp. 395–492; and "Vico's Theory of Science," *Social Research* 43 (1976) 450–83.

166. See Peirce's essay "Abduction and Induction," in *Philosophical Writings of Peirce*, ed. Justus Buchler (New York: Dover, 1955), pp. 150–56.

167. McMullin, "Structural Explanation," p. 145.

168. Hilary Putnam, *Mathematics, Matter and Method: Philosophical Papers*, vol. 1 (New York: Cambridge Univ. Press, 1979), essay 16, "The 'Corroboration' of Theories," pp. 250–69.

169. Charles Peirce, "The Fixation of Belief," in *Philosophical Writings*, pp. 5–23.

170. For a survey of the differences between a hermeneutical and a critical theory position, see John B. Thompson, *Critical Hermeneutics: A Study in the Thought of Paul Ricoeur and Jürgen Habermas* (New York: Cambridge Univ. Press, 1981).

171. For two methodologically sophisticated versions of this position, see Lee Cormie, "The Hermeneutical Privilege of the Oppressed," *Proceedings CTSA* 33 (1978) 155–81; and Matthew L. Lamb, *Solidarity with Victims: Toward a Theology of Social Transformation* (New York: Crossroad, 1982). For the neo-Marxist critique, see my "Religion and Society: Legitimation, Rationalization or Cultural Heritage," *Concilium* 125 (1979) 24–32.

172. See Habermas's contribution in Willi Oelmüller, ed., *Transzendentalphilosophische Normenbegründungen* (Paderborn: Schöningh, 1978).

173. See Joseph Raz, ed., *Practical Reasoning* (New York: Oxford Univ. Press, 1978).

174. See the discussion in relation to Hilary Putnam's paper in Frederick Suppe, ed., *The Structure of Scientific Theories* (Urbana, Ill.: Univ. of Illinois Press, 1977), pp. 424–58. Auxiliary statements should not be confused with Popper's use of "initial conditions."

175. John Losee, *A Historical Introduction to the Philosophy of Science* (New York: Oxford Univ. Press, 1980, 2nd ed.), pp. 167–70.

176. I owe this example to Frederick Suppe and his afterword to *The Structure*, pp. 689–96.

177. See nn. 152 and 155 above.

Conclusion

Fundamental theology has had a long and varied history in modern theology. It arose out of the search to retrieve the central Christian truths present in the historical sources of the faith. But it soon became an apologetical discipline seeking firm and secure foundations. At first, fundamental theology sought these foundations in historical demonstrations and the external signs of credibility. Then it sought them in the correlations between the content of belief and human subjectivity. The shift from the external to the internal, from objectivity to subjectivity, from historical to transcendental theology, and even from the term "apologetics" to "fundamental theology" may have represented progress, but the shift still remained within the bonds of foundationalism and the search for unshakeable foundations.

The foundational theology developed in this volume and explicated in relation to specific theological issues sought in three ways to avoid such foundationalism. First, each section criticized the inadequacies of the foundationalism present in the historical and transcendental approaches to fundamental theology. The theoretical critique of foundationalism as philosophically, hermeneutically, and theologically inadequate was developed in the final section. Second, the hermeneutical reconstructions developed for each issue did not seek to uncover a single belief as a foundational hinge upon which a whole set of beliefs revolved. Instead these reconstructions sought to display the diversity of theological interpretation and receptions both in theory and in praxis. Third, each section displayed that the hermeneutical reconstructions of these diverse beliefs could not in a foundational theology stand alone, but had to be placed in relation to relevant background theories and to retroductive warrants. The final section elaborated the theoretical justification of this method of reflective equilibrium among hermeneutical reconstruction, retroductive warrants, and background theories. A foundational theology entailing an equilibrium among such diverse elements avoids the foundational fallacy of previous fundamental theologies.

In the final evaluation, it might be judged that I have in fact given much more prominence to one element over the others and have therefore only inadequately dealt with the specific issues of the resurrection of Jesus, the foundation of the Church, and the mission of the Church. That may very well be true. Yet the very notion of reflective equilibrium implies an understanding of foundational theology not as a static, but rather as a continuing and self-correcting endeavor. Foundational theology takes most seriously its task when it realizes not only the diversity of its various elements, but also the need for constant revision and adjustment.

Index